We Lack for Nothing Now

"We lack for nothing now and are looking for a better future. But, my friends, to bring virgin soil, for ages untouched, to its first harvest gives one hard callouses, and much perspiration flows over one's brow before he can enjoy its produce."

*From a letter of Joseph K. Kaplan to his brother,
April 24, 1858*

We Lack for Nothing Now

Czech Settlement in Steele County, Minnesota

Michael R. Wolesky

Assisted by Susan Lindoo and Steve Wencl

Wolindoo • Saint Paul, Minnesota

© 2011 Michael R. Wolesky. All rights reserved.

Published by Wolindoo
www.wolindoo.com

Book design by Dorie McClelland, Spring Book Design
www.springbookdesign.com

ISBN: 978-0-615-43618-0

Library of Congress Control Number: 2010941180

I dedicate this book to:

My grandfather, Frank J. Wolesky, who came to America in 1902 and made my life here possible

My father, Charles R. Wolesky, who kept alive my sense of my Czech heritage

My friend and fellow historian Marie Maixner of Dolní Dobrouč

Contents

Prologue: Who Are the Czechs? *xi*

1 The Pioneers *1*

2 Civil War, Community Growth and the Rise of Institutions *23*

3 Coming to America *55*

4 1866–1872: The Post-Civil War Boom *87*

5 1875–1880: The Owatonna Czech Settlement *125*

6 The Southern Settlements to 1880 *169*

7 Czech Lodges and Organizations *209*

Epilogue: Fast Forward *229*

Appendix A: A Brief History of the Czechs to 1848 *263*
Appendix B: Czech Arrivals Who Settled in Steele County *271*
Appendix C: Origins of Local Czech Families *279*

Notes *281*
Sources *297*
Index *305*

ACKNOWLEDGMENTS

I want to express my deepest gratitude to the following people:

My wife Susan Lindoo, who was always enthusiastic and encouraging about this book; a diligent researcher and a thorough and relentless editor, she played a huge role in getting the book to print.

Steve Wencl, a Steele County native who speaks and reads Czech and knows everything and everybody connected to the Steele County Czechs; he found a great deal of information both in Minnesota and in Bohemia, translated materials and read earlier drafts of the entire work and corrected many errors.

Karleen Chott Sheppard, a St. Paul resident with Steele County ties who gathered many biographies and memoirs of Minnesota Czechs from old Czech-American periodicals, translated and published them, and generously permitted me to copiously quote from them. This book is much richer for the material that she made available to English-speaking readers.

Betty Kaplan of Owatonna for her interest in the project and for permitting me to quote extensively from the letters of Czech pioneer Josef Kaplan as published in the Kaplan Family History.

All of the many Steele County residents of Czech heritage who graciously shared their family stories, old photos, and personal memories. The times I spent talking with them were among the best parts of writing this book.

Europe in 1870

Prologue

WHO ARE THE CZECHS?

Czech is a language, and the people who speak it are the Czechs. The language is part of the Slavic language group, along with other languages such as Polish and Russian. The Slavic languages are part of the larger Indo-European language group, which also contains the Romance (French, Spanish, Italian, etc.), Celtic (Irish, Welsh and Scots), and Germanic (German, English, and Scandinavian) languages.

Bohemia is a geographic region of mid-elevation surrounded on three sides by mountains, which separate it from Germany on the north and west, Austria to the south, and Poland to the northeast. To the southeast, it drops off to the lowlands of Moravia. In Roman times, a Celtic tribe called the Boii lived here, and the Romans called the area Boiohaimum (the land of the Boii). The name Bohemia derives from this Latin term. People who live in Bohemia are Bohemians, whether or not they are Czech (in the nineteenth century, many were Germans). The Czechs living in Bohemia are both Bohemians and Czechs, in the same way that Germans living in Bavaria are both Bavarians and Germans. Before 1800, the Czech language was often called Bohemian, and the immigrants who came to America from Bohemia usually called themselves and their language Bohemian.

The use of the term "bohemian" as a synonym for someone arty or unconventional became popular in the nineteenth century. This use of the term has nothing to do with the geographic region called Bohemia, or its people. Sometime in the mid 1500s there was a large migration of gypsies into France. The French asked them where they came from, and the reply was Bohemia. It is from the French that we get the term "bohemian" when it means a free life style. The French connotation for the word was of someone living outside of conventional society and untroubled by its disapproval. It became attached to artists who lived in this way. Henri Murger's short story collection *Scenes of Bohemian Life* from 1845 popularized the term in France. Puccini's 1896 opera *La Boheme* drew on the themes of Murger's stories. In English, Thackeray's 1848 novel *Vanity Fair* introduced the term to English speaking readers.[1]

The Czech Republic is a nation in which most of the world's Czechs live, and which has Czech as the official language. The people of Bohemia, Moravia and Czech Silesia together are the Czechs. During the Middle Ages, Bohemia and Moravia were kingdoms. Later they became part of the multinational Austrian empire, ruled by the German-speaking Austrian-Habsburg dynasty. This empire contained the present day nations of the Czech Republic, Slovakia, Serbia, Bosnia-Herzegovina, Croatia, Slovenia, Austria, and Hungary, as well as parts of Poland and Romania. The empire was broken up at the end of the First World War, and several new nations were created from it, including Czechoslovakia. In 1993, the Slovaks separated from Czechoslovakia to form their own country, and the Czech areas became the Czech Republic. (For a fuller discussion of Czech history, see Appendix A.)

SPELLING AND PRONUNCIATION

For a number of reasons, some Czech names have undergone dramatic changes during their migration to America.

Probably the most important factor is the interplay with the German language. Government in the Czech lands was in the hands of German speakers for hundreds of years, with the result that Czech names became Germanized. The same sound was represented by different letters in the German and Czech alphabets. The *v* sound in English is spelled with a *v* in Czech. In German, this sound is represented with a *w*. Consequently, Czech names such as Volesky, Vencl, Vanous, or Vacek were written in Austrian records as Wolesky, Wenzel or Wentzel, Waniaus or Watzek. The *f* sound in English is represented in Czech with an *f*, but in German with a *v*. Thus, a name of German origin such as *Vaith* becomes *Fajt* or *Fait* in Czech. In both cases, the English speaker hears the word "fight." In another example, the name Schwartz becomes *Švarc* in Czech, and the English speaker hears *Schvartz*.

The German form appeared on the passports and exit documents of Czechs who left for America. Most traveled here on German shipping lines, and the German form of their names appeared on the ship passenger lists. When they arrived in America, American authorities used the German spelling in the immigrant's documents. New arrivals could decide to go back to Czech spelling, and some did. But many realized that English was closer to German than to Czech, and that the German spelling would be more comprehensible to their new countrymen. Also, many new Czech communities in America were located close to German communities because the Czechs were familiar with

German language and customs. Community news was often in German newspapers, or in Czech papers printed by Germans.

First names were also Germanized. Jan is the Czech form of John, and was often replaced with Johann, the German form. The Czech name Vaclav is frequently replaced with the German form, Wenceslaus or Wenzel. In America and in Steele County, most of the Vaclavs adopted the first name Wencl, which is an Americanization of the German spelling.

In addition, the Steele County Czechs were primarily from eastern Bohemia, which had its own regional accent. Eastern Bohemian pronunciation of the *v* was more of a *u* sound. My grandfather's name Volesky sounded more like Uolesky, which sounds much like Wolesky. In fact, my grandfather Wolesky said he didn't know why English had both *v* and *w*, since they are both pronounced the same way! The eastern Bohemian accent also pronounces the *s* like the *sh* sound in English.

Another factor resulting in spelling changes are the Czech diacritical marks. The Czech *š* is pronounced with an *sh* sound. When the name Šimek came to America, it was often spelled Shimek or Schimek. In other instances, the original spelling was retained but the diacritical mark was dropped. The earliest Simeks of Steele County spelled their names Schimek, but returned to Simek on their tombstones. To avoid confusion, I will use Simek throughout this book.

The Czech *c* without a hacek is pronounced like *ts*; thus in census records names like Moravec are often spelled Moravetz or Morawitz. When a Czech *c* has a hacek over it (*č*) it is pronounced like the English *ch*. Hence Kubiček is pronounced Kubichek.

The Czech spelling of Seykora is Sýkora. Various phonetic attempts to spell this name in the records yielded Saikora, Seikora, Sejkora, Sikora, Sykora, Seykora, and others. In Steele County, some immigrants went with Seykora, and others used Sykora. I will use Seykora for the sake of consistency.

Even Pichner, which seems straightforward, caused problems. The ship passenger lists show the arrival of Jan and Joseph Pichner aboard the *Elise* in December 1852. The passenger list was handwritten, and apparently hard to read. Three compilers who looked at the list read the handwriting three different ways. One transcribed the last name as Tichner, another as Richner, and a third as Fichner. The Pichners themselves, once in Owatonna, split on the spelling. One branch of the family changed its name to Bichner.

In this book, I will try to use the form of the name found on tombstones, or that is the accepted form at present. When I first mention someone in the book, I will use the form of the name I intend to use throughout the book and include in parentheses the name as it was in Bohemia. For example, Anton Simek (Antonín Šimek), or Frank Seykora (František Sýkora).

THE REVOLUTION OF 1848

Events occurring in Bohemia just before the first Czechs immigrated to Steele County explain much about what provoked these people to leave their homeland for a new life in Minnesota.[2] (For a fuller discussion of Czech history, see Appendix A.)

In February 1848, police in Paris fired on a crowd of unruly demonstrators, sparking a revolution that brought down the Bourbon king of France and spread to Germany, Italy, Austria and Hungary. This was the year of Karl Marx's clarion call in *The Communist Manifesto*, "Workers of the world unite! You have nothing to lose but your chains."

The Hungarians started the movement in the Habsburg domains, which included Austria, Hungary, and Bohemia. By mid-March 1848, students in Vienna who were staging violent demonstrations had been joined by angry workers. Initially, the Austrian Emperor Ferdinand rejected all petitions for social and economic liberalization. Upon receiving news about the demonstrations, Ferdinand is reported to have said, "But are they allowed to do that?" Soon, however, the Hungarian Diet demanded a new constitution with increased voting rights and civil liberties and the abolition of serfdom. On March 31, the Habsburg government granted their demands.

Also in March, the Czech-speaking delegates from Bohemia demanded religious freedom, equal use of the Czech language alongside the German language, and their own legislature. On April 8, the emperor granted most of these demands.

Because the bulk of the Austrian troops in 1848 were in the emperor's Italian territories putting down revolts, he was helpless against the unrest in his own lands. He called a constituent assembly, and on April 11 promised to free the peasants from all services and duties owed to their landlords. This new freedom was to take effect on January 1, 1849.

This tumult had the paradoxical effect of undermining the revolutionary movement. The rural population and wealthier city dwellers were satisfied with the Emperor's concessions and considered continued agitation by students and radicals to be counterproductive. German speakers worried about what they viewed as excessive gains and heightened ambitions on the part of the empire's Slavic and Hungarian residents. This ebbing of support for the revolutionaries enabled the government in Vienna to regain control.[3]

Czech nationalists called a Pan-Slav Congress that met in Prague in early June, and called for the conversion of the Habsburg empire into a "federation of nations all enjoying equal rights." This, however, inflamed the German population of the empire, and quickly led to conflict between Czechs and Germans. The Austrian military commander withdrew from Prague and bombarded the city until, on June 17, the Czech insurgents surrendered. The political liberties won only a few months earlier were withdrawn.

Due to the riots and unrest the Austrian government briefly abandoned Vienna, but it was back in place by October. In December the ineffectual Emperor Ferdinand abdicated in favor of his young nephew Francis Joseph. The war with the Hungarians continued until August of the following year, when the Hungarians were finally defeated and the constituent assembly was disbanded.

The aftermath of the revolution in the Habsburg lands was a decade of repression. Political rights and freedom of expression were withdrawn, and the borders were closely watched. All federalism in the Habsburg domains was abolished, and a uniform system of administration ran the entire realm. Industrialization and railroad building were accelerated to prevent the empire from falling behind Britain, Prussia and France. The Catholic Church was given more control over education and more freedom from government intervention than it had enjoyed in decades.

However, some reforms were instituted in the interests of modernization and preventing future social unrest. The judiciary was separated from the executive, trial by jury instituted, and the manorial courts (in which landlords were judges over their own tenant farmers) were abolished. Peasants were freed from the duty to perform a set number of hours of work per year for their landlords, and they were sold land of their own at half its market value, with twenty years to pay. In addition, it was now possible for farmers to leave the country and emigrate, although they still needed permission and passports were difficult to obtain and cost fifty silver florins.

Despite the difficulties, a few Czechs began leaving for America almost immediately. Some were political liberals fleeing the conservative backlash, and others were drawn by news of the California Gold Rush. This trickle would later become a flood.

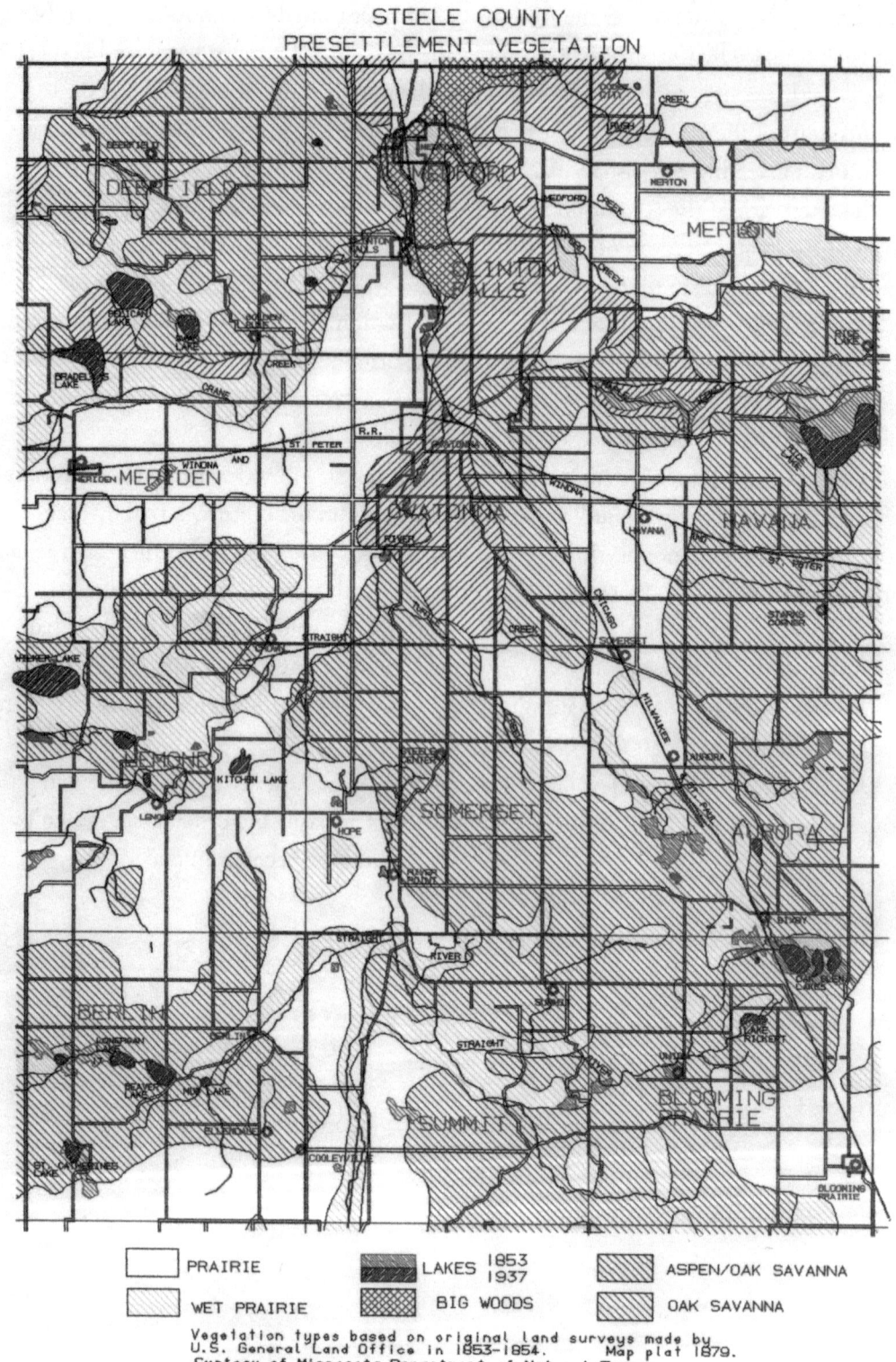

Courtesy of Minnesota Department of Natural of Resources

1

The Pioneers

THE FIRST EUROPEAN SETTLERS arrived in what would become Steele County in the summer of 1853. The territory was virgin land for European immigration. Yankees with names like Johnson, Wright, Howard and Lull staked out claims in Medford Township, and broke soil on their new lands. Two of them, Chauncey Lull and L.M. Howard, returned briefly to Saint Paul, but came back to Steele County with draft animals and built a cabin on their claim, in what is now section five of Medford Township. They spent the winter there, less than half a mile from the winter quarters of a band of Native Americans.

Technically these first settlers were trespassers. The Dakota tribe had ceded the land in the 1851 Treaty of Traverse des Sioux. Treaty ratification and financial payments occurred in 1852, and the treaty went into full effect in February 1853. However, no settlers were to move in until the survey was completed, which did not happen until the summer of 1854. It was only in 1855 that the first parcels of land from the treaty area went up for sale. The early settlers of 1853–54 had gambled that their claims would be recognized, and it turned out to be a good bet. On August 4, 1854, Congress extended preemption privileges to land in Minnesota that previously had been illegally occupied.

The land the settlers came to was rich and lovely. Steele County is a rectangle with its highest point in Summit Township. The Straight River starts in Oak Glen Lake in the southeastern part of the county, flows west to the center, then turns north and proceeds more or less straight up into Rice County to join the Cannon River at Faribault. Crane Creek flows into the Straight River north of Owatonna from the west, and Maple Creek joins it in Owatonna from the east.

> These lakes and streams in an early day were bordered with quite heavy timber, trees of maple, oak, elm, hickory, walnut, butternut, ash, boxelder, basswood, plum, cherry, crabapple, cottonwood, poplar, and probably others.[1]

The surface between the streams is a gently rolling prairie, interspersed by 'oak openings' in various portions of the county. The soil is very productive—a rich, dark loam, well adapted to all cereals common to this latitude.[2]

In a letter written in 1859, Joseph Kaplan describes the prairie to his brother:

I wish you could see our May here, how colorfully and beautifully nature is dressed. Just think of endless prairie with yard high grass which is in blossom, full of many colored flowers and most of these are a special kind of tulip. Indeed, it looks like an enormous rose sea.[3]

More settlers came to Medford in 1854, and others began to spread throughout the county. White settlers built cabins in Clinton Falls Township and Owatonna Township in the fall of that year. A party leaving Sparta, Wisconsin in May included A.B. Cornell and W.F. Pettit. The party followed a meandering route that eventually led to Medford. Most of the party returned north toward Waterford, but Cornell and Pettit followed the Straight River south for seven miles to the point where it was joined by Maple Creek. Pettit staked a claim on the west side of the Straight River, and Cornell claimed land on the east side, south of Maple Creek. This was the beginning of the city of Owatonna.

Though Yankees were the very first white settlers in the Owatonna area, Czech immigrants began arriving the next year and should be considered part of the original European settlers. The families who would be Owatonna's first Czech settlers began entering America in the early 1850s. As was true of many immigrant settlements in the New World, the first families came from the same villages in the Old World and were connected to each other through marriage or friendships. Family names of these earliest settlers are Simek, Pichner, Kubat, Fisher, Kaplan and Zednik.

The leader was **Anton Simek** (Antonin Šimek), a twenty-seven-year-old tailor from the village of Hylváty in the northeast part of Bohemia, which at that time was part of the Austrian empire. His father was John (Jan) Simek, a weaver living in house number 67; his mother, Rosalie Pichner, had died. Anton had five older sisters and two older brothers.

Anton seems to have had wanderlust. He traveled to America once or twice around 1850 and apparently lived here long enough to learn English. His early wanderings are not well documented, but he did return to Hylváty in the summer of 1852. A police file in his home region from September 1852 says he had been rambling abroad for several years. At that time it was illegal to encourage people to emigrate, and after some materials sent by a German steamship line to Simek were intercepted, the police, suspecting he was an agent for the company, began watching Anton. The file says:

> . . . according to our informers, he is a restless and eloquent young man who visits people thinking of emigration, strengthening their intentions to emigrate. However, no one believes him to be in connection with either an agent of the Jewish company Hirschmann or with another similar person. At the present time he has received a passport for a journey to North America. From here on he should be under gendarme supervision.[4]

Gravesite of Joseph Pichner, arrived in Owatonna in 1858.
Susan Lindoo

By fall 1852 Anton was on the move again, taking with him two cousins on his mother's side who were from Dlouhá Třebová, a couple of miles from Hylváty. **John (Jan) and Joseph (Josef) Pichner** and their families left for America with Anton, arriving in New York City aboard the *Elise* on December 8, 1852. The group made its way to Chicago and then on to Freeport, Illinois.

Freeport was a booming town of 2,000 people, including a German community large enough to support a German-language newspaper. Shortly after Simek and the Pichners arrived, the new Galena and Chicago Union Railroad tracks reached Freeport. Freight and passenger service began in September 1853 and, for a time, Freeport served as a camp for immigrant railroad construction workers building the line toward the west. The Pichner brothers remained in Freeport; John worked on the railroad for fifty cents per day. Over the next two years they would be joined by relatives from the old country.[5]

Joseph Pichner's brother-in-law, **Anton Kubat** (Antonin Kubát), also a tailor, was from Dlouhá Třebová. Anton Kubat's sister Catherine was married to Joseph Pichner. Anton's first wife, Anna Renchin, died in 1853 and he married Anna Kubista the next year. In May of 1854 Anton Kubat left for America with his new wife and six children. After a ten-week voyage on a sailing ship (during which Anna gave birth to a son, Anton), they arrived in Freeport in August of 1854 and joined Joseph Pichner. For the next two years, Anton eked out a living as a farm laborer in the summer and a tailor in the winter. A daughter, Antonia, was born in 1856. During his stay in Freeport Anton wrote to his friend Joseph Kaplan, encouraging him to move to America.[6]

John Pichner's brother in-law, **Benjamin Fisher** (Fišer), came from a family that had been in the milling trade for two hundred years in the region around Dlouhá Třebová. However his father had been forced to relinquish management of one of the mills in Dlouhá Třebová, allegedly due to poor management. After a similar lack of success at other mills, the family ended up in Čermná with his mother's people. In 1855 Benjamin Fisher, his wife Anna (Fibigar) and his daughter Antonia came to America and settled temporarily in Freeport, Illinois with the Pichners; John Pichner's wife and Benjamin's wife Anna were sisters. Shortly after they arrived in America, Benjamin and Anna had a son, Joseph, in Illinois.[7]

Simek returned to his home village of Hylváty in 1853 for a short time, after which he and much of his family made a final trip to America, arriving in early 1854. Perhaps accompanying Anton were his older brother Joseph, a silk weaver who had lived in Vienna during his apprenticeship, Joseph's wife Anna (Pahl) and their daughters Teresa and Anna. Joseph's wife was Hungarian and both children had been born in Hungary. Also in the party were Joseph's father John and his sisters Anastasia and Rosalia. Several

*Ben Fisher and Anna Fibiger Fisher, arrived in Owatonna in 1856.
Courtesy of Steve Wencl*

other siblings stayed in Bohemia. Joseph, his family, his father, and his sisters arrived in Boston on January 5, after an ocean voyage of 13 weeks aboard the ship *Arnor*.[8]

Anton Simek either came on the same ship or arrived soon after. No record of his ship passage has been found. Returning to the Austrian Empire after emigrating was discouraged, particularly for someone under police suspicion. So Anton may have left Bohemia under an assumed name. The first name on the passenger list for the ship that brought Anton's father and siblings to America is Louis Hirscheld. No age, occupation or country of origin is given, and it is the only name on the passenger list without additional information. Perhaps "Louis Hirscheld" was actually Anton Simek.

The Simeks joined the Pichner brothers, the Kubats and the Fishers in Freeport. Joseph Simek built a house in Cedarville, near Freeport while employed for a few months as a farmhand.[9]

Apparently these Bohemian settlers to America sought a life that would be different from the one possible in Freeport. It was soon decided that Anton Simek and his relatives

Josef Schimeck (Simek) with his great-grandchildren in 1895.
Courtesy of the Fleckenstein family files of Delphine Antoinette Hillseth Cathcart

Anton and Anna (Kubista) Kubat, arrived in Owatonna 1856. Courtesy of Tim Kubat and Dan Paukert

would travel farther to find a good place for the group to settle. Once the spot was found, they would write to the group in Freeport to join them. John Pichner's eleven-year-old son John left with the Simeks.[10]

Anton Simek appears to have traveled north in search of a place to settle. Frank Kovar, writing in 1933 about the early history of the Steele County Czechs, says Simek went up the Mississippi River in 1852 to St. Paul, Minnesota, and from there journeyed south on a post road to Albert Lea. Simek visited Owatonna, apparently liked what he saw, and returned to Illinois. Although Kovar says this happened in 1852, it was more likely to have been 1854 or 1855.[11]

It is not known why Simek came to the Owatonna area, but the probable reason was available land. In summer 1855 the federal government had completed surveying lands from the treaty of Traverse de Sioux and was offering the land for sale. Simek also may have heard of the widely publicized grand riverboat excursion to St. Paul in 1854. The excursion, planned by the Chicago and Rock Island Railroad to celebrate the arrival of the line's tracks at Rock Island, Illinois, brought well known visitors and generated much attention for Minnesota.

Esther Cornell, the widow of Owatonna co-founder A.B. Cornell, later recalled that many men had come to the new settlement in spring 1855 to select their claims, saying they would return later in the year when the grass had grown enough to feed their animals. Hundreds of wagons per week passed through the Owatonna area that summer, and many of these settlers were persuaded to stay. That year the town acquired a doctor, a preacher and a school that was initially housed in a tent.[12]

It seems probable that one of the men who checked out Owatonna in spring 1855 was Anton Simek. It is likely that Anton then traveled from Owatonna to Iowa and persuaded his brother Joseph that the newly opened territory in Steele County was the place to settle. Records show that Joseph's family had moved to Osage, Iowa, in spring 1855 and made a land claim, but stayed only a few months before moving to Minnesota and settling in the vicinity of Owatonna. Anton and Joseph and their sisters and father were all in Owatonna in fall 1855. Anton claimed 160 acres in the northwest quarter of section 11 in Owatonna Township where he and his father and sisters lived. His land was just outside of and included a small part of present-day Mineral Springs Park, and contained most of what is now the Brooktree golf course. Joseph and his family claimed land in what is now Kaplan's Woods south of Owatonna. Anton wrote letters to Hylvaty, as well as to his Czech acquaintances in Freeport, describing the Owatonna area and its opportunities.[13]

Joseph Kaplan was a young farmer in Dlouhá Třebová who may have been especially receptive to the encouragement of his friend, Anton Kubat, to emigrate. Kaplan got into a fight with a German railroad employee named Krause, and shortly after the fight a fire started in his barn that destroyed several buildings and all his crops. Kaplan accused Krause, who then sued him for slander. The court eventually dismissed the slander suit, but also found insufficient evidence to convict Krause of arson.

Kaplan decided to emigrate. He had the farm surveyed and split into four smaller farms that he sold to raise money for the trip. Kaplan married his step-cousin Barbora Zednik in the fall of 1855, just as Anton Simek was arriving in Steele County. Kaplan's approval to emigrate came in February of 1856, and his passport arrived in April. Joseph and Barbora left for America, accompanied by Barbora's parents and sister, as well as by Vaclav Pichner, a weaver from Dlouhá Třebová and godfather of Anton Simek. Vaclav was the father of Joseph and John Pichner, the brothers who had accompanied Anton Simek in 1852 and now resided in Freeport.[14]

The Kaplans' ocean voyage from Germany to Quebec took six weeks. From there, they took a series of steamboats, canals and railroads to Montreal, Toronto, across Lakes Huron and Michigan, to Milwaukee and on to Chicago. Kaplan described the next stage in an August 1856 letter to his brother:

> From Chicago we rode by train to Freeport. Here we stayed fourteen days with Czech settler acquaintances and bought equipment for farming: viz., wagons, oxen, cows; 2 wagons for $160, 4 oxen for $200, 2 cows for $50, and many other things such as stoves, plows, saws, axes, hoes, etc.
>
> The towns here are growing surprisingly, and also the railroads. The town of Freeport, for example, was founded 15 years ago and is already large, with railroads leaving it in five directions. But there are still no railroads going northwest. As we intend to go northwest to Minnesota, we have to ride from here by wagon. There are ten families of us preparing for the trip from Freeport to Minnesota over prairies and through forests. With this I end my letter till we reach our destination. Then I will write again. Goodbye![15]

The Fisher and Kubat families, the John Pichner family, and the Kaplan group left Freeport accompanied by seven other families of French and German background. The Joseph Pichner family stayed in Illinois until 1857. The band of settlers moved west into Iowa and rested at the home of some friends. The group talked it over and decided to move to Minnesota. They followed the Mississippi River north to Winona, then traveled west to Owatonna and parked their wagons in what is now Mineral Springs Park on or near Anton Simek's homestead. They arrived in Owatonna on or shortly after September 15. Kaplan's first child, Joseph W., the first Czech child born in Steele County, was born during their one week stay at the site.[16]

Benjamin Fisher recalled:

> Antonin Simek, who had already been there for two years, wrote to us that in this area were beautiful parcels of land, and invited us to come to him. We assumed that he had something picked out for us, so we took to the road.
>
> Arriving on St. Wenceslaus Day at his place, we found out something that greatly alarmed us. Simek had not expected us so late in the year. You can just imagine how it was for us, when we found out that he really didn't know anything about us. This was no small matter. We were completely thrown into such wilderness seclusion. Owatonna at that time consisted of six buildings,

Mineral Springs Park in Owatonna today; originally part of Anton Simek's homestead. Susan Lindoo

and only here and there in the area was an abandoned building. When Simek saw how troubled we were, he promised us that he would find something. However, what could be put together at this point in time? We didn't have a dwelling that could shelter us, and winter was just around the corner.[17]

The Kaplans and Zedniks stayed in their wagons in Mineral Springs Park for a month while they searched for a good plot of land to purchase. It was decided that the Fishers would help them build a house on the new land and spend the winter in the house with them. They quickly built a log house with a hay roof covered by heavy cloth. Holes were plugged with straw. On November 4, they moved from their wagons into the house. (The Kaplan-Zednik house stood on what is now 18th Street SW between Linn Street and Oak Street.) The entire group of Czech families managed to build twelve log cabins on this site, which had a spring to furnish water, before winter set in.[18]

One of the first things a new settler had to do was claim his land. Many of the early Steele County settlers claimed land under the Pre-emption Act of 1841. This act governed the sale of public lands until the passage of the Homestead Act during the Civil War. The act gave permission to settlers to enter federal land without being considered trespassers. First, the settler chose up to a quarter-section of land (160 acres) for settlement and began to build a house and clear the land. Then within 30 days the settler went to the nearest land office, swore an oath of eligibility, and filed a statement of intent to claim that parcel. Within a year of filing the claim, the settler returned to the land office and paid the cost of the land ($1.50 per acre) plus a fifty-cent fee to the registrar. In return the owner received a certificate to the land and paid no taxes for five years. However, if the settler did not pay for the land on time, it was available for someone else to claim. The earliest Steele County settlers, who came before federal land sales began, acquired their land in this way. Pre-emption claims continued until the passage of the Homestead Act in 1862 gave settlers an even better deal.

After sales of federal land began in summer 1855, another way to get a good deal was to buy land with military bounty land warrants. These were grants of land issued to military veterans after the Revolutionary War, the War of 1812, and especially after the Mexican War of 1845. Most veterans did not want to move to the frontier, so many sold their land warrants for a good price.

> Land warrants and other kinds of scrip were bought in large quantities through banks and special dealers in such papers. That there was an abundance of the warrants may be inferred from the fact that by 1860 the United States had issued them for the amazing total of sixty-eight million acres. Generally they were purchased for well under the minimum price of public land under pre-emption ($1.25 per acre). Horace Greeley of the *New York Tribune* once said that many of these rights to land were transferred by veterans for as little as ten cents an acre.[19]

Anton Simek claimed his first plot of 160 acres with military land warrant number 59,694 that had first been issued to William Holmes in 1855. Joseph Kaplan claimed his first 160 acres with an 1855 military land warrant. It is also likely that Anton Kubat and the Pichners claimed land with these warrants, since their names do not appear in the federal land database listing homestead and pre-emption claims.[20]

The new arrivals did not have an easy first winter. They gathered what grass and hay they could during the fall to feed their livestock through the winter, but heavy frosts had already come and the hay was frozen. Next, while much of it was stacked up in the fields, a prairie fire broke out during the night:

> There were no barriers to the fire, no roads or fields. The fire with the strong wind changed the wide prairie into a sea of fire, and all my efforts had been reduced to nothing. All I had left were a couple of piles of hay, had I only hauled them off earlier. The worst thing happened to Anton Kubat and John Pichner. They both had been living in wagons on the prairie with their big families. When the fire came, there was no way out, other than to struggle for life and possessions. They fought the fire as best they could and, after great effort, they survived. Not far away, a German had settled; he was a good person. The fire destroyed all his family's possessions, and from that period, misfortune after misfortune pursued him, until the poor fellow took it so bad he went insane and in a fit of madness hung himself.[21]

The winter that followed was severe. The snow was deep with a crust an inch or two thick. Travel was extremely difficult except on the few decent roads. Animals and people trying to walk on the snow fell through the crust and cut their legs. Hundreds of deer fell through the crust, and unable to escape, were clubbed to death for their meat. Deer, which had been abundant in the autumn, were scarce in spring.

Much of the damp hay gathered in the fall rotted or was eaten by deer, forcing settlers to cut more frozen grass all winter long. They sometimes traveled five miles through the snow to find areas unburned by the fire. Joseph Kaplan remembered it as a "rough time indeed. Our oxen and the cow we had barely survived the winter." Anton Kubat recalled "There is an old proverb, 'Do not despair, but hope,' and so we, in hopes of better times ahead, survived the winter with its hardships, although we often did suffer hunger."[22]

Anna Kubat remembers it this way:

> It pains me to think back to what we suffered that first winter. Worst of all was spring, when we had finished eating everything we had brought with us from Freeport. Father spent his last 50 cents for a bushel of corn, but it was very musty. We dried the corn and ground it in a coffee grinder, and from this I made cereal. The butter to put on it we had to imagine. We hardly even had any salt left. There was a lot of game, but what was the use when we had no guns to shoot it with? . . .

Winship House, probably in the early 1870s. Courtesy of Steele County Historical Society

I had a beautiful embroidered tablecloth. When we were worst off, my husband took it to town in hopes of trading it for some food. But he came back unsuccessful. What tears there were from the hungry children. Because it was near spring, herbs were coming up, and we lived on them for awhile.[23]

Kubats decided to stretch their meager food supply by sending their fifteen year old daughter Anna to find work at one of the hotels in Owatonna. She left in the morning, and returned at noon without finding the town. No wonder! Kubats lived about three miles from Owatonna, which at that time consisted of perhaps 200 people in about fifty small homes. Most lived in log cabins or sod houses with thatched roofs.[24]

Anton Kubat then led his daughter into Owatonna, where she found employment at the Sanford House, a hotel built the previous year. Anna Kubat's only pay from the hotel was her meals, and she received permission to bring any leftover food home to feed her brothers and sisters. In those early years, meals at the Sanford House and in the rest of town consisted of the basics: bread, potatoes, beans, salt pork and coffee, with infrequent additions of fruits, vegetables and dairy products as available. Catherine Pichner provided similar help to her family by working at another local hotel, the Winship House.[25]

The following description of the Sanford and Winship Houses in 1856 illustrates the conditions Anna Kubat and Catherine Pichner were working under:

> In spite of the enlargement of the Winship House in 1856, Mrs. Sheetz, one of the guests, has described it as consisting of one large room downstairs and an equally large one upstairs. A calico curtain divided the lower room into two compartments. In one corner stood the bed for the guest and her husband and in another corner of the same compartment stood the bed of host Winship and his wife. Beyond the curtain was the lobby. Upstairs the accommodations were even less inviting, but space was at a premium and frontiersmen were not given to grumbling over trivialities. In the same year Samuel W. Farmer and several companions were told there was no room for them at the Sanford House. By night they had erected a ten-by-twenty-foot addition to the hotel and thus provided sleeping quarters for four men and Rev. Solomon Wetzel and his wife.[26]

Benjamin Fisher left a description of the dire conditions facing the settlers in late winter:

> Spring was near, and distress had reached its highest peak. The flour was gone and there was no thinking about more. The children, thinking we were sleeping, in the night left their beds and looked for food as they could not sleep with such hunger. I felt so sorry for them, yet there was nothing I could do. I explained to them about our desperate situation and, crying, I told them that we would die of hunger.
>
> At this point, in a period of great distress and despondency, it occurred to me that I have a new silk scarf and an old rifle. I took them both and went to the store where I had earlier bought with cash. I asked them if they would take the scarf and rifle as collateral on 100 pounds of flour. In a breath they blew me off, told me they couldn't. I left from there and for the tears I couldn't see the road. I went into a store where I had never bought anything.

When the storeowner heard me out, he said: 'Why don't you go there where you bought with cash? Now that you have no money you come to me?' But, having listened to everything, he gave me the 100 pounds of flour and just took the scarf as security. I promised that I would pay off the debt in fourteen days, and I would never forget his humanitarian act.

At this time, Simek came over and asked if he could take in the oxen, since I didn't have any hay; at his place they would be well fed. In return, I could help him break sod in the summer. I was happy about this offer, and I agreed. I still, however, had to worry about how to pay for the flour. Simek was a friend of Doctor Morehouse, so he put in a good word for me in order that I might get some work. He listened and gave me a job chopping wood. It didn't go very well; I wasn't used to that type of work. In spite of that, however, I was able to pay the debt.[27]

By spring the settlers had run out of hay and money. Supplies had to be purchased with cash and hauled from St. Paul or Hastings by oxen teams on trips lasting four to six days. All the Czech families disassembled their log houses and rebuilt them on their new land claims. Their new land claims were covered primarily with woods or hazel brush, and had to be cleared with an iron plow pulled by teams of oxen. The Kaplan house moved east to a site near present day Highway 218, and then later moved again to the eventual Kaplan homestead. In a letter to his brother, Joseph Kaplan described the construction of a house:

> This town of ours is still built almost entirely of wood, although there are two houses of masonry. The building of a frame house that is, for example, 38 feet long, 20 feet wide, and one story tall is accomplished thus: Posts are first pounded in each corner and some more between—also crosswise. These are encased with oak boards two inches thick; these boards are placed upright. Inside them are nailed basswood boards half an inch thick. These are planed and nailed crosswise, beginning at the bottom and overlapping one inch. At the same time numerous windows are cut through. Then the building is painted white, green, or some other color. The roof is covered with boards, then with shingles. These are one and a half feet long, four to six inches wide, and made by special machinery. Here in America they do not consider durability—only looks.[28]

Bad fortune continued to plague the settlers. Charlie Fisher was badly scalded when he fell into a kettle of boiling water, and took months to recover. In addition, the Fisher's ox ran off, got mired in mud, and died before anyone found it. Joseph Kaplan's barefoot mother-in-law was bitten by a rattlesnake in her front yard and spent five weeks in bed. Ben Fisher's legs were pinned by a falling tree while he was cutting wood. His legs were not broken, but his injuries were serious enough to require six weeks in bed.

When spring arrived, Kubats planted cabbage, potatoes and corn. These vegetables, and other food shared with the neighbors, ensured that 1857 was not as bleak as that first winter and spring.

Joseph Kaplan broke ground in the spring and planted his first crops of corn, buckwheat, beans, cabbage and potatoes. These crops loosened the soil and prepared it for eventual planting of wheat in later years.[29]

A hail storm in July damaged crops throughout the county. The hail stones were so large that the marks they left in the ground could still be seen a few years later. The hail flattened most of the Fisher's lettuce crop, but profits from their buckwheat and corn crops covered the cost of flour for the next winter. The Kaplans did well; they had "at least 8,000 pounds of hay" ready for winter.

Most of the Czech families settled in an area a few miles southeast of the small village of Owatonna, near the future site of the Bohemian National Cemetery. They helped each other get started in their new lives. Fishers spent the first winter with the Kaplans and Zedniks, and the following year other settlers helped them build their home southeast of Owatonna. Anton Kubat's neighbors plowed his land until he could afford his own plow and he repaid them with labor or tailoring. Fishers loaned out their ox and were given an acre of cleared land in return.

Anton Simek also loaned out his oxen. Simek was a curious man who loved to read and was in the habit of pausing at the end of a row while plowing his fields to read for a few minutes. Simek's oxen were used to the routine, and when an old settler borrowed them, he could not understand why the oxen stopped so frequently. He thought there was something wrong and brought the oxen back to Simek, who laughed and told him to bring along a book or newspaper to read whenever the oxen stopped to catch their breath.[30]

The flow of new settlers brought changes to the region. In 1855 Steele County was carved out of Rice County, and Owatonna was platted and named, a post office was established, and at least twelve frame houses, the Winship Hotel and the town's first school were built. Most of the new arrivals to Owatonna were Yankees and they controlled the economic and social life of the town.

In 1856, the year most of the early Czech pioneers arrived, the population of Owatonna reached at least 100 and two more hotels were built. Regular stage lines and mail routes were established, several stores opened, and sawmills began to provide lumber for frame houses. New settlers included lawyers, doctors and ministers, and the first local newspaper, the short-lived *Watchman and Register*, appeared.

Between 1856 and 1857, as the Czechs struggled to survive their first winter, the population of Owatonna tripled. Two new additions were annexed to the original town plat, a bank opened and railroad fever struck as newly formed railroad companies began selling their stock. Owatonna Township's population was over 600; 106 were foreign born with Canadians, Czechs and Germans the predominant groups. Steele County's population reached 2,600.

This growing bubble of optimism burst in August 1857 when the bankruptcy of a New York insurance company started a nationwide chain reaction, known as the Panic of 1857, of bank failures, foreclosures, factory closings, and contraction of the money supply. Many Owatonna settlers lost their property to bankruptcy and foreclosures. The December 30, 1862, issue of the *Owatonna Union Express* lists Joseph Kaplan owing $16.52 in back taxes, due since 1859, on a quarter section of land. The land was to be sold on January 12, 1863, if the taxes were not paid. The stream of new arrivals dried up, and some left Owatonna for greener pastures. The town was at a standstill for three years. Hailstorms in July of 1857 reduced the food supply, adding to the misery of the financial panic and contributing to another difficult winter.

Joseph Kaplan's sister, Anna, single and 23 years old, arrived in Owatonna in December 1857. She married Dane Peterson, but died in December of 1859 at the age of 25. Another early casualty was John Simek, Anton's father. He died soon after the arrival of the second group of Czech settlers, according to Karel Srsen. He was listed in the census of 1857, but not in the census of 1860. He was buried on the Simek land, probably on what is now the Brooktree golf course.[31]

Following his father's death, Anton Simek moved from his land east of Owatonna in section 11 to a new location southeast of Owatonna to be near his fellow countrymen who had settled in that section. The 1859 tax rolls list Anton as living in section 24 of Owatonna Township, and do not show him owning the land around Mineral Springs Park.

In January 1858, Anton Simek's sister Anna married Peter Johannsen, with Anton as one of the witnesses. However, Anna and Peter's life together was short. By July 1859, Peter was dead and his estate in probate. The claims against the estate include a note by Peter promising to give Henry Leroy $38 worth of lumber, and signed by Peter's mark in place of a signature. Anton Simek also put in a claim against the estate for $55 owed,

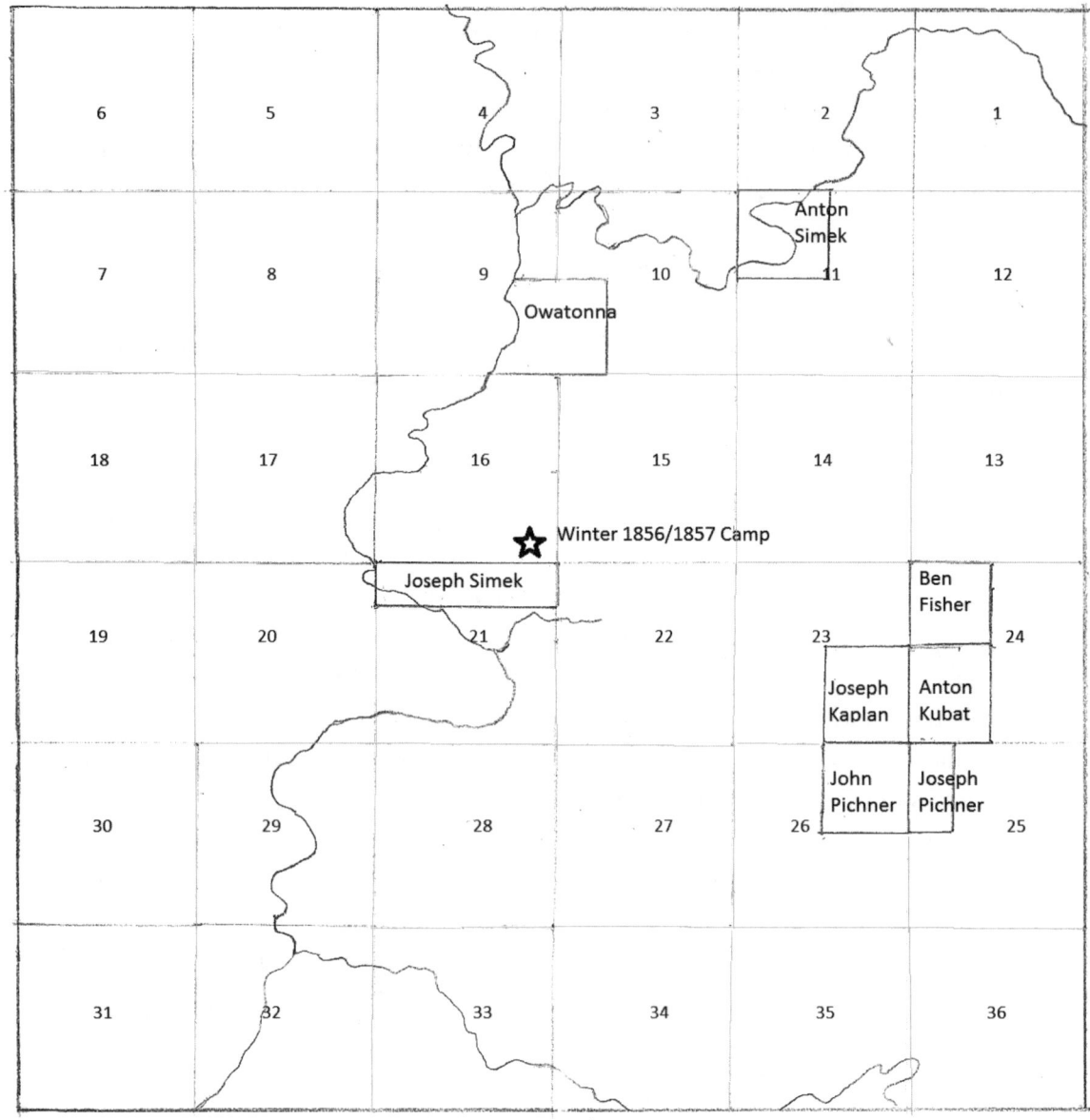

Czech Settlers in Owatonna Township 1858

in part, for a sack of meal, a sack of flour, part payment for a calf, and seven bushels of potatoes, as well as Peter's funeral expenses. The next year, in February 1860, Anna sold her land to her brother Anton, and in March married her second husband, Frederick Schuttlow (or Sattlau). Anton was once again one of the witnesses.

In 1858 Owatonna was incorporated and Minnesota became a state. The Joseph Pichner family arrived to join the rest of the group; they had left Freeport in 1857 and spent a year in Iowa's Amana Colonies. Hard times continued for the settlers. It was a very wet year and another large summer hailstorm contributed to a poor harvest. The few provisions available in the county largely went unsold because no one had money to buy them. Many families lived on bran bread or bare potatoes without salt or meat. In later years, 1858 would be known as the Johnny Cake Year because so many had subsisted on corn bread.[32]

The first attempt to build a railroad into Owatonna began in 1858. In a letter to his brother dated April 24, Joseph Kaplan wrote:

> The railroad, which I mentioned to you in a previous letter, will now be built. On April 15 of this year the matter was brought to a vote, and it passed by a 1,500 majority. It is to be built and money for building it is to be borrowed on state credit. Here in Owatonna it will be built within a year and will pass right across our section. A railroad is the most important matter for today's settler. Wherever it goes, there in a short time a marked vitality appears; or contrarily, where there is no railroad everything lies moribund. It is difficult to sell part of one's crop when one's farm is up to forty English miles away from a town. So here we have the firm expectation of being twice as well-to-do—that is, our lands will be worth that much more when the railroad comes through.[33]

The following year, in a letter of February 13, 1859, Kaplan writes that the railroad had been built and the tracks crossed his land. But all did not go smoothly thereafter for the Minneapolis and Cedar Valley Railroad. When the company was organized in 1857, it raised money, surveyed a route and persuaded the state legislature to issue land grants secured by mortgages on the right of way. The legislature also passed a loan of $5 million to be used as the basis for banks to issue currency (private banks had that right in the nineteenth century). But in the Panic of 1857, which continued into 1858, the mortgages were foreclosed, the circulating bank notes depreciated until they were worthless, and the bank failed. Hundreds of merchants and businessmen were ruined. The panic and the Civil War delayed the arrival of the railroad until 1866.[34]

Benjamin Fisher left this description of the affair:

> Contractors and workers came and started working. I slaughtered my last ox and the man who was in charge of building the track bought half of the ox, and

he told me that when he got some money he would pay me. I kept some meat for myself, but I never did get paid for the rest, not one cent. So I went to work on the railroad. I worked for thirty days, and the company then went bankrupt and I didn't get paid for my meat, for my work, no compensation whatsoever![35]

Ben Fisher and others had more land problems because of the failure of the Homestead Act. Fisher relates that he and some of the other settlers did not pay for their land claims because they were short of money and because they thought President Buchanan would give them the land at no cost. Congress did pass a Homestead Act in 1860 that would have granted land at no cost to settlers who worked it, but the bill was opposed by the southern slaveholding states, and President Buchanan vetoed it as unconstitutional. Consequently Fisher lost his land claim, which eventually reverted to the railroad. Later Fisher bought the land back from the railroad, but at a higher price.[36]

The winter of 1858–1859 came early and was exceedingly harsh, but life began to improve with the coming of spring. Due to a large crop with heavy yields, the settlers made a profit on their 1859 wheat sales despite low prices. Gradually the settlers were adjusting and learning how to survive in the new land.

In March of 1860, Joseph Kaplan wrote to his brother:

> We are looking forward to a fertile year, 1860. The winter has been dry, without snow and very pleasant. And our Minnesota is healthy and good; there are beautiful prairies and enough of woods. Minnesota wheat is one of the best in North America. A lot of immigrants have been streaming here from neighboring states of Iowa, Wisconsin, Illinois, etc., and also from Europe. Our city, Owatonna, now five years in existence since it was founded, already has 1500 inhabitants.[37]

The town had grown vibrantly and rapidly, but had not yet acquired the veneer of civilization. Visiting feminist Jane Grey Swissholm, in a letter from this period, described Owatonna as having a "woe-begone neglected look," and said "the outbuildings are of the most primitive and insubstantial kind."[38]

The federal census of 1860 tabulated 2,863 people in Steele County, with 607 of them being foreign born. Households listed as born in Bohemia included those of Joseph and Anton Simek, Joseph and John Pichner, Anton Kubat, Joseph Kaplan, Joseph Zednik, and Benjamin Fisher. The newly remarried Anna Simek and her husband Frederick

Schuttlau were farming in Merton Township (then called Orion). Also listed are the families of Joseph Hoffman, Joseph Ebenhok and Herman Prevost. Although born in Bohemia, their names indicate they were probably German speaking; Czech pioneers of the county did not consider such families to be Czech.

Bohemian-born persons living in other families included Josephine Fisher (with the family of prominent farmer John Odell), Catherine Pichner (with the family of A.B. Cornell, one of the founders of Owatonna), Josephine Kubat (with the family of David Potwin, who owned a sawmill), and Anna Kubat (with Nathaniel Winship, owner of the first hotel in Owatonna). These were teenagers working as servants to help their families' finances. They brought in some income and did not need to be fed as long as they lived with their employers.

The harvest that year was good. An agricultural society was formed, and a county fair was held. But matters on the national level were not so benign.

As the presidential election neared, several southern states threatened to secede from the union if Abraham Lincoln was elected president. When the votes were tallied in Steele County, Republican Lincoln received 523, Democrat Douglas earned 157, and pro-slavery breakaway Democrat Breckinridge trailed far behind with 8 votes.

In this same election, Anton Simek was elected county coroner in a county-wide race by a vote of 482 to 183 over his opponent, D.G. Fowle. In those days, the county coroner did not have to be a doctor. The coroner investigated suspicious deaths, calling an inquest of community members (similar to a grand jury) to hear the evidence and decide if the death was of natural causes. If medical knowledge or an autopsy was necessary, a doctor was asked to participate and testify. If the death appeared suspicious, the case was referred to the sheriff for criminal action. The coroner also served as sheriff if the sheriff and deputies were unavailable.[39]

Coroner was a position of responsibility, and it speaks well of Anton Simek that people throughout the county elected him by a wide margin. A few months earlier, in the local elections of April 1860, Simek had been elected overseer of the poor for Owatonna Township. This position, usually filled by vote of the county commissioners, involved arranging for support of the poor by their relatives, and if they had none in the area, arranging for county assistance. Children without support were set up as apprentices with families to learn a trade.[40]

In October 1860, an issue of the *Owatonna Newsletter* contained this advertisement by Anton Simek:

For Sale.

The undersigned offers the following property for sale at liberal cash prices:

A farm of 80 acres 2½ miles southeast of Owatonna, fenced in, and 13 acres under cultivation

80 acres of good prairie, 3½ miles west of Owatonna

30 acres of timberland, 2½ miles north of Owatonna

One yoke of oxen, one cow, one heifer, several pigs, farming utensils, & etc.

For particulars, inquire at this office.

A.E. Schimek[41]

There is no way to know what Simek had in mind. Perhaps he was in debt, or perhaps he planned to move into town and open a business. He apparently did not plan to sell out and leave the area, as some did, because he had just sought and been elected to public office. Whatever his plans they were overtaken by the rush of history. Lincoln's presidential election victory set in motion a momentous chain of events that would remake the United States and have powerful effects on Steele County and its Czechs.

2

Civil War, Community Growth, and the Rise of Institutions

During the period 1860–1866, several important events shaped the Czech communities of Steele County. Nationally the main event was the Civil War that raged from 1861–1865. Locally, however, this was a period of rapid settlement with new immigrants arriving weekly. As the numbers of Czech settlers grew they began to create those institutions that define community life including the Catholic Church and organizations of freethinkers, the other major response of Czechs to the question of religion.

THE WAR

After Lincoln's election victory the southern states in rapid succession announced their departure from the Union. There followed a short period of waiting and preparation that was broken on April 12, 1861, when rebel troops bombarded Fort Sumter, a Union bastion on an island in Charleston harbor. The fort surrendered the following day and on April 15 President Lincoln issued a call for 75,000 volunteers to enlist for a 90-day period. The Civil War had begun.

Both sides approached the war enthusiastically, each expecting a swift victory. As the news reached Owatonna, citizens congregated in Morford Hall where they heard Lewis McCune of Waseca call for volunteers. Twenty six men from the Owatonna area enlisted and marched to Faribault where they met up with men from other towns to join the First Minnesota Volunteer Regiment.[1]

The First Minnesota Regiment
One of the men volunteering from Owatonna was Anton Simek. On May 24, he mustered into Company I of the newly formed First Minnesota Regiment at Fort Snelling where the regiment was being trained and equipped. Volunteers and firearms were

plentiful, but at first there was a shortage of ammunition. In addition, at this early stage of the war, neither state nor federal law provided clothing for the volunteers. However, an 1860 state enactment gave colonels the authority to prescribe uniforms for their militia regiments. The First Minnesota was headed by former governor Willis Gorman who furnished his troops with red flannel shirts, black trousers and slouch hats. The soldiers of the First wore this uniform at the Battle of Bull Run, and later many felt it had made them too conspicuous to Confederate rifles.[2]

The new soldiers spent their time in drills and guard duty. When officers were told that part of the regiment was to be sent out to Indian reservations to police whisky peddlers, the troops and officers alike were incensed. They had enlisted to fight for the Union, not police the reservations. Other troops were found for this assignment.

In early May the War Department, recognizing that the war would not be over in a matter of months, asked that volunteers be requested to re-enlist; this time it would be for a term of three years. The officers did so immediately, but many of the men grumbled, viewing the request as a bait-and-switch. Being away from their families and farms for three years was far different than being away for three months. Despite considerable pressure, 350 declined to extend their terms. Soon, however, they were replaced with new recruits who agreed to the longer enlistment and the regiment again reached full strength of 1,023 officers and enlisted men.

Local newspapers followed the regiment's progress with great interest, while citizens near Fort Snelling offered what support they could. Officers were entertained in Minneapolis and St. Paul, and one day, in an effort to boost morale, six stage-loads of young women from St. Anthony visited the troops. But in mid-June rumors spread that the regiment was about to be sent east to war. On June 22, following a sendoff address by the chaplain and a parade, the regiment boarded troop transports at the lower landing in St. Paul and began its journey east to Washington, D.C.[3]

The First Minnesota was attached to General McDowell's army, which marched south from Washington. Its mission was to capture the Confederate capital at Richmond, Virginia and end the war quickly. Only about 100 miles separated Washington from Richmond. On July 21, McDowell's army met Confederate General Beauregard's force on a plateau behind Bull Run Creek, close to Manassas Junction. The Union right flank pushed back the Confederates some distance and McDowell thought the battle was his. However, the Confederates retreated to a stronger hilltop position at Henry House Hill defended by the Confederate general Thomas Jackson. Jackson would be known after this battle by the nickname "Stonewall" because of the stout defense put up by his men.

The First Minnesota, which had been held in reserve for most of the day, was sent in near the battle's climax to guard Rickett's artillery battery as it was positioned to attack Jackson's men. Other Union forces had fought for many hours and were tired and thirsty. The battery had just begun to fire when some of Jackson's 33rd Virginia Regiment came out of the woods in blue uniforms. Because of the uniforms, they were mistaken for Union soldiers and the Union army withheld fire. It was a fatal mistake. Jackson's men fired a barrage, wiping out the artillery battery and killing and wounding 30 men of the First Minnesota.

Soon after, Confederate General Johnston's fresh troops arrived from the Shenandoah Valley, eluding a Union force sent to block them. The Confederates charged into battle using, for the first time, the intimidating rebel yell. The weary and surprised Union troops began to fall back. The First Minnesota held its position until ordered to withdraw.[4]

Forty two men of the First Minnesota were killed in a half hour of fighting, including Anton Simek. The first Czech to settle in Steele County died at the age of 33 in service to his newly adopted country. A fellow member of Company I, Edward M. Kerrott, in an affidavit for the probate of Anton Simek's will, described his death:

> . . . Schimeck was there shot by a bullet or musket ball which made a wound from which I saw much blood and from which wound he died. I saw him laying on his face upon the ground apparently dead and I have no doubt that he was dead.

Earlier, on July 2, in the Union army encampment in Washington D.C., Anton Simek had prepared his will. He made bequests of real estate to his sisters Rosalie and Anastasia and a gift of $50 to his brother Joseph to buy schoolbooks for his children. He left $50 to his sister Anna in Bohemia to help pay for her children to come to America if they so desired, and he left $25 to a fellow Czech in South Hadley Falls, Massachusetts.

Finally, he left "to my friend Emily Strong of Owatonna $100 to be paid out to her within two years in case she accepts this small sum as a testimonial of friendship." This was a considerable sum in 1860, so Anton was clearly very fond of Emily. She was a school teacher in the county schools who had moved to Minnesota from Connecticut with her brother Charles and sister Minerva. A few years after Anton's death, she married Judge Nicholas Donaldson, and they had two daughters together.[5]

The Dakota Uprising

Besides the War, another major disruption during the early 1860s was the Dakota uprising. Hunger and mistreatment by government agents and traders gave rise to such discontent that on August 17, 1862, a few Dakota Indians murdered several white settlers in Meeker County. The next morning a party of Dakota attacked the Lower Sioux agency on the Minnesota River and some nearby communities. One person killed at the agency was trader Andrew Myrick, who three days earlier had said of the hungry Indians that they could eat grass or their own dung. The unrest quickly spread and by the end of August all of western Minnesota was up in arms. The worst fighting was in the Minnesota River valley west of Mankato and New Ulm. Although there was no fighting in the Owatonna area, there must have been considerable fear of the violence spreading east. By the end of December when the fighting ended, several hundred white settlers, more than seventy soldiers, and about seventy Indians were dead. Many Indians had fled to Canada or the Dakota Territory, others were shut up at Fort Snelling and thirty eight were hanged in Mankato. Federal troops continued into 1863 to pursue Indians who had fled west and north.

The Civil War increased in intensity during 1863 and 1864, with military action from the east coast states to the Mississippi River Valley. Major battles with massive casualties were fought at Antietam, Gettysburg, and other sites. The United States passed a conscription law in March 1863 to ensure sufficient soldiers for the Union Army. Relatively few people were actually drafted, but many volunteered to get the enlistment bonus, expecting to be drafted if they did not. The law allowed a drafted man to pay another man $300 to take his place. For a time Minnesota was able to meet its quota with reenlistments and new recruits, but the state resorted to the draft in May and September of 1864. After exemptions and desertions, only 269 were held for service, with an additional 272 who were substitutes.[6]

The Czechs Who Served
In addition to Anton Simek, several other Steele County Czechs fought in the Civil War. **Joseph Pichner**, age 21 (shown as Buchner in army records) and **Frank Seykora**, age 23 (apparently the son of Anton Seykora, and shown as Frantel Saikora in army records) mustered into Company C of the Second Minnesota Regiment Cavalry as it formed in December 1863. This force spent the war years in western Minnesota and the Dakotas protecting against Indian retaliation in the aftermath of the 1862 Dakota conflict. They were on fort garrison duty in western Minnesota until May 1864, when they joined General Sully's expedition into the Dakotas. The expedition lasted nearly five months, pursuing and fighting warring Dakota bands that had fled Minnesota in 1862. They fought at the Battle of Killdeer Mountain or Tah kah a kuty in July, and rescued Fiske's emigrant train in late September. For the rest of 1864 and 1865, the

mounted troops were assigned frontier patrol duty between Fort Wadsworth in the Dakota Territory, Fort Abercrombie on the Red River, Fort Ripley near Brainerd, and Fort Ridgely near New Ulm.[7]

Joseph Pichner mustered out of the army on November 17, 1865, as a trumpeter. Frank Seykora received a disability discharge on March 22, 1865, due to battle wounds; he apparently died shortly after that date as Kovar's history says he was killed in battle.[8]

John Renchin (Rencill in the records), age 40, mustered into Company G of the First Minnesota Infantry in March 1865, and mustered out just four months later in July 1865. He was paid $300 to take the place of one "Neigabauer" (perhaps this is the J. Nengibauer shown living in Somerset Township in the 1879 plat book). By the time he was trained and sent east to his regiment, Confederate General Lee had surrendered at Appomattox Court House and the war had ended. The First Minnesota, which had been involved in the siege of Petersburg, Virginia and took part in the final pursuit of General Lee, marched to Washington, D.C. in July for the victory parade. The entire unit was mustered out of service in mid-July and Renchin returned to Steele County. However, before the war's end, in June of 1865 en route to a posting in Louisville, Kentucky, the regiment was battered by heavy rains and hail. Many soldiers, including John Renchin, became ill. Renchin developed rheumatism and a couple of large tumors on his back. The symptoms faded but recurred periodically in later years, and his health never fully returned. Thirty years after the war, and after several applications, he finally received military disability pay for the injuries sustained on the June 1865 march. Affidavits filed in support of the application detail health problems he had for the rest of his life, as well as the circumstances of his illness.[9]

Wencl Watowa (Vaclav Votava) came to America in 1864 and in January 1865, at the age of 30, located in Faribault. He enlisted in Company L of the First Minnesota Heavy Artillery and was sent to garrison duty in Chattanooga, Tennessee. The Civil War ended before he saw combat and he was mustered out in September of 1865. He returned to Faribault but moved to Owatonna the following year where he spent the rest of his life.[10]

News of Lee's surrender at Appomatox Courthouse reached Owatonna at 2:00 a.m. on April 11, 1865. A cannon was dragged into the town square and repeatedly fired to wake the townspeople and spread the great news. The day was given over to celebrations that lasted far into the night.

In the following weeks and months Steele County citizens mustered out of the army and returned home to their farms and trades. The war had been a giant undertaking; more died than in any American War before or since. The north felt a sense of solidarity. The common effort of its citizens had led to victory. America's immigrant groups too were proud of their contributions to the war. Every Czech area "stressed the role played by its boys."[11]

But the impact of the war went beyond the loss of those who died. Like all wars, the Civil War threw together people and ideas in new combinations.

> The War and Reconstruction served as catalytic agents in the Czech's awareness of the American way of life. The stories that veterans on both sides of the civil conflict told about encounters and acquaintances with the new world's land and people were sources of revelation to the Bohemian and Moravian immigrants who knew the states only from busy city streets and crowded neighborhoods or from the dreary and physically taxing rural areas of the semi-frontier.[12]

THE SETTLERS

The Homestead Act of 1862, passed by Congress during the Civil War, had far-reaching effects. Members of Congress had been trying to pass a homestead bill for federal lands since the 1840s, but each time were stymied by representatives of the slaveholding states, who feared that newly settled territories might be admitted as non-slave states tipping the balance in Congress. The law passed quickly once the slave states seceded from the Union. For more than 100 years, from 1862 to 1986, settlers homesteaded in thirty-eight of the fifty states, claiming more than 10% of the land area of the United States.

A homesteader had to be the head of a household and 21 years of age. The process began when the homesteader filed a declaration of intent to settle on a piece of property. The land office checked its records to ensure no one else owned the land, and the temporary claim was cemented with a filing fee of $10 plus a $2 commission for the land agent. Now the homesteader could build a home on the land and begin farming. After five years, two persons who knew the homesteader signed a declaration attesting that improvements to the land had been made. Once this declaration was accepted, and a $6 filing fee paid, the patent for the land was issued and the homesteader owned the land.

If the homesteader had money and was in a hurry, he could homestead the land for six months and purchase it from the government for $1.25 per acre.

Wheat prices were good during the war, in part because with so many men in the army, much of the land was not cultivated. However, many new immigrants arrived during the war, and mechanization of farming sped up to allow fewer farmers to raise more food. In addition, government purchases for the war effort gave a big boost to the economy. Wheat prices in Minneapolis rose from 50 cents a bushel in 1861 to $1.50 in 1866, and the general rise of prices was of the same magnitude.[13] This inflation made it easier for landholders to pay off their farms. The price of town lots went up and Owatonna began its recovery from the bad times of the late 1850s.

Although the county history says that Steele County was half depopulated during the Civil War and settlement was at a standstill, nearly forty Czech families arrived during the 1860s, some of them in the midst of the war.[14]

Czech Arrivals in the 1860s

Slezaks—The Slezak family, Anton and Annie and children John, Frank, Anton, Josephine and Annie, arrived in New York on October 10, 1861, after a six-week journey on the sailing ship *Bavaria*. They made their way across country, traveling north on the Mississippi by boat and arriving in Hastings on November 11. There they met a group of Polish settlers from Owatonna who had brought their grain to the Hastings mill. The Poles agreed to let the Slezaks accompany them back to Owatonna. Anton Slezak, then five years old, recalled:

> The city was then bordering a wilderness, and there were but ten houses and the Winship Hotel when we pulled into Owatonna in the old fashioned ox-drawn wagon.[15]

The Slezaks stayed a year with the John Pichner family and two years with Joseph Kaplan before claiming 80 acres of land in Owatonna Township for themselves. Anton remembered these years:

> Here I spent my boyhood in rattlesnake-infested brushes and swamps. I remember well the episode when brother John and I, both barefooted, were chasing each other in play. John slipped on a rattler and skinned him from tail to head, with the reptile having no chance to strike as its skin was pulled over its head.[16]

In 1874, the Slezaks sold their land to the Sustacek family and bought 160 acres in Somerset Township.

Frank Kubista (Frantisek Kubista) and his wife Rosalie came to America with their three children on the same ship with the Slezaks. Frank Kubista was one of four Kubista siblings who came to Steele County. His sister Anna was married to Anton Kubat, and they had come to Owatonna in 1856 (see chapter 1). His sister Catherine, married to John Renchin, would come in 1863. His brother Ignac came in 1867. Frank and his family settled in Owatonna Township, and in 1866 he sold some of his land to provide a site for the Sacred Heart Catholic Church.

Departure of Joseph Simek—One of the county's Czech pioneers departed for greener pastures around this time. Joseph Simek and his family were still living in Steele County at the time of the 1860 census. However, by the time their son John was born in October of 1862, they were living in southern Minnesota in Faribault County. Joseph's brother Anton had been killed at the Battle of Bull Run in 1861, which may have caused the move. For whatever reason, Joseph and Anna and their children moved to Faribault County, where they and most of their children remained. Interestingly, Joseph was still purchasing property in Steele County in June 1864.

Joseph and Anna were important pioneers in the Blue Earth, Minnesota area. Joseph hosted Catholic services in his home until the local church was built. He also had a mill, and when it burned down, he repaid all he owed to the farmers whose flour and grain were burned in the fire. He started a brewery and hired young Paul Fleckenstein to operate it. Paul wooed and won Joseph's daughter Theresa and married her in 1865 in Blue Earth.

Joseph died in 1900 and Anna in 1893. Several of their children survived into the 1930s. The brewery finally closed in 1904 when Paul Fleckenstein died and none of the younger generation chose to continue its operation.[17]

Jirouseks—Wenzel and Anna (Kašpar) Jirousek came to America in 1862 with a son, Wenzel, and six daughters and settled in Owatonna Township. Young Wenzel married Mary Wondra, and in 1878 purchased the Wondra farm in Summit Township from Mary's sister.

Kovars—Anton and Anna (Zednik) Kovar and their children Vaclav, Anton, Barbara and Jan came to America in 1862. Anna was a cousin of Joseph Kaplan who had come to Owatonna in 1856. Her father Jan Kaplan died when she was an infant and her mother (Katerina Smola Kaplan) then married Joseph Zednik. Later, Joseph and Katerina had two more daughters, Barbara and Philomena.

Anna Zednik married Anton Kovar in 1852 and they lived on a farm in Dlouhá Třebová that Anna had inherited from her father. A few years later, her half sister Barbara married Joseph Kaplan (Anna's cousin) and the Kaplans left for America. Anton and Anna Kovar joined them in 1862.

After his death, Anna's father's cottage had been kept in trust by Anna's uncle for her, along with money raised by selling her father's loom and other possessions. When Anton and Anna arrived in Minnesota they apparently used the money from this trust to purchase a farm, livestock and farm implements. They settled in the Czech settlement just south of the city of Owatonna.[18]

Anton and Anna were accompanied on the ocean voyage by John and Barbara Kovar and their children Barbara and Anna, and by John Kovar's parents, Joseph and Katherine Kovar. Undoubtedly these Kovars were relatives of Anton and Anna.

John and Barbara Kovar spent the first two years living about 30 miles southwest of Owatonna (apparently in Freeborn County near Albert Lea). They were able to save up a good sum of money, but the sandy nature of the soil made it a poor place for farming. They moved north to Steele County by June 1865 and bought land about a mile south of Owatonna. They arrived in late fall and spent the winter in a log cabin with an abundance of cracks and no floor. They slept on featherbeds in the three-foot-deep cellar.

Their land was mostly woods. John Kovar had been a weaver in Bohemia, and did not know much about farming. However, wood was selling for $5 or more per cord, so he made a living for a time by logging his property.[19]

Belinas—Wenzel and Johanna Belina and their five children arrived in America in 1862 on the same ship as the Kovars and traveled to Steele County. They purchased a farm in section 26 of Owatonna Township and struggled for years to make it pay. Wenzel and Johanna lived on the farm until they died. Their son Anton became a wagon maker and later opened a liquor store. Another son, Charles, went on to study medicine in Iowa, and then with Dr. Morehouse of Owatonna. All of Wenzel and Johanna's sons were musicians in addition to their careers, each playing a different instrument. Their music entertained the Steele County Czechs for decades.[20]

John and Catherine Renchin—John J. and Catherine (Kubista) Renchin (Jan and Katerina Renčin) and children Barbara, Frances, John and Rosa arrived in 1863. John was 38 and had already served eight years in the Austrian army. He applied for a homestead in Somerset Township but the work was hard and money was short. When a county resident offered him $300 to enlist in the Union Army in his place, John signed on.

After his discharge John struggled for years with rheumatism and recurring tumors on his back. He could drive animal teams but could do no heavy lifting. When his ailments were particularly bad, he was taken into town lying in the back of a wagon to be treated by Doctor Morehouse. Finally in 1898, he was awarded a disability pension by the government.[21]

John Wondra (Jan Vondra) and family came to America in 1864. They traveled to Minnesota and bought a farm in Summit Township from the Hissams, becoming one of the township's first Czech families. After the shooting death of their son, young John

Wondra, in 1875 (see chapter 5), his sister bought the farm from her parents and later sold it to her brother-in-law, Wencl Jirousek. Jirouseks still lived on the farm in 2009.

John Wanous (Jan Vanous), from Dlouha Třebová, was a weaver and a soldier in the Austrian army for nine years, spending much of that time stationed in Germany doing military police duty. In 1861, he married Anna Jiroušek, but his military duty continued. After their first child was born, they fled to America. They spent two years in Chicago and then moved their family to Steele County in 1864. The family farmed rented land in Steele County for two or three years, then purchased twenty acres of land in Owatonna Township. Through thrift and hard work, their land holdings gradually grew to 455 acres as their family grew to eleven children.[22]

THE RAILROADS

Early Czechs arrived in Owatonna on horseback, in wagons, or by foot, and in 1866 arriving by railroad became possible. Railroads were still the dream of every town in America and construction of tracks toward Owatonna, first begun in 1858, resumed in 1863. One company was building from Winona, and another moving south from Mendota. In July 1866, they were both about 15 miles from Owatonna and each announced it would be the first to reach town.

The railroad companies worked night and day, through storms and shortages. The Minnesota Central from Mendota reached Owatonna during the night of Friday, August 17, 1866, laying its last stretch of tracks. The Winona and St. Peter entered town from the east the following Monday morning, August 20, completing its final segment. However, the first train, which arrived Monday to be greeted by a band, reception committee, speeches and celebrations, was from Winona. As the celebration wound down, a second train, from the Minnesota Central, pulled in from the north. Although the Minnesota Central had won the race to lay tracks to Owatonna, the first train into town was from the Winona and St. Peter.[23]

With the end of the Civil War, America became a safer and more appealing destination to Europeans. Owatonna too became a safer and more appealing destination as the railroads into town were completed. Three new hotels opened in Owatonna in 1866 and several more opened two years later. A bank opened in 1866. Farmers could now get supplies and take crops to market much more quickly and easily. The county was poised for rapid growth.

First locomotive to reach Owatonna in 1866. (Photograph taken in 1873.)
Courtesy of Steele County Historical Society

CATHOLICS AND FREETHINKERS

Czech religious history from the time of Jan Hus through the Protestant Reformation and the Thirty Year's War, and into the subsequent forced re-Catholicization of the Czechs, had generated a strong antipathy to the Catholic Church in many Czechs, particularly nationalists who saw the church as a partner with the Habsburgs in oppressing the Czechs. When they arrived in America, many Czechs reveled in their new freedom from the established church. (For a fuller discussion of Czech history, see Appendix A)

Consequently, Czech immigrants had one of the highest rates of non-affiliation with a church of any of the ethnic and national groups that came to America. Nationally, a reasonable estimate is that half of the first generation of Czech immigrants did not attend church. These freethinkers, or religious liberals as they were later called, were a mixture of atheists, agnostics, and religious Czechs who belonged to no particular denomination. They were often joined by former Catholics who had quit attending church for financial reasons or due to personality conflicts with the priest or other congregants. The percentage of freethinkers was higher in large cities like New York, Milwaukee and Chicago, and lower in farm areas. In Minnesota, it appears that about 60% to 70% of the Czech immigrants remained Catholic. Of the non-Catholics, most were freethinkers, and a small percentage was Protestant.[24]

The usual evolution of a Czech immigrant community in America began with a few families who remained close. The bonds holding these families together in a sea of people with foreign ways were a common language and culture. However, as more Czechs arrived, tensions grew between the Catholics and the freethinkers. In many locations organizations formed for all Czech immigrants began to be dominated by freethinkers as the Catholic Czechs founded parishes that became the center of their social and spiritual lives. Freethinkers did not want to attend church, were not welcome there, and could not be buried in church cemeteries. Their response was to form their own organizations.

This process of separation took a big step forward in Steele County in 1866 with the founding of Sacred Heart Catholic Church and the founding of the first secular Czech organization, the Slovanská Lípa. These were followed closely by the organization of cemetery associations.

SACRED HEART CHURCH

Owatonna Catholics were ministered to in the early years by Father Keller from Faribault, who had charge of nearly half the Catholics of Minnesota at the time. He ministered to an area stretching from Rosemount in the north to Blooming Prairie on the south, and from Kilkenny east to Pine Island. One time he walked the forty miles from Hastings to Faribault rather than use parish funds for stagecoach fare.[25]

When he first visited Owatonna services were held in private homes. He later obtained permission to offer mass in Dresser's and Burtsch's halls. While in town he stayed with Charles Schoen, a wagon maker and blacksmith, and with Sheriff Michael Toher and his wife, described by Father Pivo in his history of the local church as being "one of the most enthusiastic workers for the cause of our holy religion in this town."[26]

In 1866, local Catholics decided to build a church and formed a building committee composed of Michael Toher, Charles Schoen, Joseph Kaplan, William Leary, and James Lonergan. On September 4, Joseph Kaplan purchased the land from Frank Kubista for $189 and donated it to the church (this remains the site of the present-day structure). He also bought a parcel of land for the priest's house. Construction on the church began in 1867 and was completed in 1868 at a cost of $2,600. The building was dedicated on Christmas Day of 1868.

James Lonergan was still alive in 1901 when this first church building burned down, and he remembered the building of it in a newspaper article that year. A building "bee" had been held to raise the frame for the building. The frame was of heavy green Norway pine and very solid, as attested to by the difficulty the 1901 firefighters had in pulling it apart. The builders had great difficulty getting the posts raised and into position without having one fall, which would probably have crushed any worker in its path. Mr. Lonergan said that the memory of that fear still made him start in his sleep thirty years later.

Once the walls were raised, Lonergan went to the church in the evenings after supper and made the window frames. The tower and sacristy were built later. One year the choir gallery was added just before Christmas. Volunteers had gathered on several evenings with their tools and built the gallery in time for a choir and organ concert during Christmas service.[27]

During this period Fathers Keller (1866–1870) and Scheve (1870–1873) of Faribault ministered to the congregation. In 1873 Father Laurence Weiseler, who was also based in Faribault, began construction of a parish house that was completed in 1875. The lack of a full time resident priest for the years before the parish house was built had resulted in a sporadic schedule of services. The *Owatonna Journal* in the early 1870s listed weekly church services in each issue. The listings for Sacred Heart in 1873 were:

> Catholic—Cedar Street—Rev. Mr. Shavey [sic], pastor. Services every alternate Sunday at 10½ o'clock. Sunday school every Sunday at 3 o'clock.

In 1875, upon completion of the Sacred Heart Church parish house, Father Pribyl became the first resident pastor of the parish. Although Father Pribyl was Czech, the parish served all Catholics of the town, whatever their nationality. He was particularly suited for the post because he spoke English, Czech and German well, and also understood Polish.

BOHEMIAN NATIONAL CEMETERY

The Bohemian National Cemetery Association was created in Chicago in 1877 to fill the need for burial grounds for freethinking Czechs. Members could acquire plots by donating labor to help maintain the grounds. Many other Czech communities in America quickly founded cemeteries under the umbrella of the Association. In Owatonna Township the

Bohemian National Cemetery in Owatonna, about 1900.
Courtesy of Steele County Historical Society

Czech-Slovanic National Cemetery, originally founded as a Catholic cemetery, became an affiliate. Another affiliated cemetery was later founded in southern Steele County.[28]

In a letter to his brother written in 1910, Joseph Kaplan speaks of his role in organizing two cemeteries in Owatonna:

> That same year [1866] I had also bought five acres of land and helped organize the Catholic Cemetery. In 1867, I helped organize the National Bohemian Cemetery of Owatonna.[29]

The Catholic Cemetery he speaks of was the Sacred Heart Cemetery, located about a mile south of the Sacred Heart Church. The National Bohemian Cemetery was located further east in the area where the earliest Czech settlers built their homes, about a mile from Sacred Heart Cemetery. Its history as a cemetery apparently began in 1867 with the burial of Josef Zednik on the land of John and Anna Pavek. Frank Seykora's wife Josefa was buried there the same year, followed by Catherine Pavek in 1868. Vaclav Fisher died in 1869, Jan Pribyl in April 1871, and Vaclav Pichner in July 1871, and all were buried there. The Paveks finally sold the burial area for use as a cemetery.

This is the account of the beginning of the Bohemian National Cemetery given in the history of Sacred Heart Church, which differs markedly from Kaplan's account:

The Bohemian Catholic Cemetery in Steele County had its beginning back on October 24, 1871. This is recorded in the warranty deed by which John and Anna Pavek deeded the two acre cemetery plot to Joseph Kaplan in trust to be used 'as a Bohemian Catholic Burial Ground or Cemetery, and for no other purpose'. This same family deeded a roadway leading to this cemetery across their land from Austin Road in 1874.

During these early days this Catholic Cemetery was blessed by the pastor of Sacred Heart Parish. The pioneers do not remember which pastor it was.

In 1877 Joseph Kaplan deeded this two acre plot (of which he was the trustee) to the Bohemian Catholic Cemetery. Up to that time the land was simply held in trust by Joseph Kaplan and, as the deed read, it was meant 'for use as a Bohemian Catholic Burial Ground.' However, in the secretary's book which records the minutes of the first meetings and also the first officers chosen, the name of the cemetery is given as the 'Bohemian Slovanic National Cemetery.' Thus, while John and Anna Pavek gave the land in trust of Joseph Kaplan to be used as a Catholic burying ground, when it was organized in 1876 it became the Bohemian Slovanic National Cemetery.

This cemetery, although organized as the Bohemian Slovanic National Cemetery, carried the name of "Bohemian Catholic Cemetery" until 1897, when the book of deeds showed the name was officially changed to what it is now, Bohemian Slovanic National Cemetery.[30]

Lore passed down through the Kaplan family says that Joseph Kaplan had a falling out with one of the Catholic priests later in life, and quit attending church. However, that disagreement appears to have happened long after the deeding of the Bohemian cemetery (see chapter 8). The cemetery contains a mixture of Catholic and non-Catholic graves as part of the cemetery had been consecrated for Catholic use and some of the early burials were of Catholics.

The association for the Czech-Slavonic National Cemetery in Owatonna Township was formed in November 1876. Officers elected that day were John Pichner as President, Joseph Wavrin as Secretary, and John Seykora as Treasurer. The Board of Directors included Frank Seykora, Anton Kovar and Frank Wesely.

In 1878, new officers were elected and Articles of Operation were accepted. Members accepting the articles and rules at the 1878 meeting were Joseph Kaplan (President), John Pavek (Secretary), John Pichner, John Dusek, Frank Dostal, Frank Spatenka, Joseph Skerik, Anton Kubat, Frank Pavek, Frank Shimek, Frank J. and Joseph M. Belina and John Pichner, Jr.

Although the Sacred Heart Church history quoted above implies that Joseph Kaplan took land that John Pavek had intended for a Catholic cemetery and conveyed it in 1877 for use as a freethinker cemetery, John Pavek appears as both a member and officer of the new cemetery. Other early officers and directors include staunch Catholics John and Frank Seykora. It appears that the intent of the officers of the 1870s, including those who were Catholic, was to create a cemetery for Czechs where Catholics and non-Catholics alike were welcome.

The articles of the Czech-Slavonic National Cemetery provide for a caretaker. He was paid $3 per year for maintenance, 50 cents annually for record keeping, and $3 for each grave dug ($5 in the winter).

For $5, families becoming members received a plot 20 feet by 12 feet for their burials. A person desiring room for a single burial would be charged $2. If a poor person wished to be buried and could not afford a plot, he was to be buried free of charge.[31]

EARLY FREETHINKER ORGANIZATIONS

The first Czech organization in Owatonna was the Slovanská Lípa (Slavic Linden Tree). The earliest chapter of Slovanská Lípa in America was apparently formed in Detroit in 1857, and was named after a patriotic organization that had formed in Prague during the revolution of 1848. (The linden tree, supposedly sacred to the gods in the Slavs' pre-Christian era, was a Czech nationalist symbol in the nineteenth century.) Chapters were formed in Chicago, Cleveland, Baltimore, St. Louis, Milwaukee, Racine, St. Paul, and other cities. They served as Czech social centers and reading societies, organized cultural and gymnastic activities, and usually sponsored their city's Czech language schools. Money was raised to support these activities from plays, receptions, dances and picnics.

Slovanská Lípa originated as a joint venture of Catholic and freethinking Czechs. But in time, many of the local chapters became dominated by anticlerical members and the Catholics left. Apparently there were never more than 35 lodges in the U.S. and these tended to be absorbed later by Czech fraternal organizations that were bettered financed.[32]

The Owatonna chapter of Slovanská Lípa was founded either in 1863 (Frank Kovar) or 1866 (K.E. Srsen). One of its first activities was to obtain a supply of books, which comprised the first public library in Steele County. Joseph Rypka donated $200 for the purchase of these books. A Czech reading room was established soon after the war, and located two or three miles out of town. The Owatonna chapter survived until it was absorbed by the C.S.P.S. in the early 1900s.[33]

No records remain from the Owatonna chapter, but a description survives of an 1861 meeting of the Racine, Wisconsin chapter that gives the flavor of the organization. The Racine hall was decorated with a picture of George Washington placed between two flags, one with a Czech lion and the other with the Czech phrase for Long Live Slavdom. The program consisted of a musical selection, a talk about pan-Slavic solidarity, a comedy play, humorous readings, and ended with the singing of Arise Ye Slavs. The program was followed by a dance.[34]

A Slavic Congress, held in Chicago in late 1865 and early 1866, resolved to petition the United States Congress for land to create a free Czech homeland in America. Another resolution called for forming a pan-Slavic organization created by inviting all American Slavs to join the Slovanská Lípa. The plan for the Czech homeland failed immediately due to lack of funds to even send a delegation to Washington. The Pan-Slavic idea also died quickly. No Czechs from Minnesota traveled to the congress.[35]

SCHOOLS AND LANGUAGE EDUCATION

Attitudes toward schools and language education differed greatly between Czech Catholics and freethinkers. The differences arose from their divergent reactions to the nature of American society and their views on how they should adapt.

One thing both parties agreed on was their desire to preserve the Czech language and culture. Frequently one of the first community activities of Czech settlers was to create a Czech language school where younger generations could continue to speak Czech. According to Frank Kovar, the first Czech school in Owatonna was begun in 1864 with Joseph Kaplan as teacher. K.E. Srsen recorded that the school was first held in the rural public school building. Later, when the Czech Auditorium Hall (C.S.P.S.) was built, a Czech school operated there on Sundays. Its first teachers were Albert (Vojtech) Kaspar and Joseph Soukup, and later Anton Zajic-Donato, K.E. Srsen, Marie Moravec, Joseph Velebny, Frank Veverka, Vaclav Chott, and Otilie Moravec.

Frank Moravec, speaking much later about the activities at the Czech Hall in Owatonna, talked of the role of the Czech language school students:

> Children who attend the Czech school often prepare for us beautiful Czech programs. Everyone's personal convictions are tolerated, and there is no jealousy amongst religions. I want to announce that in our Czech hall there

is a cupboard with books which is at the disposal of our people by making a request of the caretaker.[36]

Josef J. Kovar relates his experiences in Czech language school around 1873:

When I was eight years old, we had Bohemian school for four months and I learned spelling and a lot of reading. The teacher arranged a spell-down and it included many children from Bohemia, but I won twice and my cousin won once.[37]

According to Frank Kovar, Czech was taught until World War I, when immigrants began to be viewed with suspicion and foreign language schools were banned. The school never reopened after the war.[38]

Catholics and freethinkers, however, had very different attitudes toward public schools. The common school, now called the public school, got started throughout the United States before the Civil War as part of a broader reform movement involving abolitionism and prohibition. The ideology was based on "Republicanism, Protestantism, and Capitalism, three sources of social belief that were intertwined and mutually supporting." The schools were unabashedly Protestant and used Protestant hymns, prayers and Bible readings. Many Catholic bishops felt the public school system was "both heretical and infidel." Meetings of bishops in Baltimore in 1852 and 1866 recommended that, if possible, every Catholic parish start a Catholic school.[39]

In 1869, because of the religious pluralism of the city, the Cincinnati Board of Education decided to exclude Bible reading, religious instruction, and hymn singing from the public schools. The board's action caused an uproar throughout the country. Protestants tended to view the public school system and its Protestant religious education as a bulwark of American society. Citizens who read the Bible, applying their own interpretations, were thought to have the intellectual independence and judgment necessary to a democracy and a free market economy. Removing the Bible from public schools would undercut education in citizenship skills. The public school was seen as:

God's chosen instrument for religionizing and Americanizing the youth, and they roundly castigated those who opposed it—chiefly the Roman Catholics.[40]

An article in the November 17, 1864, issue of the *Owatonna Plaindealer*, a very Republican newspaper, is an example of anti-Catholic attitudes common in America at the time. The article followed Abraham Lincoln's re-election and complains about Catholic Irish support for the Democratic Party. Under the heading "The Catholic Population," the article provides the following description of Catholicism:

> We all know that the Catholic religion is opposed to the diffusion of intelligence among the masses, and so long as they can keep them ignorant, so long will their churches prosper, but when the common people begin to read and are permitted to reason for themselves, then the Catholic fabric begins to shake from its circumference to its center.

The controversy over the nature of public schools, and whether Catholic children should attend, continued for decades; we will return to it in future chapters. However, separate schools were expensive and teachers scarce. Consequently, many Catholic parishes never founded a school. Generally, Czech neighborhoods in large cities were better able to afford Catholic schools than were rural or small town parishes. It would be many more years before Owatonna was able to support a Catholic elementary school for both boys and girls.

GROWTH OF SOUTHERN STEELE COUNTY

During the 1850s land survey Minnesota was divided into a series of townships. The townships of Steele County form a grid of three across, east to west, by four deep, north to south (see map at beginning of chapter 6).

European settlement of Steele County tended to move from north to south. The first area settled was the subdivided township of Medford and Clinton Falls, followed quickly by Owatonna Township to the south. A year or two later Europeans settled in the townships south of Owatonna (Somerset, and below that, Summit). These townships remained sparsely populated for the next few years until the coming of railroads to Owatonna in 1866 spurred their development.

The first Czech settlers in Steele County concentrated in Owatonna Township, south and southeast of the city of Owatonna. In the 1857 territorial census all Czech names in Steele County were in Owatonna Township; that pattern continued in the 1860 census. However, as more Czechs moved into the county, they found cheaper land to the south, in Somerset, Summit, and Blooming Prairie Townships.

*St. Columbanus in Blooming Prairie, about 1914.
Courtesy of Steele County Historical Society*

Blooming Prairie

Blooming Prairie was born as a railroad camp. The Minnesota Central Railroad pushed south from Owatonna in 1867 setting up temporary camps at regular intervals along the right of way to feed and house construction workers. One of those camps became Blooming Prairie as railroad workers' shacks were supplemented by a railroad station, a hotel, a blacksmith shop, a recreation hall, and, in 1868, a post office and school house.

The first known Catholic mass in Blooming Prairie was said by Father Prendegast in 1867, and the first St. Columbanus Catholic Church was erected the following year. The parish drew both construction workers and farmers from the surrounding areas.[41] In the 1870 census, the only Czech names in the Blooming Prairie area (called Oak Glen in those days) were Vincent Wencl (Vincenc Vencl), his wife Anna, and daughter Mary.

Litomysl

The 1865 census shows Czech expansion into Somerset Township, and by 1870 Czechs were moving south into Summit Township as well.

Somerset Township lies directly south of Owatonna Township, and is watered by the Straight River flowing north, and Turtle Creek flowing west. The first European settler was Thomas Thompson in 1855. He was joined the following year by more than three dozen new residents, mostly native-born Americans. The village of Somerset was platted in section 20 in 1856, but never developed. By the end of 1856 most of the best government land had been claimed. The first Czech settlers arrived about 1863.

The southern Czech settlement in Somerset and Summit Townships was separated from the original Czech settlement in Owatonna Township by a few miles of land claimed by other nationalities. The center of the southern Czech settlement was about nine miles from Sacred Heart Catholic Church in Owatonna. This was a long distance by horseback, thus the southern settlement developed largely independent of Owatonna Township. It eventually had its own Catholic church and school, public schools, stores, creameries, and social halls. This region, the second major Czech settlement in Steele County, never became an incorporated town; however, it came to be known as Litomysl after a city in eastern Bohemia. No one knows why the new settlement was named after this city since the settlers were not from the city of Litomysl, but from small villages to the east, and Litomysl in Bohemia was neither the religious seat nor the nearest market city for the immigrant's home villages.

Seykoras—The extended Seykora family was one of the first Czech groups to settle in Somerset and Summit Townships. (Although Joseph Simek purchased land in section two of Somerset Township in July 1857, he apparently never lived there, but continued to live in Owatonna Township.) Anton Seykora and his family arrived in America in 1862, and John and Frank, their families, and their sister Rosalia arrived in 1863. Rosalia settled in Owatonna Township and remained there. After a short stay in the Owatonna area, Frank and Anton and their families moved to Somerset Township. John and his wife Emilia and children Anna, Emelia and Rosalia settled first in Owatonna at the site where presently stands the West Hills complex. In 1864, John moved his family to Summit Township and settled in section 4, near his brothers. His land was located a mile south of the future Litomysl Church. The family's log house had an entryway, one large downstairs room, and one room upstairs where the children, eventually numbering eleven, slept.[42]

The three Seykora brothers were among the founders of the Litomysl community and church.

> Although all three were more or less gruff and short-tempered, they were the type of men of which frontiersmen were made. Anton was known as the most prudent of the three brothers. He was known to be very considerate of others, and was ever ready to help his less fortunate neighbors. Anton was also remembered as being deliberate and slow in his actions.[43]

Anton Seykora bought land in section 26 of Somerset Township on June 12, 1863. Anton Schattlau and his wife Anna (the sister of Anton Simek) bought land in the same section on the same day. Anton's brother Frank Seykora purchased land in the section on July 17, and on September 23, Joseph Rypka and Joseph Horsky also purchased land in section 26. In the same year other Czechs arrived in other sections of Somerset Township. On September 23, Joseph Pichner purchased land in section 34 and on October 10, Wencl Wanous purchased land in section 24.

Several of the settlers expanded their holdings the following spring. On March 22, 1864, Joseph Pichner, Joseph Rypka, Frank Seykora, Anton Schattlau and Anton Seykora bought more land in section 35 of Somerset Township, just south of section 26. Anton Seykora purchased 40 acres from Christian Borchert; the others purchased 20 acres each. This section would eventually become the home of the Litomysl church.

Kaspers—Joseph (Josef) and Dorthea (Brožek) Kasper (Kašpar) and their seven children from Ustí nad Orlicí came to the United States in 1864. Joseph had planned to emigrate in 1848, but his older brother hurriedly left Bohemia to escape military service in the Austrian army. Since the oldest son was unavailable, it fell on the next son to perform the service. When his time with the Austrian army ended, Joseph saved the necessary twenty dollars in gold per family member to secure permission to leave and pay passage to America.

Upon reaching America, the Kaspers traveled first to Wisconsin to visit Joseph's older brother and then ventured on to Owatonna. They rented a house in Owatonna for six months, then moved to a farm in Havana Township (the biography of his son Anton Kasper in the 1910 county history says the farm was in Aurora Township). Around 1868, they moved to southern Somerset Township. By 1879, Joseph owned 160 acres of land in section 22, and another 160 acres adjacent to it in section 27.

Joseph's oldest son, Albert Kasper (Vojtěch Kašpar), began his schooling in rural schools and continued on to Owatonna High School. He taught school in Owatonna Township in 1873–1874, and moved to Somerset Township where he taught in 1874–1875. Around 1875 he bought a farm in section 28 of Somerset Township.

In a 1931 letter, Albert described purchasing 160 acres of wild land to improve. He had not constructed a shelter for his first night on his new property. This was summer and as darkness fell he was surrounded by swarms of mosquitoes. To escape their relentless biting, he waded into a pond where he slept through the night with only his head, covered by a handkerchief, above water.[44]

Joseph Kasper's second son, Anton, also bought a farm in section 24, adjacent to those of his father and his brother. Another son, Frank, eventually opened a store on Cedar

Albert Kasper (arrived in Owatonna in 1864) and Joseph Kaplan (arrived in Owatonna in 1856). Courtesy of Tim Kubat

Street in Owatonna. A fourth son, Joseph Kasper Junior, was a watchmaker who moved to Chicago.

The 1870 U.S. census enumerates a substantial Czech colony in Somerset Township. The families of Anton Masser, John Bulva, John Slavick, John Brosek, Joseph Horsky, Frank Dusek, Ignac Pavek, Vincent Skalicky, Frank Moravec, Frank Pavek, Frank and Anton Kubat, Ignac Kubista, Frank Wesely, Frank Motl, George Motl, and John Renchin had swelled the ranks of earlier Czech settlers.

In the 1865 Minnesota census, there were no recognizably Czech names in Summit Township; by 1870, Summit Township included the families of Frank Renchin, John Simek, Wenzel Hanous, John Seykora (who had moved from Owatonna Township), Frank Fisher, John Wondra, and Joseph Vaith (a Bohemian German from Ostrov).[45]

Frank Renchin was an early Czech settler in the Cedar Rapids, Iowa area. His son, young Frank, enlisted in the Union army during the Civil War in an Iowa regiment. Elder Frank moved to Summit Township with most of his family sometime between 1862 and 1870. His son Frank was still in Iowa in 1870, but moved to Steele County to join his family by 1875. (See section at the end of this chapter.)

John and Maria Simek came to America in the fall of 1864. They either had no children, or their children were grown by the time they emigrated. They were probably related to the Simek family who came to Steele County in 1855. They settled on a farm in northeastern Summit Township that would play a role in the drama of the 1873 Blizzard (see chapter 4).

Frank and Theresa (Rehak) Fisher and two children arrived in New York in early September 1863 on the same ship as the families of Frank Belina, Wenzel Wanous and Joseph Wavrin. They also settled in northeastern Summit Township. Their son, Joseph Fisher, born in 1865, wrote about his childhood memories:

> I remember how dad used to go to town with a yoke of oxen. I was little then. I had to stay home. We didn't have any horses then, neither did our neighbors. That was really a great day when dad traded off two yoke of oxen for a team of horses.
>
> The winters were very severe. I remember driving over snow that was packed and hard high over the wooden fences. Those days there was no such thing as a wire fence. The farmers built them out of poles; the better fences were made out of board rails. In the winter those fences didn't mean anything. We used to make a beeline and head off for whichever direction we wished; the snow was so high. And it was hard, too. The oxen stayed right on top.
>
> The houses were built of logs. We had one big room for the kitchen, dining room and bedroom all together. The children slept upstairs when it was not too cold. There were many cracks. The snow used to blow in. When it was too cold, the children slept under the parents' bed downstairs. They had a board frame which slid in under the big bed. That's where the kids slept.
>
> It is fresh in my mind how one night the wolves howled. We didn't get up, but wished that we had done so after the neighbor lady had spoken to us. They had killed her sheep.
>
> There was an abundance of foxes and deer. You had to look out for your chickens with the foxes around.
>
> The farmers raised ducks, geese and chickens. But of course not very many. The chickens wouldn't lay all winter as they do now. The hen houses were too poorly built. Then too there were no incubators in which to hatch the chicks. You had to use setting hens. There were a few turkeys around, too.
>
> All of our corn was planted by hand with one of those hand planters that you stab into the ground for every hill of corn. Then it was hoed by hand.[46]

Saco/Moravia

The bulk of Czech settlers in the Litomysl settlement were in southeastern Somerset Township and northeastern Summit Township. However, another Czech cluster had begun to form as early as 1866 in the northwest corner of Somerset Township, north and west of the future Litomysl settlement. This would later become known as Saco (although the Czechs called it Moravia), and eventually would have its own small Catholic church.

Frank and Barbara Moravec may have settled here as early as 1860 according to the Sacred Heart Church history, although they first appear in the census records in 1870. In any event, they were among the earliest Czechs to settle this area, and the story is that the settlement was named Moravia after them.[47]

Frank Kubat (František Kubat), a nephew of pioneer Anton Kubat, and his wife Thekla (Tekla Bělina Kubat) were among the earliest settlers to the Saco area. They left Dlouhá Třebová and arrived in New York in June 1866 aboard the ship *Mobile* with their children Frank, John and Anna. They homesteaded by the Straight River about seven miles south of Owatonna, in section 7 of Somerset Township. More children were born and three small daughters who died of diphtheria were buried on a small hill near the house.

Their first home was a log cabin with a dirt floor that grew lower over time from frequent sweeping. The family was very poor and the children could attend the Saco school only in the three warmest months; they could not attend in cold months for lack of warm clothes. They went barefoot all summer and in winter wrapped their feet in rags or wore shoes made of rabbit skins. The children slept upstairs and in winter their feather quilts were edged with frost from their breath. The log house was replaced with a frame house after daughter Rosa married in 1890.

The Kubats picked wild hazelnuts in the fall that were stored in barrels to be eaten in winter. They rarely had sugar and the children remember visiting a kindly neighbor whom they asked for sugar. When they couldn't afford coffee, the family roasted wheat in the oven and ground it up to make a hot drink. Frank used extra eggs and anything else the family could spare to trade for necessities. After the Rock Island Railroad was built nearby in 1900, he walked into town on the railroad tracks when the roads were covered with snow.[48]

Weselys—Another Saco family from this early period was Frank Wesely (František Vesely) and his wife Rosalie (Rypka) Wesely. They left Lhotka for America and arrived in New York City aboard the *Mobile* in June 1866 with their children John and Frank. They made their way to Owatonna, and settled on a farm in Somerset Township.

*Wagon train in downtown Owatonna, 1864.
Courtesy of Steele County Historical Society*

Frank Wesely was one of several siblings who came to Minnesota. The oldest child, Jan, married Theresa Rypka and remained in Bohemia, making a living as a blacksmith in Dlouhá Třebová. However, Frank's sister Theresa married Joseph Deml of Parnik, and they came to Steele County and lived in the Litomysl settlement, as did sister Anna and her husband Joseph Hudrlik (also of Parnik). Sister Rosalie married Frank Styndl of Svinna, a blacksmith. They also came to the Owatonna area and settled in Bixby. Finally, sister Paulina married a Rypka and was known to be living at Cromwell, Minnesota at one point.

The 1860s were just the beginning of Czech immigration to Steele County. During the immigration boom of the following decade, Somerset and Summit Townships experienced the greatest growth in Czech population.

THE QUIET PERIOD

The decade of the 1860s was a quiet period in Steele County Czech settlement and few accounts of it remain. Several of the earliest settlers left vivid descriptions of their first few years in America, but usually had little to say about their later lives. Settlers who arrived during or shortly after the Civil War left very few first hand accounts of their experiences.

Newspaper records are of little help. The 1860s Owatonna newspapers that survive are spotty, and their local news coverage is surprisingly sparse. Most of the space is devoted to national and international news and advertisements. There are very few obituaries or marriage notices, even for the Yankee middle and upper classes whose concerns tended to dominate local coverage. Most mentions of local Czechs are legal notices such as probate and delinquent tax notices, or paid ads for sale of lands.

Local Czechs lived outside of the city of Owatonna; newspapers covered the city but generally ignored the rest of the county. Czechs came to town to shop and attend various functions, but most of their lives took place in the countryside out of the notice of the press. In the glimpses we catch of their lives they worked hard, built better houses, cleared their land claims for farming, and stayed out of debt. They went to church, raised their children, and visited each other. It appears that many Czech settlers spoke little English and had as little contact as possible with the English speaking majority. They were not elected to public office (with the notable exception of Anton Simek).

All this would change in the decades that followed. By the 1870s, Czechs who had settled in the early 1860s had acquired property and learned some English. Their children were grown or nearly so, and the new generation, fluent in English, was comfortable in both its parents' world and the wider culture. Czechs began to hold public office, first in Owatonna Township, then in county-wide and city offices. They founded local organizations, and joined groups that were predominantly non-Czech. They opened businesses in Owatonna and Blooming Prairie.

The newspapers also changed. During the 1870s and the decades that followed, local papers offered more local news, more obituaries, and more coverage of the county outside the city of Owatonna. Czechs were more visible, in part because of the large influx of new immigrants from 1865 to 1890. The county began to develop a sense of its history, and newspapers mirrored that by writing about the deaths of the first settlers, whatever their place of origin.

For all these reasons, in the 1870s Steele County Czechs emerged from their quiet period and assumed their place in the broader life of the county.

FRANK RENCHIN

Frank Kovar's history of the Czechs of Steele County mentions a local Czech Civil War veteran named Frank Renchin who returned crippled from the war. However, no Frank Renchin appears in the Minnesota Civil War records. It turns out that Frank Renchin was a veteran of an Iowa unit, and moved to Minnesota later.

An older Frank Renchin, born about 1808, and his wife Rosa came to the Cedar Rapids, Iowa area in 1854. The census of 1860 shows Frank (age 52), Rosa (age 40) and their children Frank (19), Rosa (17), Joseph (16), Agnes (11), and Anton (9). Mother Rosa is described as a washerwoman, and daughter Rosa as a servant. Young Frank is also listed in the census for Cedar Rapids Township living with the Andrew Steinagle family. Steinagle is a master brickmaker, and he has six journeymen brickmakers living with him, one of whom is Frank Renchin.

When the Civil War broke out in 1861, young Frank enlisted in Company D of the 12th Iowa Infantry Regiment. The unit was sent to Tennessee and engaged in a number of actions, culminating in the Battle of Shiloh on April 6 and 7, 1862. Renchin was shot in the right thigh at Shiloh and much of his regiment was captured and imprisoned by the Confederates until November 1862 when they were paroled and exchanged for Confederate prisoners. Renchin was discharged from the army in January 1863 because of his injuries.

Meanwhile, his parents had another child, Louis, born in Iowa in 1862. Sometime after that, but before the census of 1870, the older Frank and Rosa moved from Iowa to Steele County, Minnesota. The 1870 census shows them living in Summit Township with their children Anton and Louis. Their daughters Rosa and Agnes were apparently married by then, either in Iowa or Minnesota.

Their older sons, Frank (the Civil War veteran) and Joseph remained in Iowa when the rest of the family moved to Minnesota. The *History of Czechs of Cedar Rapids* reports that Frank Renchin was one of the founders in 1868 of the Czech reading society of Cedar Rapids. The purpose of this organization was to encourage reading among Czech immigrants, and to sponsor lectures and dramatic presentations. At the time of the 1870 census, he was single, living alone in the 1st ward of Cedar Rapids, and employed as a clerk in a store.

At the time of the 1875 Minnesota state census, young Frank had moved to Minnesota and was living with his parents and brothers in Summit Township. In 1880 the U.S. census still shows him living with them. Anton had moved out by then.

Frank was listed on the 1883 pensioner's census index for Steele County because of his bullet wound in the thigh. The 1890 U.S. census records for most states (including nearly all of Minnesota) were destroyed in a fire, but the Civil War Veterans Schedule for 1890 records the veteran Frank Renchin as living in Pratt, Summit Township, Steele County, Minnesota. This is not entirely reliable, however, since Pratt is not in Summit Township. His mailing address is listed as Blooming Prairie.

By the time of the 1900 U.S. census, Frank Renchin is listed as a boarder with the Anton Renchin family in Stevens County, Minnesota. Based on their ages as recorded in the census, this Anton Renchin seems to have been Frank's brother. In 1910, the census shows Frank living as head of the household in Westfield Township of Dodge County, Minnesota. His occupation is listed as "own income." He is living with his other younger brother, Louis, a farm laborer. Both were unmarried.

Frank Renchin eventually died in Hennepin County in 1913 and is buried in Lakeview Cemetery in Minneapolis. His tombstone lists him as a veteran of the GAR (Grand Army of the Republic).

CZECH SETTLERS AND NATIVE AMERICANS

The Indians of Steele County had signed a treaty giving away their land rights only a few years before the earliest Czech settlers arrived. Many had moved west or lived on the small reservation between Waseca and Mankato. Yet in the 1850s and 1860s some Indians still lived in or passed through Owatonna, Somerset, and Summit Townships. Several of the early Czechs left vignettes about their encounters with these first residents of Steele County. Sometimes the encounters occurred because Indians were asking for help and sometimes because Indians were offering help.

The Cornells were one of the two founding couples of the city of Owatonna. Many Indians were still in the area during their first winter, which was the very cold winter of 1854–1855. The Indian agent told the Cornells not to resist if Indians came for food or to take their animals. However, the Cornells encountered no problems, and often invited Indians in to warm up and share their food.[49]

Anna Kubat, in remembering the hardships of the winter of 1856–1857, writes:

> Deer came to us in winter for hay, Indians came to beg a piece of bread.
> When they saw that we ourselves had nothing, they sometimes brought us a piece of game.[50]

When the young child, Charlie Fisher, was badly scalded during the 1856–57 winter, some Indians arrived at the cabin soon after, having been drawn by the screams. They made a preparation using cold ashes to put on the wound before bandaging it, saying this was better than putting bandages directly on the wounds. At other times, Indians would look in the windows of the cabin until someone went to see what they wanted.[51]

While John Renchin was in the army, his wife Catherine moved with her children to a log house closer to town, on a farm located at the present-day address of 3469 Austin Road. One day, two Indians on ponies rode up to the farm and asked for food. As Catherine was baking bread they waited until the bread was done. She gave them all of the bread she'd baked, and they rode away.[52]

Lula Rysavy describes events told to her by her grandparents, Bernard and Josephine Ressler, after their arrival in 1873:

> After they moved to a farm in Litomysl, Minnesota, grandma told about
> Indians coming to get water from their well, and wanting to hold one of their
> babies. At first, she was nervous about it, but later they became friends.[53]

Joseph Fisher, born in 1865, relates:

> The Indians around here were a friendly lot. They came at times begging for food, but never molesting anyone. When they were given some, they were satisfied and went their way. I didn't see any myself, but folks told me about them. [54]

Other times the settlers' stories describe Czechs' observations of a culture that was in many ways different from, but in some ways similar to, their own.

In a letter to his brother dated January 1, 1857, Joseph Kaplan wrote his impressions of the Indians he encountered:

> Quite often one sees Indians, about whom you read various reports in Bohemia. They are people with tough constitutions, red streaks around the eyes, brown skin, and good dispositions. They can walk long distances, and their only work is hunting. Their clothing consists of white woolen breeches and a sort of outer cloak. They carry a long rifle over the shoulder. The poorer ones walk, and the more prosperous ones ride horses. In the winter, they put up canvas tents in the woods, leaving an opening at the top for smoke; in the center they build a fire, around which they lie in a circle, feet toward the fire. Once a year they have a festival. Then they shoot game and boil it in a kettle, unsalted. When they eat, no one may throw away a bone, but after the feast they give them all to the dogs. After that they form a circle and hop from one foot to the other to the accompaniment of various rattles and tinkles. They are good-humored. When you read about battles between whites and Indians, it is the whites who are to blame.[55]

Joseph Kaplan was involved in calming a controversy between Indians and European settlers around this time. A little south of Owatonna and east of the Straight River, in what is now Kaplan's Woods, there used to be an area of springs and a dry area rather like an island. Near this island stood the largest, roundest, tallest tree in the area. This tree had great meaning to the local Indians.

The operator of a saw mill on what is now Lemond Road cut the tree down without asking anyone. The Indians were very upset, and Joseph Kaplan helped to calm them down. Perhaps his sympathetic attitude toward them resulted in their trusting him more than most settlers. When Highway 14 was built, the area was destroyed and now lies beneath the highway.[56]

In the autumn of 1859, Joseph Kaplan had a disquieting experience, which he described in a letter to his brother:

> I cannot pass over in silence a curious story I experienced in September of last year.
>
> On a certain business matter I set out with one Yankee of our place for a journey over one hundred miles westward from Owatonna; we had to travel through large woods—dense, dark woods, overgrown with diverse shrubs, so that the traveling was very difficult. When evening came, we still had a long way to go. We were really not cheerful about it. So we were proceeding as quickly as possible. We reached a plain and saw smoke in distant woods. We rejoiced at it saying to ourselves, it must be a farm. We hurried, came close—ho! Indians they were.
>
> They had a man's head stuck on a kind of stake, and they were dancing around it. What now? It was too late to run away, they had seen us already. We had to join them, regardless of consequences. One group of Indians who did not dance was sitting around fires, and those we had to join . . .
>
> The head they were dancing around belonged to a chieftain of another Indian tribe which they had just defeated in a battle. That was why the feast was made. I do not know how many of them there were. There were about 30 tents. We were told one belonged to each family. These tents looked like the gingerbread maker's booths at your country fairs except there were openings at the top for smoke. We stayed overnight and ate smoked meat.[57]

When the Indians ceded their territory they agreed to go onto reserved sections of land. One such reservation was west of Owatonna in Waseca County. The unrest Kaplan writes about may have been an early symptom of the Indians' discontent over the life they lived on the reservations that would explode in the Dakota Conflict of 1862.

In time, as the area became more densely inhabited and developed, the Indians left the region and stories about settler and Indian encounters ceased.

3

Coming to America

WHERE THEY CAME FROM

Nearly all of Steele County's Czech immigrants came from the Lanškroun district in the highlands separating eastern Bohemia from Moravia. This area borders on the mountains that separate Bohemia from what is now Poland, but in the mid-1800s was German Silesia. Three quarters of the villages in the Lanškroun district were predominantly German-speaking.[1]

The district was named for its largest town, Lanškroun, which had about 5,000 inhabitants in the 1850s. Next in size was Čermná with about 3,000 people. The remaining 41 towns and villages of the district were smaller yet, but it is from these smaller settlements that most of the Steele County settlers migrated.

On the western edge of the Lanškroun district the Třebovska River flows nearly straight north from the Moravian border to meet the Tichá Orlice River at the town of Ústí nad Orlicí. The name Třebovska is derived from the Old Czech word "trieb" meaning forest clearing. The first settlers cleared the river valley by cutting trees but leaving the stumps in place and planting crops in the soil around the stumps. This process of "triebing" gave the river its name. The river runs between high, wooded hills on its way to the town of Česká Třebová, which spreads out on both sides of the river.

Records from the year 1278 mention Českou Třebovou, founded earlier that century by Premonstratensian monks from nearby Litomyšl. In the fourteenth century the monks built Česká Třebová's beautiful church of St. Catherine. It is a round church with an onion dome roof style reminiscent of the Russian and Greek Orthodox churches. In 1452 the town's weaving guild was founded and weaving was the town folk's chief livelihood until the arrival of the railroad from Olomouc to Prague in 1845. Another railroad was built from Česká Třebová to Brno in 1849. The railroads brought heavier industry and, beginning in 1849, the construction of several factories. Emigrants from the area,

Original home of Anton and Anna Kubat in Dlouhá Třebová, Bohemia. Courtesy of Tim Kubat

including Wencl and Rose Haberman, who came to Steele County traveled on the new railroads to German ports for their trip to America.

Lhotka

The Třebovska River flows out of Česká Třebová through Lhotka and into Dlouhá Třebová. The small village of Lhotka was the home of Steele County immigrants Frank and Terezie Spatenka, Frank Vesely, and Frank Styndl. Frank Styndl, born in nearby Svinna, had married Frank Vesely's sister Rosalie, and they lived in Lhotka's house number 69 with their children until coming to America in 1886. [Note: although these house numbers were assigned several centuries ago and the numbering revised in the 20th century, visitors to villages in the Czech Republic often use the old numbers, with the help of local residents, to find their ancestors' homesteads.]

Dlouhá Třebová

Most early Czech settlers to the Owatonna area were from Dlouhá Třebová, a few miles downriver from Česká Třebová. The town's oblong shape gave it the early name Trebovia Longa Villa, and later its Latin name of Longo Trebovia. Reference to its shape continues as the Czech name dlouhá means long. The eroding current of the Třebovska River cuts the village into a higher part where the main road and most of the houses stand, and a lower and smaller part. In the nineteenth century the village did not have its own parish. The southern part of town was in the parish of Česká Třebová, and the northern part in the parish of Ústí nad Orlicí. In 1893 a non-denominational cemetery was established, and in 1905–1906 a parish church was built. After settling in America, Steele County residents Joseph Kaplan, Ignac Kubista, and Anton Renchin sent money back to the old country to help build and equip Dlouhá Třebová's new church.

Family names from Dlouhá Třebová that are familiar to Steele County residents include Pichner, Kaplan, Seykora, Renchin, Rypka, and Belina. The Pichners lived in house 74 on the south end of the village near the boundary with Lhotka. The Seykoras lived in house 136 in the middle of the village, and the Kovars in houses 64 and 65 at the north end near the future site of the church. The Kubats were from house 144. The Kaplan house was number 36. Benjamin Fisher worked at the mill and lived with his family at house number 75 where his oldest daughter was born.[2]

Hylváty and Ústí nad Orlicí
Hylváty, the next village downriver from Dlouhá Třebová, was the home of Steele County's Simeks and Frank Kovar. From Hylváty the Třebovska River flows into the town of Ústí nad Orlicí. Ústí nad Orlicí featured a Baroque church built in the 1770s and a picturesque town square with an arcade and a statue of the Virgin Mary. The Joseph Kaspar family of Steele County came from Ústí nad Orlicí.

Zhoř, Přívrat, Řetová and Řetůvka
A line of high hills on the west side of the Třebovska River valley is the site of the villages of Kozlov (which today has a downhill ski area), Zhoř, Přívrat, Řetová and Řetůvka.

Zhoř lies on the main road from Česká Třebová to Litomyšl. It is a small village built on a ring of hills and along a narrow, middle valley. In the mid-nineteenth century Zhoř contained about sixty houses and a chapel and was home to the Wolesky and Broulik families that would migrate to Owatonna.

Přívrat is situated in the hills a few miles west of Lhotka. In 1450, a fortification stood at the present site of Přívrat to protect a fish pond, streams and fields of the Doník family. The village probably arose around the fort. In 1659, the largest landholders included Jan Volesky, Martin Kubat and Jakub Coufal. However, all of Přívrat's landowners were required to pay rent to the lord of the manor in the form of goods and services and, as the rent steadily increased, some landowners abandoned their farms to become paid laborers. In 1674, Jan Vanous abandoned his farm, the largest in the area.

After 1700 the most common names in Přívrat were Coufal, Dostal, Jasansky,

Kolar, Kovar, Vencl, Volesky, Vavrin and Vanous. Members of nearly all these families migrated to the Owatonna area in the nineteenth century. The John Vondra family of Steele County lived in Přívrat until emigrating with help from Joseph Kaplan, whose mother was Ludmilla Vondra. When a new stone altar was added to the Přívrat church in 1901, contributors included United States citizens Mrs. Frances Klasek and Mrs. Anna Vencl.[3]

Řetová (or Velká Řetová, which means big Řetová) had a stone church built in 1755 and dedicated to St. Mary Magdalen. The Jirouseks of Steele County once lived in house number 66. Nearby is Řetůvka (or Malá Řetová, meaning little Řetová) situated in a low-lying valley of Řetůvka Creek, called Goose's Neck by local residents. It contained its own school and a stone chapel dedicated to St. Wenceslaus on a hill at the edge of town.[4]

Litomýsl
West of the Lanškroun district, in the valley of the Loučná River, lies the city of Litomýsl. Although few, if any, Steele County Czechs came from Litomýsl, the Czech settlement south of Owatonna was named after it. The Czech chronicle of Kosmas from around 1110 wrote of a hill fort named Litomysl in existence in 981 guarding the trade road between Bohemia and Moravia. The name may have come from the personal name Lutomyssl, but no person of that name from that time can be found in contemporary records. Litomýsl has a scenic town square, a Renaissance-era castle, and was home to the famous Czech composer Smetana.[5]

Dolní Dobrouč
On the eastern side of the Třebovska River valley, the stream Dobrouč runs roughly parallel to the Třebová River. The two valleys are separated by a high, forested ridge. The stream courses through Horní Dobrouč (which means Upper Dobrouč), a mainly German-speaking village, and a mile or so later enters Dolní Dobrouč (Lower Dobrouč), a Czech town.

In the nineteenth century, three hundred people left the small town of Dolní Dobrouč for America. Founded in 1292, Dolní Dobrouč was the home town of Steele County Kubiceks, Meixners, Rysavys, Waceks, and Horaks, some of whose forbearers had shown a streak of independence. The local leaders of a 1775 farmer's revolt, part of a larger uprising across much of Bohemia, were Matěj Maixner, Tobiáš Skalický, Jindřich Kubíček, Josef Šubert and Jan Šilar. They were caught and imprisoned in Chrudim for a time, then flogged and sent home.[6]

On the east side of the stream and the main road through Dolní Dobrouč stands the Catholic Church of Saint Mikulase (Nicholas), built about 1870. The old church and

*Original home of Frank Kubicek in Dolní Dobrouč, Bohemia, about 1900.
Courtesy of Marie Meixner*

Original home of Frank Kubicek in Dolní Dobrouč, Bohemia, 2002. Michael Wolesky

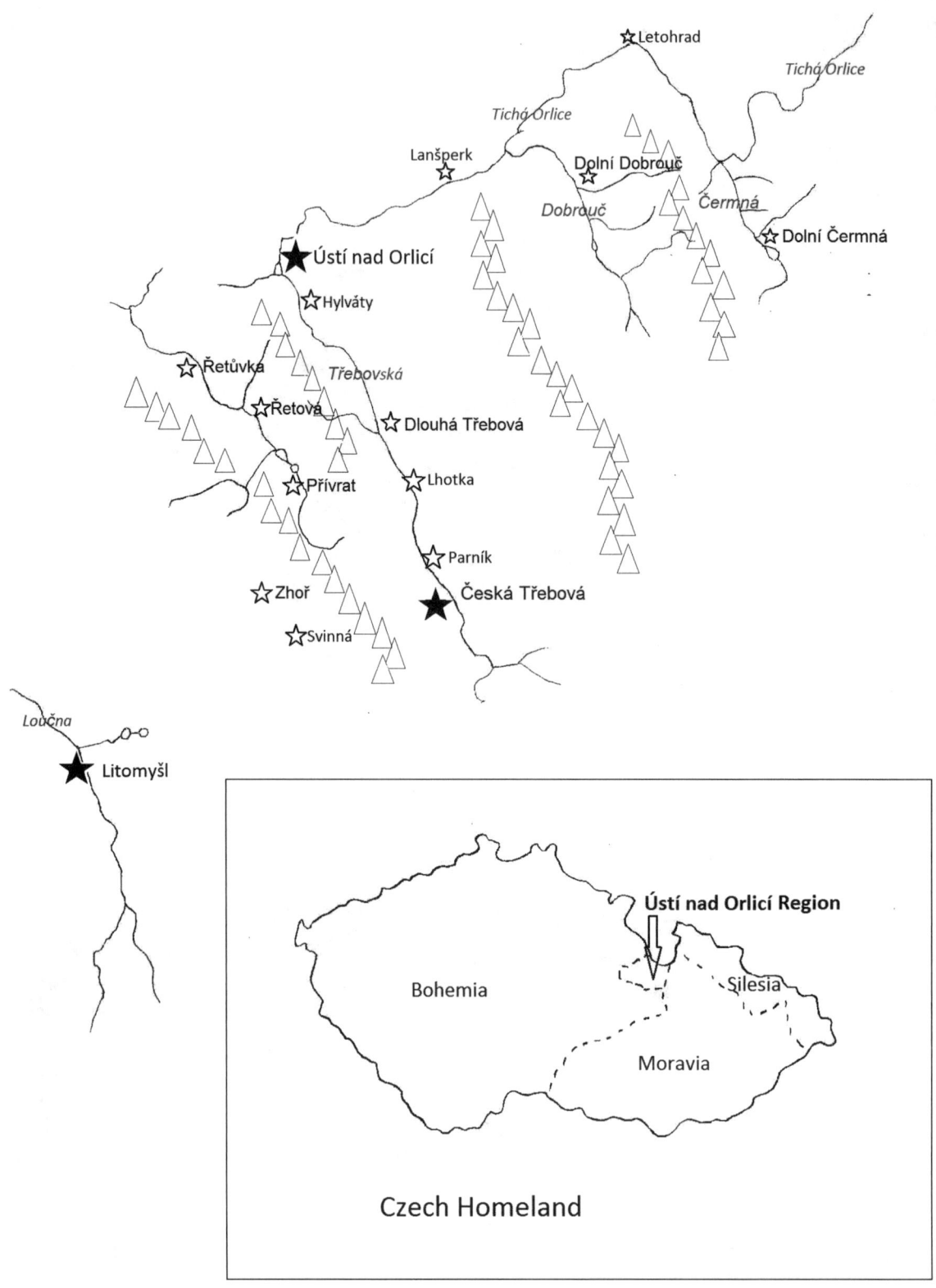

cemetery are behind it. Across the road and in the hills to the west of town is Horak's Chapel. The local story is that Bernard Dusek from house 33, whose nickname was Horak, fell ill. He promised the Virgin Mary he would build her a chapel if he recovered. He got well, but lacking the funds to build the chapel, he erected instead a statue of the Virgin at a spring. Before long, he was ill again. He dreamt that the Virgin Mary confronted him about his broken promise to build the chapel. He apologized and again promised to build a chapel. Once again he recovered, and in 1866 he built a lovely white chapel in a small clearing on a wooded slope.[7]

Lanškroun and Čermná

In the next valley to the east of the Dobrouč valley flows the Čermná River. The district capital of Lanškroun, a primarily German-speaking city in the nineteenth century, occupies the south end of the valley. Farther north, the river flows through Horní and Dolni Čermná. In the nineteenth century, these two towns were one village called Čermná, which was eventually divided in 1936.

The name Čermná derives from the old Slavonic word for red, čermný, which later became červený in Czech. The town was apparently named either for the clay coloring the stream, or for nearby weathered iron ore in the soil. Čermná was founded as a German town and was in existence by 1292. It became predominantly Czech during the Hussite disturbances of the fifteenth century. However, the battles of the Thirty Years War resulted in a depopulation until the town was re-filled by German settlers. More than 180 secretly Protestant serfs fled to German Saxony in 1736.

A prominent feature of the town is Mary Hill, where pilgrims heading for Maria-Zell in Austria would gather at the start of their pilgrimage. The Church of Our Lady of the Snows was built on the hill in 1875. The cottagers of Čermná labored in farm fields and on construction sites in the summer, and spun flax and wove sack cloth in their cottages in the winter. The Betlachs who settled in Blooming Prairie came from here.[8]

The Čermná River, like the Třebovska and the Dobouč rivers, flows north into the Tichá Orlice River, which continues southwest into Ústí nad Orlicí and beyond. Most of the Czech immigrants to Steele County, particularly the earlier ones, left for their new life in America from these three river valleys in the Lanškroun District.

WHY THEY LEFT

The exodus of Czech emigrants to America began soon after the Revolution of 1848, and continued until the First World War. However, the flow to Steele County slowed after 1880 as most Czechs who arrived in America after that date went west to Texas, Nebraska or the Dakotas where they could still find free land for homesteading.

Why did so many Czechs leave their homeland during that time period? First, it was because they were finally able to leave. Before the Revolution of 1848, Czech farmers were in a semi-feudal state. They worked the land but did not own it; instead they paid a form of rent by working a set number of hours each month for their landlord. They also needed permission from the landlord, which was rarely granted, to leave their area. The 1848 Revolution abolished these remnants of feudalism. Following the revolution farmers could buy the land they worked with long-term loans and citizens could more easily obtain permission to emigrate.

Before 1848 most people did not find their condition so difficult that it was worth overcoming the obstacles to leave. However, in the wake of the revolution, rapidly changing economic, social and political conditions made the idea of emigration more appealing.

Political conditions in Europe were deteriorating, involving the Austrian empire, of which Bohemia was a part, in several military actions. First was the Revolution of 1848 that unsettled much of Europe. Then in 1854, after forty years of peace following the Napoleonic Wars, the Crimean War broke out. Britain, France and the Ottoman Empire fought Russia for control of access to the Black Sea. Prussia stayed neutral, but Austria was pressured to join Britain and France. After considerable maneuvering, Austria narrowly avoided joining the war, which ended in 1856.

This was followed in 1864 by a short war by Prussia and Austria against Denmark for control of Schleswig and Holstein. Two years later, the victors fell out over division of the spoils and fought a seven-week war that included a major battle on Bohemian soil. In 1870, Prussia joined the rest of the north German states in a war with France that resulted in the creation of a united Germany on the northern borders of the Austrian Empire.

Austria was also engaged in battles on its southern borders; it had long controlled land in northern Italy, as had France. The Pope controlled part of central Italy in the form of the Papal States. The rest of the peninsula was divided into a number of different political units. Between 1859 and 1870, the Austrians were driven from northern Italy as the various Italian states united to create the Italy we know today.

Austria's many military engagements required soldiers, and support in the form of modern industry and agriculture. Many analysts believe that avoidance of military service as a reason for emigration from Bohemia has been overstated, but there is no doubt it was an important reason for some. Joseph Kaspar's older brother fled Bohemia to escape military service, which greatly delayed Joseph's own intended emigration. John Wanous was already in the Austrian army when he fled with his family to America in 1862 to avoid more years of service. Frank Wolesky came to America in 1902 at the age of fourteen in part to escape military service. In 1869 some of the pressure was relieved when the period of military service was shortened from seven years to three years at the urging of landowners who wanted more readily available farm laborers.

The freeing of farmers from the last vestiges of serfdom in 1849 had also brought major changes to agriculture. Large landowners who had relied on the labor of their tenant farmers for several days each month now had to replace that help. The response of landowners in parts of the country with fertile soil and good agricultural conditions was to mechanize their farms and buy more land to farm in the American style, putting farm laborers out of work. Large mechanized farms were not practical in the hilly and stony Bohemian-Moravian highlands where most of the Steele County Czechs originated, so small farms continued. However, these small operations found it increasingly difficult to compete with the large farms in other areas or with the huge quantities of wheat imported from America after the Civil War. Most farmers could not survive without borrowing money, but banks were usually owned by wealthy landowners who set the terms of the loans to their own advantage. If the loan could not be repaid the land was foreclosed or sold, often to wealthier farmers, thus further concentrating the land into holdings by only a few.

Another factor affecting agriculture was the pattern of inheritance. The end of the old land laws in 1849 allowed farmers to buy the land they had worked using long-term credit. A law of 1867 allowed these farmers to sell their land as well. However, with land ownership came the dilemma of inheritance. Under the old inheritance laws, land was usually passed to the oldest son and younger sons had to find other ways to make their living. After the estate laws were changed in 1868 land could be divided among several children. As this happened each son received land, but what had been a sufficiently large farm for one family was broken up into smaller portions that had to support several families. After several generations, the result was many people living in poverty on tiny "handkerchief plots." The situation was worsened by a financial crisis in May of 1873 that led to a depression in which farmers received less money for their crops but had to pay more for everything they needed to grow crops and sustain life.

Industry was also changing. In the 1840s and 1850s rural industry in eastern Bohemia was primarily textiles; several Steele County Czechs were listed on official records as weavers or tailors. Until 1866, textile production in eastern Bohemia was done on home looms under the control of local guilds. However, in 1866 Austria changed its traditional protectionist policy after it was excluded from the German Zollverein (customs union) dominated by the Prussians. Austria signed trade agreements with France and England that opened her markets to western products resulting in a flood of low priced manufactured textiles. This was particularly hard on ironmakers and cotton spinners. These industries modernized, building efficient production facilities to compete with foreign imports. Between 1870 and 1900, the home-based textile industry in eastern Bohemia was almost completely wiped out by the factories of Brno and Jihlava.[9] Some rural Czechs moved to cities and industrial towns to work in factories, but in the early periods of industrialization, factories did not create as many jobs as their products and imports destroyed.

Finally, even in these chaotic times, the population of the Czech-speaking areas rose from 6.6 million in 1845 to 10 million in 1910. With many more people to feed and employ, but with small scale farming and cottage industry disappearing, Czechs in eastern Bohemia saw America as the land of opportunity.[10]

America became an especially attractive destination after passage of the Homestead Act and the end of the Civil War. Some of the earliest Czech emigrants to America were political liberals who fled the failure of the 1848 revolution. They were usually students or intellectuals who settled in cities such as New York, St. Louis, Cleveland and Milwaukee, and started the first Czech newspapers in America. They were joined in the mid-1850s by political prisoners from the revolution just released from prison.

The California gold rush of 1849 received enormous publicity all over the world, and a few Czechs came to seek their fortunes in the gold fields. For others, the story inspired wanderlust to see a new and exciting land. Anton Simek, the earliest Czech settler in Steele County, may have been cut from this cloth. He seems to have left Austria for the first time soon after 1849. A police report from 1852 describes him as restless and implies that he had made more than one trip abroad.

Recruitment of emigrants began in the 1850s. In 1852, the Hamburg shipping line Morris and Co. Columbia began distributing leaflets in Bohemia printed in German and English, and attempted to induce a network of local innkeepers to act as their agents. In November 1852, the Austrian Interior Department issued a ruling on these agents, who were said to be committing "criminal enticement." This ruling was used as the basis for surveillance of people suspected of being agents, usually activists from the uprising of 1848.

A package from J.E. Weigel in Leipzig, Germany addressed to Anton Simek in Hylvaty was intercepted by the authorities in August of 1852. It contained posters promoting emigration. The authorities in Prague instructed the regional authorities to discover if Anton Simek was acting as an emigration agent. The Lanskroun county executive, Baron Poettin, replied that Anton Simek was a restless and eloquent young weaver who had been rambling abroad for several years, and who encouraged people to emigrate. However, he was not believed to be an agent of the Hamburg Hirschmann Company or of anyone else. He remained under police supervision until he again left for America in late 1852.[11]

Within a few years, shipping companies from both Hamburg and Bremen had agents active in Bohemia. One of the most successful was Alois Kareš from Vamberk. He was active in 1854 in the Česká Třebová and Lanškroun region of eastern Bohemia, where most of the Steele County Czechs originated. He later expanded his network to cover most of Bohemia. In 1856, he published *Conditions for Transfer from Bremen to the United Settlements of North America* and letters from satisfied Czechs who had settled in America.

These letters from the first Czech settlers were another enticement. Letters to friends and relatives generated interest in their home villages, and drew more townsfolk to join those already in the New World. Shipping company agents, like Alois Kares, found the letters to be useful recruiting tools.

Austrian authorities fought back by harassing the agents and publicizing negative aspects of emigration. They released stories of Czech returnees stuck in Bremen with no money and nowhere to go, and of Czechs who had found that America did not live up to their dreams.

American companies, states and cities were also involved in recruitment, particularly after the Civil War. Railroads such as the Northern Pacific and St. Paul Pacific advertised and recruited for laborers to lay the tracks and for settlers to buy some of their extensive land holdings. The Northern Pacific set up an immigration department in 1866 that peaked in activity in 1872 and 1873.[12]

Wisconsin appointed a Commissioner of Emigration who resided in New York. Soon after the events of 1848, he sent materials to the Habsburg lands, including Bohemia. These were published as newspaper ads and leaflets to be distributed on ships, in hotels, and in bars. They stressed low taxes, freedom of religion, a countryside similar to Bohemia, cheap land, and political freedom, as well as the right to vote.[13]

Minnesota's territorial legislature also began an effort to attract immigrants. In 1855, Minnesota had a commissioner to meet immigrants, distribute literature about

Minnesota, and advertise in newspapers in the United States and abroad. Commissioner Eugen Bernand directed most of his efforts toward Germans, Belgians, Swiss, and French immigrants. Czechs were not targeted, yet much of the German material made its way into Czech areas where many Czechs read German. In addition, Czechs normally emigrated from German ports.

This effort lapsed after a few years, to be revived in 1867. Minnesota appointed special agents in various ports of entry for different nationalities. The agent for Germans, B. Kieholz, was in New York and was furnished with 2,000 copies of an immigration pamphlet to be distributed in Germany. In 1871, a Minnesota agency was established in Germany to distribute 5,000 pamphlets about Minnesota and secure fare reductions for travelers to the state. The commission again lapsed and was revived in 1879. Between 1879 and 1882, 55,000 pamphlets were distributed in Germany.[14]

In 1869, the state of Minnesota published *The Minnesota Guide*, a book for "travelers, pleasure seekers and immigrants." It contained a history of Minnesota and descriptions of the geography, transportation, institutions, population, agriculture and climate ("the healthiest in the world"). The text is accompanied by maps, drawings and advertisements, and includes descriptions of most of the state's settlements. Owatonna is described in part in this way:

> The town was laid out in 1856, but as lumber had to be hauled over fifty miles, the town did not grow much until the completion of the two railroads in 1866, since which it has increased rapidly. The population is now about 3,000. There are five churches, a fine school house that cost $25,000, and a number of fine stores, dwellings and other substantial buildings, besides an elevator and two depots and freight houses.[15]

Owatonna and Steele County found ways to get their message out. The *Owatonna Journal* for September 3, 1868, contains a letter to the editor, titled Our Somerset Letter, by an unidentified writer calling himself Old Settler. After describing the early history of Somerset, current acres planted, and yields of its various crops, he gives this enticing description:

> This town is composed of about equal proportions of prairie and timber: the surface gently undulating or rolling, has a rich, deep soil; is watered by running streams. Straight River crosses the town from south to north. Several small streams empty into it within the limits of the town. A majority of the settlers are from Eastern and Middle states; the balance are Germans and Bohemians

and in intelligence and enterprise will compare favorably with those of any other locality. We have four school houses in town, and three more near the town line. And last, though not least, we are near one of the best markets west of the Mississippi. The city of Owatonna, one of the great Railroad centers of the West—in fact, no better place can be found to invest capital in Real Estate or in any business pursuit, in all the growing west, than in Steele County, and for the laboring man, who has but little capital but his hands. So come, all who are seeking homes in the West, and breathe our pure air, and reap the rich harvests of our inexhaustible soil, and enjoy the spirit of liberality and enterprise which pervades our community.[16]

The Homestead Act of 1862 was a powerful magnet for people from areas such as Bohemia where land was scarce and expensive. Before 1840, lands west of the Mississippi River were thought to be unsuitable for settlement, and the Great Plains considered a desert. Europeans had discovered that prairie sod was very difficult to break apart as prairie grass roots grow deep and are thickly intertwined. Native Americans living in the eastern United States had been transferred to these western lands and European settlers were happy to let them keep it. However, this attitude changed in 1839 with John Deere's introduction of the steel plow that broke apart the prairie sod allowing its conversion to agriculture. Following the Civil War, the Union Army engaged in actions against Indian tribes that occupied the west; by 1890 the tribes had been defeated and confined to small, scattered reservations of poor land. This confinement of the Indians opened vast tracts of prairie for settlement that the Homestead Act could offer to new settlers for next to nothing except their sweat.

Large quantities of land virtually were being given away to those willing to clear and work it; a farmer with little education could better himself and his family through hard work and perseverance. The Minnesota Guide devotes a full page to explaining the homesteading process and listing land offices where claims were to be filed. However, most of those who immigrated to Steele County after the Civil War found all the land already homesteaded, and had to purchase land from the railroads or earlier settlers.

THE LIFE THEY LEFT BEHIND

The life that our ancestors left behind in Bohemia was, in some ways, hard, monotonous and grinding, and in other ways, close-knit, supportive and joyful. The transition to American culture would be difficult, and the structure of many Czech-American communities is explained by attempts to recreate what they had left behind.

Czech farmers did not live at a distance from each other as farmers do in the United States. Farm families clustered in villages of around 30 houses, inhabited by perhaps 200 people. Village farmland radiated out from the village until it came to woods, mountains, or the lands of adjacent villages. Fields were not laid out in a patchwork of squares, but in long strips that started at the village and extended to the village land border. Consequently, many farmers had merely to step out of their door to be on the closest portion of their farmlands, but had to travel some distance to reach their land's farthest extent.

Czech villages were largely self-contained and stable, occupied by extended families whose ancestors had lived in the area before them. The village was usually dominated by a Catholic church or chapel with a spire, and a two-story building containing the government functions of courts, administration and revenue gathering. Protestant churches, when they existed, were by and large unpretentious structures without towers. In front of these buildings would be a small central square or village green, normally rectangular, and often containing a duck pond and the village water pump.

The wealthy lived in homes of brick and stone near the church. Their homes usually had a Baroque style façade that was often in a color of yellow-gold loved by the Empress Maria Theresa who had encouraged its use. Shops and businesses faced the square. Most villages had a primary school, and often a parsonage, cemetery and town hall.

Peasants lived in wooden houses close to each other, painted white with colored trim and shingle roofs. Often the window coves contained pictures or small statues of saints. Flower gardens were placed in front, and barns and vegetable gardens in the back. Cow sheds were nearby and a fence enclosed the buildings and sheds.

Many peasant homes consisted of three or four buildings attached to each other in a U-shaped or quadrangle configuration, with a middle courtyard that often contained manure. Stables and living quarters were usually under the same roof, the living quarters composed of one or two rooms. Furniture might be a wooden table, benches along the wall, a tile stove and brick oven, and a spring-less bed with a feather mattress. The floor was bare, utensils few and simple, and the whitewashed walls covered with holy pictures and perhaps a clock.

When a farmer retired and his son took over working the land, the parents retained ownership of the main house but moved into a smaller structure attached to the main house, called the výměnek. Father helped son farm, but the son was in charge. However, the parents had their own garden and their son was required to give them a set quantity of crops and animals.

Most farmers kept geese, chickens, rabbits and possibly a pig or goat. Crops were usually rye, barley, potatoes, flax, cabbage and peas. Farm machinery was rare, except for hand tools such as scythes, hoes and flails. Farmers either sold their crops to wholesalers who traveled from village to village negotiating with farmers, or transported their produce to the nearest city for sale there.[17]

Social Hierarchy

Bohemian social structure of the nineteenth century was clearly stratified. Large landowners farming fifty or more acres of land were at the top. Nearly all were German-speaking and many dabbled in banking or industrial enterprises. The wealthiest of this group owned more than 250 acres.

Next were farmers, or sedláks, who owned twelve to fifty acres of land, sold grain for the market, hired farm help, had some horses, and often ran small businesses on the side such as blacksmith shops. They were a relatively small but prosperous group, yet near the end of the nineteenth century even they had trouble competing against mechanization and imports.

Less well off than the sedláks were the cottagers (chalupniks or malorolníks) who owned ten or twelve acres of land and usually sold some of their produce in the market. Some could afford to hire farm labor. If they had livestock, these were dairy cattle rather than draft animals; humans performed the physical work. Many of the emigrants to America were cottagers.

Subsistence farmers were next down the ladder. They owned five acres or less and all of their crops went to feed their families. Generally the family could not manage on what they grew themselves, and hired out as farm laborers to earn a small income.

At the bottom were the landless farm laborers (čeledín) and hired maids (děvečka). Laborers made their living as farmhands, moonlighting as craftsmen or construction workers. As the nineteenth century wore on, these laborers were increasingly displaced by the use of machinery in farming and the production of manufactured goods to replace craft goods. A large percentage of Czech immigrants were čeledín.[18]

Local Government

After 1866, farmhands were governed by a labor contract and passport called a knížka. Laborers needed a knížka to find work; farmers hiring a laborer without one could be fined. The contract held for at least one year, clearly specifying the laborer's obligations while leaving vague the employer's obligations. Laborers were furnished with room and board and usually ate with their employer's family. Their annual wage of $160 to $190 was paid in quarterly installments. A laborer might also be given use of a garden plot in which to grow food for his personal use. In theory, laborers received about 100 days off each year, counting weekends and the many holidays and feast days. However, an employer could ask his laborer to work on any of those days. The laborer could refuse, but the employer had the right to dismiss a laborer at any time for any reason. Conversely, it was much more difficult for a laborer to quit his employment. Disputes were arbitrated by the mayor of the nearest town. An employer could also control with whom the laborer met and when, and could inspect the laborer's belongings to ensure he was not pilfering the employer's goods.

The same terms, for the most part, applied to maids, except that they were paid less money than the male farm laborers.[19]

Frank Moravec, speaking of why he left for America in 1879, describes the rural conditions, along with military service, as deciding factors:

> In Bohemia, it disgusted me and also pained me to see poor people hauling liquid manure in a wheelbarrow to a distant rented field, and in the same wheelbarrow bring the pitiful yield of that field back home, and how people of both sexes would be hitched to a plow! Sad, but true! Before the war [the Prussian-Austrian war of 1866], people found work to sustain them in nearby factories, fewer people worked in the fields. Young people were happy enough; now bad whiskey has damaged and destroyed domestic peace. In my own case, at least, I never knew hunger.[20]

Village affairs were administered by a justice of the peace or magistrate. In the 1860s, the Austrian government gave villages their administrative autonomy. Village aldermen became decision makers in charge of police, schools, charity and local property. Although everyone in the village was legally entitled to participate in public affairs, the local elite, fearing loss of status and power, reacted by raising taxes on the less prosperous. Many wealthy farmers left their villages rather than share power with people they considered their inferiors, and many poorer farmers left rather than suffer heavy taxes and contempt.

Political and social issues facing Czech decision makers in the nineteenth century included control of dancing, length of military service, taxes, and tariffs. Wealthy farmers wanted to limit dancing because they believed dancing contributed to out-of-wedlock births that later led to high unemployment and drained local charity funds. Farm employers wanted military service limited to three years and military exercises forbidden during harvest season to assure adequate farm labor. Wealthier farmers wanted reductions in taxes, and poorer farmers wanted protective tariffs against farm imports.[21]

The Catholic Church, supported by a special tax, played a dominant role in social and political life. The priest was a leading figure in every village and town. All persons were required to belong, at least nominally, to a church. Churches maintained the local history, recording births, deaths, marriages and confirmations. After 1781, Lutheran and evangelical Protestant churches (but not Hussite churches) were legal and existed in some towns. Marriages between those of different religions were difficult, if not impossible, during most of the nineteenth century.[22]

Czech Education

Elementary education was opened to everyone following the 1848 revolution. In the late 1860s children began attending school from age six to fourteen; prior to that it had been age six to twelve. However, school attendance was not compulsory, and as tuition was charged, children of poorer families attended only as the family could afford it. Girls usually attended until about the age of ten when they could be hired out as maids. Boys had a bit more opportunity and stayed in school longer. Secondary education was available in larger towns and cities, but also required payment of tuition.

As time passed the annual school term was lengthened and material was taught in greater depth. Later immigrants to America were better educated than those who had come earlier. Almost all Czechs were sufficiently schooled in the Czech language to use the hymnal, prayer book and Bible. In 1900, literacy among Czechs in the Austrian Empire stood at 97%, higher than for the empire's Germans.

In the Czech-speaking areas there was no attempt to teach German in elementary schools. In mixed areas of Czechs and Germans, however, Czechs also learned German. Indeed, ambitious Czechs were anxious to learn German as a path to advancement, and this was particularly true for skilled workers and their families.

Descriptions of rural schools often tell of an old soldier, a permanent resident of the village, teaching sixty to eighty pupils.[23] The memoir of Frank Moravec, a Steele County Czech who grew up in Dolní Dobrouč, has just such a story. Frank describes his childhood education in the 1860s this way:

> This town of 2,500 inhabitants, more or less, had a school, but with only three grades. The schoolroom was packed with students and there was no ventilation—well, I won't say any more about that, you know how it is. The teacher

at that time, Mr. Jan Sic, was neither fish nor fowl, but I would say more German than Czech, and this sentiment showed in his teaching. We were taught religion 100%, but only a smattering of everything else. I remember how we were asked about what we knew about Asia: 'Jesus Christ was born there.' Africa? 'People with black faces live there.' Australia? 'It's an island.' America? 'Christopher Columbus discovered it.' And arithmetic, I didn't know until I came here what fractions were. Those who didn't study on their own, had little knowledge to take them through life.[24]

Terezie Spatenka, born Terezie Jasansky in 1835 in Lhotka near Česká Třebová, did not attend school until age twelve, and then for only a few weeks. Her teacher was a retired soldier named Kubista who smoked all through the school day and, before and after his teaching duties, worked on a loom he had set up in the school. On Saturdays, every member of her class brought a penny for the teacher. She learned to read and write and for several years received religious instruction on Sundays.[25]

Czech Social Life

For the lower classes, meals did little to liven their days. The diet of small farmers consisted primarily of potatoes and grains cooked in small pots, cabbage eaten raw or pickled, and occasionally dried fruit. Meat was reserved for special occasions, and might be salami or liver sausage. Breakfast was usually a cup of weak coffee or soup, and the evening meal a piece of rye bread or cheese. On Sundays, breakfast would be coffee and bread, with a lunch of soup and cake, a piece of bread for a snack, and a dinner of coffee and bread. Beer was the most common beverage for all social classes. On festive occasions, women made kolačky (Bohemian baked pastries), and a folded version of a kolaček, the buchty, could be carried out to the fields for lunch.[26]

In the nineteenth century, Czech villagers abandoned their traditional village dress, or kroj, for regular use, and on weekdays began dressing in town clothes, reserving their best clothes for Sundays. Traditional dress, with its distinctive design and embroidery designating the wearer's home region, was still worn for festive holidays.[27]

Village social life centered on the church and inn. Most villagers attended church services and events on Sundays, and took part in frequent holy days and saints' days with costumes, processions, and pilgrimages. Additional, less predictable events that enlivened an otherwise hard life were weddings, funerals and besedas, or social gatherings.[28]

Weddings were the most festive, beginning the afternoon preceding the ceremony and lasting several days. Dressing of the bride was a humorous event, and the wedding party sang and played instruments all the way to the church (or tavern, where most weddings in the nineteenth century were held). On the day of the wedding, the whole village joined the bride and groom's families in eating, drinking, and dancing that often lasted through the night.

Funerals were emotional events as relatives and neighbors said their goodbyes to the deceased, but also played a role in village social life as a time of coming together. Villages held harvest celebrations in the autumn and holy day celebrations throughout the year. Most events, including saints' days, featured drinking, music, singing and dancing.[29]

Terezie Spatenka of Owatonna remembered the carefree days of her youth at these celebrations:

> I enjoyed going to dances. Back then, girls went to dances wearing most often blue skirts, and barefoot. Any girl who had a calico skirt could consider herself a young lady. The floor of the tavern was of well-tramped down earth, and it was better to dance on and we had a better time there than today's young people in those enormous dance halls.[30]

While Czechs who came to America were glad to leave the poverty and rigid social strata behind, they missed the close-knit social structure of their villages. They would try to recreate this support in their churches and fraternal organizations.

LEAVING HOME

Czechs needed permission to leave their home country for America. Emigration policy in Bohemia was quite restrictive in the early years of emigration to America, but liberalized later.

Until the 1850s the Austrian government considered its inhabitants part of the national wealth, and did not favor emigration. In 1851, a leaflet on emigration was issued by the government, and records began to be kept on those who emigrated. An 1857 decree liberalized passport policies, and in 1859 more power over who was able to emigrate was given to local officials at the expense of the royal government. The Austrian government attempted to use the emigration process to funnel people toward under-populated parts of its empire such as Serbia; this was most successful during the American Civil War. But for the most part, internal emigration could not compete with the promise of America.

Policy was determined by the Emperor and the Interior Department, with some input from the provincial governments, and was enforced by two competing national police forces. The Interior Ministry under Bach was somewhat more liberal about emigration than the Ministry of Police under Kempen. Consequently, emigration policies varied in different times and places. Common threads were that permission was less likely if the prospective emigrant was dodging his military service, behind on taxes, or in debt. Conversely, permission was more likely to be granted if the applicant was a criminal or considered a revolutionary or troublemaker. In areas with economic problems and large unemployment and poverty, local officials were often happy to let poorer citizens leave. And if permission was refused, some left the country illegally.

Illegal immigration numbers were often higher than legal numbers. Some people simply left, not realizing they needed permission. Others, considered undesirables or trouble makers, left while officials turned a blind eye. Still others who were in trouble with the law or were evading debt or military service fled, sometimes under an assumed name.[31]

From 1785 until 1860, emigrants were required to pay a fee (abfahrtsgeld) to leave. After January 20, 1860, emigrants to the United States and Mexico were exempted from the fee.

The prospective emigrant could apply for either a travel passport or an emigrant passport. If he chose to apply for an emigrant passport, he would lose his Austrian citizenship as well as rights in his town. Joseph Kaplan's application for emigration contains the age, religion, occupation and marital status of Joseph and his wife. It also lists his place of residence, where he planned to settle, and why he was emigrating (Kaplan's response to that question: "America in a hope of improvement of living.") The passport application also lists how much property he was taking with him, and contains certification from the military and civil authorities that they had no objection to his departure.

The travel passport (Reise-Pass in German) was good for three years. Documents varied over time and from region to region. The pass for Vincenz Starch, a German from northern Bohemia who emigrated in 1855, allowed him three months to depart before the pass expired. Nine years later the pass for Joseph Kaspar, from Usti nad Orlici in eastern Bohemia, was very similar. The pass for Vincenc Pecháček, from Čermna in eastern Bohemia, is simpler in form. Other than Imperial boilerplate language, the only information it contains is Vincenc's name, occupation, and place of residence before departure. Emigrants who had a change of heart were usually allowed to return if the term of the pass had not yet expired.

Not every Czech was happy in his new home, and many returned penniless, often becoming a drain on their home village. Though rarely discussed in standard American history books, a surprisingly large number of European immigrants to America returned to Europe. This was true in colonial times, and continued until the close of large scale immigration in 1924. Some had come intending to work only a few years before returning to their home country, but many of the returnees were immigrants who had been disappointed in their plans to establish a new life in America. The Czechs fit this pattern; in the period from 1908 to 1923, 19% of Czech immigrants returned to Europe.

The royal official in Lanskroun, Count Pötting, issued a decree in March of 1853 that attempted to deal with the problem of returning immigrants:

Circular to All Villages, Circular Nr. 1726, 11 March 1853
It has repeatedly occurred that people who have cashed in their property and emigrated to America, have found no success there, that they have returned to their homeland as beggars and become a burden to their country and to their own villages. Such cases have forced the Austrian Empire to require that whoever wants a travel document to America must show:

What arrangements he has there,

How long he requires for these dealings before being required to present the travel document,

Whether he has the necessary assets to travel to America and back, and

What preparations have been made for this voyage.

Whoever wishes to emigrate to America forever with his family from Austrian land must:

Fulfill the requirements of the first clauses contained in the Emigration Law of 24 March 1832,

Either at the Imperial or Royal sub-regional office, in the form of a declaration or by presenting documents from the native village and from two witnesses as signatories, he must renounce his Imperial Austrian citizenship and hometown residence.

By this renunciation he will lose his Imperial Austrian citizenship and the right of residence in his native community and he may not come back, or only do so after obtaining permission to emigrate to the Austrian Empire, and if one or another person should return without permission, as a foreigner, he will be investigated and ejected from the Austrian Empire. The local administration is required to proclaim this to the attention of each citizen.

From the Imperial and Royal sub-regional office at Lanskroun, 11 March 1853, Imperial and Royal sub-district administrator, Count Pötting.

In 1855, and again in 1857, the number of Czechs returning from America rose due to high unemployment in the States. When they arrived in Bremen, the Saxon government refused them admission to its territory as the Austrian government no longer considered them citizens. They were stateless people with nowhere to turn. Austrian Interior Minister Bach intervened on March 23, 1857, by ordering that returnees be readmitted to the Austrian Empire and allowed to apply for citizenship.

The process of applying for emigration, which in the 1850s was often a complicated and lengthy affair, was streamlined in 1865 to a matter of a few weeks. This lax control continued until 1881, when the process once again became more difficult.[32]

Emigrants from eastern Bohemia could catch a train at several points including Česká Třebová and ride through Bohemia and Germany to the North Sea coast. Nearly all immigrant ships taken by Czechs left from either Bremen or Hamburg, and, until 1891, primarily from Bremen. Both Bremen and Hamburg were inland from the sea. Because of silting in the rivers, only some sailing ships were able to reach the cities. Steamships, once they became the dominant mode of transportation, were too large to even attempt the journey. Therefore, both cities created ports on the North Sea connected to their home cities by railroad.

Ports of Departure

Bremerhaven, located 38 miles north, was the deep sea port for Bremen. Between 1850 and 1862, departing passengers were transported by rail from Bremen to Bremerhaven where they could stay at the Karlsburg emigrant house, which had sleeping and eating accommodations for 2,000 to 3,500 people, a hospital and a chapel. By 1862, as scheduling and rail service improved, it was possible for passengers to stay in Bremen until their ship was ready for departure, take the train to Bremerhaven, and immediately board ship. At that point, the Karlsburg, no longer necessary, was closed.

Hamburg created a similar arrangement with the city of Cuxhaven, 68 miles to the north on the North Sea.[33]

The last step in the immigrant's process of departure was to make it out to sea. Shipping companies were insistent that only healthy immigrants left port on their ships. Immigrants refused admission at the port of entry to America because of ill health had to return to Europe. Since most would not have money for the return ticket, the passenger company was faced with transporting them back for free. To make matters worse, beginning in 1891 the United States charged a $20 penalty for every immigrant passenger who was rejected. As a result, health checks were performed in Bremen and Hamburg, and unhealthy emigrants were not allowed aboard ship. Temporary housing for passengers awaiting departure was closely policed for health problems, as were conditions aboard the ships. Finally, passengers were coached on how to pass the health examination and questioning by immigration officials that awaited them in America.

THE OCEAN VOYAGE

Getting to Minnesota was an arduous undertaking for the earliest Czech immigrants. Early immigrants made the voyage to America on sailing ships, enduring weeks of cramped and uncomfortable conditions. Joseph Kaplan's account described six weeks aboard the *Emma*, which carried about 300 people in addition to the captain and crew. John Renchin's family traveled nine weeks on the ocean to reach Baltimore (at first, not realizing it was included in the fare, John politely refused the food on the ship). Anna Kubat and her husband and six young children had an even longer trip:

> The trip across the ocean took ten weeks. We went through several heavy storms. The ship was old, and it was terrible listening to the creaking and cracking during the storms. When we neared the shores of America, a son was born to us. During the journey, three other babies were born on shipboard. They were dressed up to celebrate their baptisms, and the captain became godfather to each of the newborns. Our son was named Antonin. The new mothers were given tasty foods, and even the newborns were given gifts as a remembrance.[34]

Steamships began regular crossings of the Atlantic in the 1850s, but for the next two decades were too expensive for most immigrants. Steamships made good time regardless of winds and currents, and crossed much faster than sailing ships. They came into widespread use by immigrants in the 1870s, and in the 1880s replaced sailing ships for passenger travel. In 1856, five percent of immigrants landing in New York were aboard steamships; by 1870, that number had reached 88 percent.[35]

Two steamships bringing Steele County Czechs to America in the 1860s were the *New York* and the *Hansa*, both operated by the North German Lloyd shipping line. They were built around the same time, were of similar design, and were typical of early steamships. The ships were powered by steam engines through a single propeller, had one smokestack, and traveled at speeds of about 13 miles per hour. In addition, each had three masts for sailing should they encounter good winds, lack of fuel, or engine failure. They were about 320 feet long, 40 feet wide, and made of iron. The *New York* accommodated sixty passengers in first class, 110 passengers in second class, and 400 passengers in third class (or steerage).[36]

A Czech-language advertisement for the Hamburg-American line listed prices by ship from Hamburg to New York as $28 for steerage, $72 for second class, and $120 for first class.

An advertisement for Morris and Company of Hamburg touted the conditions of passage on the Hamburg Line vessel *Columbia* going to America. It quotes the order of the Senate of May 28, 1851, requiring that every passenger have a personal space of 14 square feet. The order enumerates the weekly provisions to be served to each adult passenger, including 2.5 pounds navy biscuits, 1 pound wheat flour, 5 pounds oatmeal, 2 pounds rice (to be replaced by potatoes in season), 1 pound salted beef and a few ounces of tea, sugar and molasses. Each person was to receive 3 quarts of water daily, and cooking fuel and facilities were to be furnished.[37]

Frank Kubicek left Bremen in 1872 on the steamship *Ohio* and arrived in Baltimore nineteen days later—less than three weeks! He was a curious seven-year-old, and after a few days of sea sickness, "I felt fine and got to going around the big ship. I guess I crawled through and saw everything that could be seen on the ship."[38]

The trip was not always smooth. Joseph Petranek and his family set out across the Atlantic for America in 1883 on a sailing ship with auxiliary motors. However, because of rough seas, the ship used all its fuel and was forced to make most of the voyage by sail. The usually three-week trip took six weeks.

On the Petranek's voyage, children under twelve traveled for half price, and babes in arms were free of charge. However, there were other costs. Water on board was rationed and sold to passengers. When the length of the trip doubled from three to six weeks, the Petraneks did not have enough money to cover expenses and subsisted on a daily kettle of potato soup. Joseph Petranek played musical instruments, his own and other people's, to entertain the passengers and crew. As they finally neared port, Joseph used the last of his money to splurge on a kettle of prune soup. But as his family gathered around the kettle to eat it, the ship rolled and the soup spilled. They spent their last day on board ship hungry.[39]

ARRIVAL

During the early nineteenth century the United States had 101 ports of entry, regulated only by the cities themselves and the states. In the 1840s, in response to problems with disease on board overcrowded ships entering U.S. ports, the United States government passed laws regulating the number of passengers for a given ship size.

New York had surpassed Philadelphia as the largest port of entry shortly after the opening of the Erie Canal in 1825. The canal made it possible for settlers to go north from New York City on the Hudson River, take the canal to the Great Lakes, and sail the lakes to points far inland where land was cheap. A few years later, railroads would serve the same purpose.

Shipping companies from Bremen and Hamburg began recruiting Czech emigrants in 1852. In these early years, the Hamburg line, Morris and Co. Columbia, offered service from Hamburg to New York, New Orleans, Boston, Baltimore, Philadelphia, Quebec and Galveston.[40] Most Steele County Czechs entered through New York or Baltimore.

Castle Garden

Until 1855, immigrants simply left the ship they had come on at their port of entry and proceeded to their destination in America. In that year, the state of New York opened the nation's first immigrant receiving station at Castle Garden, a small island just off the tip of Manhattan. It opened for business on August 3, 1855.

The common perception is that most immigrants to the United States were processed through Ellis Island in New York. In fact, Ellis Island did not open until 1892. Its predecessor, Castle Garden, began existence as one of the fortifications built after an 1807 attack by the British navy on a ship in New York harbor. The fortification, called Southwest Battery, was constructed on a small island just off the tip of Manhattan. It was a circular building about 200 feet offshore, connected to Manhattan by a timber causeway with a drawbridge. It stood ready to repel the British during the War of 1812, but never actually fired a shot in anger. It was renamed Castle Clinton after the war, and the War Department transferred it to the city of New York in 1821.

The castle reopened as an entertainment venue in 1824, an open-air band shell with gardens and a fountain. It hosted fireworks and band concerts, speeches and receptions. It had a promenade atop its walls, and a bar. A roof was added in the 1840s, and it accommodated operas in concert form including *The Semiramide* and *The Barber of Seville*. In 1850, the European singing sensation Jenny Lind, "the Swedish Nightingale," made her American debut in Castle Garden.

Within a few years, the castle's entertainment career came to an end. When it reopened in August 1855, it was as the immigrant reception center for the city of New York. Shortly before reopening, quantities of earth were dumped in the water between Manhattan and the castle, joining the island to Manhattan Island with a fence to separate the castle from the rest of New York City.

Pictures and an eyewitness description from the mid-1860s give a sense of the immigrant experience. The circular castle walls were topped by a roof sloping up from all sides to a peak that contained a cupola with skylights to provide illumination. Inside, the circular perimeter wall was a ground floor and upper arcade, supported by columns and arches. Another ring of columns in the center held up the apex of the roof. The rest of the floor was taken up by benches for immigrants to sit or sleep on, and work stations where a dozen or so immigration officials performed their various tasks.

The building was divided into two halves, and immigrants were assigned to one or the other based on nationality. Each half was divided again into two parts, one for women and one for men. Coal fired stoves heated the building, and gas lights illuminated it at night. Each half had a refectory to provide food, and pumps to provide water. Watchmen patrolled to prevent problems.

Before Castle Garden opened, immigrants were often victimized by thieves and con men who hung around the docks ready to prey on naive passengers arriving from all parts of the world. At Castle Garden, these vultures were kept at bay by the fence and immigration officials. Inside immigrants could receive medical help, exchange currency at reasonable rates, learn about travel routes and fares, or find lodging and employment. They might also find help with letter writing and mailing, baggage delivery, and funds transfers to or from relatives. Eight million immigrants arrived at Castle Garden between 1855 and 1889.

Nonetheless, over time Castle Garden acquired a bad reputation. Its design protected immigrants from ruthless con artists on the outside, but on the inside it became a haven for corrupt immigration officials.[41]

> Castle Garden's terrible reputation seems justified—it was shot through with corruption. Inspectors, service personnel and outsiders all preyed on the new arrivals, taking advantage of exhaustion, language difficulties and culture shock to rob tens of thousands of immigrants of their money and other possessions.[42]

Another function of Castle Garden was to prevent people with infectious diseases from entering the country. Federal doctors boarded arriving ships from small boats as the ships entered New York harbor. The doctors examined passengers, looking for disease or physical defects. If they found a person not fit for admission, he could not enter the U.S. This was fairly uncommon for passengers from German ports because of Germany's strict examination standards and health code.

František Vlček arrived at Castle Garden around 1890, bound ultimately for Cleveland. He recalled how passengers stood in rows inside the ship as doctors quickly made their way along the lines. Each person was given a superficial examination, the doctors looking under the eyelids of a few passengers in search of eye infections. After the doctors had left, passengers went up on deck to watch as the ship continued into New York harbor.[43] As nerve-wracking as the physical examinations must have been for passengers—their quest for a new life in a new country could come to an abrupt end—it was actually not a major hurdle to immigration. In the years between 1892 and 1900, 3,727,245 people entered the United States as immigrants. Only 1,309 (0.04%) were rejected for health reasons. More than 10 times as many (15,070) were rejected as likely to become public charges.[44]

The end of the Civil War and the resulting economic boom in the north led to a flood of new immigrants. In 1875, Congress passed a law forbidding entry to the U.S. for criminals and "women brought for lewd and immoral purposes." The law was challenged in the courts, but the United States won. Congress had asserted its right to control immigration. The United States government now shared responsibility for the entry stations with states containing the ports.

In 1882, Congress passed a law forbidding entry to convicts, lunatics, idiots or anyone unable to care for himself and who would need public charity. In 1890, Congress terminated its contract with the state of New York and took complete control of immigration into New York City. Joint control was ended in all other ports of entry the next year. When New York refused to let the United States use Castle Garden for a federal immigration station, an old barge office at the foot of Manhattan Island was used for twenty months while a new federal reception area was built on Ellis Island, a low piece of land well out in the harbor.

Ellis Island

Ellis Island was New York's entry point from 1892 until 1924, except for a short period beginning in 1897 when a fire destroyed the main building, and the barge office was again pressed into use. A larger building, the one that tourists are shown today was constructed and opened in 1900. Czechs called Ellis Island Ostrov Vzdechu, or Island of Sighs.

The greatest rush of immigrants in American history occurred during the period when Ellis Island was the New York receiving station, making the island legendary in American history. However, since the vast majority of Steele County Czechs came to America before 1892, most who entered at New York went through the Castle Garden receiving station.[45]

Port of Baltimore

The second busiest port for Minnesota Czechs was Baltimore. Many Germans had settled there, creating a thriving community that enticed still more German immigrants to remain in Baltimore rather than move farther west. By 1861, a fourth of the city's population was of German ancestry. Many local German businessmen befriended their non-German business colleagues.

In particular, Albert Schumacher, German consul for several northern German cities, was a friend of John W. Garrett, head of the Baltimore and Ohio Railroad, and became a director of the railroad himself. The B&O signed an agreement in January 1867 with the North German Lloyd Steamship Line which allowed passengers in Germany to buy tickets good for the trip across the ocean and the subsequent railroad trip to Chicago, Cincinnati or St. Louis. Within a few years, the Hamburg-American Line and the Baltimore Mail Line signed similar agreements.

Until 1868, immigrants to Baltimore arrived at Fell's Point. However, the Fell's Point facilities, built for sailing ships, were too small for the new steamships. In 1868 the railroad built new piers and facilities for steamships at Locust Point, in Baltimore's inner harbor. The railroad built two terminals, one for the steamship lines and one for the railroad. Immigrants could disembark from their ship, cross the pier, and immediately board a train. This was possible because health inspectors boarded each ship as it entered Chesapeake Bay, and inspected passengers as the ship moved up the bay toward Baltimore. As was the case in New York, passengers coming from north German ports were well-screened for health problems before leaving for America, and rejection rates for health reasons were low. By the time the ship docked, many passengers were ready to start on the next leg of their journey. Most of the rest could leave within a few hours.

Passengers delayed by disease or paperwork could stay at a boarding house on pier 9 run by Mrs. Koether. Several steamship lines had signed a contract to pay her 75 cents per day for each passenger for whom she provided room and board.[46]

Frank Kubicek remembered his swift passage through Baltimore at the age of seven in just a few words:

> We were on the ocean for nineteen days. We landed in Baltimore, and the same day we boarded a train going further west. On the third day, we were in Chicago.[47]

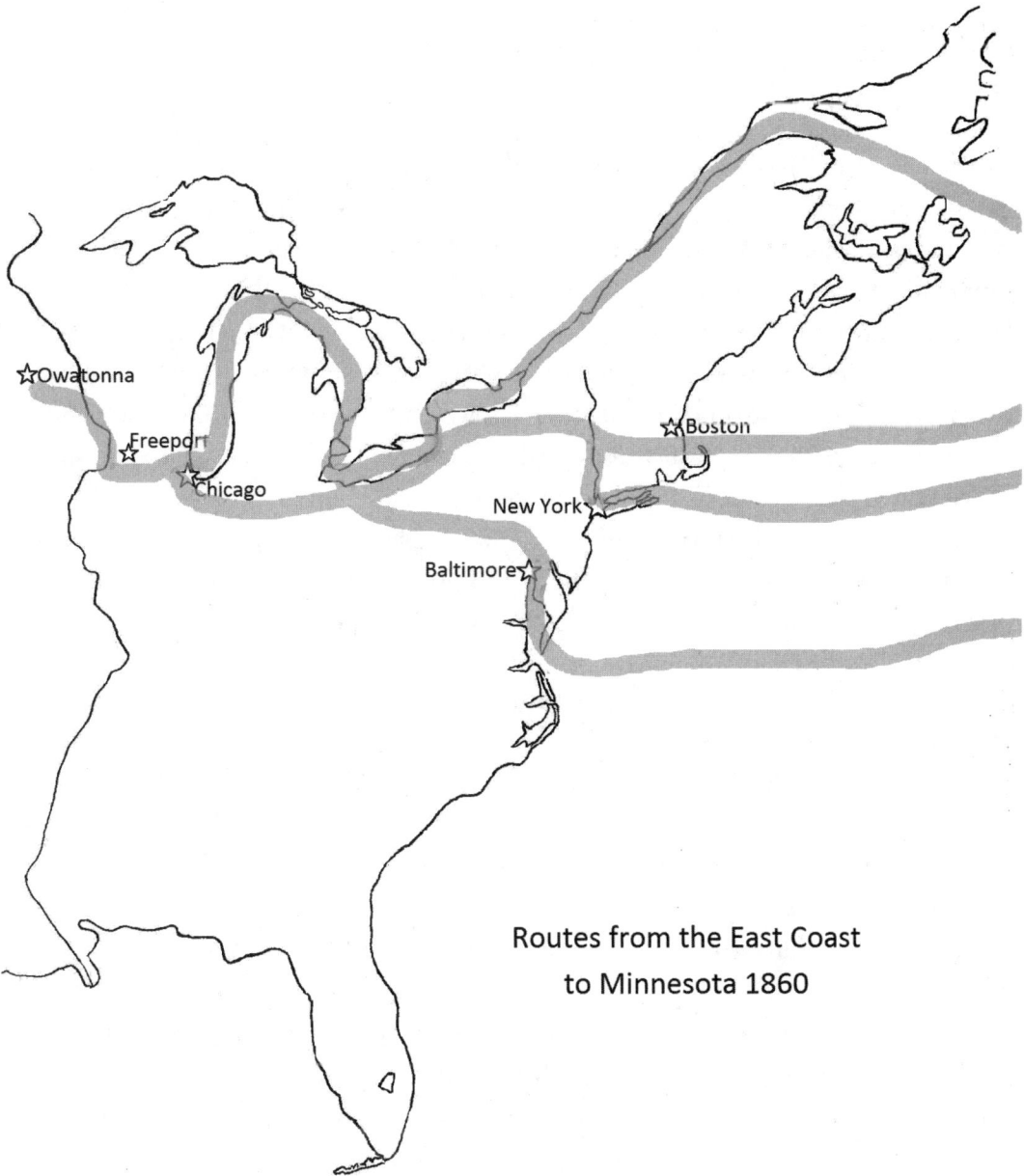

Routes from the East Coast to Minnesota 1860

ON TO MINNESOTA

Once in the U.S., settlers had to find their way to Minnesota. Before the Civil War, the American rail network was intermittent and trains ran at slow speeds. Railroads that connected were often of different track gauges, necessitating numerous transfers from one train to another.

Besides rail, travelers might also reach the interior by water. Some immigrants entered the U.S. at New Orleans and traveled up the Mississippi River. This was the route by which many Germans and Czechs reached St. Louis. German shipping lines used New Orleans as a major American destination until the Civil War, although even before the war the port had been periodically closed by yellow fever outbreaks. The Civil War accelerated the shift from the port of New Orleans to New York and Baltimore.

Some immigrants entered the continent via New York, journeyed up the Hudson River to the Erie Canal, and then on to the Great Lakes. Others entered the continent via the St. Lawrence River, which also delivered them to the Great Lakes. From the Great Lakes settlers might travel to any of several destinations. Many Czechs arriving in Milwaukee, Chicago and Cleveland took this route.

Anton Simek and the Pichners landed in New York in December of 1852, and likely traveled to Freeport, Illinois by rail since ice on the Great Lakes probably prevented them from using the Erie Canal–Great Lakes route.

Joseph Kaplan's family entered the continent in July 1856 at Quebec City. They would have landed west of the city at the immigrant receiving station in Wolf's Cove. They switched to a steamship that took them to Montreal. Kaplan described it as

> . . . a huge steamboat: 100 feet long, more than 20 feet wide, and three stories high—the third very magnificent. It carried 1150 persons and sailed almost as fast as the steam engine on a railroad.[48]

These steamers left Quebec every afternoon at 5 and arrived at the Lachine Canal in Montreal early the next morning. The Kaplan party arrived in Montreal on July 29, then boarded one of the Royal mail steamships which departed from Montreal every day at 10:30 bound for Kingston, Ontario. From Kingston, the Kaplan party traveled on a canal along the north shore of Lake Ontario to Toronto. A railroad carried them to Lake Huron (probably the newly opened stretch of the Grand Trunk Railroad from Toronto to Sarnia), where they boarded a steamship to Mackinaw, Michigan and entry into the territory of the United States. Another steamship ferried them across Lake Michigan to Milwaukee, where they caught a train to Chicago. From Chicago they journeyed by train to Freeport, Illinois for a reunion with their countrymen, the Anton Kubat family, the Pichner brothers, and the Benjamin Fisher family. After a two week rest, they made the rest of the trip to Iowa and on to Owatonna by covered wagon, finally arriving in mid-September.[49]

The Kubat family also entered at Quebec City, and the Benjamin Fisher family may have, as well. The John Renchin family, arriving in 1863, traveled by train from New York to Chicago or beyond, then by ox cart to Winona. In 1861, it took Anton Slezak's family a month to travel from New York to Hastings, Minnesota. They arrived in Hastings by boat on the Mississippi River, and had probably traveled from New York to Illinois (or La Crosse, Wisconsin) by train, and then up the river from there.

After 1870, when the rail network was much improved and passenger travel by steamship had begun to replace the old sailing ships, it took a month or less for a Czech immigrant to journey from Hamburg or Bremen to Owatonna. The transportation networks had improved just in time to handle the flood of immigrants headed for Minnesota at the end of the Civil War.

Threshing party, Owatonna settlement, about 1893. Adults standing in front: Anna and Anton Kovar, Mary Jirousek, Anton Stancl with hands on pitchfork, Barbara Truhlar holding daughter Mary; two men standing behind the Kovars, Mr. Jirele and John Pichner; man lying behind children, Frank Kovar; woman on far right, Anna Zednick Kovar.
Courtesy of Steve Wencl

4

1866–1872: The Post-Civil War Boom

In the summer of 1866 the American Civil War was over, most of the troops had come home, and the American economy in the north was booming. In Owatonna workmen were constructing tracks for two railroads that would soon reach town, and local citizens were organizing the first Catholic Church in Steele County, the Church of the Sacred Heart.

Early Czech immigrants had survived the first few years in their new home and now were taking their place within the larger community. The situation in the Czech homelands was much grimmer. That summer, eastern Bohemia was about to be caught up in the maelstrom of war.

THE AUSTRIAN-PRUSSIAN WAR OF 1866

Prussia and Austria had fought together as allies in a short war against Denmark in 1864 over the status of Schleswig and Holstein, two small German-speaking states near Denmark. Soon after the war ended, however, the victors disagreed on the future status of the two provinces. The disagreement was actually part of a larger conflict as the North German Confederation, with Prussia as its most powerful member, tried to unite a group of northern and central German-speaking states and exclude the influence of the Austrian Habsburgs. This small group of German-speaking states, Bavaria, Baden, Wurttemberg and Saxony, lay between the Austrian Empire on the south and east, France on the west, and the North German Confederation to the north. King William of Prussia and his Chancellor, Otto von Bismark, intended to gather these remaining small German states with Prussia into a new, unified German kingdom. Their actions would exclude Austria from any participation in the affairs of the northern German states.

In the treaty that followed the 1864 war, Austria was made the protector of Holstein. When Austria decided to hold elections in Holstein, the Prussian government declared the elections an "intrigue" that broke the treaty. Prussia invaded Holstein and forced the withdrawal of the Austrian troops, thus starting a war between Prussia and Austria.

As the spring of 1866 turned to summer, Prussia enlisted the King of Italy as an ally, forcing Austria to fight a two-front war in the north and the south. Austria quickly defeated the Italians, knocking them out of the war. However, the Austrian troops that had fought the Italians in the south then had to be moved north to counter the Prussian threat.

In the interval, Prussia had invaded the southern German states of Hanover, Kassel and Saxony. The Saxon king retreated into Bohemia with 20,000 troops to join the Austrian forces against the Prussian armies, which invaded Bohemia from two directions in late June.

The Prussians possessed superior training, weapons and leadership, but the Austrian troops were in their home territory and led by experienced generals. In short order, the local population also turned against the Prussians.

The Prussian 1st Army had crossed into Bohemia near Reichenberg (modern Liberec) occupying the town for three days and requisitioning wagons, horses and food, and charging the local people a war tax. As word of the Prussians' actions spread, towns in the surrounding area hid their food, livestock, supplies and the handles to well pumps. Without access to these necessities, the Prussian troops were left hungry and thirsty.

The Prussians continued marching southeast toward the Austrian fortress of Königgrätz (Czech Sadová), near the larger city of Hradec Králové. At the town of Podol, they defeated a force of Austrians and Saxons, who lost a thousand soldiers. The Austrians retreated to the vicinity of Münchengrätz (Turnov), where they held their own against the Prussians in another battle until the Austrian generals ordered a retreat. The thirsty Prussians, pausing to celebrate at nearby Wallenstein brewery, let the Austrians escape.

The Austrians retreated to Gitschin (Czech Jičín) and awaited arrival of the main Austrian army under General Benedek that was approaching from the south.

A second Prussian army had invaded Bohemia from the east, entering near Náchod and moving southwest intending to meet up with the western Prussian army. As they moved, they pushed back Austrian forces in their path, until the Austrians won a costly victory at Trautenau. But delay and poor communications by the Austrians allowed the Prussians to regain their momentum. Austrian General Benedek, who had intended to meet up with the Austrian forces in Jičín, decided the movements of the Prussians made this course of action too dangerous and determined to make a stand at the fortress of Königgrätz, ordering the Austrians and Saxons in Jičín to join him there.

Retreat through the city of Jičín was costly for the Austrians. Fighting between the advancing Prussians and the Austrian rearguard lead to the capture of 876 Austrians who had blundered into a swamp. The rest of the Austrians marched hard with very little food and water for more than two days before joining the main Austrian army at Königgrätz on July 1. It was raining as they arrived, and the muddy ground and inadequate latrines sped an outbreak of cholera that had just begun.

The Austrian troops rested for a day as Austrian commanders made their plans and put artillery and defenses in place. The Prussian 1st Army was approaching from Jičín, and the Prussian 2nd Army was hurrying to join them from the northeast, setting the stage for the largest battle ever fought on European soil to that time. The Austrians and Saxons fielded 205,000 soldiers to fight a combined Prussian force of 225,000 soldiers on a battlefield of about nine square miles. The rumble of the cannons could be heard in Řetůvka, 35 miles distant.

Austrians and Saxons occupied high, wooded ground between the Bystriz (Bystřice) and the Elbe (Labe) Rivers. Behind them, on the far side of the Elbe, was the fortress of Königgrätz, reachable by crossing three pontoon bridges.

July 3 dawned foggy and rainy as the Prussian 1st Army advanced on the Austrian forces. Austrian artillery killed or wounded many Prussian soldiers as they attempted to outflank the Austrians and overrun their cannons. The Prussians forced one Austrian artillery battery to retreat, but the Austrians counterattacked and by late morning, appeared to be on the verge of winning the battle.

At that moment, the advance guard of the Prussian 2nd Army approaching from the northeast arrived to help turn the tide. With their arrival, the Prussians nearly doubled their number of troops, and began pushing the Austrians back toward the center of their position, the village of Chlum.

The Austrians ordered a retreat about three o'clock in the afternoon. Their cavalry launched one last charge against the Prussians before retreating toward the fortress of Königgrätz behind them. Under cover of Austrian artillery, the Austrian infantry moved east toward the fortress. But when they arrived at the Elbe River, they found the pontoon bridges had been removed by the fortress' commander under the mistaken impression that all Austrians had already crossed. In desperation, soldiers began to wade or swim to the other side and many were drowned.

Those soldiers who made it across now approached the fortress through a haze of smoke and fog. The fortress commander, thinking they must be Prussians, refused to open the fortress. As more and more soldiers crowded in on the walls, the commander ordered sluice gates to be opened, flooding the low ground around much of the fortress.

Mass panic ensued. As Austrian soldiers rushed toward the fortress, fearful that Prussians were on their heels, the plains around them started to flood. Only one narrow road stayed above water. One hundred and fifty thousand soldiers pushed desperately forward, toward that road, to escape the rising water and the crush of soldiers behind them. Hundreds of soldiers drowned, and more were crushed against the walls of the fortress by the mass of humanity. The fortress only opened its gates to the survivors long after nightfall.[1]

The Austrian army lost nearly 45,000 officers and men on July 3, many if not most of them Czech. The Prussians captured 20,000; the rest were dead or wounded. One Czech soldier who died that day was Joseph Kubicek. According to the story passed down through the family, Kubicek drowned. His sisters, Josephine (Mrs. Joseph Skalicky) and Anna (Mrs. Anton Mikyska), and his cousin Frank Kubicek, left for America after the war ended and settled in the Owatonna area.[2]

After the battle, the Austrian army retreated south to protect Vienna from advancing Prussian forces. Prussian army generals and Prussian King Wilhelm intended to advance all the way to Vienna, crush the Austrians, annex a great deal of Austrian territory, and charge the Austrians a large sum of money to help pay for the war. Prussia's chancellor, Otto von Bismark, argued against this idea. He reasoned that as the Austrian army still had considerable strength, defeating it would be difficult and would bring the French in on the side of the Austrians. There were also Prussian political considerations that needed attention, particularly the diplomacy of bringing Saxony, Bavaria and Hesse into the unified Germany he was trying to create. He argued that the best policy was to give the Austrians a lenient peace and return Prussian troops to Prussia. He was supported by Crown Prince Frederick Wilhelm. After a few weeks of diplomacy, a provisional armistice was signed on July 26, and a final one on August 23.[3]

While these issues were being settled, Prussian troops moved to the south, following the retreating Austrians. A Prussian contingent of more than 2,000 soldiers and 400 horses arrived in Řetůvka on July 8. As they neared the village, many local people fled into the forest with their livestock; young men of conscription age in particular hid to avoid being forced into the military. Prussian conduct, for the most part, was peaceful and respectful, although the local magistrate was briefly jailed for failure to carry out Prussian orders. The initial Prussian force moved on and was replaced with a succession of other contingents before the last Prussian troops departed on August 31.[4]

Retreating Austrian troops passed through nearby Lanškroun, followed closely by pursuing Prussians. The two armies met and skirmished at the adjacent villages of Rudoltice and Damníkov, destroying crops and confiscating food, as well as bringing cholera to the area. In the town of Cermna alone, 68 people died of cholera.[5]

Local Accounts of Austrian-Prussian Recollections

Franta Moravec of Owatonna was a child six years of age in Dolní Dobrouč when the war started. He remembered ". . . the Prussians in the year 1866, and those great Hungarian oxen when they were being herded through our town over the paved roads after the army."[6]

Terezka Jasansky Spatenka of Česká Třebová was 31 years old during the Prussian occupation. Her uncle Frank Simek was forced to house some Prussian soldiers and was put in charge of a Prussian cash box. When the cash box turned up missing, Simek was charged with its theft and hauled off to Prussia in shackles. Later, the cash box, which had apparently been taken by Prussian soldiers and hidden in Simek's hay loft, was found and Simek was released. The cash box episode became the talk of the village, and a local joker wrote a song about it. Disgusted with the teasing from his neighbors, Simek sold his farm and immigrated to America. He arrived in Steele County in the fall of 1866.[7]

The villagers' ingenuity in coping during wartime is clear in the following anecdotes from Steele County Czechs who recalled stories from two different wars.

Frank Spinler had a mill in Dolní Dobrouč. His son Rudolf, born in 1865, immigrated to America and the Owatonna area. He told his descendants how in the old country his family had hidden food from foraging armies. When word came that an army detachment was approaching, the family threw their bags of flour into the millpond. The kids jumped into the millpond and flailed about, pretending to play. This churned up mud concealing the bags of flour. After the soldiers left, the flour bags were dragged from the pond. The water had soaked into the flour only to a thickness of about ¾ of an inch, after which the wet flour formed a shell that kept the rest of the flour in the bags dry.[8]

Agnes Rajnet Rysavy, also from Dolní Dobrouč, told of hiding food from the Austrian army and police during World War I. One method her family used was to pull up floorboards and dig out the dirt, disposing of the dirt in the creek. They would then hide 10 or 12 sacks of potatoes in the hole, replace the floorboards, and use dry dirt to fill in cracks between the boards to make it appear as though nothing had been altered. They also hid sacks of flour at the bottom of the creek (as the Spinlers did in the millpond) or in the hog scalding trough, covered by drying clothes. Wheat might be dumped on the floor of the hay mow and covered with loose hay or straw. Bags of flour were covered with layers of oilcloth and hidden at the bottom of the manure pit under the hog pens. Lard was stored in partially-full crocks in plain sight, but with the top halves of the crocks filled with milk that hid the lard. Agnes' brother buried potatoes in a hole on the edge of the woods, replacing the sod in such a way that the potatoes remained exposed to air.[9]

Effects of the Austrian-Prussian War

Prussian troops departed Bohemia by the end of summer 1866, but the effects of the war were long lasting. A new constitution of 1867 recreated the Austrian empire as the Dual Monarchy, or Austro-Hungarian Empire. The same ruler led both parts of this new entity, as Emperor of Austria and King of Hungary. The armed forces, foreign policy and financial affairs were jointly run, but otherwise the two halves operated as separate nations. Seeing this, Czechs began to agitate for a triple monarchy, with Czech lands receiving the same rights as Hungarians achieved in 1867. One author described the reorganization as a deal between the Empire's German and Magyar minorities at the expense of Slavic groups that together comprised the majority of the population. The eventual effect was to change the Slav's desire for autonomy into a desire for independence.[10]

In 1868, following defeat by the Prussians, military service in the empire was reformed. Before this time, soldiers were drafted when and in the quantity needed. Beginning in 1868, all males were required to serve three years of active service, followed by nine years in the reserve. Other reforms included a new electoral law that began representative democracy, changes in church-state relations that decreased the powers of the Catholic Church over education and marriage, and increased rights for members of other religious faiths.

Despite these reforms, the great migration of Czechs from their homeland to America, for the reasons examined in chapter 3, was just getting underway.

THE RAIL REVOLUTION AND AGRICULTURE

Most early settlers in Steele County were farmers and the arrival of railroads revolutionized their work. Before the Civil War, a farmer living near Owatonna might spend five or six days on a round trip to Hastings, Red Wing or Winona to sell his wagon load of wheat for river shipment. The money he received in that town as payment for his wheat, he also spent in that town for supplies.[11]

After the arrival of railroads in 1866, farmers could ship crops directly from Owatonna, saving time and greatly increasing the likelihood that they would spend the money received as payment for their crops on purchases from merchants in their own community. Thus, railroads would appear to have been a boon. However, certain railroad practices and the freight rates they charged generated resentment in farming communities.

Among other questionable practices, friends of railroad owners would be given advance notice of proposed routes and locations of planned towns, allowing them to buy choice land and turn a considerable profit when the railroad opened.

One of the first structures built in a town that had been opened up to rail traffic was the grain elevator. As crop yields became too large for storage on the farm, farmers hauled their produce to town to sell to the grain elevator. However, the price they received often was less than the standard price posted for a bushel of wheat or oats, and was based instead on the elevator owner's judgments about dirt in the crop, color of the grain, weight and other factors. Farmers, suspecting they were victims of a kind of shell game, began to call for regulation of elevators. The Minnesota legislature finally required a public grading system for grain in 1885.[12]

In fall 1878 the *Owatonna People's Press* published items that expressed the resentment against the elevators. The first was a reprint from the *Mankato Review*:

Who the Gougers are:
No. 3 wheat will yield within one pound as much as last year's No. 1, and the flour is allowed to be particularly good. That is, the difference in point of yield between the two grades is only a fraction over four per cent. But the difference in money which the mills and elevators offer for these grades is still nearly forty per cent after the recent revision of prices by the Millers' Association. How is this? Farmers ought to be able to get more yet for their No. 3 wheat.[13]

A month later, a farmer wrote in with a humorous account of how he dealt with the gougers:

A Joke on the Atmosphere.
Last week I hauled a load of wheat to the Owatonna elevator to sell. As usual the buyers applied their brass testers, and it weighed but fifty one pounds per bushel. Previous to that time my wheat had weighed fifty-three pounds. When I asked for an explanation, they told me that it was owing to the damp weather; that my wheat had gathered moisture from the atmosphere, and did not weigh so heavy; consequently they could give me but thirty five cents per bushel. I well knew that the Hon. Brass Kettle could not be at fault, and under the circumstances I will own that I inwardly thought, d__m the atmosphere. I was obliged to raise a little money, so I sold a part of my load for thirty-five cents a bushel, and hauled the remaining eighteen bushels and twenty-five pounds to Clinton

mills, and atmosphere or no atmosphere, I got five hundred and fifty-five pounds of very good flour for the seven-eights of my wheat.

FARMER[14]

Railroad rates also seemed irrational and capricious. As with airline rates in the 21st century, 19th century railroad rates varied bewilderingly based on distance and line. The Winona and St. Peter railroad charged 3 cents per ton per mile to haul wheat from Owatonna to Winona, but charged six cents per ton per mile to haul it from Rochester to Winona on the same line, even though Rochester was closer to Winona than Owatonna. Four years after Owatonna became a rail city, Republicans in the Owatonna area denounced railroad practices they felt were abusive.[15]

In December 1867 a young Minnesotan named Oliver Kelley founded the National Grange of the Patrons of Husbandry, and in September 1868 founded the first Minnesota chapter. He reasoned that farmers needed a way to cooperate on statewide and national levels, and he looked to the model of the Masons for inspiration. He foresaw Grange activities to be education, collecting statistics, protection of farmers from fraud and corporations, and establishing depots in cities for the sale of farm produce. The Grange movement quickly caught on. By the end of 1870 Minnesota had 50 granges, and by mid-1873 more than 200.[16]

Steele County's 12 granges passed resolutions against railroad and elevator charges and the cost of farm machinery, and designated a local grange store. Civic leaders of Owatonna organized the Board of Trade in May 1873 to ensure fair treatment for farmers and push for better treatment from the railroads. Occurring at the height of the Grange movement, this was another sign of the discontent with farm policies and the railroads.[17]

Prominent Minnesota politician Ignatius Donnelly, author of a famous book on the lost continent of Atlantis, took advantage of the surging Grange movement and agricultural discontent to issue a pamphlet urging the Grange to form an independent political party. According to Donnelly, this party should take back government for the people, who, he said, were no longer adequately represented by the two major parties. In response to his call, a county convention was held in Mower County in July that nominated independent candidates for the fall election. The meeting also called for a statewide convention to carry the movement far and wide.

The result was the Anti-Monopoly Party convention that opened in Owatonna on September 2, 1873. The convention came out against corporations, high tariffs and corporate favors to legislators, and nominated a full slate of candidates for state offices. However, attendance at the convention disappointed the organizers.

The Democratic Party and the splinter group Liberal Republicans also nominated the Anti-Monopoly candidates to run as candidates for their parties, making them fusion candidates. The Republicans still won a majority of the legislature, but a smaller majority than usual. Many of the Republicans were also Grangers, which made the legislature ripe for passage of reforms.[18]

The Grange movement did succeed in getting three "Granger laws" passed in the Minnesota state legislature in 1871, 1874 and 1875 that called for the appointment of state railroad commissioners and state-regulated railroad rates. However, the laws were not as effective as proponents had hoped, in part because railroads' finances were shaky after the Panic of 1873 and the state feared driving them into bankruptcy.[19]

The Grange movement peaked in Minnesota in 1874. In Steele County, the educational and social efforts of the organization paved the way for the later cooperative creamery movement.[20]

Steele County farms in 1860 primarily grew oats, corn, potatoes and barley according to the census of that year. However, because of high demand for wheat during the Civil War, most cropland was switched to wheat production. A settler who arrived in Owatonna in 1865 complained that he could hardly find butter because farmers were raising wheat instead of dairy cattle. The price of wheat peaked in 1869 at $1.53 per bushel, but quickly slid to 95 cents due to overproduction.

Crops were not rotated in the fields during this period, leading to decreased soil fertility and decreased yields. At the same time more lands west of Minnesota were opened to settlement resulting in increased wheat production and lower prices, while railroad and elevator storage charges did not decline.

Besides the Grange movement another response to the needs of local farmers was the creation of the Steele County Agricultural Society in 1871. Members met to discuss the best ways of farming under the new conditions. The Society recommended that members grow less wheat, diversify into other crops and raise dairy cattle. Many farmers did not follow these recommendations, however, and continued to suffer from low wheat prices for many years.[21]

Cheese factories began to appear in Steele County in the mid-1860s. The factories made use of dairy farm output providing a market for farmers who converted from wheat farming to dairy cattle. The owner of the Horton and Case cheese factory in Owatonna loaned money to farmers at 12 percent interest, allowing them to buy cows and ensuring a steady supply of milk for the factory. Three more cheese factories opened in Steele County by 1873, and another opened in 1882. A news item early in 1873 illustrates their impact on the farm economy:

> **200,000 Pounds of Cheese.**
> . . . The actual facts as given us by Titus Case, Esq., the proprietor of three of the factories of this county, are as follows: the Owatonna factory, using the milk of 300 cows, manufactured 57,891 pounds [of cheese]. The Dodge city factory, using the milk of 270 cows, manufactured 47,288 pounds. The Havana factory, using the milk from 225 cows, manufactured 38,000. The Berlin cheese factory manufactured over 50,000 pounds. So it will be seen that the four factories of this county have in the aggregate manufactured in the neighborhood of two hundred thousand pounds during the past year. This has been marketed at an average rate of twelve cents per pound. When we have the Medford factory in operation, as it will be during the coming season, we shall have five factories in the county, and of course the amount of our annual product will be proportionately increased.[22]

Only five weeks later, the *Journal* addressed the issue again:

> Another cheese factory is being started in this county. This time it is Meriden that is to be accommodated. The Meriden factory will be the sixth in this county. Now let us have the ear of our farmers one moment while we say that to properly avail yourselves of these advantages you must improve your stock. Let it be a part of a matured plan with each farmer, to make each season mark an increase in the quality of the cows that form his dairy.
>
> Raise only the best calves; have no others. Go at it systematically and determinedly and while you are making money from the cheese product of your dairy, you will also make money by the improvement of your stock.[23]

When the cooperative creamery boom came to Steele County in the 1890s most of these cheese factories were converted to creameries.[24]

SCHOOLS IN THE CZECH SETTLEMENTS

From the original log school in Owatonna in 1854, the county school system had grown to employ sixty teachers by 1866. Superintendent A.A. Harwood organized a teacher institute to improve the qualifications of the county's teachers. The institute held week long meetings in the spring and fall with lectures in mathematics, science, logic and government that covered topics such as corporal punishment.[25]

The country school for the original Czech settlement southeast of Owatonna was commonly known as the Pavek School (district 23), in section 22 of Owatonna Township. It was founded in 1858, two years after Czech pioneers settled in the area. In the 1860s and after the surrounding land was owned by the Pavek family.

The earliest record remaining from the Pavek School is an account ledger that was begun in 1867 and ended in 1906. Most of what was written in the early years is in Czech. The account book itself was purchased used at a cost of 75 cents. A sum of $35.50 was carried over at the start of the ledger, since the school had been in operation before 1867.

The ledger records the school officers from 1867 to 1869 as: Ben Fisher, Director; Joseph Kaplan, Clerk; and Anton Kovar, Treasurer. In 1869 and 1870, Wencl Belina served as Clerk, Anton Kubat as Treasurer, and Wencl Jirousek as Trustee. John Pichner served as Director in 1871, 1872 and 1875, along with Joseph Kaplan as Treasurer and Joseph Kubat as Clerk. Later officers included Joseph Racek, Joseph Wavrin, and John Pavek.

The school year started in November and ended in March. In 1870, 64 children were assigned to the district. Subjects generally taught were reading, writing, arithmetic, geography, and the Czech language.

According to the ledger, the woman (unnamed) who taught in 1867–1868 was paid $130 for the year, or about $25 per month. By 1882, John Czezinski was paid $175 for teaching (about $35 per month). Other teachers listed during the 1870s were Lucinda Caps, Mary E. Titus, Pauline Pichner, and Albert Kasper. The teacher for the three winters of 1876–78 was Miss Frances McAlona. According to the county superintendent of schools, the children in this district made good progress in English under her instruction.[26]

Teachers during the 1880s included John Czezinski, A.L. Hickock, Clara Hays, N. Hays, E.B. Calhoun and Amanda Smith. W. Wood, C.M. Parker and Amanda Smith taught in the 1890s. In the early years, teachers usually boarded with a family in the area for the length of the school year.

Frank Kovar's history states that Czech language lessons were taught in the Pavek School by Joseph Kaplan beginning in 1864. According to school records Joseph Brozek taught Czech for a month in 1869 for a salary of $20. John Pichner was paid for teaching Czech in 1875. However, after the Auditorium Hall in Owatonna opened in 1896, Czech language lessons were taught there on Sundays and discontinued at the school.

Supplies for the school included brooms, chalk, books, drinking glasses, locks, firewood, and repairs. In 1869, $1.65 bought two brooms, a stovepipe elbow and a drinking cup. In 1891, the school purchased a Webster's dictionary (Slovnik Vebstru) for $3.50. In 1887, Godfrey Kaplan was paid $8.50 for building an outhouse, and in 1888, $4.00 was paid for building a coal bin. Other expenses included laundering, cleaning and curtains. One of the largest expenses, in 1894, was $92.80 for what must have been a very nice

District 23 School, Owatonna settlement, 1920. Courtesy of Steele County Historical Society

bookcase. A school tax on personal property helped pay the cost of public schools. The tax rate for District 23 in 1873 was 2%.[27]

The following report on the Pavek school appeared in 1880:

> **School Report.**
> The following is the report of the six months school in District 23, which closed April 22:
> No. scholars enrolled: 54
> Total attendance in days: 3946
> Total days school: 118
> Average daily attendance in term: 34
>
> Charley Belina took the first prize in A class in spelling; Francis Kovar in B class; Joseph Jirousek in C class; Joseph Sikora in writing and John Pichner in reading.
>
> John H. Czeszinski, Teacher

> We learn that Mr. Czeszinski has taught a very successful school during last term in District 23; also that throughout the entire term the pupils were all industrious, well behaved and made remarkable progress.[28]

Joseph Kovar was an early student in the Pavek School. He was born in Minnesota in 1864, and moved as a child to the Owatonna settlement. One of his first experiences at his new home was school:

> The second year I had to go to school, although I was only four years and eight months old. It was a mile and three-quarters through woods to reach school. Dear parents who have small children, it is not right to send them such a distance to school when they are so young. I had three older sisters, and the oldest gave us orders. I was thin and weak, and my sisters chased me along faster than I was able to go, until I had sticking pains under my ribs. If I didn't know my lessons in school, I was not allowed to eat dinner, and at home I was thrashed. Anyone with any sense at all can imagine how much such a child is capable of learning. Often I could have frozen along the way if it hadn't been for my neighbor Franta, who was four years older than I. When I was seven years old, in the morning I had to help my father stack either hay or wood. That was bad, too, because I had to go to school alone and I was always late.[29]

County superintendent Rev. G.C. Tanner had this advice for how to teach English to children who lived in foreign language households:

> In some of our schools much time is wasted in spelling words which are not useful to the pupil—I now refer to schools in which German, Bohemian or Norwegian is spoken at home. First, only the simple words of the language should be taken and the pupil should be shown the object for which the word stands unless the teacher is sure the pupil understands the meaning of the word. Few words a day—and more than this can be done—will give the pupil quite a vocabulary in a single term.[30]

The Havana School (District 11), established in 1857, also served some Czechs who were part of the original settlement just south of Owatonna. The 1879 school superintendent's report gave this description:

Miss Esther Adair has taught the school the past year. This is one of our largest schools. While the number of classes is large yet the teacher has so conducted the work as to show marked improvement, and the pupils have been well advanced in their studies. This district has been for the most part fortunate in the selection of its teachers.[31]

Silvin Pribyl, who lived right across the road from the school, remembers the way it was in 1928 when he first went to school:

We were so near to the school that we wanted to go all the time. I went when I was five, but did not last long. There were two teachers and forty some students, this all in a one-room school. This scared me and I quit after about a week. I didn't go back until the next fall when I had to go.[32]

Other school districts of importance to Steele County Czechs included the Litomysl School (District 57) in Section 26 of Somerset Township, where Catholics in the area met for religious services until they built a church in 1877. Riverpoint School (District 37) was established in 1860 in section 33 of Somerset Township; a larger school was built in 1921. Saco area Czechs were served by the Matejcek (or Saco) School (District 69) in section 8 of Somerset Township. Farther south was the Hope School (District 12), in section 19 of Somerset Township. The first Summit School (District 51), in section 11 of Summit Township, was a log building built in 1867; its teacher for that year was Ellen Donaldson. Unfortunately, few if any nineteenth century records from these schools survive today.

Minnesota's policy from the earliest territorial days had been to make primary education available to everyone, so schools were supported by aid from the state school fund as well as by township taxes. Since it was assumed that everyone would want to take advantage of this free option, education was not mandatory. However, year after year the numbers of children attending school in districts around the state were far smaller than the numbers of children eligible to attend. No attempt was made to enforce primary schooling until 1885, and even that law was ineffective. A tougher law was passed for cities and villages in 1899, but statewide truancy enforcement did not begin until 1909.[33]

Henry Pribyl, born 1897, gives an account illustrating the difficulty of enforcing attendance even in 1910:

I went to school in Summit Township, District 95 for the first two years, and District 51 in the same township for grades three through seven. My last year of school I went nine days and I was thirteen years of age. There was much work, husking corn by hand, herding cows and plowing.

Right after Christmas I came down with smallpox that lasted three weeks. Then my brother Frank came down with them. Three weeks later the rest came down with them and we were quarantined for nine weeks. By that time we had to get ready for spring work the next year.[34]

Religious Education Question

The question of religious education in public schools arose in Minnesota, as it had in Ohio and other states (see chapter 2). Folwell describes the situation in this way:

> In the rapidly filling counties of the frontier there was a mixture of native and foreign-born people (in 1870 more than one-third of the people of Minnesota were foreign-born) and their children in the schools. Catholics could not tolerate the reading of the King James translation of the Bible; Protestants would have no other. Doctrinal instruction was, of course, impracticable. The reasonable and practical treatment of the impasse, it was thought, was to relieve the public schools of religious observances.[35]

The *Owatonna Journal* in 1873 printed a strong statement of the Catholic attitude toward public schools:

> Division of the School Money—The Rev. Father Phelan, Catholic, savagely assails the American public schools in the *Western Watchman*. He says, speaking for his church:
> We are convinced that the present school system is a curse to this country, and the cause of its profligacy, its crime and corruption. We express no opinion of this or that school, or one or other corps of teachers; we form our judgments upon the corruption of the *system*. Our present system of public schools, by its forbidding all instructions in the principles of morality, and its ignoring the authority which alone can give sanction to moral precepts, fosters and encourages immorality, disarms virtue, and opens the floodgates of sensuality and of social, civil and national corruption.

He wildly declaims that the public schools of the country are the principal reservoirs which feed the houses of prostitution, insists that children "will go to the devil if they are not forced to confess," and says, in conclusion, that Catholics will be satisfied with no schools except those which have a confessional for shield and defense. He then demands a portion of the public school money for the training of Catholic children.[36]

A few years later, after proposals to share public school funds for Catholic education or to allow Catholic religious education in public schools during school hours were defeated, the Catholic Church took a different approach and backed the abolition of all religious instruction of any kind in public schools. From the *Owatonna Journal*:

Another Attack on Our Common Schools.
A bill to prohibit religious exercise, and sectarian practices, and the use of sectarian books, papers, &c., in the public schools and institutions of learning of this State.

Section 1. That all religious exercises, singing of sectarian hymns, or other sectarian practices, and the use of any sectarian or religious books, papers or other things, in any of the public schools, or public institutions of learning of this State, are hereby prohibited and forbidden therein, between the hours of nine o'clock in the forenoon, and four o'clock in the afternoon of the days in which public instruction is required to be given therein, or at any other time when such instruction is required to be, or is given therein by the trustees or proper officers thereof.

Sec. 2. Any teacher of any school or institution of learning, or any other person, who shall violate any of the provisions of section one of this act, shall pay a fine of not less than five, nor more than fifty dollars for every such violation; and such teacher shall be deemed to have violated his contract, and shall have forfeited all right to recover compensation for services rendered thereunder; and any officer of any such school or institution of learning, who shall authorize, direct, permit or consent to any such violation, shall be guilty of malfeasance in office, for which, upon due proof thereof, he shall be removed from office by the Governor.

Sec. 3. This act shall take effect and be in force from and after its passage."
The above bill introduced by Senator McDonald, who represents a Catholic constituency, is a covert, yet direct attack upon the common schools. We

regret to say that the measure bids fair to receive the support of the Democratic party in the Legislature. . . .[37]

A week later the paper weighed in on the issue again:

If the agitation of the question of sectarianism in the school as it has been called, shall result in the exclusion of all sectarian teaching, we shall be glad, and if the Bible, even, shall be excluded, and as a result we shall have more home teaching, more pains taken to inculcate moral and religious ideas at the hearthstone, and by the precept and example of professed Christian parents, we cannot say that we will regret the change. We, as a people, have relegated to the school and the Sunday school, those duties which God and nature intended the parents to perform, to a dangerous extent. Our streets are sometimes made hideous by their horrid profanity, and this largely because their parents have not inculcated right thoughts at home, because the children have been allowed to run in the streets without proper restraint, and because something else has been put in the place of right precepts at the fireside and by the mother's knee.[38]

In 1877, the Minnesota legislature passed and voters ratified an amendment to the state constitution on the subject of schools and religion. It provided that no appropriation of money or property be made "for the support of schools wherein the distinctive doctrines, creeds or tenets of any particular Christian or other religious sect are promulgated or taught."

Many people feared that the threat of eternal damnation was all that would enforce proper conduct, and chaos would result when religious instruction was removed from schools. Others felt that proper conduct and morals could be taught in schools in a nonreligious manner. In 1881, the Minnesota legislature easily passed a law authorizing (but not requiring) the teaching of hard work, punctuality, thrift, patience, health, temperance, honesty, justice, courtesy and other virtues. The teaching method was to give a short talk on a virtue each day. The next day students were required to produce illustrations of that virtue and thereafter to practice it in their daily lives.[39]

In annual reports written after this 1881 law, the state superintendent of education argued that morals could be taught in schools while religious teaching was left to families and churches.

The 1877 constitutional amendment removing religious instruction from schools was understood to apply to Bible reading, and thus was applied. The use of school houses for

Sunday school and religious services outside of school hours was not considered a violation. Hence, the Litomysl Czechs held religious services in the local school until their church was built.[40]

During the 1870s, as many school systems around the country began secularizing public schools, the Catholic hierarchy split into two factions over the issue. One group of Catholic bishops wanted to work with public school systems, possibly by using government funding for both Protestant and Catholic schools. This never came to fruition, but Bishop Thomas Grace of St. Paul, and his associate and eventual successor John Ireland, were in favor of Americanizing Catholic immigrants, and of working with the public school system when possible. Another group of bishops, led by Bernard McQuaid of Rochester, New York, pushed hard for Catholic schools in all parishes.

When the Third Plenary Council of bishops met in Baltimore in 1884, the hardliners won out. The education policy enunciated by the council had four parts: every Catholic parish that did not then have a Catholic school should build one within two years, parish priests who did not start a school could be removed from their parishes, and parishes that refused to found a school could be put under interdict and refused sacraments. A fourth idea, to refuse sacraments to parents who did not send their children to Catholic schools, was narrowly voted down. The Vatican later reviewed the education policy and softened it to some extent.[41]

In addition to difference in attitudes toward the public schools, Catholics also differed in their views toward assimilation. Most of the American Catholic hierarchy was Irish, spoke English, and were in favor of immigrants learning English as quickly as possible. However, most non-Irish immigrants wanted to keep their language and culture alive and pass it on to their children. German, French-Canadian and Polish Catholics (and to a lesser extent, Czech and Slovak Catholics) wanted Catholic schools to teach in their native languages. They viewed public schools as a threat to both their faith and their cultures.[42]

Nonetheless, separate Catholic schools were expensive and much harder to establish and maintain in rural areas than in concentrated urban neighborhoods. Therefore, they would come later than most other institutions to Czech settlements.

ARRIVALS

The *Owatonna Journal* complained from time to time that misleading advertising by railroads and corporations caused new immigrants to bypass Owatonna and other suitable sites for settlement in favor of the desolate and inhospitable prairies. Even so, Owatonna continued to attract its share of new settlers:

> Immigration has commenced in good earnest. From every train numbers of the hardy yeomanry, with baggage in hand, proceed to the interior, and many of them are securing homes in this county. Prairie schooners are also seen frequently, and our State will get a good share of settlers this season notwithstanding the damaging reports which have been circulated in relation to the weather of the past winter. We are glad to see so many of these comers settle where they have good markets and all the essentials of pleasant homes, instead of pushing to the extreme frontier, where land is but little cheaper than it is here, and where hardships are numerous.[43]

Frank Simek, fresh from his scrape with the Prussians over the missing cash box, arrived in America in late 1866 or early 1867 and made his way to Owatonna. He was probably related to local Czech pioneer Anton Simek, or to John and Maria Simek who arrived in 1864. **Jan and Florian Brozek** also arrived in 1866.

Theresa (Jasansky) and Frank Spatenka came to America in 1867. She was from Lhotka, near Česká Třebová. She married Frank in 1855, and they made a living on a field he had inherited that was next to a river. They processed linen for the army and other customers in their weaving shop, laundered the linen in the swift flowing river on a scrubbing board that Frank built, then bleached the linen and laid it on the field to dry in the sun:

> I will never forget the beautiful evenings and nights we spent watching the linen. I knew how to blow military calls on a horn, but in spite of our watchfulness, sometimes a thief would succeed in cutting through the buckles holding the linen pieces and steal a few.

Soon after the dislocations of the 1866 war, a spring flood in 1867 washed away the scrubbing board and covered the bleaching ground with sand. They sold their property and sailed for America a few months after her Uncle Frank Simek had begun his journey.

Theresa and Frank arrived in Owatonna just in time for one of the worst growing seasons on record. After buying the most urgent necessities they had but $20 remaining. They used the $20 plus $15 of borrowed money to buy a cow, and paid off the debt by working for 40 cents a day. In 1868, Frank went to work for the Chicago, Milwaukee and St. Paul Railroad, then being built through their area, for $1.25 a day.

The Spatenkas bought a team of oxen and rented a farm, but suffered from the low farm prices that followed the Civil War. After three years they managed to save $100 and bought 80 acres of wooded land in section 25 of Owatonna Township, where they cleared the land and built a log house and grass or straw out-buildings.

Theresa suffered a broken arm and internal injuries when her skirt caught in the moving chain of a threshing machine and threw her to the ground. The crush of work to maintain the farm forced her return to her labors before she was fully recovered.[44]

Wencl and Anna (Srsen) Suchanek made the voyage to America in 1867 and settled on a farm in Somerset Township that is still owned by their descendants. By 1880 the farm acreage was a combination of woods, meadows and cropland growing hay, oats, corn, wheat, sorghum and potatoes. The farm supported two horses, two milk cows, four pigs and 110 poultry birds.

Wencl and Anna had nine children. In addition they also raised Joe Srsen as one of their own. According to Joe's descendants, his birth mother asked Wencl and Anna to watch him after they landed in New York, but she never came back for him. Anna was a Srsen, but apparently not related to Joe Srsen.

Wencl and Anna's son John lost his arm in a threshing machine accident; it was buried beneath the maple trees on the farm. Son Joseph took over the farm from his parents, and had an ice house where he kept river ice packed with sawdust from the mill he ran with his Kubista inlaws for use during summer.[45]

Ignac Kubista came to America in December 1867 with his first wife (identity unknown) and children John and Mary. Prior to leaving, Ignac had served in the Austrian army for eight years tending horses. Like so many of the earliest Czech arrivals, they were from Dlouhá Třebová. In Minnesota his wife bore a child, daughter Maria, but died during childbirth or shortly thereafter. Ignac then married Rosa Pišorna who lived in Owatonna, and they had a daughter, Rosa, in December 1869.

Ignac Kubista and his family settled in Somerset Township, in the area later known as Saco. They homesteaded 500 acres of land, but neglected to register the land as required by the homesteading law. Their family history says this happened because they could not afford to subscribe to the newspaper in which the notice to register was published. In addition, they did not read English and no one had told them about the registration requirement. As a result, someone else registered for part of their land and they lost about 200 wooded acres.

Like other early farmers in the area, Ignac took his wheat to Faribault by ox cart to have it ground into flour. One time on the way home his oxen smelled the rain-swollen creek ahead and rushed forward to drink from the creek. Ignac was unable to keep them in check and the jouncing about caused all the freshly ground flour to spill on the ground. This was the creek just south of Owatonna near the future location of the Monterey Ballroom.[46]

The big group of newcomers to Owatonna in 1866 arrived in New York harbor on July 18 aboard the *Mobile*. The passengers included **Frank and Anna Blazek, Frank and Rosalie Wesely, and two Kubat families, Frank and Thekla as well as Anton and Paulina**. As described in chapter 2, the Kubat and Wesely families settled in the area that would become known as Moravia or Saco.

Alois and Frances (Hanzlicek) Simon from Dolní Dobrouč came to America in 1866 or 1867 with their children Alois, Frank, Frances and Anton. They settled on land in Summit Township and farmed. Frances's brother, Frank Hanzlicek, would come to Steele County in 1882.

Joseph and Katerina Pribyl arrived in America aboard the sailing ship *Western Metropolis* in November of 1867 with their children John, Mary, Peter, Charles and Joseph. (Steele County residents **Anton and Marie Maca** and their family came on the same ship). A daughter, Victoria, was born in early 1870. They lived in Somerset Township for two years, then bought 200 acres of land in Summit Township.

Peter Pribyl married Mathilda Kubicek, the younger sister of Steele County immigrant Frank Kubicek. They took over the Summit Township farm after Peter's parents died. Another son, John, farmed, and his son John eventually purchased part interest in the Srsen Iron works in Blooming Prairie. Victoria grew up to marry Joe Miller.[47]

Frank Kubicek was a wheel maker in Dolní Dobrouč and owned a few acres of land. His shop was in the house his wife Matilda had inherited from her parents. After finishing his military service, and after the deaths of his father and parents-in-law in rapid succession, he decided to leave for America.

In the spring of 1872, Frank and Matilda sold everything they owned and split the proceeds with Frank's sisters-in-law. What remained was just enough to pay for passage to America for Frank, Matilda, and their young son Frank. They felt their infant daughter Matilda was too young to make the voyage, and left her with her Aunt Vavra; she traveled to America eight years later by herself and joined her family in Owatonna, where she married Peter Pribyl.

The Kubiceks departed from Bremen in June 1872, and settled in Chicago, staying initially with Alois Jirousek, an old friend. Frank had difficulty finding a job since he did not speak English, but eventually found work as a longshoreman for $2 a day. After leaving the Jirousek household, the Kubiceks rented a house for a month on what Frank Kubicek called Bankers Street because the families living on it were well off. However, the neighbors were so cruel to them that they quickly moved to 164 Dekoven Street in the Bohemian neighborhood near St. Wenceslaus Catholic Church and school. The block they lived on was where the great Chicago fire had started a year earlier. Young Frank learned Bohemian and English from the nuns at the school.

When the river froze for the winter and no more ships came into the Chicago harbor, Frank was out of work. The family used up their savings and had bills to pay in the spring of 1873. At that time, Frank's brother Vincent came to America and stayed in Chicago with the family. He also could not find a job and moved on to Minnesota, settling in Owatonna where he immediately found a wheel makers job with good pay. Frank left his job as a longshoreman to work on a construction crew, but found the work dangerous. At the end of October 1873, he moved to Owatonna and joined his brother Vincent.

Frank and his family worked over the winter repairing sleds and wagons for local farmers. In the spring they moved onto the farm of Anton Maca and helped him clear his land. In the fall of 1874, Frank bought 80 acres of land in Summit Township from the railroad for his own farm.[48]

A clutch of **Skalickys** arrived in Steele County in the mid-1870s. The first to come was the **Frank and Matilda (Fisher) Skalicky** family from Dolní Dobrouč. They arrived in New York in July 1865 with their children Frank, Matilda and Frances. Their young son Frank, born in 1855, left an account of his life.

The family took a train from New York to Buffalo, made their way to Chicago and on to Watertown, Wisconsin. They stayed with a widow ten miles out of town until after the harvest, and rented a farm from a German the next year with an arrangement that allowed them to keep half the crop. However, the German died and the family did not get on well with his widow, so they moved to Monroe, Wisconsin.

In Monroe the family purchased forty acres of land that included a log cabin roofed with sod on one side and shingles on the other. In heavy rains when the sod side leaked they moved to the shingle side of the house. After six years in the cabin, they built a log house and lived there for two years before moving to the Owatonna area in March 1875. They settled in Somerset Township and began clearing the land. Young Frank recalled digging out many stumps and roots; the advantage to the family was that they did not need to buy firewood.[49]

Joseph and Josephine (Kubicek) Skalicky grew flax on their farm in Dolní Dobrouč and dried it in large ovens. One day an oven caught fire and burned down all the buildings; shortly thereafter they decided to move to America. Josephine's cousin Frank Kubicek sent them money to pay for the trip. They left Hamburg on a sailing ship, landed in New York, then took a train to Chicago where they joined Frank Kubicek in 1873 before moving to the Owatonna area.

Joseph and Josephine were met at the train station in Owatonna by their friends, the Kupkas, with whom they stayed for a time. They eventually settled on wild land in Somerset Township across the road from the future site of the Litomysl church. They later donated the land for the church's cemetery. Catholic priests from Owatonna who visited Litomysl to minister to local Catholics often stayed overnight with the Skalickys.[50]

Another (and younger) **Joseph Skalicky** arrived in Minnesota in 1874. He was born in 1855, and educated in Bohemia. After his parents John and Emilia Skalicky died, he came to America. He worked as a farm laborer for two years, then bought forty acres of wild and unimproved land in Blooming Prairie Township. In 1878, he bought another 120 acres adjoining the original plot. He married Matilda Pirkl in 1876.[51]

Still another Skalicky family, **Wencl and Sidonia** and three children arrived in America in 1875. At the time of the 1875 census they were living with the Suchanek family in the Saco area. By the time of the 1880 census, they were farming in Blooming Prairie Township.

Finally, **Frank Skalicky and his wife Frances (Brusenbach)** came to America in 1875 after living in Prague, Bohemia for a time. He was a farmer and blacksmith. Both could read and write, but only in Czech; they never learned English. They farmed in Summit Township.[52]

Bernard Pirkl and his wife Josephine (Matejcek) were married in Dolní Dobrouč and lived in nearby Letohrad. Bernard was the village postal clerk and farmed a narrow strip of land running away from the back of the house. They sailed to America in 1870 with their children and settled for a year in the Wisconsin Dells area before coming to Steele County. They purchased a farm in Blooming Prairie and built their house into a hillside; the children discovered they could easily walk on the roof, which nearly drove their mother crazy.[53]

Bernard and Josephine Pirkl's daughter Josephine married Bernard Ressler in Bohemia. The couple moved to America in 1868 under assumed names to escape the military draft for a war they did not believe in. They moved to Pennsylvania, then settled in Wisconsin on a farm near Portage in what is now Wisconsin Dells. Around 1873 they moved to Steele County to be near their relatives and bought a farm in the Litomysl area in Summit Township.[54]

Kaspar Slezak, apparently a cousin of Anton Slezak (who came to Owatonna in 1861), arrived in America early in 1871. His wife, **Anna (Pelinka) Slezak** and children Anna and Barbara arrived in New York in May 1871 aboard the *Rhein* and joined him in Steele County. They moved to Somerset Township and farmed there for eleven years, then moved into Owatonna and lived with Dr. Francis M. Smersh, who had married their daughter Amelia. They also owned a land claim in Cromwell, Minnesota, where they spent five or six of their summers. Although Anna gave birth to two sons and six daughters, only three daughters survived the couple. Kaspar's brother Wenzel Slezak came to America and Steele County in 1882.

Kaspar and Anna Slezak's daughter Anna married Joseph Amon Kubat, son of pioneers Anton and Anna Kubat. Joseph moved to Owatonna and opened a butcher shop in 1874 that he operated for 18 months. Later, he opened a billiard parlor and liquor store.[55]

Frank Rypka arrived as a single young man in the U.S. in 1869. He moved to Cedar Rapids, Iowa for three years, then to Steele County. In 1875, he was living with the Kaspar Slezak family on their Somerset farm, and in November of that year married Kaspar's daughter Barbara. They lived in Steele County until 1900, then moved to Cromwell in Carlton County.

Frank's brother, **Anton Rypka**, came to America in 1877 and lived a year in Cedar Rapids, Iowa before moving to Steele County in 1878.[56]

Another arrival during 1873 was the **Joseph and Katerina (Janoušek) Škeřik** family. Katerina was from Sloupnice, near Litomysl, and married the widower Joseph in 1863. They had four children together and Joseph had a son from his earlier marriage. They settled on a farm in Havana Township where they lived the rest of their lives. One son, John, remained in Moravia and became a Protestant minister. Another son, Frank, took over the farm from his parents and was Presbyterian, which was unusual among Steele County Czechs.[57]

Joseph Skerik received a letter in February of 1883 written by his sister's husband and another acquaintance, both from Joseph's home village of Sloupnice. Milan Jerabek reproduced part of it in his thesis on Czech immigrants to Minnesota:

> . . . We were greatly comforted by your letter, and your sincerity, which you proved by offering to help us pay the fare to America to your place. You ask how much money we'll be able to raise for the journey. That, my dear friend, is very little—about 80 fr. č. . . .

Two years ago we burned out during the night just after harvest. All our grain, straw, and furniture were destroyed—nothing was saved. Also, Terezie was ill. . . . After you have read this letter, you will best know what we will need. If you would be so kind as to take care of us until we get to your place, we will with God's help, work for you until all is repaid. . . . We shall anxiously await your reply and in the meantime go to Cermna and get ready; only take care of us as soon as possible, for you see what straits we are in.

How is your brother and his wife and all the rest of your children? All the relatives near and far we heartily greet.

(Signed) Jan Herman and your sister Terezie

Another part is added to the letter after Herman's:

Also I, the writer of this letter, an acquaintance of yours . . . greet you.

If it isn't too far, send our greetings to Josef Škeřik and his family, František Dostal and his family, and Jim Vostov and his family. I should like to hear about John Vašina and Helen his wife and the children they took along, if they are alive and how they are faring . . . I often think of you, and am sorry I hadn't gone to America long ago. It is hard living, the weaving trade is getting worse and worse, and farming is likewise bad; if only my brother-in-law Oliva from Kansas could help me, but he can't, unless later; they are faring a little better now, and had a good crop last year. We had an exceptionally good crop here last year, the best that anybody can remember, but we had too much rain and part of the crop spoiled. Grain is coming in from Hungary; it isn't expensive if we only had the money.

(Signed) Jan Kumpošt[58]

LOCAL EVENTS

Much of our understanding of the lives led by Czech immigrants in the years following settlement comes from articles and notices in the local newspapers.

The 1870 Federal census counts taken in the summer months described Steele County as populated with 8,271 people, of whom 2,183 were foreign born. Almost all Czechs in the census were farmers, laborers, housekeepers or servants. The only exceptions were apprentice watchmaker Joseph Kaspar and shoemaker Joseph Grisel (spelling uncertain), both living in the city of Owatonna. Czech occupations would show much greater variation in every future census.

Steele County, the new home of the Czech settlers, was changing. Trees were less plentiful than in earlier times. Farms and the building of towns had consumed much lumber, and railroads finished the job. Timber was needed for railroad ties as the lines were constructed, and wood to burn was needed to propel early steam engines. By the late 1860s, local timber of good building quality was hard to come by, and it was lumber imported by rail that enabled the county to continue to grow.[59]

By the end of the American Civil War the earliest Czech settlers had lived in the Owatonna area for a decade. The quiet period mentioned in chapter 2, during which little is mentioned about Czechs in local newspapers and histories, was coming to an end.

The *Owatonna Journal* of January 9, 1868, under the heading, Leading Business Houses, lists "Frank Janesk, Cedar Street" under the sub-heading "Boots and Shoes." This may have been Frank Janish, who arrived in Minnesota between 1864 and 1868.

Another article that same day concerns Bohemians in another town; the paper likely printed it because of the large number of Bohemians in and around Owatonna. The tone is disparaging:

> In Helena, Scott County, a young Bohemian last week commenced a school in a German and Bohemian district, he being cleverly versed in both these languages but not at all in English. Some Bohemian children came, bringing English textbooks, and were indignantly sent home. The parents came to remonstrate but remained to fight. . . . A trial is taking place at Shakopee today, where an interior view of Bohemian life may be obtained cheaply.

A few weeks later, on February 13, 1868, the *Journal* ran this item:

> Found on Main St., Owatonna, a large leather pocket book containing a tax receipt, tax notice, and other papers, evidently written in Bohemian. The owner can have the same by calling at this office and paying charges.

Some of the items in the local newspapers were publicity the Czech settlers would rather not have had. This item appeared in the March 23, 1871, issue of the *Owatonna Journal*:

> **Squabble**—We have been furnished with the following: On Tuesday night of last week a party of Bohemians met at Dick Joos' saloon on Bridge Street,

in order to enjoy his fine stock of benzene. Having partaken too freely of the good thing, they became quarrelsome and began to attack some Germans who were there, with knives and clubs, which caused them to take the outside of the house. Finding themselves in danger, they called in the assistance of the officers, who came promptly at the call, and with some trouble, arrested four of them and locked them up for the night. The next morning they were taken before the City Justice, and the leader of the gang was fined five dollars and costs.

The *Journal* for September 17, 1871, contains another Czech misfortune. It is a notice of upcoming sale of the land of Wenzel and Therezie Hrdlichka due to default on their mortgage. They owed $407.16 to George B. Hall, and their land would be sold on October 27, 1871, unless the amount was paid before that time. The land in question was the south half (1/2) of the southwest quarter (1/4), and northeast quarter (1/4) of the southwest quarter (1/4) of section 21 in Owatonna Township. Apparently, the Hrdlichkas did lose the land, because by 1879 they had relocated to a farm in Somerset Township.

Other newspaper items suggest the social climate in which the Czech immigrants found themselves. The conquest of the Papal States and the city of Rome in 1870 by Italian nationalists was followed by the First Vatican Council held in Vatican City. The chief result of this council was to declare the infallibility of the Pope, a doctrine that caused outrage in the United States among a population already largely anti-Catholic.[60] This attitude is clear in the following advertisement, intended to recruit speakers against Catholicism, which appeared in the *Owatonna Journal*, January 11, 1872.

> **Popery**
> **The Foe of the Church and Republic**
> What it has done. What it is doing and what it means to do. Its despotism. Its infallibility. Its fraud. Its relics. Its miracles. Its idolatry. Its persecutions. Its hatred of our public schools and of civil and religious liberty. Its startling crimes. Its horrid wickedness and its New York riot.
>
> Agents wanted everywhere. Permanent employment at liberal pay offered. Young men, ladies, teachers and clergymen in every town and county. Send circular to Ziegler and McCurdy. 518 Arch St. Philadelphia, PA (also offices in Cincinnati, St. Louis and Springfield, Mass.)

That Steele County Czechs were becoming part of the fabric of the county, is apparent by their inclusion in more routine newspaper items. Anton Kubat is listed as a grand juror for the April 1872, court term, and the city school honor roll on April 4, 1872, lists Agnes Kaplan for perfect deportment, as well as Mary Racek for perfect scholarship and perfect deportment. A notice of the marriage of Anton Wavrin and Franciska Wondra on September 22, 1872, at the home of Joseph Wondra appears in the October 3, 1872, issue of the *Journal*.

Czechs begin to take their place as elected public officers in this period. After the early offices held by Anton Simek before the Civil War, no Czech in Steele County held public office until the late 1860s. They first appear as officers of School District 23 in Owatonna Township (see discussion on schools above). The first appearance at the township level is in April 1869, when John Pichner is elected Township Supervisor. After a gap of a few years, Joseph Kubat is elected Township Treasurer in 1875. After this Czechs hold township offices in most years through the late 1870s and 1880s. County-wide and Owatonna municipal office would take longer.

Returning to Bohemia

An interesting piece of news for Czechs thinking of going back to Bohemia to visit friends and relatives, or of giving up on America and returning permanently to Bohemia, appeared in the *Owatonna Journal* in December of 1872. It was a convention between the United States and the Austro-Hungarian Empire concerning citizenship and naturalization, signed September 20, 1870, and proclaimed August 1, 1871. It set the terms by which an Austrian emigrant was considered by the Austrians to have become a United States citizen, and to what extent that person was still liable under Austrian law for misdeeds committed before his departure.

A former Austrian citizen who had resided in the United States continuously for five years, and during that time had become a naturalized citizen (declarations of intent not sufficient) was considered a citizen of the United States. The same was true reciprocally for an American becoming an Austrian citizen.

An Austrian who had become a naturalized citizen of the United States, but wanted to return to Austria, would have to renounce his American citizenship and apply for renewed Austrian citizenship. Such a person was still liable for "actions punishable by the laws of the original country committed before his emigration, saving always the limitation established by the laws of his original country and any other remission of liability to punishment." Included in particular was non-fulfillment of military duty:

> 1st. If he has emigrated, after having been drafted at the time of conscription, and thus having become enrolled as a recruit for service in the standing army.

2nd. If he has emigrated while he stood in service under the flag, or had a leave of absence only for a limited time.

3rd. If, having a leave of absence for an unlimited time, or belonging to the reserve, or to the militia, he has emigrated after having received a call into service, or after a public proclamation requiring his appearance, or after war has broken out.

Non-fulfillment of military duty in any way other than as described in items 1, 2 and 3 would not be punishable for a person now a U.S. citizen.[61]

The Winter of 1872–1873

The winter of 1872–1873 was a bitter one, and storing produce was a serious problem. The *Owatonna Journal* offered this advice:

> The exceedingly cold weather that has visited us this winter has frozen the vegetables in nearly all the cellars in town. The consequence is many have to eat frozen vegetables. Let every farmer who has a supply in his cellar, if they have escaped thus far, see to it that they are protected for the future against any amount of cold. They may be worth something when the weather gets warm enough to bring them to town, and in the spring.[62]

Early in the new year Steele County was engulfed in a ferocious blizzard that struck southern Minnesota on January 7 and 8. January 7 began as a fine winter day, but the many who went out visiting, traveling to town or about on business suddenly found themselves surrounded by a fast-moving storm. Temperatures dropped to about minus 15 Fahrenheit, and the fine, dry snow driven by vicious winds reduced visibility to nearly zero. Many people were caught and could not find their way to safety. At first it was feared that 800 people had died, but the final count put the death toll at 70. Many more were badly frostbitten. The state legislature eventually appropriated disaster relief to persons in 34 counties.[63]

As with recent blizzards, towns fared better than rural areas. The *Owatonna Journal* summed up the Owatonna experience:

> Of the fury of the terrific storm that swept over us on Tuesday and Wednesday of last week, the fortunate denizens of this little city, protected by its surrounding hills and timber, saw but little. It was mainly on the broad prairies that it sought out and gathered up its victims.[64]

However, farther down the same column, a much grimmer tale is told of southern Steele County. Edward Veith, a farmer in northern Summit Township, and his neighbor (Joseph Fisher in his memoir says it was one of the Pribyls) went to Blooming Prairie to sell wheat. On arrival they were told that a big storm was on the way. They headed back, but when they reached the home of John Simek, Veith stopped with the intention of spending the night. Pribyl continued toward home; by then, the storm was at full force.

Veith stayed with Simek for some time, but as Simek had no warm stable for Veith's horses, Veith left to continue his journey home.

> This was the last seen of him, and Schimeck supposed he had gone home, until on Friday, when his team with the harness on came back to his house. He then took the team home, where he learned that nothing had been seen of Veit since his leaving home for Blooming Prairie on the Tuesday previous. A company of his neighbors was organized to search for him, and from fifteen to twenty have been out ever since, engaged in the fruitless search. His sleigh was soon found, in which was a feather bed which he had taken with him to keep him warm. Still further search has resulted in finding his pipe, and tracks known to be his from the impressions made in the snow by a patch on one of his boots. It is almost certain that his body is buried in the snow drifts somewhere, and the search will probably be continued, although there is a possibility that he may not be found until the snow goes off in the spring. Our informant says Veit was a middle-aged man and leaves a family.[65]

The story continued the following week in the *Journal*:

> **Still Missing.**
> Although diligent search has been made for the body of Edward Veith, whom we mentioned last week as having probably perished in the storm, it has not yet been found, and his whereabouts is still a mystery. The gentleman who was with him came very near losing his life, we have since been informed. Instead of stopping, as did Veith, he proceeded homeward, and his team turned around and was traveling in the wrong direction, as he knew by the wind. He accordingly turned the team and succeeded in reaching his house, but when he found the door he was too weak to either open it or arouse the family, and exhaustedly, fell against the door, where he remained for some time, until his mother, thinking she heard a noise, opened it, and he fell into the house. He

did not seem much frozen, but was thoroughly chilled, and would have perished had he had a short distance further to travel.[66]

The final chapter in the story appeared in the *Journal* two months later:

The body of Edward Vaith, who was lost in the January storm, was found about one mile east of Schimeck's, in the town of Summit, on Thursday last. He was lying on his back with one arm across his breast. None of his effects had been disturbed.[67]

As the brutal winter turned to spring tragedy again struck the local Czech settlement. Anton Sattlau, the longtime husband of local Czech pioneer Anna Simek, committed suicide.

Suicide.
Anton Schatten [sic], a German about 45 years of age living in the town of Somerset, committed suicide by shooting himself in the stomach with a shotgun, at his home on the night of 8th last, at about the hour of midnight. He had been suffering somewhat, with a disease supposed to be neuralgia, for some time past, yet his sufferings were not considered of a nature sufficiently excruciating to induce a desire in a sane mind to so hastily shuffle off this mortal coil. It appears from the statement made by his wife that after having gone to bed as usual, and while she was soundly sleeping, he arose and, placing his shotgun so that the muzzle pointed directly to the pit of his stomach, he fired the fatal shot. He was, so far as worldly goods are concerned, in fair circumstances, and was quite generally respected by his neighbors.[68]

The Pribyl family had an eventful year in 1873. Only a few months after one of the Pribyls narrowly escaped death in the January blizzard, this story appeared:

Fatal Accident.
On Saturday last a team belonging to and driven by Joseph Wandra, of Summit, ran away and threw Mr. Wandra and Michael Langmichel from the wagon, when they were about six miles from town. Our first informant states that Wandra and a man named Prebble [sic] were racing horses, and that the two men were thrown directly before Prebble's team, both team and wagon passing over them,

while another says that they were pitched forward and Wandra's wagon ran over them. Be this as it may, the two men were dreadfully injured, both externally and internally. Langmichel died on Sunday evening and Wandra lies in a critical condition. Langmichel was about 25 years of age and had not family.[69]

Joseph Wondra survived and recovered, only to be involved in another tragic event a few years later.

As 1873 came to an end, several items in the local paper illustrate the acceptance of local Czechs into the fabric of the community:

Married.
At the residence of L.F. Pike, in Somerset, July 27, 1873, by L.F. Pike, Esq., Mr. William Bohn to Miss Tachela Kasper, both of Steele County, Minn.

At the residence of the bride's father, November 11th, 1873, by L.F. Pike, Esq., Mr. Frank Wenzel and Miss Sarah Kubister [sic], both of Steele County, Minn.

Taken Up.
By the subscriber, in the town of Somerset, Steele County, Minn., November 22d, 1873, a black horse colt, seven months old, white spot on forehead. No other marks. The owner will please prove property, pay charges, and take the same away. FRANK KUBISTA[70]

WORLD AND NATIONAL EVENTS

German Unification
In 1870 Europe was again embroiled in war. As part of his plan to unite the north German states in a new German empire, Prussian Chancellor Bismark goaded the French into a war with Prussia. Bismark knew the one thing that would entice the suspicious southern German states, particularly Bavaria, into a union with Prussia was war with their common enemy, France.

The Germans made rapid progress, quickly defeating the French. While German troops remained in Paris until the French could gather and pay them a large sum of money, Bismark announced the creation of the German Empire. All German-speaking states north of the Austro-Hungarian Empire were united creating modern Germany, although with much broader boundaries than those of today.

Following the departure of the German troops a worker's revolt in Paris set up a revolutionary municipal government called the Paris Commune. It was defeated by the French government later that year in a bloody battle followed by the execution of thousands of people.

Italy also was reunified in 1870. Since 1860 the Risorgimento movement under Garibaldi and Mazzini, originally based near the Alps, had gathered more and more territory on the Italian peninsula. The war between Prussia and France gave the Italians cover to finish the job by conquering the Papal States, leaving the Pope in charge of only Vatican City.

American news

In the United States, the nation's first transcontinental railroad was completed with the driving of the golden spike near Utah's Great Salt Lake on May 10, 1869. Congress had already granted charters for building three more transcontinental railroads, which would eventually be the Northern Pacific, the Southern Pacific and the Santa Fe. The lands between California and eastern Nebraska and Kansas had very few European settlers at the end of the Civil War. However, the coming of the railroads sparked a huge land rush that, by 1890, resulted in the defeat and banishment to small reservations of Native Americans and their replacement with European settlers.[71]

In the five years following the Civil War, President Andrew Johnson was impeached, Ulysses Grant was elected President, Reconstruction began in the defeated Confederate states, and a series of Indian wars was begun. And in the early 1870s, the country endured the Panic of 1873.

The Panic of 1873

The increase in public debt necessary to support rapid industrialization of the Austro-Hungarian Empire led to an Austrian stock market crash in May 1873. The crash resulted from overconfidence, financial over-commitments and speculation, and revealed widespread corruption in the railroad industry. For the rest of the decade, higher interest rates and underemployment led to more emigration from the empire to America.[72]

A similar phenomenon began a few months later in America. In the boom years between the end of the Civil War and 1873, wheat production in the U.S. doubled, as did national railroad mileage. Railroads were expanding rapidly, but generally not in a sound financial manner. Tracks usually preceded settlers, so the advancing railroads ran for some time through largely empty territory yielding little revenue. In addition, many were sloppily built and had overvalued stock. In early September 1873 banks that had invested heavily in railroads began to fail. The Panic of 1873 caught fire on September

18 with the collapse of the New York banking firm of Jay Cooke, whose innovative bond sales had largely financed the Union side in the Civil War. The usual progression of chain reaction bank failures, tight money and calling in of loans followed. Railroads, already suffering from high expenses and inadequate revenue, were badly hurt and rail expansion ceased for a few years. Because the Minnesota legislature was unwilling to make matters worse for railroads under these conditions, Granger laws passed during this period were less onerous and more lightly enforced than their sponsors had hoped.

The *Owatonna Journal* was sanguine in its initial assessment of the Panic on September 25, 1873:

> The last week has witnessed another of those financial panics which occasionally occurs and which for a time unsettles affairs. It was opened by the failure of Jay Cooke & Co., which caused a run on many other banks, because of the suspicion this first failure created. The result has been numerous important failures, the last of which, up to this date, is the banking house of Henry Clews & Co., which among the list of failures ranks next to that of Jay Cooke & Co. in importance. The failure of the last named firm was occasioned by their extraordinary efforts to carry through the Northern Pacific Railroad, which enterprise will probably suffer some delay, at least, as a result. It is thought that confidence has been restored, and that the list of failures will not be increased materially. The most noticeable effect of these failures in the West has been the reduction of the price of grain.[73]

For investors with available funds it was a time to acquire failed companies at bargain prices. Future household names like John D. Rockefeller and Andrew Carnegie took this opportunity to enlarge their growing industrial empires.

A deep depression lingered for six years. In large cities many were thrown out of work, and many businesses failed. Farmers who owed money might find their loans called in or money scarce for additional borrowing. However, for a farmer who owned his own land, life continued almost as usual.

For the people of Minnesota, the Panic resulted in tight credit, low grain prices and high transportation costs on the railroads. Still, they were not hit as hard as older states to the east. By the end of the 1870s the economy had returned to its previous level and resumed growth.[74]

Matejcek-Ressler store, 300 block, North Cedar, Owatonna. From left to right, Joseph Matejcek, unknown woman, Bernard J. Ressler, unknown man, and Frank Hudrlik. Courtesy of Steele County Historical Society

5

1875–1880: The Owatonna Czech Settlement

1875 CENSUS

In the 1870s the growth pattern of Czech settlements in Steele County continued to shift to the south. Counts of Czech households in county townships in 1870 and 1875 illustrate this shift:

Location	1870	1875
Owatonna City	7	8
Owatonna Township	26	37
Clinton Falls	1	1
Havana	1	6
Somerset	33	60
Summit	13	24
Aurora	0	1
Blooming Prairie	1	1

The original settlement based in Owatonna Township and the City of Owatonna lapped over at its edges into southern Clinton Falls Township and western Havana Township. This settlement added 17 new Czech households between 1870 and 1875.

The southern (or Litomysl) settlement based in Somerset and Summit Townships lapped over at its edges into Aurora and Blooming Prairie Townships. This settlement added 39 new Czech households between 1870 and 1875, more than twice the growth of the original settlement.

Even in 1870, the Czech settlement in Litomysl was larger than the Owatonna Czech settlement (47 households compared to 35), and the gap had widened by 1875 (86 households compared to 51). This pattern would continue through the second half of the decade.

GROWTH OF OWATONNA

Owatonna's white population was about 100 individuals in 1855 when Anton Simek arrived.[1] Twenty years later, the white population had increased to 2,800. The town grew quickly, attracting a variety of businesses. In 1868, with a population of 1,500, Owatonna had doctors, lawyers, dentists, photographers and blacksmiths, eleven hotels, sixteen grocery stores, jewelry and hat stores, and a book and stationary store.

As the population grew, economic and cultural life deepened. The Lowth and Howe machine shop began producing farm machinery in 1865 and a large flour mill built in 1874 began milling. The Steele County Agricultural Society was formed in 1871 to improve county farming, and the Board of Trade was established in 1873 to encourage business and industry. A cheese factory was started in Owatonna in 1869, and by 1873 there were five cheese factories in Steele County. In 1877 commercial sale of spring water began from the future site of Mineral Springs Park.

The town acquired wooden sidewalks, telegraph lines downtown, street signs, and a bridge across the Straight River. Ordinances cracked down on noise, littering, prostitution, roaming livestock, vagrants, confidence men, and horse thieves. The town established a fire department in 1875.

An 1880 map of Owatonna shows two banks, an opera house, eleven hotels, nine churches, four mills, two breweries, two wagon works, plus a public and a Catholic school and an academy. Musical groups such as the Beethoven Society, German Centennial Band, and Owatonna Cornet Band performed locally and around the state. The Czechs and Germans organized their own choral societies to sing in English and their native languages. Local and traveling lecturers and theater troupes performed in town, such as dance performances by Professor Donato and the Lyceum debates on eternal punishment described later in this chapter, and this presenter who was described in an 1880 newspaper announcement:

> On Monday evening Robt. Reitzel, of Washington D.C., a German Freethinking lecturer, delivered his lecture in German on "Christianity and Atheism" at Germania Hall. The hall and necessary expenses were paid by the freethinkers of this city. After the lecture the band serenaded Mr. Reitzel and had a good time.[2]

Owatonna claimed several reading rooms intended by their founders to provide cultural uplift for local citizens. Lodge organizations such as the Masons and Odd Fellows provided another social outlet.

Along with the increase in social activities came the appearance of temperance groups. Alcohol abuse pushed some families with marginal income into destitution, as well as increasing fist fights, crimes, domestic abuse, and accidents with horse teams and wagons (see examples later in this chapter). On the other hand, ethnic groups such as Germans and Czechs from cultures where beer or wine was part of daily life experienced the temperance movement as a threat to their way of life. The issue took on a certain religious dimension as the Catholic Church had a more tolerant attitude toward moderate use of alcohol than many Protestant denominations. As the Democratic Party became more pro-immigrant and less pro-temperance, Czechs, who were nearly all Republicans during and immediately after the Civil War, began switching political parties.[3]

Horse racing and baseball were very popular during the 1870s, and lacrosse, croquet and bicycling gained followings. Bars, bowling alleys, skating rinks, gymnasiums sprang up. Families went on picnics, held parties and dances, and made social calls.[4] There was even a beauty contest that "broke up in disorder when the supporters of Miss Lena Larson accused the firemen of illegal voting."[5]

SOCIAL CONDITIONS IN OWATONNA

In the earliest years of the county's settlement, Czechs such as Anton Simek and Joseph Kaplan were quickly accepted by the small community. All inhabitants lived in primitive conditions and worked in close proximity to each other, the shared hardships and lifestyle creating close bonds between native born and immigrant settlers. Growth and prosperity brought changes.

As the town grew, native-born citizens comfortable with the language, culture and legal system of America and with connections to influential and wealthy patrons tended to do well in business, politics and the professions. The newly influential set the social standards and looked askance at new arrivals from other lands who did not understand or did not want to abide by those standards. Before long, social classes were replacing the old frontier equality.

> Ethnic groups also clashed with each other on occasion. Peter Prahm, a Danish settler, told how a group of Irish armed with sticks and clubs broke up a Scandinavian dance at Burtsch's Hall. A second dance was about to be ended

in a similar manner when the Irish discovered that the Scandinavians were likewise armed. Not all friction was physical. Pulpit and press denounced the Germans for serving beer at a Sunday picnic, and a well-patronized beer garden two miles from town was viewed with suspicion. Although the foreign-born groups scattered and made no united efforts to maintain their cultural traditions, they found the process of assimilation somewhat slower than in the earliest years of settlement. In 1873 the editor of the *Journal* observed "Our people generally are too exclusive and clannish."[6]

Ethnic stereotypes and humor were prevalent then as now. One entertainment satirizing the Germans is announced in this advertisement:

Don't fail to hear the repetition of the Haymakers at Chambers Hall next Tuesday evening—to close with the "side-splitting" farce of what Hans Zaur Kraut knows about farming.[7]

In another instance, the *People's Press* printed an angry letter from three Czechs in response to an apparently derogatory article published by another newspaper:

Answer to Wanted Jerry to Pull Her Tooth
We were not aware that the *Owatonna Review* is for the purpose of picking up and publishing news of the character last copy contained, about a Bohemian woman that wanted to have her tooth pulled. Really, news must be very scarce, since he publishes an article like that. Did he publish it for the purpose of making one's mistakes public? Or was it meant for an advertisement to Mr. Searle's business? We don't know and will not pretend to say, but you can rest assured that there is far more of that which is commonly termed ignorance among Americans, if he is to be taken as a specimen, than among foreigners, be they Bohemians or Germans; and to testify to the fact we will only say, that anyone possessed of some common sense and with the least perception of right and wrong, would never publish such an article. We could point him out something far more interesting than his article contained did we desire to, but at present it would be only a waste of space and time, and we will only add that if he is short of news and subscribers, and Mr. Searle of customers, he will hardly gain either in this manner.
                                          Owatonna, April 26th
                                          THREE BOHEMIANS[8]

However, much journalistic coverage of the growing immigrant groups was neutral or positive, particularly in the *People's Press*. The following educates readers about the favorite dance of local Germans and Czechs:

> **Origin of the Polka**
> About 1830 a peasant girl, being in service in a tradesman family at Elbesteinitz, in Bohemia, beguiled herself one Sunday afternoon in her kitchen by endeavoring to invent a new step, which she tried to adapt to a village song. While thus disporting herself she was surprised by her employer, who, quite interested, made her repeat the experiment the same evening in the parlor, where Joseph Neruda, an eminent musician, happened to be present, who noted the air and step. Not long afterwards the new dance was danced at a citizens ball in the town, and in the 1830s came into fashion at Prague, where in consequence of the half step which occurs in it, it was called the Polka, which means in Czech, half. Four years later a band of Prague musicians brought the dance to Vienna, where it had a great success, and in 1840 a dancing master of Prague, named Raab, danced it for the first time in Paris.[9]

In November 1876 the *Owatonna Journal* summarized recent naturalizations:

> Since the 14th day of October last, Recorder Burch has issued 171 naturalization papers to foreigners in this county. Of these, 29 were issued on the 1st inst.[sic], 14 on the 3d, 32 on the 4th, 25 on the 6th, and 19 on the 7th. Of the whole number issued, nine were from England, twelve from Austria, seven from Switzerland, sixty-five from Bohemia, thirty-two from Denmark, twenty-one from Norway and Sweden, and twenty-five from Prussia. Of the Norwegians and Danes naturalized, nearly all were Republicans, as were also a majority of those from England and Bohemia.[10]

Two years later, the *People's Press* reported that local Germans intended to establish a German language newspaper. It went on to say:

> With the same propriety, there ought to be a Bohemian and a Norwegian paper started.[11]

A German weekly, the *Minnesota Post*, was begun that year and published for a time. Only in 1900 did the local Czechs get their own newspaper when Joseph Velebny started the weekly *Northwest Herald* (Severo-západní Herold); however, it only lasted a few weeks. Later and even more briefly there appeared the *Free City* (Svoboná Obec).[12]

STATE, NATIONAL AND INTERNATIONAL EVENTS

The United States underwent a period of ferment from 1875 to 1880. Rapid growth of industry and railroads, accelerated in northern states by the Civil War, was briefly interrupted by the Panic of 1873 and its aftermath. Increasingly harsh competition in industry began a long period of labor strife. The underground Molly McGuire movement created fear and consternation among business owners in the coal fields of Pennsylvania until in 1877 its leadership was captured and hanged. That same year a 10% pay cut for railroad workers on several major U.S. railroads led to an apparently spontaneous national strike. Railroad workers and large mobs of unemployed persons rioted in several major U.S. cities. More strikes would occur over the next sixty years.[13]

In 1876 the United States celebrated its centennial, but also witnessed the highly contentious and disputed presidential election between Samuel Tilden and Rutherford Hayes (more on this later in the chapter). This was also the year of Custer's infamous rout at Little Big Horn. An 1868 treaty had granted the entire western half of South Dakota to the Dakota Indians. Unfortunately in 1875 gold was discovered in the Black Hills and European Americans swarmed onto Indian lands. The U.S. army tried for a year to keep them off the Dakota reservation, but the trespassers had many allies in Congress and among settlers in surrounding areas. The pressure proved too great. With the treaty breaking down, many Indians left the reservation. Custer's force was sent to bring them back, but suffered a stunning defeat.[14]

In Minnesota, the big news of 1876 was the attempted robbery of the First National Bank of Northfield by the Jesse James-Cole Younger gang. The following year, 18 workers in Minneapolis lost their lives in the Washburn A-Mill grain dust explosion. With an 1876 constitutional amendment, women won the right to vote in school elections and to hold school offices.[15]

According to the 1880 census, from 1870 to 1880 the population of Minnesota grew by 78% to 781,000 people. Of these, 268,000 were born outside the United States: 68,000 were English-speakers, 108,000 Scandinavians, and 67,000 Germans. During this period, settlement moved beyond the hardwood forests of southern and central

Minnesota into the prairies of western and southwestern Minnesota, and north along the Red River Valley. The evergreen forests of northern Minnesota remained sparsely populated. The average Minnesota farm grew from 139 to 145 acres, and while wheat was still king, farm production began to diversify.[16]

The Owatonna newspapers in the late 1870s carried articles about this land rush. An example from 1878:

> The rush for new lands that set in soon after the departure of the grasshoppers, exceeds anything ever before witnessed, not excepting the high pressure times of 1856. The railroads leading to the frontier are crowded, and the hotels along their lines are overflowing with eager land hunters. Nor does this make up the sum total of emigration, for all the thoroughfares leading from the old settled counties to the new, are lined with emigrant wagons containing the families and household goods of thousands, who, having acquired comfortable homes in the eastern part of the state, have been tempted to sell out and again push out for cheap lands on the frontier. The rapidity with which the public lands are being taken up, may be estimated from the following report of land sales for three months, ending April 1st 1878, compiled by the *Pioneer Press*:
>
> | | |
> |---|---|
> | Northern Pacific | 119,300 |
> | St. Paul & Pacific (main) | 44,456 |
> | branch | 75,000 |
> | St. Paul & Sioux City, | <u>56,000</u> |
> | | 295,656 |
> | Western Minn. Land offices | 497,215 |
> | Fargo land office, estimated | 415,000 |
>
> These are the lands actually disposed of in three months, and does not include the sales of large tracts to colonies, &c, under contract or in course of negotiation. For the last seven months, the amount of lands disposed of by the United States land offices and railroad companies in Minnesota and northern Dakota, is almost 2,550,000 acres.[17]

NEW ARRIVALS

The Austro-Hungarian Empire banking crisis of 1873 led to higher interest rates and underemployment for the rest of the decade. As a result, Bohemia strengthened its position in factory production of textiles, machinery, glass and beer, but cottage industry continued its decline and emigration from Bohemia to America remained strong.[18] The conscription law of 1868, which required three years of active military service and nine more years in the reserves, also contributed to emigration.

John and Mariana Sustacek (Jan and Mariana (Maschova) Šustáček) were among those joining the Owatonna Czech settlement in the 1870s. In November 1873, they and their children Frank, John and Alois arrived in Baltimore aboard the *Ohio*, took a train from Baltimore to Minneapolis, and traveled south to Owatonna.

The Sustaceks were from the village of Řečice, located in Moravia to the southwest of the area that produced most Steele County Czech immigrants. However, the straight line distance separating the two areas is only about forty miles. Řečice was a very old village and Sustaceks lived in the oldest part of it, a horseshoe shaped group of houses looped around the old village magistrate's home.

Another Sustacek family, the Joseph Sustaceks, lived in the eastern part of the same village. They left for America in 1874 and made their way to Hutchinson, Minnesota unaware that the John Sustacek family lived only about 80 miles away.

Upon arriving in the Owatonna area, John and Mariana Sustacek settled on the Anton Slezak farm in section 26 of Owatonna Township. Some months later in July 1874, Sustaceks bought the 80 acre Slezak farm for $1,000, allowing the Slezaks to move to the Litomysl settlement to the south. John and Mariana sold the farm in 1906 to their son Joseph Walter Sustacek with the understanding that he would furnish them with a good home until they both died. Joseph Walter farmed the property until the 1940s.

Another Sustacek son, John J., loved books. As a young adult he often caught the train on the railroad near his family's farm and rode to Minneapolis where he would check out books from the public library and walk to Minnehaha Park to read. One day in the park he met a young Czech woman who rented a room in Minneapolis and worked at a photography firm. She often ate her lunch in Minnehaha Park. As they made their introductions they discovered they were both Sustaceks! She was a daughter of the Joseph Sustacek family of Hutchinson.

Within a few years they were engaged and were married in 1899. Their meeting brought the two families into contact, resulting in an exchange of letters and visits. The identical last names, combined with several identical first names, led to confusion for the post office. As a consequence, some Sustaceks changed their names to Sustak.[19]

Frank Kovar came to Minnesota in 1875 at the age of nineteen. There was an abundance of work available, but Kovar was paid only forty cents per day for his first season of farm labor. After the ground froze and the snow fell, his employer paid him five dollars a month to haul firewood by ox cart twice a day to the local brewery four miles away. It was a very cold winter and he was not well dressed for the conditions, so he often ran ahead of the ox cart to stay warm. Still, he enjoyed watching the sun rise as he loaded the cart with wood, and remembered the shimmering beauty of the winter.

The following winter, Frank and his brother chopped and split firewood for forty cents per cord. They ate at their sister's house and so managed to save fifteen dollars over the winter.

In the 1880 census Frank Kovar was recorded as a farm worker on John Steinbauer's farm in Havana Township.

> In those days, everyone was contented; one person had a little, the second had less and the third maybe nothing at all, but we lived a beautiful social life. The young people went to dances, where there was not much room, and a rather primitive band. I used to say, "We know how to dance even if in a keg of salt.[20]

Frank Kovar married Josepha Belina in 1879 and took up farming. The first three years were dry, and the farm was attacked by chinch bugs, so harvests were small and debts grew. However, Kovar began making good money raising horses and selling them for $250 per pair to settlers in the newly opened Dakota Territory. Then he went into the dairy business providing milk to the butter factories and, after seven years, paid off his debts.[21]

Vaurin and Josephine Dusek and their four children left Bohemia in May 1875 for a 44 day voyage on a sailing ship to Baltimore. They arrived by train in Owatonna just in time for the 1875 census, where they are listed as living in Somerset Township with John and Anna Rypka. They moved to Deerfield Township and in 1879 bought a small farm on the west shore of Swan Lake in Section 34.

Frank Spinler was married to Josephine Dusek's sister Frances. The Spinlers also immigrated to Owatonna, but once there, they and the Duseks discussed moving further west. In summer 1882 the Dakota Territory was opened up for settlement and Vaurin and Frank set out for it on foot in search of good land by a lake. Eventually Vaurin returned to Steele County to tend the crops while Frank persisted in the search for a place to settle.

Frank Spinler found what they were looking for in Jerauld County, South Dakota, by a lake in Crow Lake Township. Vaurin joined his brother-in-law and they staked their claims, Duseks on the north side of the lake and Spinlers on the south. The land, newly surveyed, still had bright stakes with legible numbers.

Dusek returned to Minnesota to pack up and move his family. They arrived in Dakota in October 1882. At twilight on the first day, as the two families relaxed on the grass near Spinler's sod house, coyotes began to howl, sending the children sprinting for shelter. The eight Duseks spent their first night with the Spinler family in their 6 ft. x 14 ft. sod house. The next morning, Vaurin began breaking the soil to build his own sod house.

Within a few years, Frank Spinler decided he wasn't meant to be a farmer. The Spinlers sold their land to Duseks and moved to Oregon while the Duseks stayed on in South Dakota.[22]

The Smersh family arrived in Owatonna in 1878. Thomas Smersh (Tomas Smrz), a weaver from Moravia, and his wife Rosalie (Maca) Smersh, a Bohemian, arrived in New York in November 1867 aboard the *Western Metropolis*. This ship also carried the Joseph Pribyl family and the Anton Maca family, both of whom moved immediately to Steele County.

The Smershs, who probably were inlaws of the Macas, moved first to Pittsburg. After nine years they moved to Davenport, Iowa, and a couple years later resettled in Owatonna. In 1880, the family lived in the city of Owatonna and Thomas worked as a laborer. Their daughter Frantiska was a servant in an Owatonna household.

Thomas and Rosalie's son Francis (František) Smersh was eight years old when the family came to America. He was educated at night schools in Pittsburgh, and after moving to Owatonna at age 19 he attended Owatonna High School and worked as a blacksmith. He left Owatonna to attend Kings Medical College in Des Moines and the Bennet College of Eclectic Surgery, graduating in 1888. He attended the Homeopathic Hospital College in Cleveland before opening a practice in Allegheny City, Pennsylvania.

When Francis found the climate in Pennsylvania did not suit him, he returned to Owatonna. In 1891 he married Amelia Slezak and the couple became pillars of the community. Dr. Smersh practiced medicine in Owatonna for many years, and his name is on the death certificates of many Steele County Czechs. He became chairman of the board of health in Owatonna in 1894 and still held the position in 1910. He was active in the county, state and national medical associations, the American Public Health Association, the Anti-Tuberculosis Society, and had an interest in the Smersh and Kubat Drug Company.

In addition to his medical activities, Dr. Smersh was an alderman for the third ward and served on the library board. Francis and Amelia were active in local fraternal organizations, including the C.S.P.S., the Sons of Herman, the Eagles, the Foresters and the Ancient Order of Aztecs. Dr. Smersh died in 1928, and Amelia in 1955. Their son Jerome also became a doctor.[23]

Frank Moravec arrived in Owatonna in 1879. Born in Dolní Dobrouč in 1860, he was the sixth of ten children of Jan Moravec and Josefa (Maixner) Moravec. His father died in 1870 and five years later his mother gave the farm to the second son and moved into a small cottage with the younger children.

Frank finished school at age thirteen and became a cowherd. After a year he was apprenticed to a carpenter for two more years, and earned thirty gold pieces each year while living with his mother to save expenses. In a short memoir he wrote for the Czech publication, *Hospodář*, he says that because of "my impudent behavior" his apprenticeship did not go well, and he was intrigued by stories of the good life being led by young men who had immigrated to America to avoid the draft. His older brother Leopold left first and settled in Wisconsin. A year later, Frank departed for America.[24]

Moravec and others from Dolní Dobrouč left on March 13, 1879, and arrived in New York on March 31. The group went out sight seeing in New York on a Sunday, but returned to their hotel when a group of juveniles threw stones at them.

After a three day train ride, they disembarked in Owatonna on April 4. Within a short time they crossed paths with local butcher John Stransky, who could tell by their clothing they were newly arrived Czechs. Stransky took them to his parent's apartment for a good meal. Moravec met other local Czechs in town that day, and through them found work with a local German farmer.[25]

Frank worked on several farms over a ten year period, saving his money to buy a farm in Havana Township. He married Mary Kaspar, and they raised two daughters and farmed for 32 years before moving closer to Owatonna. In retirement, Frank and Mary lived on five acres of orchard land near the Owatonna town line. They raised cattle, chickens and bees and had a fruit orchard. Moravec wryly described his retirement:

> In our town there are a number of retired people like myself, in fact there is almost a whole street full of them, and when they start talking in a steady stream of politics or some other serious matters, I take refuge in a game of cards. What all could be written about those people; they reap not, nor do they sow, but in their diligence they manage to keep gaining weight![26]

Anton Rypka, the younger brother of 1869 arrival Frank Rypka, came to America in 1879. Like his brother, he moved first to Cedar Rapids, Iowa, before coming to Owatonna Township a year later. At the time of the 1880 census, he was living with his brother Frank's family. The following year he married Frantiska Kubat, daughter of county pioneers Anton and Anna Kubat. They farmed in Owatonna Township until 1917 when they moved into town.[27]

CZECH BUSINESSES

On November 30, 1876, an announcement in the *Owatonna Journal* stated that "Joseph Kubat has opened a new meat market on Cedar Street, first door north of C. Zamboni's gun smith shop. The public patronage is respectfully solicited."[28]

The Kubat meat market became a partnership the following summer and the *People's Press* announced the new firm name as Kubat & Stransky.[29] An advertisement for the establishment appeared the following week:

> NEW FIRM, NEW MEATS
> KUBAT & STRANSKY
> Cedar Street, Owatonna, are ready to supply the people at all times with the best meats of all kinds, poultry, lard, sausage tallow, etc. at the most reasonable prices. A share of the patronage is respectfully solicited.[30]

This partnership lasted little more than a year according to a notice in the *Press*:

> Dissolution of Partnership
> The partnership heretofore existing between Joseph Kubat and John Stransky has been this day dissolved by mutual consent.
>   All debts must be paid on or before November 1st, to J. Kubat.
>   JOSEPH KUBAT
>   JOHN STRANSKY[31]

This same **John Stransky** made the newspaper again a year after the partnership's breakup. At that time, he had his own butcher shop at the corner of Cedar and Pearl St. in downtown Owatonna. According to the newspaper account, on Thursday evening, October 30, Stransky was drinking in Wencl Watowa's saloon on Bridge Street. He met Vincent Novotny, another butcher who lived about three miles south of town. Stransky called Novotny into the alley between Watowa's saloon and Newsalt's building on Bridge St. Novotny, thinking that Stransky wanted to talk with him, followed him into the alley. Stransky struck Novotny three or four times in the face knocking him down, then kicked him several times breaking two of his ribs. Stransky took all the money Novotny was carrying, amounting to $8.45, left him in the alley gasping for breath, closed the door to the alley, climbed into his buggy and drove off.

At first Stransky was charged only with assault and battery, but it soon developed that there was a witness. A young employee of John Shea named Albert Lich (or Leik) was passing the alley at the time of the assault. After hearing Lich's account, Stransky was charged with highway robbery.[32]

Other Czechs starting businesses in town included **Benjamin Meixner**. In January 1877, the *People's Press* announced that Meixner had purchased the blacksmith and wagon shop of the late Henry Nuttleman.[33] Meixner's handiwork included a new fire truck for the city:

> The new hook and ladder truck, which has just been built by B.J. Meixner, carriage builder of this city, under the superintendence of Chief Engineer Hadley, is a credit to the city. It is finished in first-class style and is made not only for ornament but also for use. The addition of two good roof ladders to the fit out, has greatly improved it.[34]

Meixner had one of the same problems business owners in all times and places have had—deadbeat customers:

> **Johnson vs. Meixner**
> It appears that Andrew E. Johnson, a farmer of Berlin, recently purchased a wagon from Mr. B.J. Meixner, of this city, giving therefore a note signed by parties whom he represented to be responsible. On inquiry Mr. Meixner found that the note he held was worthless, and took back his wagon. Johnson next replevined it and the case came before City Justice Cornell, who gave judgment in favor of Mr. Meixner, it appearing that Johnson knew the note was worthless when he gave it to Meixner.[35]

John Janisch, who had been a "gentleman's assistant" at a local clothing store for several years, purchased an interest in the Dennerline clothing store in fall 1877. The store went under the name of Dennerline and Janisch and was still in business three years later.[36]

Albert Kasper arrived in Steele County in 1864 at the age of eleven. By the 1870s he owned land in Somerset Township and was teaching school. On December 30, 1880, he married Rosa Bartosch, the daughter of a gamekeeper for one of the Austrian Emperor Franz Joseph's hunting parks. Albert and Rosa moved into Owatonna in 1881 and opened a general merchandise store at 214 North Cedar Street. At first the couple lived above the store, but as their family grew, eventually to 10 children, they moved to larger quarters. Albert gave apples to children who came into the store and every year before Easter Rosa colored bushels of hardboiled eggs as gifts for the town's children.

By 1897, Kasper had gone into business with **Joseph Matejcek**, who was married to Rosa's sister. Kasper stayed involved in the store until 1905; it continued under Matejcek ownership well into the twentieth century.[37]

Czechs were also present in Owatonna's saloon trade. In February 1877, the city council approved the surety bond of **Wencl Hrdlichka** to operate a saloon.[38] Later in the year, the council also approved a saloon bond for **Wencl Watowa**.[39] The following year, it was **Anton Pehler** who received approval.[40] A year later, **Joseph Kubat and Peter Ganser** were licensed to run saloons.[41]

Wencl Hrdlichka's saloon enterprise may not have lasted long. Fifteen months after the city council approved his saloon bond, the *People's Press* announced that "V.F. Hallichka" had opened a boot and shoe shop on Broadway, and that he made a specialty of repair work.[42]

Three weeks later, the *Press* called attention to "V.I. Hallichka," located on Broadway, advertising pure California wines and cigars.[43] His advertisement appeared a week later:

> **Agency of pure wines.**
> From Bella Vista Vineyard, in Gordelia, Sedano [sic] county, California. Also, all kinds of liquors and best brands of cigars, always kept on hand. Therefore, I solicit patronage and guarantee satisfaction to all. Call and convince yourself that our wines are pure California grape wines and everything as represented.
> V.J. Hrdlichka,
> Proprietor[44]

Wencl Watowa's saloon license was called into question in September 1878. The city council referred his license to sell beer for twenty months to the license committee to "investigate the character of the place Watowa keeps, and also his personal character." Two weeks later, the license committee reported and recommended approval of his license.[45]

One of Steele County's many **Frank Seykoras** ran a blacksmith shop just south of town. This ad appeared in the *People's Press* on May 18, 1878:

> **Found.**
> On my premises, on the 11th day of May 1878, one mare colt about two years old; the owner can have her by proving property and paying expenses. FRANK SIKORA, blacksmith on the Austin road, two and a half miles from the city.[46]

1890 Owatonna store. Courtesy of Tim Kubat

The shop was flattened the following year in a violent storm that destroyed several buildings on the outskirts of Owatonna:

> The house and blacksmith shop of Mr. Frank Sikora, a Bohemian, living five miles southeast of town on the Austin Road, was blown down and the debris scattered several rods along the ground. Mr. Sikora and family miraculously escaped any serious injury.[47]

Probably the best known Czech business news of this period was the February 16, 1879 fire in the downtown Owatonna store run by **Joseph Kaplan and Frank Seykora**. Joseph W. Kaplan, son of the Czech pioneer Joseph K. Kaplan, was the first Czech child born in Steele County. He was born in a covered wagon in what later became Mineral Springs Park in September 1856. Frank Seykora was a son of one of four Seykora siblings who came to Minnesota in 1862 and 1863. Seykora had apparently clerked for the Morehouse store the previous year.[48]

At about 8 p.m. Sunday night, February 16, 1879, J. Hrdlichka (Mr. Houdek's clerk) discovered a fire in the back of the small grocery store operated by Kaplan and Seykora. He yelled for help, and two men who were nearby ran over, but could not get into the store. John Kinyon, S.R. Kruner, Jerome Johnson and W.H. Hill broke into the store and saw a fire in the ceiling just in front of the chimney. They ran up the outside staircase to the upper floor, through the open door, and used snow and water to put out the fire. There was much straw lying around on the upper floor, and beneath the upstairs floorboards Kinyon found a roll of heavy brown wrapping paper soaked in kerosene. Another roll of this paper was found in the flooring the next day. It was a type of wrapping paper used in the Kaplan and Seykora store.

The store building was of wood frame construction, as were several adjoining buildings. If the fire had not been discovered when it was, several buildings would probably have burned.

The initial newspaper account said the store's stock was insured for $300, but was thought to be worth only $100, and that public opinion thought Kaplan and Seykora knew more about the fire than they were letting on. They were arrested the following Wednesday, and their fathers posted bail.

Their court hearing began the following day. Henry Zichrick and Jerome Johnson testified that the fire was probably started about 7:30 p.m. The defense said that J. and W. Hrdlichka, F. Larson, Kaplan and Seykora were drinking beer in the store on the afternoon of the fire. After supper they went down to Anton Renchin's to "have a good time." They sent J. Hrdlichka to get a fiddle, and he saw the fire while passing the store on his way back to Renchin's. Larson testified that they locked up the store when they all went to supper about 6:00 and returned to the store about 7:30, according to the store clock. However Kaplan said the clock was not running. Consequently, the whereabouts of the defendants during the half hour preceding the discovery of the fire at 8:00 p.m. was in doubt. Kaplan said he had fastened the door to the upper floor with string several days before to keep out the snow, and had no ideas who had opened it.

The prosecution introduced evidence that the stock of the store was worth about $150, but the defendants moved that independent experts be appointed to make an impartial estimate. Michael Leary and Ed Downy were appointed and arrived at an estimated worth of $337.50, thus eliminating the argument that arson had been used to collect on the destruction of an over-insured store.

The prosecution also called witnesses who said Kaplan and Seykora had spoken of leaving Owatonna in the spring and going west. They admitted they might have said this, but only as a way to get customers to pay up their accounts.[49]

The following June the grand jury met and indicted Kaplan and Seykora for setting fire to a store building in the night. The case went to trial in December 1879 and the defendants requested separate trials. Both cases were taken from the jury and decided by the judge. The judge held that there was no testimony in the case that would justify the court in upholding a verdict of guilty and dismissed the charges in both cases.[50]

CZECHS AND CRIME IN THE CITY

Unfortunately, during this period, the Czechs of Steele County made the papers as both victims and perpetrators of crimes. Luckily none of the crimes against Owatonna area Czechs were fatal. Some of the stories:

> Peter Stevens stole a horse from Anton Kubat and a clock from a schoolhouse in Frank Chambers' district on Thursday, the 28th of May, and the next afternoon at four o'clock, Sheriff Toher had him in the Faribault jail. Toher started at five of the same morning that the thief made the raid on Kubat's stable. The thief had about three and a half hours start, but Toher left without breakfast, and in consequence was light and made good time. That fool that stole that hoss better go where the Sheriff don't pursue till after breakfast to engage in his business after he gets out of prison.[51]

> Last Tuesday, the 19th inst., Mr. Joseph Kubat had a Buffalo Overcoat containing a pair of kid gloves, stolen from Chambers' Hall. Mr. Kubat was called up for interpreter, and while there his coat was stolen from his seat where he left it. If Mr. Kubat ever sets his eyes on the coat he will know it—the thief had better take care.[52]

> On Monday of last week a tramp entered the house of Mr. Koovar, living six miles southeast of the city, whose wife was alone at home, took twenty five dollars, and meeting with resistance from Mrs. Koovar, drew a knife and cut an ugly gash in her left arm, and has not since been caught.[53]

An article in 1880 about John Janisch, a partner in the clothing store of Dennerline and Janisch, suggests he was the hero of an earlier affair:

The "brave man" Janisch who it will be remembered one night last summer started downtown for a pistol when the ladies about Scale's corner were in imminent danger of adulation from a drunken Norwegian, has been out of town for the past week.[54]

A serious assault case involved a "drunken Bohemian named Joseph Ceipult," who went to Bion's brewery to beat up Joseph Veith. During the fight, Veith's very pregnant wife tried to intervene and was kicked in the abdomen by Ceipult. At first it was feared she and her baby might not survive, and Ceipult was kept in the county jail until her condition was determined. When she and her child recovered, Ceipult pled guilty to assault and was given the choice of spending 90 days in jail or paying a $75 fine. He paid the fine plus an additional $100 to settle a civil lawsuit against him. The *People's Press* described him as "a dangerous character and the people living in his neighborhood greatly fear him, as he usually goes about armed with a knife and is especially dangerous when partly intoxicated."[55]

Another drunk and disorderly man about town was one of several Joseph Kaplans living in the county at the time.

> **A Sudden Knock Down.**
> Last Friday a man named John King was going along Cedar Street in front of Hill and Luers drug store when he met Joseph Kaplan, whom he mistook for a friend, and said "Hello Charlie." Kaplan retorted, "I'm not Charlie" in an angry insulting manner. John King began talking with another man when Kaplan walked back and charged him with making game of him (Kaplan) and squared up with King. King then knocked him, without any ceremonies, giving him a tremendous clip on the side of the nose which was badly barked and gave him another punch after he fell. Marshall Whipple was at the seat of war in about two seconds and soon King and Kaplan were on their way to the City Justice office where they were fined $6 each, which included expenses. King paid his fine like a man but Kaplan did considerable whining before he settled after which both started on their way rejoicing.[56]

Two weeks later the paper included an item to make clear that this Joseph Kaplan was not local Czech pioneer Joseph K. Kaplan, nor apparently his eldest son Joseph W. Kaplan:

The Jo. Kaplan that King knocked down recently, is not the Jo. Kaplan many people suppose. It appears that he is now working for Mr. H.J. Cassidy, near River Point.[57]

Six months later, this same Joseph Kaplan again made the paper. His story was intertwined with that of saloon keeper Wencl Haebell. On Friday, January 7, 1881, John Thorsen complained that Wencl Haebell was selling whiskey without a license. Haebell was tried the following Monday, found guilty, and fined $30 and court costs of $12.50.

The next night, Joseph Kaplan and J.D. Cassidy (probably the son of Kaplan's employer H.J. Cassidy) became disorderly at Haebell's establishment and broke some glass. They were arrested, brought before Justice Cornell the same day, and pled guilty. They were charged a $7 fine plus $2 for the broken glass and $5 court costs. The paper reported that they paid the amount and rejoiced that they did not end up in jail.

Wencl Haebell sold his business to C. Jahreiss during this same week, possibly because of the fight, and used the proceeds to pay the fine he had been assessed on January 7.[58]

ASSORTED NEWS STORIES

1870s newspaper stories featuring Czechs in all facets of life mirrored the settlers' integration and acceptance into the Owatonna community, including political and civil positions.

In November 1874, Anton Kubat Jr. was chosen for grand jury duty in the next term of District Court. In March 1878, Joseph Bickner was elected Township Supervisor, and Anton Kubat Township Treasurer, of Owatonna Township. The following March, Kubat was returned as treasurer and Frank Seykora replaced Bickner as one of the supervisors. Kubat and Bickner were delegates to the Steele County Democratic Party convention in October 1878, and Bickner was appointed to the county party committee for the following year.

Czechs also made their appearance in the civil courts. In addition to divorce and probate notices and the occasional defaulted mortgage, Joseph Pichner took on the township government:

> **District Court.**
> Joseph Pichner against the Supervisors of the Town of Owatonna. In this case the court decided that the Supervisors had not jurisdiction to lay out the road.

This decision applied to five other cases on the calendar, which were appeals from the decision of the Supervisors in relation to the same road.[59]

The severity of a February 1875 storm was illustrated by the following anecdote:

> During the terrific blow on Tuesday of last week Joseph Kubat, of Owatonna Township, noticed a large goose pass swiftly by his window under complete control of the wind. The goose stopped at Mr. Kubat's premises, and he was greatly mystified as to whence it came until he met Mr. Wenzel Euroshek, who lives over a mile distant and who claims that said goose was very summarily enticed from his place. So it seems that even a goose could not stand the pressure of the breeze, but was compelled to do its bidding.[60]

In 1880 Joseph Kaplan hosted an event for the general public:

> **A Grand Picnic.**
> A Grand Picnic will be held in Kaplan's grove, one mile south of City Park on Sunday, June 6th, 1880, under the auspices of the Centennial Cornet Band. A cordial invitation is extended to all, both old and young. Come and have a good time.[61]

HORSING AROUND

At a time of rapid population growth when the horse was the primary means of transportation, it is no surprise that newspapers frequently reported on deaths, injuries, and narrow escapes involving horses. Deaths by train or horse teams were the car accidents of their day.

> **Runaway.**
> On Saturday last a runaway occurred in this city, which, considering the circumstances, was remarkable in that no serious results followed. Dr. S. Blood and wife were driving down Cedar Street toward the public square from the south, a gentleman of the Bohemian persuasion (we don't mean a newspaper man) was driving out of town, going south in a two-horse sleigh. Both of his horses were running, evidently nearly at the top of their speed. The Doctor's

horse became excited as this running team passed, and almost immediately became unmanageable, running and kicking in a frightful manner. The Doctor, finding himself unable to hold the horse, reined him out of the road at the residence of C.S. Crandall, running him into the trees in front of his place. Upon striking the trees of course, there was a sudden stop, the horse being cleared from the cutter instantly, and the Doctor performing a somersault in the air at the height of about five feet from the ground, striking terra firma flat on his back, while Mrs. Blood was violently thrown out on the opposite side. The great wonder was that neither of them, although somewhat advanced in years, appeared to be seriously injured.[62]

Fatal Accident.
Havana, Dec. 16, 1879.
On Friday of last week, as a son of Mr. Joseph Ripka, residing in Aurora upon a farm of Mr. A. F. Anderson, was on his way to Owatonna, and, when near the house of Mr. F. K. Hickok, his team became frightened and ran away with him. As near as can be ascertained, he had the front bob sled with a box fixed upon it, and where the team left the road, they ran on to some plowing throwing him out completely smashing his skull and killing him instantly. At least Mr. Eugene Hickok who ran to his assistance thinks so, for he found him dead, and his team standing by him. The team had dragged him about twenty rods from the place where he was thrown out. It appears that the deceased had put the lines about his neck, so as to keep his hands warm. His parents who are in rather poor circumstances, are nearly heartbroken, he being their only son and about twenty-two years of age. Mr. Ripka thinks that they are having more than their share of trouble. Early in the fall they had four stacks of wheat burned, and now, worst of all, he has lost his only means of support in his old age. Mr. and Mrs. Ripka have the sympathy of the entire community in their great trouble.[63]

This brief article describes vehicle malfunctions:

Last Saturday evening as Mr. John H. Czeszinski was starting from town on North Cedar street for home in company with Mrs. Jos. Fisher, the bolt of the clevis fastening the whippletree came out and the team started, very much frightened being struck on the back and heels by the whippletrees.

Mr. Czeszinski was thrown out on the sidewalk on his back and succeeded in holding the team though he was severally bruised. Mrs. Fisher was also thrown out and one wheel ran over her ankle spraining it. The harness was broken in several places.[64]

In the following story, it is difficult to know whether the newspaper editor deliberately mangled the name for humorous effect.

Wencel Moronshek started out of town Monday evening and ran Mr. Pribyl's team through north Cedar street, contrary to the ordinance which forbids fast driving. Marshal Whipple overtook him and brought him before the City Justice who assessed him $5, which included costs. He was refractory, however, and wouldn't pay, but after he rusticated Monday night in the City cooler, he came down Tuesday morning, and thus our educational fund is growing, and our city officials are getting rich—slowly.[65]

Finally, there is the dangerous career of Frank Kubicek Sr. The local paper for late July 1881 tells the tale of Frank's first close call (that we know of):

A Mad Runaway.
Early last Monday morning, Frank Kubicek's team ran away. The animals suddenly started up at D.O. Searle's corner, while Mr. K was in the wagon and had hold of the lines. He was thrown from his balance and rolled out, and the wagon ran over him, but without inflicting any serious injury. At Clarke's corner the wagon struck Mr. Frank Srsen's horse and buggy, overthrowing animal and vehicle and breaking the rear axle of the left wheel. Mr. S. was also bruised. The animals continued the race down Cedar Street, until they struck the same telegraph pole that wrecked P.J. Tuttle last spring. Here the telegraph pole was broken down, the wagon smashed and the horses liberated from it without either of them receiving any hurt.

Kubicek's horse adventures continued into the 1890s. Young Annie Skalicky, before her 1895 marriage to Joseph Seykora, had an earlier boyfriend. This boyfriend was riding his bicycle back to town in the dark when he was killed by a team of horses driven by Mr. Kubicek.[66]

A few years later, in July 1897, Frank had a final mishap with horses which seems an eerie echo of this boy's death. Kubicek was hauling a load of lumber from Owatonna back to his farm in Litomysl. He was sitting on the side of the lumber when two boys on bicycles unexpectedly approached from behind. Their appearance scared the horses, who bolted, knocking Frank from the wagon. He fell under the wagon and was run over by the rear wheel. He was taken to the hospital but died six days later.[67]

SACRED HEART CHURCH

Owatonna's Catholic parish, Sacred Heart, was poised for growth. Father Keller, based in Faribault, had helped in its birth and erecting its first building. His successors in Faribault, Father Scheve (1870–1873) and Father Wieseler (1873–1875) managed the Owatonna parish and oversaw construction of a rectory.

Weekly listings of church services in the *Owatonna Journal* during the pastorates of Father Scheve and Father Wieseler announce Sunday school at Sacred Heart every Sunday at 3 p.m., but Catholic service only every alternate Sunday at 10:30 a.m. This was the best that could be managed without a resident pastor.

Even so, Sacred Heart parish was thriving. In 1871, the parish recorded 43 baptisms, of which at least a dozen were children of Czech immigrant families. (It is difficult to be exact because of odd spellings and because some names like Fisher may or may not be Czech). The parish celebrated six weddings that year, and in four of the weddings one or both of the newlyweds were of Czech ancestry. By 1874 there were 117 baptisms, of which at least 30 were Czech-Americans, and eight weddings, with at least three involving a Czech-American member.

At some point the parish began an annual parish fair that was open to the public. This would have served for entertainment, fund raising, recruiting new members, and as a way of introducing the church to non-Catholics in the community. The first newspaper announcement was in February 1874:

> A fair for the benefit of the Catholic Church of this city will be given shortly. A cutter, settee, buffalo coat, and a summer suit are among the articles to be disposed of.[68]

The fair may not have been held immediately, as no date is given. Another ad appeared a few months later:

CATHOLIC FAIR
AT BURTCH'S HALL
OWATONNA
June 8, 9, & 10
ENTERTAINMENT FOR ALL
Consisting of
VARIOUS AMUSEMENTS
Refreshments, &c.
ALL ARE INVITED[69]

In 1875 the church was ready for its first pastor. Father Francis Pribyl was born in Římov, near České Budějovice in Bohemia, in 1852. His family came to America in 1864 and settled in Winona. Francis went to St. John's College in Collegeville, Minnesota in 1868, and completed his studies at St. Francis Seminary near Milwaukee. He was ordained in St. Paul in March 1875, and later that year was assigned as first resident pastor of Sacred Heart Parish in Owatonna.[70]

Father Pribyl spoke English, Czech and German, in addition to being somewhat conversant in Polish. This made him well suited to minister to the multilingual parishes that he was assigned to lead. Besides his Sacred Heart responsibilities, he frequently performed mass at Holy Trinity Church in Litomysl and St. Columbanus Parish in Blooming Prairie. In addition he occasionally visited the Catholics in Moravia (Saco), who, as they had no church building, held services in the country school house.

In the spring of 1876, he had the church lathed and plastered, and furnished the recently completed rectory. Father Pivo, pastor from 1891 to 1936, in his brief history of Sacred Heart Church, described Father Pribyl as "renowned for his zeal of building churches in all his outmissions."[71]

Because he lived in Owatonna, Pribyl became a visible presence in the community. The parish and Father Pribyl appeared in the local papers with increasing regularity.

In spring 1876, the *Owatonna Journal* informed its readers about a visit by future bishop, Father Cotter of Winona:

> Rev. Father Cotter, of Winona, will deliver a temperance sermon at the Catholic church of this city on Sunday next at 10:30 a.m. All are invited to attend.[72]

In the following weeks, news of the annual Catholic fair appeared:
> The Catholic Fair is in progress at Chamber's Hall. A large number of domestic and fancy articles are on exhibition and there seems to be plenty to amuse.

Two very fancy cakes from the Parcher and Arnold houses attract special attention. The fair closes tonight, when a cutter, sewing machine and other articles will be disposed of by lottery, and refreshments served."[73]

The Catholic Fair, held last week, was a success financially, and the voting of prizes created a great deal of interest. A silver pitcher was voted to the Parcher House cook, the contest lying between him and the cook of the Arnold House. A very fine lap robe was voted to Dr. Morehouse as the most popular physician in the city, after a lively contest. Chauncey Easton drew the fine cutter which was disposed of by lottery, and a party from Waseca drew the $80 sewing machine.[74]

A dedication ceremony was held during the summer to celebrate completion of Sacred Heart Church:

There was an immensely large attendance at the Catholic church in this city on Sunday. It was the occasion of the dedication of the church, which was beautifully decorated with evergreens and flowers. Bishop Grace, of St. Paul, was present, and delivered the sermon in the morning. In the afternoon about two hundred ladies and gents were confirmed.[75]

Father Pribyl made the paper later that year for the building activities noted by Father Pivo:

Rev. T.[sic] J. Pribyl, pastor of the Catholic church of this city, is pushing the interests of his church rapidly forward in this part of the state. He has made arrangements to have a Catholic school, costing $15,000, built at Waseca next year, and is just finishing a fine church, valued at $5,000, in that town. Mr. Pribyl, although a comparatively young man, is fast becoming one of the leading ministers of that church in southern Minnesota.[76]

A further development appeared a few months later:

A New School.
We understand that the Franciscan Sisters have made arrangements, through Father Pribyl, for building a $6,000 school house, on the land near the Catholic Church, in the city. This is good news for our citizens. Every educational

*Sacred Heart Church and Academy, Owatonna.
Courtesy of Steele County Historical Society*

institution built in our midst, will add materially to our fast increasing prosperity. An institution of learning, such as contemplated, is always a permanent benefit to the city in which it is located.[77]

The 1996 Sacred Heart Church booklet commemorating the 130th anniversary of the founding of the parish provides background on why the school, originally intended for Waseca, was built in Owatonna.

> Mother M. Alfred of the Sisters of Saint Francis of Minnesota had come west from Joliet, Illinois at the invitation of Father Alexander Christie of Waseca to found an academy for the education of young women. With sites offered in Waseca and Owatonna, she decided in favor of Owatonna and, with the cooperation of the pastor, Rev. Francis Pribyl, set immediately about the task of building.
>
> The new academy was made of brick and had dimensions of 50 feet x 32 feet. It was three stories high with a mansard roof. Its estimated cost was $8,000.[78]

Mother Alfred founded the Joliet convent in 1865 and oversaw it for 10 years. When she was replaced as Superior she was free to move west and continue founding schools, an effort undertaken by her order in several Midwestern states. In January 1877, she was given authority by the new Superior in Joliet to purchase property for schools in Waseca and Owatonna.

Mother Alfred stayed with the Breen family in Waseca while assessing the situation. She did purchase property in Waseca for the school, but the site did not get the approval of local parishioners. Deciding that conditions were not right for construction of the Waseca school, and at the invitation of Father Pribyl, she turned her attention to Owatonna.

She purchased the site for the school in Owatonna with her own funds. The favorable site combined with local support convinced her that the school would be a success.

While construction on the Owatonna school was underway, she was asked to build a similar school in Rochester. Construction of the Rochester school, Our Lady of Lourdes, was begun in summer 1877.[79]

The local papers followed construction of the Owatonna school. In mid-July it was reported that the walls of the basement and first story were completed. By early August, construction of the mansard roof was underway. On August 14, the *People's Press* called the new building "a model of architectural beauty." The September 1st report described work on the fourth story. Finally, an article announced the completion.

> **New Catholic School.**
> This institution has just been completed. The work on the building was done by C. Bohn, of Winona, and is excellent. The painting and graining by A. Johnson is very fine. It is called the Sacred Heart high school and is taught by the Franciscan sisters. The school will open next Monday, October 1st, and children of all denominations are admitted. All the branches usually embraced in elementary and high school courses will be taught as well as German. Tuition will be one dollar a month for each pupil. French will also be taught for which there will be an extra charge. Music lessons on piano or organ ten dollars a quarter, use of instrument for practice one dollar a month. Extra lessons in fancy work, such as wax flowers, wax fruit, hair flowers, fine leather work, gold, silver, silk and zephyr embroidery can be obtained. A few young lady boarders can be accommodated at the institution. Further information can be obtained by addressing the Superioress of Sacred Heart High School, Owatonna, Steele County, Minnesota.[80]

The academy opened in October 1877 with about 60 pupils. Sister M. Augustine was the principal, Sister M. DeChantal, Sister M. Columba (who was Father Pribyl's sister), Miss Mary Froelich, and Miss Mary Kelly comprised the staff.[81]

The following month, an item in the *People's Press* announced a fundraiser:

The Catholic Fair.
Benefit of Sisters' School, of Owatonna
At Chambers Hall, on Nov. 26th, 27th, 28th, and 29th.
Beautiful Fancy Work of the Sisters—Wheel of Fortune—Raffle—Interesting Voting—Cheap Meals—Oysters etc.
During this fair next week ample opportunity will be afforded to all to answer and enjoy themselves in various ways, and by patronizing the fair to contribute their share towards it success, and thus practically to show their estimation of the improvements made in this city, within this year, by the Catholic community.

Among the many beautiful articles which will be offered or sold, we might mention as the most prominent, a valuable and very beautiful wax cross, nearly two feet high, encircled in wax flowers, under a glass globe.[82]

Soon after the Owatonna and Rochester schools began operating, Bishop Foley of Chicago ordered the Minnesota Franciscan sisters community to separate itself from the Joliet motherhouse, culminating a contentious relationship between Mother Alfred and Bishop Foley. The sisters in Owatonna and Rochester were given ten days to decide whether to return to Joliet or stay in Minnesota. Twenty five sisters chose to stay and teach in the new schools.

Bishop Grace of St. Paul welcomed them, approving of their decision to separate from Joliet. He gave Mother Alfred permission to found an independent Franciscan community based in Rochester, and appointed her as Mother General.[83]

FATHER PRIBYL

Father Pribyl was perhaps the first Czech-born citizen in Owatonna to become a public figure. He was certainly the first to receive substantial notice from the local newspapers. Articles about him give a sense of the man and a glimpse of Czech immigrant life and Catholicism in the 1870s.

In addition to his role as builder, Father Pribyl became a spokesman for the Catholic faith to the broader community. On three consecutive Monday evenings in January 1878, he participated in a discussion about hell and eternal punishment hosted by the Owatonna Literary Association. The Lyceum participants were Charles G. Early, Universalist minister Reverend H.G. Butler, and Father Pribyl. The first Monday's discussion generated considerable interest and drew a large crowd to the second week.

> **Lyceum.**
> Last Monday evening at the appointed time of meeting, the spacious room occupied by the Owatonna Literary Association was literally crammed. The interest taken in this matter of eternal damnation seems to be very great. There are about as many opinions as there are men, for we found by careful listening that no two men who spoke held precisely the same views on the subject.
>
> Rev. F.J. Pribyl spoke for considerable time, giving in an able manner the reasons for eternal punishment, and concluded by giving proofs of it from Revelations. He was listened to attentively, and followed by Rev. H.G. Butler, who assigned some of the reasons why he believed that there was in store for men, no such place as an unending hell in the next world. He took the ground that the word everlasting did not, in every case, mean unending duration of time, but that in some cases only a limited period . . .[84]

The discussion attracted so much attention that the *People's Press* printed a stenographic report of Father Pribyl's speech the following week:

> Rev. F.J. Pribyl, after alluding to the great public interest manifested at the present time on this question, said that the very fact of such a great sensation being created, showed that a great number did believe in the doctrine of Hell. He showed further, that this doctrine was common in the days of old, before the time of Christ, by quoting Virgil, and ancient pagan authors. He then

defined the belief of the Catholic Church as follows: That there is a Hell, or place where the souls of the wicked suffer punishment for all eternity, but only those who died in a state of mortal sin, are guilty of grievous offense against God. Only those are committed to the flames of Hell. Not those who commit a slight fault, or who die in a state as we might say, of venial sin. These latter are not cut off from God forever, but are placed in an immediate state, which is called purgatory, and after a greater or less duration of time, proportionate to the crime committed, will be admitted into Heaven. I do not consider that it is necessary for us to bring proofs of this dogma of hell, because it is the accepted belief of such a large number; not only of Christians, but of other religions. Now what has reason to say about this doctrine. We shall find reason has a great deal to say in favor of it. Reason teaches us that God created us, and placed us here to know him, serve him, love him, and be happy with him forever in Heaven. He gave us laws also, to guide us to this end. Now we know if we start from Rochester to go to Owatonna, and there is but one road, and we do not follow that road, we shall not get to Owatonna, but to some other place; so if we do not follow the path God made for us—the path of morality and religion, we fall away from God into Hell. This separation from God is one of the greatest punishments of hell. One that violates the commandments of God in any grievous matter, insults him and commits an infinite offense, because to do right, to be served by his creatures, is infinite, and an offense infinite in malice, must be met with an infinite punishment, and as this punishment could not be infinite in intensity, it must be infinite in duration. God is not only merciful, but he is also just; and being just must not only reward the good, but he must also punish the wicked. Being infinite in his mercy, it is only reasonable that he must also be infinite in his justice. Then another argument from reason: but reason can tell us but little about our future destiny. Our Lord and his disciples distinctly taught the eternity of punishment. But do not think God punishes anyone from love of vengeance. It is from the love of order. Order is the first law of Heaven. Thus we see easily, that as God is infinite just as well as holy. The eternity of punishment for those who separate themselves from him by mortal sin, is not incompatible from his infinite love of his creatures.

    Rev. H.G. Butler, after some preparatory remarks said: I understand the word hell to mean a place of endless punishment, of endless unquenchable fire. I wish to call attention to the fact that the word rendered "hell" in the

Old Testament, signifies, according to the best authorities, the end of the world, or a subterranean abode where departed spirits go without distinction. It is rendered "pit" and very often "grave" as when the Patriarch says . . .[85]

Other newspaper items noted that Father Pribyl attended a temperance rally in Faribault in March 1879 where 300 people signed the pledge to give up alcohol. In August of that year, he attended a conference in Milwaukee of Bohemian priests of the United States.

Even Father Pribyl's family made the papers. The *People's Press* for December 6, 1878, had this news item about his father on p. 4:

Father Pribyl, Sacred Heart Church pastor, 1875–1880. Courtesy of Sacred Heart Church, Owatonna.

> Mr. Pribyl the father of Rev. F. Pribyl, pastor of the Catholic church of this city, who had several bones in his ankle broken some time ago by an out house falling on him, is now, so far recovered, as to be able to go around with the aid of a stick.

The ever present hazard of runaway horse teams did not exempt the clergy:

A Narrow Escape
Last Monday afternoon as Rev. R.[sic] Pribyl, of Owatonna, and Father Christy, of Waseca, were driving near the depot, Mr. Pribyl's horse took fright from the cars and ran off oversetting the carriage and throwing both of them out violently upon the ground. Father Pribyl's right leg was badly bruised as was also Father Christy's head, but otherwise they escaped uninjured. [86]

An 1879 newspaper story describes the Catholic school's July 4th picnic and spotlighted yet another talent of the ubiquitous Father Pribyl:

Catholic School Picnic.
The picnic for the benefit of the Catholic school passed off pleasantly on the afternoon of July 4th.... The plays and recitations were all originals being written for the occasion by Rev. F.J. Pribyl, on whom they reflected great credit as an amateur dramatic author of considerable ability.[87]

Father Pribyl may have had another priest assisting with the Owatonna duties for a few months in 1879. This priest, Father Felix Sumtrey (the *People's Press* says Smutny) died late in the year:

Death of a Catholic Priest.
Rev. Felix Sumtrey, a Catholic priest who came to this city last June, died on Tuesday of last week at the residence of W.B. Fisher. The Reverend Father was only twenty-five years of age, but had already endeared himself to a wide circle of acquaintances. He was a native of Bohemia, and came to this country two years ago at the earnest solicitation of a priest sent to that country from Nebraska to obtain priests to administer to the wants of the Bohemian settlements in that state. His death was from rapid consumption, contracted while in the discharge of pastoral duties. His funeral on Saturday was very largely attended. Rev. F. Pribyl, of whom the deceased was a classmate in Europe, delivered an address at the Catholic church upon the life work of his departed friend. Reverends Burton of Rochester and Christie of Waseca, together with a number of other Bohemian priests, were in attendance at the funeral.[88]

Sacred Heart Church lost Father Pribyl in 1880 when he was transferred to Madelia and St. James parish. The *People's Press* for April 9, 1880, remarked that:

He takes with him the good wishes of all who have had the pleasure of making his acquaintance.

Father Pribyl's replacement at Sacred Heart was Father Walter (Qualterus) Raleigh, who served from April 1880 until January 1885. Father Raleigh had been an Episcopalian rector in Hastings, but converted to Catholicism and was ordained a priest. However, as he was Irish and did not speak Czech, Father František Šulák, a Jesuit from Chicago, and Father Šimoník from Heidelberg visited Sacred Heart periodically to minister to Czechs in the congregation.[89]

Bishop John Ireland of Saint Paul visited Sacred Heart church in early October 1880 and performed the sacrament of Confirmation.[90]

A few weeks later, Father Pribyl made a return visit to Owatonna and apparently he did not like what he heard. Rumors were abroad that when Father Pribyl left, he had taken some church funds that should have stayed at Sacred Heart. Father Pribyl was not happy and fired off an angry letter to the *People's Press*:

Interesting Letter from Father Pribyl.
St. James, Minn., Nov. 16, 1880
EDITOR OF PEOPLE'S PRESS;
In my visit to Owatonna a few days ago I was pleased to learn of the harmony and good will prevailing among the people of my former congregation, for when we love the good God even in a small measure we rejoice in whatever good is done, it matters not by whom, when only our dear Lord is honored and not offended. But I was also not a little grieved when I heard that my good name had been assailed by some persons accusing me of injustice towards the Owatonna congregation. If this was simply a personal matter, if I could lose my good name, which is very precious to me, without bringing disgrace upon the church of which I am a Priest, I would willing remain silent, remembering that our Divine Master calls those blessed who suffers wrongs unjustly for his sake. Yet as my life reflects on my religion I cannot permit on my account the holy Catholic Church, the Spouse of Jesus Christ and my spiritual mother should suffer, nor do I wish to increase my merit through the guilt of my friends. For the last five years that I am priest some $30,000.00 passed through my hands for improvements, much of which I was obliged to collect by small amounts, and in Owatonna alone some seem to find crookedness in my accounts. These are open to all who have a right to examine them, yet some have judged and condemned before examining rightly, hence I will now give a short statement of those accounts to all through your paper, as at present I have no opportunity to do so otherwise.

Expenditures of Owatonna Catholic Congregation in improvements on the church, school and cemetery from Oct. 9, 1875 to April 1, 1880	$7,173.59

Receipts on above for the same space of time by subscriptions, fairs and collections	3,965.74
By my own donation to the congregation	<u>1,518.83</u>
Sum Total of Receipts	$5,484.57
Leaving the congregation in debt	1,691.02
Of the above $653.50 belongs to me to apply on my own debts.	
Due on my salary for 4 ½ years at $400 per annum	$1,800.00
Receipts by pew rent to apply on my salary during same time	<u>1,590.50</u>
Balance due me on salary	209.50

This is due me from some who have failed to pay their pew rent, and from them I expect what they owe me.

The itemized statement of the above accounts are found in their proper books. These I revised myself carefully and Bishops Grace and Ireland after an examination also found them correct. . . . When I came to Owatonna 5 years ago I had a little money; on leaving I have debts, yet not more than I could pay if I receive my just dues from my former missions. If ill health disables me from performing mission work I am dependent on my relatives or the cold charity of the world.

Hoping this statement may dispel any misunderstanding that persists, and again thanking all friends for their past kindness to me, I am

Yours respectfully,
REV. F. J. PRIBYL[91]

This may have been the end of it as nothing more about the affair appeared in the newspapers.

FATE OF THE CZECH PIONEERS

By the time of the 1880 census, 25 years had passed since the first Czech families settled in Steele County. What had become of those pioneer families?

Anton Simek and his family were the original Steele County Czechs. Anton's father died between 1857 and 1860 and was buried on his farm. Anton himself, as we have seen, was killed at the start of the Civil War in 1861 at the first Battle of Bull Run.

Joseph Simek, Anton's brother, moved with his family around 1862 to Blue Earth, Minnesota in Faribault County. He claimed and cleared land, and by 1895 owned 870 acres. He built a steam-powered flour mill, started a brewery, and was one of the founders of the first Catholic church in the area. He died in 1900.

Anastasia Simek, Anton's sister, married Peter Johannson in 1858. In 1860, after Johannson's death, she married Anton Sattlau. Sattlau committed suicide in 1873. In 1875, Anastasia was still living on their farm in Somerset Township. By 1880, she was living in the city of Owatonna and occupied as a laborer. She died in 1882 and is buried in the Bohemian National Cemetery in Owatonna under the name Anna Sattlau.

In contrast to her twice married sister, **Rosa Simek** never married. She farmed Anton Simek's property in Owatonna Township for a time, but in 1875 was living with Anton and Anna Kubat. In 1880 she was back on her farm. She moved in with the Kaplan family in 1895, and died the next year. Joseph Kaplan described her as "very saving and lived common." During her lifetime she contributed $400 to the Central School fund in Prague, $100 to the Bohemian National Cemetery, and $1,018 to the building of the C.S.P.S. lodge hall in downtown Owatonna. In her will, she left another $500 to the Central School fund, $1,000 to the poorhouse in Usti nad Orlici (very near her home town), $300 to a home for the elderly in Chicago, and $100 to the J.C.D. women's fraternal lodge in Owatonna. She also left $1,000 to Joseph Kaplan Jr. She is buried in the Bohemian National Cemetery in Owatonna.[92]

Accompanying Anton Simek when he arrived in New York in 1852 were his cousins, the brothers **John and Joseph Pichner**, and their families. John and Joseph were joined a few years later by their father Vaclav Pichner.

Vaclav died in July 1871. In 1872 Vaclav's grandson William, son of Joseph and Catherine Pichner, died from a kick by a horse. William's brother John, determined to move to Iowa, walked from Steele County to Cedar Rapids in five days, settled there and married Theresa Hrdlichka from Owatonna. Joseph and Catherine sold their homestead to Anton Seykora in March 1874. Joseph died two months later and Catherine died in 1879. The *People's Press* ran the following:

DIED—March 23, of liver complaint, Mrs. Catherine Bichner, aged 58 years and three months. The deceased has lived in this country since 1852, raised a large family and was universally beloved by all who knew her. She was the mother of Mr. Joseph Bichner, who is well known in this community. The funeral last Tuesday was largely attended, more than forty teams forming the procession.[93]

Vaclav, Joseph and Catherine are all buried in the Bohemian National Cemetery in Owatonna.[94]

Vaclav's younger son John Pichner died in 1874, and his wife Paulina died in 1875. However, their ten children continued to live in the county, and their son John's farm in Owatonna Township was still in the Pichner family in 1998 as one of Steele County's Century Farms.

Anton and Anna Kubat came to America in 1854 and joined the Pichners in Freeport, Illinois. They claimed federal land in section 24 of Owatonna Township, and lived there until their deaths. This item appeared in an Owatonna paper in 1879:

Happy Family Gathering.
Quite a large family gathering occurred last Sunday at the residence of Mr. and Mrs. A. Kubat, who live three miles south of Owatonna. Mr. A. Kubat is 64 years of age and is still quite hale and hearty. There were present on that occasion seven of his children, who are all married, having families of their own, in all numbering forty persons. A fine dinner was served and liberally partaken of by all present. The gathering was a very happy one, the memory of which will be long cherished by all who were in attendance.[95]

In an article in the 1883 *Kalendar* that described the first hard years as a pioneer in Steele County, Anton summed up the rest of his life this way:

The time had come when fortune began smiling at me. Each year I worked a larger part of the land, and then, piece by piece, I began buying more land until I ended up with 400 acres of good farmland. Hardship and troubles had to be put out of my mind, because the children were my main concern now. Their future, and especially their education, had to be secured. Schooling did not come as easily for them as for many others, but I did teach them to speak, read and write in Czech, which should be the duty of every of Czech father. In conclusion, I want to tell you that I have willed my five children each 80 acres of land, and the others—four (because it pleased nature to give me nine) will receive their father's assets. Today I still live on my original 80 acres, and I expect to remain until the day that my children and my grandchildren, which now number 30, see me off to that place from which there is no return.[96]

Anton Kubat died in 1891, and Anna in 1903.

Benjamin and Anna Fisher lived on their homestead in Owatonna Township until sometime between 1870 and 1875, when they moved to Clinton Falls Township and purchased a farm in sections 35 and 36. In an 1882 letter to *Amerikán Národní Kalendář*, Fisher describes his life after the initial pioneering years:

> I sold my acreage and bought half a section, and now my three sons are farming on acreages I divided up. Both of my daughters are married and living on big farms, so large that all the farms are connected.
>
> And those Americans who were witnesses to our experience are amazed that we made it. The person who has gone through the experience that we went through, perhaps understands the best what we have and what we have done for ourselves as we in return respect and understand him.
>
> In closing my letter, I want to mention that now in the area of Owatonna there are about 200 Czech families, and for the most part they are doing well.[97]

Anna died in 1889, but Benjamin continued in good health until 1902. At the age of 86 he suffered serious injuries when he was butted by a ram on his farm. He died the next day. Anna and Benjamin left six sons and six daughters. Their Clinton Falls farm was sold by some of their descendants to Ed Warner in the 1940s. However, other Fisher descendants purchased farms nearby, and some of Ben and Anna's direct descendants are still farming in Clinton Falls in the 21st century.[98]

Joseph Kaplan and his wife Barbara (Zednik) Kaplan homesteaded in Section 23 of Owatonna Township in the original Czech settlement, which was southeast of the city of Owatonna. Over the years, they acquired other property, including land in Section 21, directly south of Owatonna. The land now occupied by Kaplan's Woods Park and Gainey Farm Conference Center was originally part of Joseph Kaplan's property.

Joseph and Barbara had seven sons and three daughters. In June 1881, their young daughter Marie was killed by a train near their home. Following the tragedy Barbara Kaplan became very ill and died in October 1881.

Joseph remained a widower for more than a year. On New Year's Day 1883 he left on a visit to Bohemia to see his relatives and homeland. While there, he met and married 20 year old Anna Rypka. They returned to America and had twelve children, two of which died in infancy. Anna Kaplan died in March 1907 and Joseph in April 1918. His original farm (and part of his original farmhouse) was still in family hands in 2009. Joseph and Anna's sixth child, Christine, married Wencl Meixner. Christine and Wencl's second son Vernon now lives on the Kaplan homestead, Kaplanka.[99]

The parents of Joseph Kaplan's first wife Barbara were **Joseph and Katherine Zednick**. They and their young daughter Philomena came to America and Steele County with Joseph and Barbara. In a November 1857 letter to his brother in Bohemia, Joseph Kaplan says his mother-in-law had survived a rattlesnake bite and was back on her feet and being more careful. The September 1857 census records 59 year old Joseph living with Sarah, aged 30, and 4-year-old Philomena. Sarah may have been from another settler family and helping out while Katherine recovered. Katherine does not appear in the census.

The 1860 census records Joseph Zednick as living with Rosalie, age 33, and 7 year old Philomena. Katherine never again appears in the census records, and has probably died. At some point, Joseph married Rosalie. They are living together in the 1865 census and in 1867, when Joseph died, the probate records refer to Rosalie as his wife.

Joseph Zednick was the first person buried on the land that would become the Owatonna Bohemian National Cemetery. After his death, Rosalie married Frank Seykora (one of the original three Seykora brothers) in November 1867. The 1870 census records Frank Seykora living with his 40 year old wife Sarah and 18 year old Philomena. It would appear that Rosalie Zednick/Seykora went by both Rosalie (1860, 1865) and Sarah (1857, 1870).

In November 1870, Philomena Zednick married Frank Seykora Jr., her step-brother.

A FAMOUS CZECH RESIDENT OF OWATONNA

For a few years Owatonna was home to a world-renowned Czech named **Anton Zajic Donato**. Donato was born in 1840 as Antonin Zajic in Golčův Jeníkov, central Bohemia. He was orphaned at an early age and eked out a living until discovered by a circus owner. He performed as an acrobat, but tired of the circus and ran away.

Zajic claimed that during the early 1860s he fought under the charismatic Garibaldi for the reunification of Italy and lost his right leg when he was wounded at the Battle of

Magenta. He said that he convalesced for some time in Italy and started back to Bohemia. But while passing through Geneva he was impressed by a one-legged Spanish dancer named Donato, and stayed for five months to learn how it was done. Then, when the Spanish Donato died in 1865, Zajic took Donato for his stage name.

That, at least, was Zajic's story. According to a 2004 Prague Radio broadcast, Zajic was not an amputee, but used an old trick favored by beggars and acrobats. The trick was to bend his lower leg back, strap it to his thigh, and dance on the remaining leg.

Whatever the truth about his leg, Zajic/Donato passed as an Italian dancing Italian folk dance while wearing the red shirt worn by followers of Garibaldi. He also wore a cape and brought the crowds to their feet by concluding his dance with a fast whirl accentuated by the cape.

Donato teamed up with other artists to tour the world for ten years. He performed in Paris, at Covent Garden Theater in London, at the royal Spanish palace at Alcazar, in Vienna and Berlin, in Prague, Constantinople and St. Petersburg. The French newspaper *Le Monde* and the Czech newspaper *Hlas* gave him enthusiastic reviews.

From Europe, the group moved on to Russia, Turkey, Egypt, India, Sri Lanka, Japan, Singapore, Australia, New Zealand, and Samoa. Donato became famous and wealthy.[100]

In 1872 Donato tired of the nomadic life and came to America. He danced in various venues, this time in Czech or Slovak folk costumes to acknowledge his true identity. After performances in New York, he contemplated returning to Bohemia. He decided instead to visit western states and performed in Wisconsin, Illinois, Nebraska, Iowa and Minnesota.

By chance, he visited and performed in Owatonna. While there he met fellow performer and Owatonna resident Mathilda Skalicky, the daughter of Frank and Mathilda Skalicky of Somerset. He may have met Mathilda at one of the performances reviewed by the Owatonna paper:

> Bohemian theatrical entertainment at Chambers' Hall, Monday night, given by Prof. Donato, seemed to be highly appreciated by our Bohemian friends. The hall and gallery was crowded. The remainder of the night, was spent in dancing; in which all participated—old and young. Perfect order and harmony prevailed throughout. It was a noticeable fact that a majority adopt our latest style and fashion in dress; and for grace and beauty, many of them are not excelled by any of our Yankee belles.[101]

The following week, the *People's Press* ran a notice of another Donato performance:

> Prof. A. Donato, the one-legged comedian and songster, will perform at Chambers Hall next Monday evening.

The paper's review of this performance appeared a week later:

> Prof. Donato gave his second concert in Chamber Hall Monday evening. A good audience was in attendance, and a big time was had at the dance after the performance. The best of satisfaction was expressed, except when some young sport had his gay Bohemian girl taken from his care by a less pretentious fellow.[102]

In his autobiography, *Around the World on One Leg: Travels and Episodes From An Artistic Career*, Donato says he met Mathilda several more times with the help of Mr. Renchin.

Following his Owatonna performances, Donato moved to New Prague where he met Dr. John Habenicht and his friends V. Bros, Fr. Kolar, Voy. Burak and Jan Kodadek. He bought a lot from V. Bros and with the help of his new friends opened a saloon. But he did not want to operate it alone and returned to Owatonna to marry Mathilda Skalicky at Sacred Heart Church in October 1878.

Anton and Mathilda first resided in New Prague where their son Anton was born in late 1879. Then they moved to Owatonna and opened another saloon. Donato writes that he quickly realized it was a mistake, since New Prague was growing quickly and his saloon there had provided a good business. Donato is listed in the 1880 census in the city of Owatonna as Anton Zajic, saloon keeper, age 40, with his 23-year-old wife Mathilda and 7 month old son Anton. Mathilda gave birth to a daughter, Otilie, in 1881.[103]

In early 1881 Donato helped organize the local C.S.P.S. chapter. Although married in a Catholic Church, Donato was a freethinker. He was an admirer of the Italian Garibaldi, the scourge of the Papacy. He speaks in his book of Jacob Steinbauer of Winona, and says it was remarkable that Steinbauer, a Catholic, took a freethinker like Donato as his sincere friend.[104]

Donato also taught Czech language courses in Owatonna, apparently separately from the long-running Czech courses already being offered at the District 23 schoolhouse in the original Czech settlement.[105]

Donato gave another performance in Owatonna in February 1881:

> The Grand Concert and Social Dance given by Prof. A. Donato, at Germania Hall last Saturday evening, passed off very pleasantly. The concert part of

the entertainment is very highly spoken of by all who could understand the language in which it was rendered. The dance had begun when we arrived, and the way waltzes, schottisches and polkas were performed spoke well for the artistical [sic] tastes and terpsichorean abilities of those who danced. The music by the New Prague Brass and String Band was excellent. This concert and ball gave entire satisfaction to all in attendance.[106]

In 1882, Donato moved his family to St. Paul, Minnesota and opened still another saloon. He again felt he had made a mistake, for he fell ill and had no friends there to help him. After a year in St. Paul, the family moved to Cedar Rapids, Iowa for two years, but didn't see a future there, so in 1886, after the birth of son Frank Z., moved to Schuyler, Nebraska, near Columbus. Anton started a Czech language school where he taught for twelve years. Every year the children gave him a gift; his favorite was a cane with a gold handle. He also tried to interest the local Czechs in theater. The Donatos added daughter Sylvia to the family in 1885.

By 1897, the school was not providing a sufficient livelihood, and the Donatos moved to Omaha. The 1900 census records Anton Z. Donato living in Omaha, Nebraska and working as a newspaperman. His wife Mathilda is employed as a teacher. All four children are still living with them.[107]

By 1910 the family had moved on to Lincoln, Nebraska. Anton and Mathilda were living with their two sons, Anthony Z. and Frank, and Anthony's wife Milada and young son Anthony Z. Donato III, born in 1908. Anton was retired and Mathilda worked as a cashier.

The 1920 census is the last that records Anton and Mathilda Donato. They are living in Stocking, Nebraska with their son Anthony, a lawyer, and his family. Anton and Mathilda died in Wahoo, Nebraska, he in 1922 and she in 1935.

Dr. Habenicht, in his 1910 book *History of Czechs in America*, devotes a paragraph to Anton Zajic Donato. He summarizes Donato's life in America, and claims:

> The money he earned in Czech America was lost because of blind confidence in his wife. . . . He wrote his autobiography and a book of travel, however, in a non-Czech style. It was published by August Geringer in Chicago.[108]

CZECHS AND THE FOURTH OF JULY

For the most part, Owatonna did little to celebrate the centennial of the Declaration of Independence on July 4, 1876. The Owatonna Cornet Band was hired to play for the Rochester celebration, while part of the Owatonna firefighters squad was in Mankato to help it commemorate the event. In Owatonna, there were informal gatherings at the Methodist camp meeting grounds north of town and at the German beer garden northeast of town. People from the country who came to Owatonna expecting to find numerous festivities looked in vain.

One of the few exceptions was the performance of the Owatonna Bohemian band:

> Our streets were remarkably quiet most of the day on the Fourth. The Bohemian band was drawn through the street in an opera bus, the horses decorated with flags, and their music was one of the few things that reminded one that the day was not Sunday. Our foreign born citizens exhibited far more patriotism than the native population."[109]

Steele County Czechs continued to celebrate the Fourth of July. The *People's Press* for June 20, 1879, carried this notice:

> There will be a first class picnic July 4th on the farm of Mr. Joseph Kubat, about four miles southeast of Owatonna, near the Austin road. The Bohemian brass band will be in attendance and a speech in the Bohemian language is being prepared by Messrs. Anton Pirker [sic] and A. Kasper, which will be delivered on that occasion. Be sure and remember if you want to enjoy yourself, go to this picnic.[110]

The town's Catholic school had an event the same day:

> The picnic for the benefit of the Catholic school passed off pleasantly on the afternoon of July 4th. The attendance was quite large and the good things furnished by the ladies were liberally patronized. Cake, ice-cream, blueberries, lemonade and fruits were offered for sale at tables on the grounds at very reasonable rates. The school children gave an exhibition which consisted of singing, declamation, and drama. Miss Brennan did excellently in the character of the "country school marm" as also did all the others who took part

in that laughable play. Miss Maloney, Willie Toher, Willie Leary and Johnnie Pribyl, performed their parts excellently, also some others whose names we did not learn. . . .[111]

CENSUS OF 1880

In the 1880 federal census, Steele County had a population of 12,460, of whom 8,576 were native born and 3,884 foreign born. The city of Owatonna had 3,161 residents.[112]

The 1880 Czech population of Steele County is 764 Bohemians born in Bohemia, and 471 born in the U.S. of at least one Bohemian-born parent. This count includes several German Bohemian families, and omits a number of Czech families whose origin is listed as Austrian or German. Nonetheless, it is a good reflection of the Czech community's size. The corresponding numbers for the 1860 census were 48 Bohemians born in the old country and 20 born in the U.S. of Bohemian parents.[113]

Count of Czech households in 1880 by township:

Merton Township	1
Havana Township	13
Aurora Township	3
Blooming Prairie Township	25
Clinton Falls Township	9
Owatonna Township	44
City of Owatonna	20
Somerset Township	58
Summit Township	36
Deerfield Township	5
Meriden Township	1
Berlin Township	0
Lemond Township	0

The original Owatonna Czech settlement based in Owatonna Township had spread into the city of Owatonna, Havana Township on the east, Meriden Township on the west, and Deerfield, Clinton Falls and Merton Townships on the north, for a total of 93 Czech households.

The southern settlement based in Somerset and Summit Township had lapped over into Aurora and Blooming Prairie Townships on the east for a total of 122 Czech households.

As of 1880 the earliest Czech settlers had been in Steele County for twenty or more years. Their children, who were born in Minnesota, were comfortable in the new land and had grown up learning English as well as Czech. Both the county and city of Owatonna had increased in size and had developed more complex economies that supported a range of occupations.

In 1880 most Czechs (as well as most Americans) were still farmers, laborers and servants. However, in Owatonna Township, Thomas Wanous was working in a shoe store, Leopold Spatenka worked in a flour mill, and Frank Seykora was a blacksmith. In the city of Owatonna, John Janisch was a clothing merchant, another Frank Seykora and Joseph Kaplan were selling farm machinery, Benjamin Meixner was a wagon maker, Kaspar Slezak, Wencl Watowa and Joseph Kubat were saloon keepers, John Stransky was a butcher, Joseph Srsen was a store clerk, and Frank Smersh was a blacksmith.

In the southern settlement, where most people regardless of origin were still farmers or farm laborers, Frank Schisler in Blooming Prairie was a tailor.

The slow process of Czech immigrant assimilation into the wider society had clearly begun.

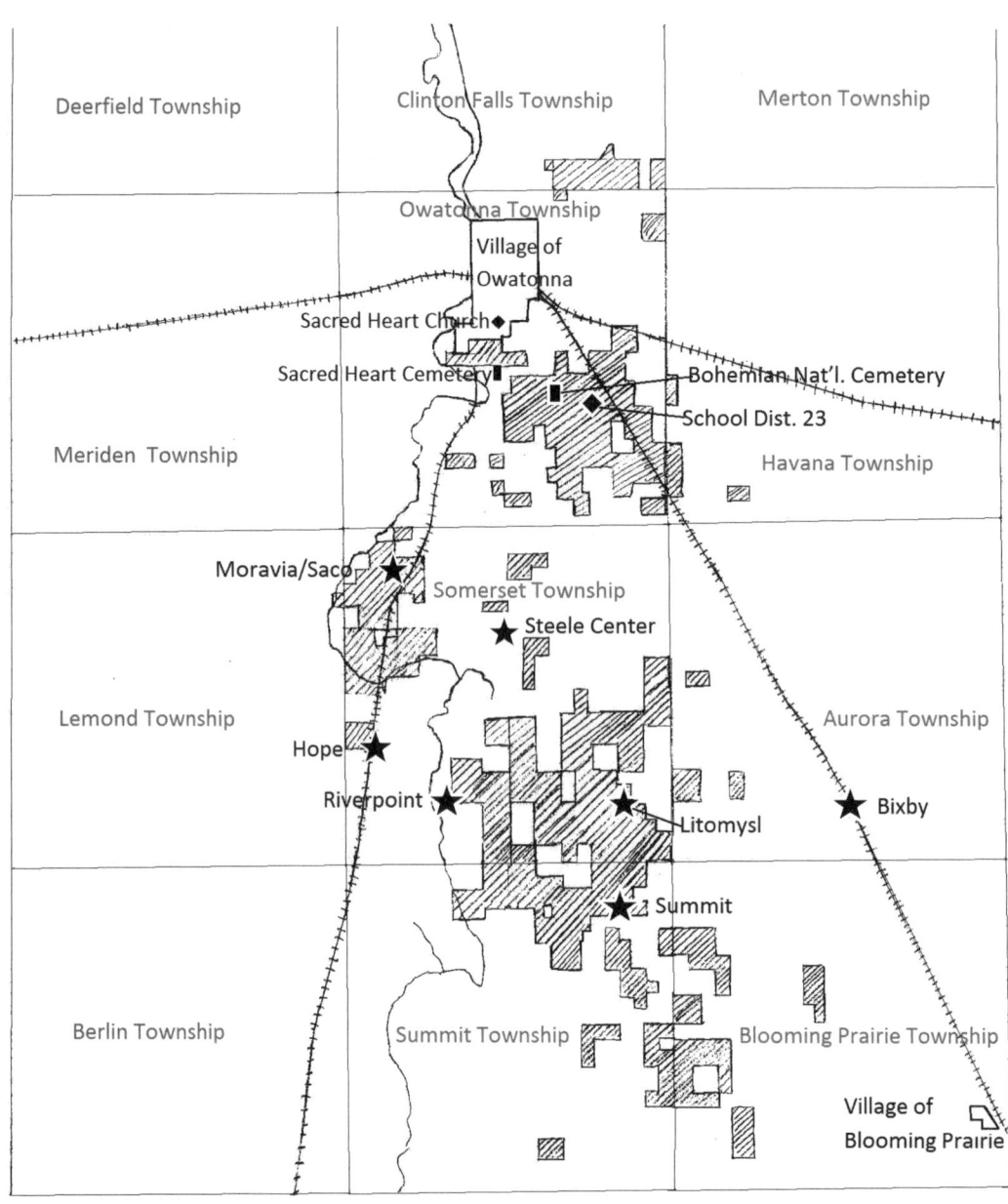

Land in Steele County Owned by Czech Settlers, 1879

6

The Southern Settlements to 1880

According to Frank Kubicek's memoir, by 1873 the land near Owatonna contained only prairie and stumps; all the trees had been cut to build houses. Newly arrived Czech immigrants traveled south of Owatonna in search of unsettled land. The areas they settled included Moravia (also called Saco) and Litomysl, which straddled Somerset and Summit townships.

MORAVIA (SACO) SETTLEMENT

The small Czech settlement of Moravia, or Saco, was located at a bend of the Straight River in the northwestern corner of Somerset Township, about seven miles south and a little west of the town of Owatonna.

Chapter 2 told the story of this area's settlement in 1866 by Frank and Thekla Kubat, Anton and Paulina Kubat and Frank and Rosalie Wesely. They were joined in 1867 by Ignac and Rosalie Kubista and Wencl and Anna Suchanek. By 1870 Frank and Barbara Moravec, Frank and Rosa Pavek and Ignac and Rosa Pavek had moved into the neighborhood.

More Bohemian settlers arrived in the 1870s. **Karel and Katherine Srsen** and their children Joseph, Anton, Edward, Charles, Anna and Frances arrived in New York on July 3, 1875. They spent the night in a small hotel and awoke to sounds resembling gunfire. Fearing they had landed in a country at war, they discovered the American tradition of Fourth of July firecrackers!

The Srsens came from Dlouhá Třebová where they had lived on a twelve acre farm purchased from their cousin Joseph Seykora, who had departed earlier for America. In Bohemia, Karel apparently did not farm, but sold textiles that he bought from village weavers. His oldest son Frank had emigrated to America in 1874. Sons Frank and Joseph were from Karel's first marriage to a Rypka.

From New York, the Srsens traveled to Chicago, then on to Owatonna. They were met at the train station by Joseph Seykora, and stayed with the Seykoras until they purchased their own farm in April 1876.

The Srsen farm was at the south end of the Saco settlement, and a bit north of what would become the village of Hope. Although inexperienced at farming, the Srsens made a living in their new home by farming.[1]

In the 1880 census, their older sons Frank and Joseph are recorded as living in Owatonna. Frank is listed as a laborer, and Joseph as a store clerk. Joseph was also a local agent for the Hamburg America Line, one of the German shipping lines bringing immigrants to America.

Joseph Srsen's work as an agent for Hamburg is part of a story in Frank Kubicek's memoirs. When Frank's family came to America in 1872, they left behind his little sister Mathilda because she was too young to travel. She stayed with her aunt and uncle Vavra. However, Mr. Vavra died about 1879, and as his family was struggling financially, Mathilda moved in with another aunt, Mrs. Stoline. In 1880, Mathilda was twelve years old, and her family decided she should join them in America. Young Frank described the process this way:

> My father went to Owatonna to get information about sending her the money. He was to contact Hamburg America Association, Joseph Srsen in charge. This was about the middle of September. Father turned over the money to Mr. Srsen. He was to make all the arrangements for her trip and passport. Father expected she would get all of this and be on her way in a few days. He also wrote a letter to her so she would know what was what. Pretty soon my folks got a letter from her stating that she was not getting any money or heard about any passport or anything else.

After conversations with Joseph Srsen, and a letter to Mr. Vosatke, general manager of "some association in America," Frank's father heard the news he wanted:

> In a few days he received a letter from him [Mr. Vosatke] stating that he just received the money and card to be sent to sister Mathilda from Mr. Joseph Srsen and it was taken care of right away that day.[2]

Another Saco resident, **Frank Miller** (František Milar), emigrated from Dolní Dobrouč. His father died when he was five years old, and at the age of seventeen, Frank left for America to avoid military conscription. When he landed (probably in New York), he was pinned with a tag giving his name as Frank Miller and his destination as Owatonna. At his arrival in Owatonna, where he was met by a relative, all he had with him was a little clothing and fifty cents.

Frank acquired twelve acres of wooded land by the Straight River, not far from Frank Kubat's property. He lived alone and kept an axe by the door to protect himself from the wolves he heard howling at night. In winter when he chopped a hole in the river ice to provide water for his cows, the wolves drank there, too.

Frank worked hard and improved his farm. He also had a small blacksmith shop that brought in extra income. In 1882, he asked Frank Kubat's permission to marry his daughter, Rosa. Frank Kubat said Anna was the oldest and she must marry first. So Frank Miller asked to marry Anna. They were married in January 1883.

Frank and Anna worked the fields and had four children. But something went wrong as Anna was giving birth to their fifth child in February 1890, and she and the baby died. Rosa came to the house to tend the children. A few months later, Frank Kubat gave permission for Frank Miller to marry Rosa and in April 1890 they were finally married.

Rosa gave birth to fourteen children. Only one, Marie, died in infancy. At first, the children attended the Saco school. However, Frank heard that District 17 School across the river in Lemond Township was better and provided free textbooks. He bought a small piece of land across the river, making his children eligible to attend school in that district. To get to school, the children crossed a footbridge over the river and walked about 1½ miles. They spoke only Czech, so had to learn English along with the other subjects.

Frank's mother, Frances (Spinler) Miller, came to America to stay with Frank and his family. However, the house was crowded, personalities clashed, and she soon left to live with another family.

Frank bought a violin from a peddler for fifty cents. He repaired and strung it, and taught himself to play. He acquired a reputation as a good fiddler, and was part of a group that played for parties and dances. The players shared whatever money listeners tossed in a hat, plus were given free beer. Rosa tended bees in their apple orchard, and was very good at carpentry.[3]

Wencl Hrdlichka and his wife Rosa (Seykora) were married in 1872, and living in Saco by 1875. Wencl's father, Wencl Hrdlichka, had come to Steele County by 1861 when he filed a declaration of intent to become a citizen of the county. The whole family was in Steele County by 1863 and Wencl and his wife Theresa entered into a mortgage for land in Owatonna Township, just south of the Straight River. However, they defaulted on the mortgage in 1871, and the land was sold at auction.

The parents, Wencl and Theresa, were living in Owatonna in 1875, but by 1880 had moved to Barnes County North Dakota, with their three youngest children. Their oldest daughter Theresa was working as a servant in Owatonna at the time of the 1870 census. Not long after, she moved to Cedar Rapids and married John Pichner, who had moved there from Owatonna. The younger Wencl Hrdlichka stayed in Steele County, married Rosa Seykora, and lived in Saco for many years.

Several Matejcek siblings from Dolní Dobrouč made their way to Steele County. **Vincent and Mary (Motl) Matejcek** and their children came to America in 1868, lived in Wisconsin for a few years, and then settled in Saco in the early 1870s. Vincent's younger brother **Peregrin Matejcek** and his wife Mary arrived in Saco by 1880. Their older sister **Josepha** married **Bernard Pirkl** in Bohemia and they also came to America in 1870 with their children and were living in Summit Township by 1875.

Anna (Svercl) Matejcek was married to **John Matejcek**, the older brother of Vincent and Peregrin. He died in Bohemia in 1874, after which Anna and her children came to Minnesota in the late 1870s. At the time of the 1880 census, Anna was living with her sister Caroline and Caroline's husband Frank Stransky, who also lived in Saco. When long-time Saco resident Frank Moravec's wife Barbara died, he married Anna Matejcek in 1883.

Several members of the Matejcek/Svercl clan moved on to Walsh County, North Dakota, in the northeast corner of the state. This area opened to widespread settlement about 1881 as land became available for homesteading and the Great Northern Railroad provided easy access and transportation for farm produce.

Three of Frank and Anna Matejcek's children homesteaded there. Young Frank married Mary Skalicky at Sacred Heart Church in Owatonna in 1882, and they left for the Dakotas not long after. Daughter Anna had married Joseph Pic in Bohemia. They came to Steele County around 1879 or 1880, lived there for some years, and then left for North Dakota. The youngest brother Alois (Louis) also homesteaded in North Dakota. He remained single and made a living as a farmer, mason and carpenter. Frank and Anna's fourth child, John, married Mary Vasicek in Litomysl and stayed in the Blooming Prairie area.

After Anna Matejcek married the widower Frank Moravec, they followed her three children out to North Dakota and homesteaded. In 1886 Frank Moravec obtained a loan to start construction of the Saint Peter and Paul Catholic Church in Bechyne, North Dakota, where Frank and Anna are buried. Anna's niece, Mathilda Stransky, married Joseph Maixner in 1880 at Sacred Heart Church in Owatonna. They farmed in Summit Township for a time, moved to North Dakota in 1886, but eventually moved back to Olivia, Minnesota. In 1894, Anna Matejcek and Caroline Stransky's brother, Frank Svercl, came to America with his family. After staying in Steele County for a few years, they also moved to North Dakota.[4]

Other Czechs living in Saco by 1879 were **Frank Stransky, D. Wacek and Frank Motl**. After Frank Stransky's death, his wife Caroline (Svercl) Stransky married widower Frank Kubicek. More Svercls immigrated to Steele County before 1900.[5]

The Catholics of Saco, like Catholic pioneers in other areas, first met for prayers and services in each other's homes. Frank Miller started by leading prayers on Sundays in his home. Soon several neighbor families were praying together. Later they met for Sunday prayers in the Saco schoolhouse.

Establishment of Saco Church

Catholic priests from Sacred Heart Church in Owatonna began visiting Saco each month to say Mass. These visits were continued by Fathers Pribyl, Sulak, Simonik, Solnce and Singer. On the remaining Sundays, residents gathered in the schoolhouse to read the Gospels, sing hymns and pray. Frank Miller frequently led the prayers.

The Saco Catholics wanted a church in their settlement, and by one account they started planning for it in 1869, not long after the founding of Sacred Heart parish in Owatonna. The mission was organized in 1888 and Wencl Pavek donated land for the site. In 1891, the church was ready. It was named St. Wenceslaus after the Czech patron saint and Wencl Pavek, the donor of the land. The first Mass was said in 1891 by Father Pivo of Sacred Heart.

St. Wenceslaus remained a mission parish without a resident priest. At different times it fell under the jurisdiction of the pastor of Sacred Heart Church in Owatonna or of Holy Trinity Church in Litomysl, once that church had a resident pastor. Like other Catholic churches of that era, St. Wenceslaus charged families pew rent. A quote in Frank Miller's biographical material puts the rate at $6 per year. The church building was eventually moved to the Village of Yesteryear in Owatonna.[6]

A cemetery was started on land across the road from the church. The earliest recorded burial is from 1900. The cemetery remains to this day and contains about fifty graves. The most common family names are Kubista, Srsen, Vasicek, Wanous, Houdek and Appl.

The closest school for most Saco families was the Matejcek or Saco school, District 69. The county school superintendent's report for 1879 says of this school:

> This district is one of the last organized. A new school house has been built and our Bohemian citizens are deserving of praise.[7]

A nearby school was District 17 in Lemond Township where Frank Miller eventually sent his children.

Because Saco was relatively close to Owatonna and Steele Center (and later to Hope)

Saco Church, 1927. Courtesy of Steele County Historical Society

Saco residents frequented the businesses in these communities. No commerce or industry developed in the settlement and it remained a small farming village with a mission church and school.

GROWTH OF THE LITOMYSL SETTLEMENT

The 1870 census recorded continued growth in Somerset Township's Czech colony. Earlier settlers had been joined by the families of John Slavick, Joseph Kaspar, John Brosek, Ignac Pavek, Vincent Skalicky, Frank Moravec, Frank Pavek, Frank and Anton Kubat, Ignac Kubista, Frank Wesely, Frank and George Motl, and John Renchin.

Czech settlers took longer to reach Summit Township, south of Somerset. The thirty families enumerated in the 1865 state census of Summit include no recognizably Czech names. By 1870, Summit Township included the families of Frank Renchin, John Simek, Wenzel Hannus, John Seykora (who had moved from Owatonna Township), Frank Fisher, and John Wondra. There were also Bohemian Germans, including the families of Joseph and Edward Vaith.

Summit Township was some distance from towns of any size. The northern boundary of Summit was about ten miles from Owatonna. Traveling this distance on horseback or by wagon was time consuming and done infrequently. Frank Kubicek, who lived at the south end of the Litomysl settlement, said that in 1878 his father replaced their slower oxen with horses:

> We had 13 miles to Owatonna. We had to do all of our own hauling to and from Owatonna, like grain, lumber, etc. The roads were poor, and there were hardly any. Traveling with a team of oxen took us about six hours one way, so when we wanted to go we had to start out before sunrise in the morning and come back late in the night.[8]

Frances (Rysavy) Buryska, born in 1914, lived closer to Owatonna than Frank Kubicek, but said that as a child her family would travel to Owatonna only once or twice a year because of the time involved. Her father went more often on business.[9]

As a result, the Litomysl Czech settlement in Somerset and Summit Townships developed apart from the original Owatonna settlement, with its own economic, religious and social institutions. Its growth accelerated when the railroad nearby was completed, allowing quicker and easier transport of goods and people.

Frank Kubicek Jr.'s memoir covers this period in considerable detail. After arriving from Chicago in 1873, Frank's family spent the first winter with his uncle **Vincent Kubicek**, a wagonmaker in Owatonna. Frank Kubicek Sr. could not find work in Owatonna, so he spent the winter in the country helping farmers repair their wagons and sleds.

In spring 1874, the Kubiceks moved to the Anton Maca farm to live and work with them through the summer.

> Most of their work was grubbing out stumps and clearing the brush. Mother worked with father doing the same work until haying and harvest. Then, they helped with that. I had to stay home and take care of my brother, Bowman. Sometimes my folks would help other people and did not get home all week

so I was alone with Bowman [young Frank was aged nine at this time, and Bowman was a one year old infant].

That fall Frank's father bought 80 acres of land and built a one-room house for his family. The home, without protective woods around it, was vulnerable to prairie fires.

> Now, there was the danger of prairie fires with the big dry grass and some dry brush. When the fire started, there was nothing to stop it. There were no plowed fields round yet so Father hired a neighbor, Alois Simon. He came over with three teams of oxen and plowed a strip about two rods wide around the place so if the fire started it would have something to stop it.[10]

Young Frank began school in the nearby school house, but attended for only two months before the school burned down. Apparently the fire was no accident. The Owatonna paper ran this short item a few days later:

> We are informed that a schoolhouse was burned in the town of Summit a few nights since. There are strong suspicions of incendiarism.[11]

In spring Frank helped his father clear their land. By fall they had removed trees and brush from 30 acres and hired a neighbor to break the soil. In fall 1875, more Bohemian families from the Dolni Dobrouč area immigrated to Summit and Somerset townships and needed places to spend the winter.

> There was no place for them to move, so my folks asked one family to move in with us. They were Wm. Hartle, his wife and two children, Wm. Jr., 13 years old and Francis, who was 5 years old. In our one room house we were crowded. But that wasn't all. My father was still making new wagon wheels and other parts of wagons out of wood, and Wm. Hartle was weaving willow baskets so with all of this and a cook stove, some beds, and a table, we kids did not have much room to run around in.[12]

Frank's memoir describes the growth of his family's farm—purchasing teams of oxen, buying and clearing more land, pasturing cattle on the prairie grasses, and harvesting the grains.[13]

In 1876, an ominous cloud that had been hovering over Minnesota for several years finally made its appearance in Owatonna. In June 1873, clouds of Rocky Mountain locusts (most of the newspapers called them grasshoppers) had swarmed into Minnesota, Iowa and the Dakotas from farther west. They first appeared in thirteen counties in southwestern Minnesota. The insects devoured most of the standing crops, mated and died, but left eggs that would hatch the following year.

This process continued in 1874 and 1875, with the infestation gradually moving closer to Steele County. State newspapers were full of stories about the plague and suggestions on how to fight it. Farmers in eastern Minnesota feared it was only a matter of time.

In fact, a few locusts had landed in Steele County in fall 1875. The *Owatonna Journal* carried this story:

> GRASSHOPPERS—James Harris, who lives about four miles west of this city, has left with us about a teacup of grasshoppers, which are said by many who have examined them, and who profess to know, to be the genuine destructives which have infested our frontier, while others hold a contrary opinion. He gathered them in an open field and says they were quite numerous. They are about half grown and the impression is that they hatched last season, as the frost does not injure them. We are bringing up the pests in the bottle and they seem to thrive well. We have not learned that they have been found elsewhere in the county.[14]

In 1876, the summer of the national centennial, the locusts arrived in force. In July hatchlings from eggs laid in fall 1875 were joined by a swarm from Pembina, North Dakota. The left flank of that mass came nearly to Steele County. In August, a swarm from southwestern Minnesota, reinforced by a multitude from the Dakotas, massed over southern Minnesota to the Mississippi River and beyond. Steele County wasn't spared.

The *Owatonna Journal* made a note of the first appearance:

> A few grasshoppers were seen flying over this city Friday afternoon and Saturday morning. They were evidently out prospecting, and examining the condition of the country, preparatory to future movements.[15]

Governor Pillsbury issued a call to the public to assist the suffering counties. Representatives of the states being assaulted by locusts met to plan common strategy.

By August most of the grain in the easternmost counties had been safely harvested, so crop loss was not as bad as it might have been. However, the eggs were laid, and the real threat was to the following year.[16]

Young Frank Kubicek gives this description:

> Grasshoppers came along right after harvest this same year. There were just millions of the---! Luckily the grain was out of the way, as they ate everything that was green-even the leaves on the trees. The trees were bare just like winter. They laid so many eggs the people were afraid what was going to happen the next year when all those eggs would hatch. Many thought that they would not even put in any crop, but save the seed and labor. But after all the worry, there were very few that hatched.[17]

The state legislature went into session early in 1877, appealed for federal assistance, and offered a bounty on grasshoppers. Advice from other states described methods of destroying the eggs. One method that would be tried in Minnesota was dragging long metal sheets coated with tar through the fields to snare young locusts.

The state government's application to Washington for help was to no avail. In the spring of 1877, an appeal to a higher power was tried:

> Governor Pillsbury, at the request of the various religious denominations, has appointed Thursday, April 26, a day of fasting and prayer, for deliverance from the grasshopper plague.[18]

When the hatching began that spring, the tarred sheets and a type of mite that attacked locusts made a difference. Still, many locusts survived and at the beginning of July began rising to the sky in swarms. But instead of landing a short distance away, gorging themselves, and laying eggs as they had done in previous years, most flew off to the west and northwest and left the state. By the end of August, the locusts were gone from Minnesota.[19]

What followed that fall was the largest bumper crop in state history. The locusts had done little damage and the weather was perfect. What was true in the rest of the state was true in Steele County:

> Our crop turned out to be the biggest since we started. Wheat went 30 to 40 bushels to the acre. It weighed 61 pounds to a bushel, normal is 56 pounds. We never saw such wonderful wheat before or since.[20]

However, 1878 was a very wet year, delaying the farmer's harvests, and crops were of poor quality. Frank Kubicek also recalled poor crops yields in 1879. Then in February 1881 a monster snow storm hit Minnesota, and Steele County suffered along with much of the rest of the state. The effects were worst in the rural areas where wind swept the landscape unhindered by buildings:

The Recent Snow Storm.
One of the most severe Minnesota snow storms known in the past ten years occurred Friday and Friday night and Saturday and Saturday night of last week. . . .

In the country a terrible state of affairs existed. In many cases the hogs and stock of the farmers were so snowed under as to be in imminent danger of perishing for lack of food and water. On the farm of Joseph Kubat, Esq., who lives four miles southeast of town, they were compelled to cut another hole into the stable in order to feed and water their cattle and horses. It was simply impossible during the storm to dig the snow away so as to get in at the door. Their well was covered over to a depth of over twelve feet and they were compelled to melt snow in order to give a little water to their stock. It took two days to shovel out their hogs, but happily none of them died from their fast and exposure. At P. Iunker's the snow drift was higher than the ridge of the stable.[21]

NEW ARRIVALS IN THE SOUTHERN SETTLEMENT

Frank Horak arrived in Steele County in 1875 at the age of 18. One of ten children of Jan and Amalie (Maixner) Horak from house 209 in Dolní Dobrouč, he was the first of four brothers to come to Owatonna. In 1878, he married Dorothy Kasper at Sacred Heart Church. They homesteaded a farm in Somerset Township, seven miles south of Owatonna, and raised six children.

Frank's brother Adolf came to America at age 19 in 1882 at the urging of Frank and his friends, the Spinler brothers. Adolf lived in Owatonna and made his living as a bartender and saloon owner. He was a partner in the Clausen and Horak saloon at 328 North Cedar, and later the Martinek and Horak saloon at 137 West Bridge Street, with Emil Martinek. He married Philomena Horak (not a close relative) in 1894.

Another Horak brother, **Alois**, born in 1867, came to America in 1887. He was living in Owatonna in 1900 with his wife of two years, Katia.

The fourth brother, **Joseph Horak** arrived in America in 1890 at the age of twenty. He married Agnes Pachl in 1915. They both worked at Pillsbury Academy for many years, and had no children.

The four brothers kept in touch with relatives in Bohemia. Of their siblings who remained in Bohemia, two sisters died in infancy, another sister married a Sisser, two brothers were killed in World War I, and the last brother married and lived in the same house in which they had all been raised.[22]

Wencl and John Jirele were sons of Joseph and Katherine (Pavek) Jirele. Wencl married Barbara Rypka in Bohemia and their son Wencl was born in 1873. They came to America in 1877, settled first in Blooming Prairie Township, but moved to Aurora Township where they farmed until 1903 when they retired and moved to Owatonna. After Barbara died in 1898, Wencl married Anna Simek. All three of Wencl and Barbara's sons, Wencl, Louis and Joseph, farmed in Aurora Township.[23]

John Jirele, Wencl's younger brother by five years, may have come to America at the same time as Wencl. He married Anna Dostal in 1878 and by 1880 they were farming in Owatonna Township, close to Anna's parents, Frank and Marie Dostal, who had come to America in 1870.[24]

Frank and Josephine (Matejcek) Hanzlicek, both born in Dolní Dobrouč, came to America in 1882 and settled in Blooming Prairie Township. Frank had been drafted into the Austrian army for a year of military service. At the age of thirty he married Josephine and they had four children. Frank's older sister Frances preceded him to America. Frances, married to Alois Simon, immigrated to Steele County in 1867. On word that Frances and her husband were doing well in America, Frank decided to emigrate. He came to America for a one year stay in 1881. Satisfied with what he found he returned to Bohemia for his family.

Frank and Josephine rented land for four years and Frank worked at odd jobs to save up money. In 1886 they bought eighty acres of land, farmed it, and then bought forty more acres in 1896. They had five more children. Their son Frank moved to North Dakota. Frank Sr. was both a practicing Catholic and a C.S.P.S. member.[25]

NEWS ITEMS IN THE SOUTHERN SETTLEMENT

Wondra Shooting

The summer of 1875 witnessed a tragedy that involved two of the early Czech families.

Anton and Anna Slezak and their children arrived in Owatonna in 1861 (see chapter 2) and claimed a homestead in Owatonna Township. In 1874 they sold it to the Sustaceks and moved to section 33 of Somerset Township.

The Joseph Wondra family, living in section 4 of Summit Township, was among their new neighbors. The Wondras had moved to this location in 1864, shortly after arriving in America (see chapter 2). The younger generations of the Slezak and Wondra families soon got to know each other.

Anton Slezak, twenty years old in 1875 wanted to marry 17 year old Anna Wondra. Anna's brother Joseph, 25 years old and married to Mary Pribyl, got along well with Slezak but thought his sister too young to marry.

On Sunday May 30, 1875:

> Anton Slazeck [sic], a neighbor, went to Wundroe's [sic] house at about six o'clock for the purpose of borrowing a gun. The gun was handed to Slazeck; when he asked if it was loaded, Wundroe replied that it was not. Slazeck then called for a cap, after receiving which he remarked to Wundroe that he was going to shoot him, which remark was at the time considered as a jest. The gun was pointing directly toward Wundroe when Slazeck adjusted the cap, and Mrs. Wundroe told her husband that he had better take the gun out of doors. He had scarcely moved before the gun was discharged, the whole charge entering his abdomen and causing instant death. Slazeck made no attempt to flee, but remained at home until arrested by Sheriff Toher on the following morning. Slazeck declares that the shooting was purely accidental, while others think it was premeditated, though the parties had always been friendly and no cause for such a rash act can be assigned.[26]

The story passed down through the Wondra family was that the fatal shot went between Joseph Wondra and his infant son Joseph John Wondra, sitting on his father's lap, and found its mark in the father.[27]

The grand jury examined the case in June and found insufficient evidence to indict Slezak.

Despite this tragedy, Anton Slezak and Anna Wondra were married in February 1876. In a brief memoir of his life written more than fifty years later, Slezak never mentioned the shooting. He described his early life with his parents, his marriage to Anna, and their subsequent life together. They farmed in the same area where their parents lived until 1894, then sold their farm and moved closer to what is now the village of Hope.

Joseph Wondra's wife Mary was pregnant at the time her husband was killed. The son, born about a month after the shooting, died in September of the same year. Joseph and Mary also had an older daughter and son. The couple had no will and Mary Wondra filed to claim half of the farm under the intestacy laws. However, Joseph owed his parents money when he was killed, so Mary's mother-in-law, Frances Wondra, filed a claim for one third of the farm under the law of dower (meant to protect a widow from destitution when her husband died, but in this case the husband of Frances, John Wondra, was very much alive).

Frances and Mary settled their claims in fall 1877. The farm eventually went to Frances Wondra's daughter, and Joseph's sister, Mary, who was married to Wencl Jirousek. The Jirouseks moved from their original farm in Owatonna Township to the Wondra farm. This property has been in the Jirousek family ever since, and is one of Steele County's century farms.

Joseph Wondra's widow Mary married Frank Rysavy in January 1877.

Joseph Wondra's parents seem to have separated after the shooting. Frances Wondra filed for divorce from John in March 1878, but the request was denied by the court in June. John Wondra left Minnesota and settled in Portland, Oregon, where he died in 1885. Frances apparently remained in Minnesota. The 1880 census records Frances Wondra, age 58, residing with and keeping house for Joseph Wanous in Summit Township.[28]

Joseph Kubat Injured
The *Owatonna Journal* for July 13, 1876, carried the first news of the massacre of General Custer's troops at Little Big Horn and, on page three, ran this story of Joseph Kubat's close call:

> Joseph Kubat, of Somerset, was coming into town on Saturday last for the purpose of having repaired the remains of what had once been a buggy, but having participated in a celebration behind a runaway team on the 4th, it needed remodeling. The buggy was following, as best its crippled nature would allow it, in the rear of Joseph's wagon. When within a couple of miles of town, a bolt coming out caused the whiffletree to drop and the horses to

take fright and run. Mr. Kubat was thrown from the wagon violently, injuring his right side and hip severely though not dangerously. The wagon took a bee line for a fence and leaned up against it to rest. The horses ran into another wagon nearby, and becoming entangled in their harness, received some ugly bruises. And now, not only his buggy, but Mr. Kubat himself, his horses and wagon, all need repair.[29]

Election of 1876
The Presidential election of 1876 was one of the most contentious in American history. The Democrats ran against rampant corruption in the federal government during the Grant administration. Republicans countered by calling the pro-southern Democrats the party of rebellion. The Democratic contender, Samuel Tilden, won a majority of the popular vote. However, vote totals in four states were in dispute, and if all four states went to the Republicans, the Republican candidate Rutherford Hayes would have a majority of electoral votes and become President.

The issue went to the House of Representatives where a commission of eight Republicans and seven Democrats was to decide the outcome in the four contested states. The commission apparently decided to let Hayes win in return for withdrawal of Federal troops from the south and end of Reconstruction. On March 2, 1877, the commission declared Republican Hayes the winner.[30]

This election was also contentious in Steele County and led to accusations of voter fraud and duping of Litomysl Czechs:

> The result of the election in Steele County is surprising, and still it is not so much to be wondered at when we look and compare the figures. Two years ago when Mr. Dunnell ran for Congress the total vote was 1694 taken from the head of the tickets. Last year the total vote was 1472; this year it was 2,539 or 1,067 more than last year, or 845 more than two years ago.
>
> It is a wonder where all these votes come from. . . .It is said on good authority that a large number of Bohemian residents in Somerset, were cajoled into voting the Republican ticket, by one "Kabbage" who tells the last man he meets that he will work for his ticket, but the man who pays him cash is the man and party he works for. This man it was thought was brought up by the Republicans and he got the Bohemians to vote the Republican ticket, they doubtless supposing it was a Tilden ticket, which they wished to vote. . . .[31]

The "Kabbage" mentioned might have been Julius Kabage, a German-American born in Wisconsin and aged 21 at the time of the election. He had married Barbara Kovar in 1877 and was living in Somerset Township at the time. His biography in the 1910 county history says he was a member of the Republican Party.[32]

Civil Court Proceedings
The Litomysl Czechs, as people do everywhere, argued among themselves, fell behind on their mortgages, and filed for divorce. Among the many names in the 1870s District Court proceedings were some Czech names:

> Franceska Wacecek against Wenzel Wacecek; action for divorce. In this case the parties have relented and concluded not to do it.[33]

> The case of John Ranchin vs. F. Sikora, in which Ranchin claimed damages from Sikora for driving over grain, was tried, and Ranchin was awarded damages to the amount of five cents.[34]

> Frances Wondra vs. John Wondra; action to obtain a divorce; H.E. Johnson for plaintiff; decree refused.[35]

> Wenzel Hanus vs. Anna Hanus, action to obtain a divorce; H.E. Johnson for plaintiff; decree granted.[36]

> Notice of Mortgage Sale by Advertisement
> Default has been made in the conditions of a certain Mortgage executed and delivered by Wencel Hanus and Barbara Hanus, his wife, mortgagors, to A. L. McCaslin, mortgagee, dated the 19th day of August A.D. eighteen hundred and seventy-eight . . . [37]

> Notice of Mortgage Sale by Advertisement
> Default has been made in the conditions of a certain mortgage executed and delivered by Dominick Wacek and Franciska Wacek mortgagors, to Lyman Goodhue mortgagee . . .[38]

> Horsky vs. Kowas-Last Monday the celebrated dog case of John Horsky against John Kowas took place before City Justice Cornell. J. M. Burlingame

was attorney for the plaintiff, and the matter was settled by Horsky, when Kowas offered to give up the dog providing Horsky would give up the suit. Horsky had no money to pay the costs which amounted to $2.25 but offered the Justice the dog. Horsky says he paid his attorney $5 so that he is out that amount besides the expenses. Kowas went on his way rejoicing.[39]

Herdina Case

A notorious, and ultimately troubling, affair involving the local Czech community hit the newspapers in July 1877. It involved the Herdina family (Hrdina in Czech), who had arrived in the U.S. in 1875.

Murderous Assault.

On Saturday evening last W.R. Knickerbocker, his wife, little son about 4 years old and two little daughters, together with Frank Bailey, all of Somerset, and William Barker, of Lemond, were going home in Knickerbocker's wagon. When part way home they overtook and passed two teams. In one of the wagons they passed was Frank Herdina, Sr., Frank Herdina, Jr., and a woman, in the other was Otto Herdina and John Kroulik. The parties passed were Bohemians living in the town of Summit. As the party with Knickerbocker passed the others the Bohemians set up a yell calling them s__'s of b____'s and numerous other vile epithets. They did not appear to be intoxicated as they could walk and run as well as anyone and gave no evidence of being under the influence of liquor except their fiendish actions. After Knickerbocker drove past the Bohemians gave chase with yells and curses and several times ran the tongue of their wagon into the back endboard of Knickerbocker's. It is probable that nothing worse than this would have transpired had not Knickerbocker's little boy's hat blown off. When this occurred William Barker got out and ran back to get it. When he got beside the wagon in which was Otto Herdina and John Kroulik they both jumped out and attacked him with blows, kicks and knives. Seeing this, Frank Bailey, a young man about 18 years old jumped out of Knickerbocker's wagon and ran to his assistance, followed by Knickerbocker himself. By the time they got there all four Bohemians were engaged in the melee, attacking Bailey as soon as he came, and Knickerbocker as soon as he reached the place, with knives, cutting and slashing indiscriminately.... News of this terrible affair spread rapidly and before the Bohemians reached home, Oscar Gross, constable, L.F. Pike, Justice of the Peace, and

Gardiner Story had overtaken and arrested them and started with them for this city, where they were lodged in the lockup. Dr. Twiford of Geneva was sent for immediately, arriving at Smith's at about 11 o'clock. An examination of the wounds revealed the fact that a part of a knife blade is yet in one of them. While the injuries received by both Knickerbocker and Barker are of a serious and very painful character, it is hoped that with good care both will recover. . . .[40]

The arraignment the following week brought out a few additional details:

The Herdina Case.
The examination set for Monday occurred as expected, the Herdinas appearing. It appears from the evidence the Bohemians threw stones and struck Mr. Knickerbocker on the head, knocking him senseless, and while in that condition knifed him; cutting him badly on the right arm, a gash across the right eyebrow, besides the stab in the left shoulder.

"In matter of Mr. Barker, the old man Herdina backed him into a ditch, and Barker falling down, the old man fell on to him. Young Herdina tried to cut Barker, but Barker shoved the old man from one side to the other, and he received several severe cuts from his own son. But in spite of this Barker received cuts and bruises which are yet serious. . . .[41]

The trial was held five months later:

District Court.
The grand jury found two indictments against the Herdinas and Kroulik, one for their murderous assault on Barker and the other for their assault on Knickerbocker. The trial in the Barker case commenced on Tuesday. A jury was secured without much trouble and nearly all the evidence for the State submitted on the first day. Yesterday the examination for the defense commenced, but it is conducted slowly and tediously owing to the fact that the accused can not speak English and their testimony is taken by the aid of an interpreter. The testimony for the State substantially corroborates the account given of the affair by the *Journal* at the time of its occurrence. The civil actions, brought against the accused for damages, will probably be heard after the State trials during the present term of court.[42]

The verdict and sentence were issued a week later, but the *People's Press* was troubled by additional evidence that came out at trial:

> **District Court.**
> The district court adjourned on Wednesday after being in session a little over two weeks. The most important cases tried were those of the State against the Herdinas. The cases occupied the attention of the court *(illegible)* in a verdict of guilty *(illegible)* all the defendants, except Kroulik, who was found guilty of assault only. The sentence of the court was as follows: that Kroulik be confined in the county jail for one year; that Frank Herdina, Sr., be confined in the State Prison one year, Frank Herdina, Jr., two years, and Adolph four years.
>
> There were several things connected with the trial of these men that strike us as being unfair. The first of these was the fact that in each case the jury was composed entirely of Americans, no one being allowed to sit in the jury box who could speak their language. It seems to us like trying an American in a jury of all Bohemians or Norwegians. Next, the evidence showed that the Bohemians had been drinking, and that before the fight commenced, Bailey, one of the Knickerbocker party, stripped off his coat and told them to come on, that he could lick them all. It also showed that if they had tried in the least, to have kept out of their way, no one would have been hurt.
>
> These facts and many others do not seem to have been taken into consideration by the court in pronouncing his sentence. That Barker threw a stone and knocked the old man Herdina down, is an undisputed fact—and this he had done before anyone was hurt. While we believe in punishing the guilty, we believe in having the punishment proportionate with the crime. . . .[43]

The case was in the newspapers again the following spring and summer as the appeal by Frank Herdina Senior reached the Minnesota Supreme Court, and the civil lawsuit of Knickerbocker and William Barker against the Herdinas was heard. At that time, the *People's Press* apparently printed the entire transcript of the original case as a thirty-page pamphlet. Unfortunately, copies do not seem to have survived.

Frank Herdina Senior's appeal to the Minnesota Supreme Court was decided on July 2, 1878. Herdina's lawyers, A.C. Hickman and Amos Coggswell, argued that the jury should have been instructed:

If the father's motive in participating in the melee was to protect his sons, he should be found not guilty;

The father could only be found guilty of assault with a dangerous weapon if he helped the sons arm themselves beforehand;

The father could not be found guilty if the evidence indicated he was so drunk that he did not know what he was doing.

The Supreme Court concluded that a parent had no right to protect his children in the commission of a crime; that once the father came to the aid of his sons knowing they were armed with a dangerous weapon, he was guilty as well; and that while there was evidence the father was drunk at the time of the assault, there was no evidence he was so drunk that the did not know what he was doing. Consequently, the conviction and sentence were upheld.[44]

William Barker's civil suit for $1,500 in damages against the Herdinas and John Kroulik was also decided in summer 1878. The jury found in favor of the defendants Frank Herdina Jr. and John Kroulik, but found for the plaintiff to the amount of $750 against Frank Herdina Sr. and Adolph Herdina.

Mr. Knickerbocker also sued and collected $675 from all three Herdinas, but the court found in favor of defendant John Kroulik.

After serving time for this affair, John Kroulik had apparently been out of prison only a few months when he was in trouble again, though for a less serious offense:

A Five Dollar Fight
Wednesday John Kroulik and I. Pavek were arrested by Constable Williamson at Blooming Prairie and charged before the City Justice with assault and battery upon J. Junik on Tuesday morning. There had been a dance at Pavek's, and it appears from the evidence of the witnesses on both sides that Junik had called Johnny a "kluk," which being interpreted means a little boy, or, when applied to an older person, a disreputable fellow among the fair sex. Johnny naturally wanted to know what kind of a "kluk" he was, and then Junik pushed him, when they clinched and fell and Johnny being the most active, got on top soonest and thereupon pounded Junik a few. . . . the Court fined Johnny $5.00 and costs. It seemed as though Johnny might as well have the other fellow charged now as they all agree that he begun it. Pavek was dismissed from the case.[45]

Finally, the aftermath of this assault case may have led to the loss of the Herdina family farm. From Frank Kubicek's memoir:

In the spring of 1881, Father bought another 120 acres from Herman Schmidt of Owatonna. This farm was owned by Frank Herdina. At one time he lost it on account of poor crops and poor management. He could not meet his payments, so Herman Schmidt took it over as he had a mortgage on it.[46]

Farming was a tough and unpredictable business then as now. The additional stress of having the head of the family in jail for a year, and two sons locked up even longer, plus the costs of attorney fees and civil damages may have made it impossible to keep the farm going. The 1879 plat book shows the Herdina farm in Summit Township, just across the road to the north of Frank Kubicek's farm. However, the 1880 census records the Herdina family living in Blooming Prairie.

Drunk Driving and Assault
A less serious story involving Litomysl Czechs appeared later in the year:

> Marshall Stowers has not had such a genuine hug as the one he received last Monday for a long time. It happened thus: A Bohemian resident of Somerset indulged too freely in corn juice. He started home with two women in the wagon. He was too drunk to drive and the woman on the seat with him attempted to take the lines, but he refused and struck her several times. Stowers went to take him to jail when the woman, supposed to be his wife, held on to him and clasped Stowers around the neck, vainly pleading to have the man released. But the Marshal pushed him on a dray, when the two women pulled him off, but he was pushed on again and taken to the caboose.[47]

Joseph Bichner
Local newspapers also tracked the everyday life occurrences in the Czech southern settlement. Joseph Bichner of Summit was mentioned a number of times, often due to his involvement in politics. The September 1, 1877, edition of the *People's Press* did a little self promotion by noting that Joseph Bickner, "one of the best farmers in Summit," came to the newspaper offices to have some auction posters printed in Czech and English. "He knows the place to go to get his printing done promptly and satisfactorily."

In October, Bichner announced he was a candidate for County Treasurer. However, he was defeated by a Mr. Canadell by 250 votes.

The following summer Bichner's assessment of farming in Kansas and Minnesota appeared:

> Joseph Bichner, Esq. of Summit, returned from a three week visit to Kansas, Thursday. He reports that there is an immense flow of immigration into that state, and that in two or three weeks they will begin to harvest. He still believes that there [is] no place like Minnesota, and that Kansas as a wheat growing state, does not compare with it.[48]

In October, Joseph Bichner of Summit was chosen as delegate to the county convention of the Democratic Party. (A Joseph F. Bichner was chosen as a delegate from Owatonna.)[49]

The following year, Bichner was one of six members of the Democratic Party's county committee that met to choose delegates to the state party convention.[50]

Bichner was also a member of the county Democratic Party Hancock and English Club. The club's executive committee consisted of two persons from each voting precinct and one from each city ward. Joseph Bichner was one of two members from Summit Township, John Wavrin represented Owatonna Township, and Wencl Kovar represented Somerset.[51]

In the 1879 elections, Wencl Pichner was elected Somerset Township Supervisor, and Wencl Wencl was elected Blooming Prairie Township Supervisor.[55]

Miscellaneous News Items
The Kovars of Somerset Township had a frightening experience in summer 1878:

> On Monday of last week a tramp entered the house of Mr. Koovar [sic], living six miles southeast of the city, whose wife was alone at home, took twenty five dollars, and meeting with resistance from Mrs. Koovar, drew a knife and cut an ugly gash in her left arm, and has not since been caught.[52]

Accidents involving horses continued to plague the settlers.

A Fatal Accident
Alois Rishavey, a Bohemian, in attempting to jump out of Ressler's wagon in the Town of Summit, while the horses were running away, was caught in one of the wheels and died of injuries received Wednesday of last week. His friends sent for the coroner Thursday, but as the facts were known regarding

his death, that officer thought his presence unnecessary. He was buried Friday. The deceased had been in this country only about six months.[53]

Fatal Accident

John Wanous, an aged Bohemian living six miles south of the city, was killed, about one and a half miles south of town last Saturday evening, about five o'clock p.m., by falling off a large load of bran, which he was taking home for food. He left town about four o'clock, and being old and feeble, he was assisted in mounting his load by two young men. It is supposed that in going down the hill beyond the Catholic burying ground, where he was found, that he lost his balance and fell head foremost, killing himself by dislocating his neck and breaking in his skull. The same evening he was brought back to town and taken to Dr. Rossbach's office, but was found to be quite dead.[54]

Settlers also risked great loss from fire.

A poor man named Wencl Pukert [apparently should be Paukert] living in Blooming Prairie township last Tuesday, lost a fine span of horses, a set of new harness and a stable by fire, set by his little six year old son.[56]

Frank Wencl

Marital discord and the resulting side effects resulted in court actions involving Frank Wencl:

Frank Wencel, a Bohemian who lives about five miles south of town, assaulted Frank Kubishka, his brother-in-law. Kubishka brought an action before City Justice Cornell, which was heard Wednesday when Frank Wencel was fined $10 and costs . . .[57]

District Court.

The following cases are marked for trial and will be noticed when disposed of: No. 21. Rosa Vencl vs. Frank Vencl, divorce. No defense.[58]

Default has been made in the conditions of a certain Mortgage executed and delivered by Frank Vencl and Rose Vencl his wife mortgagors, to Joseph Newsalt mortgagee, dated the first day of April A. D. eighteen hundred and seventy eight and . . .[59]

Child Support
>Last Friday night John Sikora was held in the sum of $500 bonds on charge of bastardy. Agnes Herdina had the child with her at the justice court during the entire trial, and the sympathy of those in attendance seemed to be with her in her misfortune. Sikora's father went on his bonds.[60]

Death of Frank Seykora

Frank Seykora, one of the three Seykora brothers who came to Steele County during the Civil War, died January 19, 1881. His death certificate says he froze to death. The newspaper's account:

>Frank Sikora, Jr., in company with his youngest son, left town Wednesday evening for home in good health. When they arrived home the son found his father dead.[61]

Death of George Motl

One of the early Czech settlers of Somerset County, George Motl, killed himself on July 24, 1881. He had visited his son Frank that morning and given him his will, telling Frank he would not live much longer and there was enough money in his trunk to bury him. He also insisted that Frank and his family come over that day for dinner. Later in the day George quarreled with his younger son, Joseph, and then went to his room. Joseph left the house to work in the fields, leaving his wife and hired hand Frank Pavek in the living room. They heard a shot and opened the bedroom door to find that George Motl had shot himself.[62]

HOLY TRINITY CHURCH

Since Catholics in Somerset and Summit Township lived too far away to easily attend church services in Owatonna or Blooming Prairie, they began gathering at private homes for prayer. The homesteaders rang a bell to announce the service and Czechs families gathered to sing hymns, pray the rosary, and listen as someone read a Czech sermon from a book lovingly brought from Bohemia. When the school building for district no. 57 was built near Litomysl, believers used it as a temporary church.

Until 1875, occasional visits by missionary priests were the only opportunities to hear Mass and receive the sacraments. Father František Tichý (stationed in St. Paul from 1877 to 1880, and New Prague until 1906) and Father František Šulák (a Jesuit from Chicago) visited the congregation about four times a year. This changed when Father Pribyl became resident at Sacred Heart Church in Owatonna in 1875. He spoke Czech and frequently visited Litomysl. In time, he convinced fifty families (not all of them Czech) to build a Catholic church in the Litomysl settlement.[63]

The Holy Trinity Church of Litomysl was organized in January 1878. In March, Anton and Anna Seykora donated land for the church and Joseph and Josephine Skalicky donated an acre for a cemetery. Construction began in early spring on a wooden church 40 feet long by 28 feet wide. The first Mass was celebrated in the partially completed building in late June 1878 on the Feast of Corpus Christi, and the first wedding (of Joseph Pirkl and Josephine Skalicky) was celebrated on May 23, 1879.

In 1881, the community painted the church inside and out and adorned it with two bells and the Stations of the Cross purchased with parishioner donations. The Seykora brothers donated and installed the main altar and two side altars were built, one for the Virgin Mary and one for St. John Nepomuc, a famous Czech martyr. Three paintings by the Bohemian artist John Umlauf were brought to America and donated, one for each altar. In 1884 the congregation added a bell tower. The horses' hitching rail was an 80 foot long steel pipe supported by wooden posts under a clump of shady trees.

A major event every year for the Litomysl Catholics was the Feast of Corpus Christi. In 1940 a new stone church was built and a commemorative booklet printed at the time described the day:

> Dating back even to the time before the church was built, this celebration was one of great note. Many days before the feast, preparations were made to make this an outstanding day in giving tribute to the King of Kings. Three portable altars were erected in various places to which the entire congregation marched in procession, praying at each in turn. At first these altars were placed on the lawns of nearby homes. Later, and at the present time (1940), these altars are put on the church grounds. . . .
>
> In the early days, one of the parishioners announced the arrival of the great feast to the countryside by firing a cannon long before dawn. After Mass, as various organizations formed ranks, the procession formed. Led by a boy carrying the cross the rest of the congregation followed in order. Directly preceding the Blessed Sacrament, which was carried by the priest under a canopy, marched the tiny flower girls who strewed flowers in the path of the Divine Master. The singing of songs, recitation of the rosary and the playing of the

Holy Trinity Church, Litomysl, 1927. Courtesy of the Alfred Wondra family

local band added to the tribute. The procession slowly wended its way from altar to altar where prayers were said and the choir sang for the Benediction of the Blessed Sacrament at each.[64]

Father Pribyl, who had left the pastorship of Sacred Heart Church in Owatonna the month before to serve in Madelia, returned in late May 1880 to lead the Corpus Christi ceremonies at Holy Trinity Church:

> The object of this grand solemnity is the honor of our Saviour in the Blessed Sacrament and to invoke the blessings of the Almighty upon the crops of the earth.[65]

Interior, old Holy Trinity Church, Litomysl, before it was torn down. Courtesy of Kathye and Wayne Beebe

This custom continued well into the twentieth century. Frances (Rysavy) Buryska, born in 1914, remembers the processions from her childhood:

> We had Corpus Christi processions every year. There was a small building on the cemetery grounds that housed the grave digging and cemetery upkeep tools. This building was cleaned up, an altar made and decorated with many flowers, and to this altar the procession marched. First, the flag bearers, then a long stream of boys and girls with small baskets of flower petals to strew on the way, then the priest with the monstrance under a canopy held by four strong men. Then came the choir, followed by the

Klecker Band and the rest of the congregation. The little girls were dressed in white, and I remember carrying my little basket. It was especially pretty with blue satin ribbons on it. Sometimes there weren't many flowers, so we'd rob mother's geraniums and snip some grass to put in the basket to add quantity. We ran out of flowers long before we reached the cemetery because we'd toss them by the handful. The music of the band kept the people moving briskly. After the Benediction, everyone took off on their own There was a time or two where instead of the cemetery, we walked to the Frank Skalicky farm. They had a large open porch, and the altar was set there, with great bunches of peonies all around.[66]

Holy Trinity did not have a resident pastor until 1898 when Father Ottmar Miller was appointed by Bishop Cotter to lead the congregation. Earlier a succession of priests, usually based at Sacred Heart Church in Owatonna, served the congregation. Typically, they visited Litomysl one Sunday each month. They were met by an "honor guard" of Skalicky brothers on horseback and escorted to the home of Joseph and Josephine Skalicky where they boarded during their stay. On Sundays when no priest was present, services were led by members of the congregation who read from the Bible and led recitations of the Rosary and, during Lent, Stations of the Cross.[67]

St. Joseph Society, a fraternal insurance organization associated with the church, was established in 1883. The charter members were Wencl Wanous; Joseph Skalicky; Joseph Hudrlik; Frank Skalicky; Joseph, Anton, Frank and John Seykora; John Seykora Jr.; Joseph Pirkl; Joseph Steinbauer; John Matejcek; and Frank Motl. St. Joseph Society was affiliated with the First Central Catholic Bohemian Union national organization (see Catholic Lodges in chapter 7).

In 1889 St. Joseph Society joined other lodges in many western states in breaking away from the First Central Catholic Bohemian Union to form the Zapadni Česko Katolicka Jednota (Z.C.K.J. or Western Czech Catholic Union). This was a fraternal group that paid death benefits and helped widows and orphans. Only Catholics in good standing could be members. The Western Czech Catholic Union eventually merged with the Katolicky Delnik (Catholic Workman) organization.

In 1897 the lodge built a hall across the road and to the northeast of the church on land that had belonged to Joseph Skalicky. Known as the North Hall, it hosted dinners, plays and dances. The building was 30 feet by 50 feet and painted white. The interior was unpainted, and consisted of a dance floor, bar, small stage and balcony. An adjacent barn sheltered horses during winter church services.

In 1934 a new and larger lodge was built adjacent to, and replaced, the old one. This new Hall was later moved to Blooming Prairie where it now houses an antique store.

Holy Trinity Church and North Hall formed the center of the Litomysl community. Between 1898 and 1940 more than a thousand children were baptized in the church. In 1940, parishioners donated field stones to build a new stone church next to the old one. When the new church, built by the Wacek Brothers, was finished the old wooden church was torn down. The 1940 Holy Trinity Church still stands today.

School district No. 57, known as the Litomysl School, was located about two miles north of the Holy Trinity Church. The county school superintendent's report of 1879 dismisses it with this short summary:

> Here is a small school which has been taught two or three terms by Mr. Albert Kasper. The children have made some progress in learning English.[68]

BOHEMIAN NATIONAL CEMETERY OF SUMMIT TOWNSHIP

Just as in Owatonna, the southern settlement needed a burial place for unchurched Czechs. A squabble within the Holy Trinity Catholic congregation gave birth to such a cemetery.

Sometime before 1892, an individual (no record of the name has been found) living in southern Summit Township and belonging to Holy Trinity died. After the funeral, the casket was carried down the road to the Catholic cemetery. However, because the individual's family was behind on its pew rent Church elders stopped the funeral party at the cemetery gate, refusing burial unless the delinquent pew rent was paid on the spot!

An argument and fight broke out, and the deceased was taken away to be buried on farmland. That family and several others broke from the church because of the episode. Soon after, the Vavra family donated $35 to buy 1⅛ acres of hilltop land from Fred and Rosalie Haberman for a cemetery. Local farmers used horse scrapers to cut the hilltop into the shape it has today. Established on December 2, 1893, as the Česko-Slovanský Národni Hřbitov, or Bohemian Slavonian National Burying Ground Association, its name was eventually shortened to Bohemian National Cemetery. According to the Ruzek family, the first burial in the new cemetery was William Ruzek, who died January 20, 1894.[69]

Although the Bohemian National Cemeteries provided a burial option for Czechs who could not or did not wish to be buried in a church cemetery, they were open to all

Blooming Prairie Bohemian National Cemetery, today. Susan Lindoo

Czechs including Catholics in good standing. Frank Ruzek, who died in 1936, was a founding member of the Blooming Prairie ZCBJ Lodge 83. According to his obituary in the *Fraternal Herald*, his funeral, at Blooming Prairie's St. Columbanus Catholic Church, was attended by many lodge members, and he was buried in the Blooming Prairie Bohemian National Cemetery. Other Catholic families who attended Holy Trinity and St. Columbanus, including the Betlachs, Jansas, Pelinkas, Pechaceks and Skalickys, also have members buried in the Bohemian National Cemetery.

SURROUNDING VILLAGES

The Litomysl Czech settlement was surrounded by several small villages, including Summit, Steele Center, Riverpoint, Bixby, and Hope. The villages served as commercial units where much of the day to day business could be done, minimizing the need for business trips to Owatonna or Blooming Prairie. The villages usually included a creamery, general store, school, and perhaps a post office.

Summit

In the early days of Summit Township's settlement there was a house, called Omro, about one and a half miles south of Holy Trinity Church. It served as the post office for nearby farmers from 1898 to 1902. A little farther south, in section twelve of Summit Township, was a creamery built in 1893. From its beginnings, Czechs were involved in organizing and running the creamery. In 1893, the president was J.B. Pribyl and the secretary was Frank Kubicek. For the first four years the key role of buttermaker was filled by J.K. Bennett and Carl Nelson. They were succeeded by Joseph Wondra, and in 1907 he was succeeded by Frank Wolesky.

The creamery was a wooden, two-story building with dairy operations on the ground floor and a room above where the buttermaker lived and the creamery board met. The creamery paid off its early debt by 1902. In 1915 it was upgraded with a gasoline engine and steam boiler. The creamery provided a substantial economic boost to area farms. In September 1899, the creamery received 6,500 pounds of milk per day, paying patrons 20 cents per pound of butterfat. In one week in 1915, twenty two boxes of butter (each holding 60 pounds) were produced and hauled to Bixby for shipment by rail.

In early 1918, on a day when the board was meeting on the second floor, the creamery caught fire and the building and most equipment were destroyed. The creamery was rebuilt in the same location and opened for business in November 1918.

In 1919 Sam Blockhus became buttermaker and held that position until 1949. Blockhus lived at the Chris Lynard house and walked to work until a new creamery house was built just east of the creamery in May 1920 (now the home of Bob and Carol Prokopec).

The creamery produced 102,875 pounds of butter in 1920, 194,225 pounds in 1926, and 203,800 pounds in 1944. The butter was sold for 59 cents per pound in 1920, 43 cents per pound in 1926, but in 1934, during the depths of the depression, sank to 23.45 cents per pound. Farmers were paid an average price of 68 cents per pound of butterfat delivered to the creamery in 1920, 49.2 cents per pound in 1926, 28.2 cents per pound in 1934, and 37 cents per pound in April 1935. This represented a substantial degree of economic activity for area farmers, even at the lower prices of the Depression.[70]

A general store was located just east of the creamery. Frank Kubicek bought the store in February 1896 at a price of $300 for the building and $616 for the merchandise. Frank lived on a farm a short distance west of the creamery. His daughter Mary clerked in the store until her marriage in 1908 to Adolph Ressler. The store prospered, mainly from the business of creamery patrons, and Frank was able to repay his debt on the store and nearby farm.

During the night of August 12, 1909, the store was struck by lightning and burned to the ground. It was a total loss and as the $1200 worth of insurance did not cover the $2000 loss of building and inventory, Frank decided not to rebuild. He thought the creamery was on shaky financial ground and the store would not be economically viable without the creamery.[71]

Brothers Louis and Frank Schisler built a new store on the north side of the road across from the creamery. Frank Schisler was a cabinetmaker who lived in the farm formerly owned by Frank Kubicek. After a few years, Frank Schisler left the store and Louis became the sole proprietor.

When the creamery was operating the store was open from 6 a.m. to midnight. Louis sold nearly everything his customers might need. He sold coffee by the pound that he ground in an old coffee mill, and plugs of tobacco for 10 cents that he cut off of slabs 15 inches by 4 inches. He sold shoes, straw hats, underwear, shirts, beer (3 bottles of Flecks beer from Faribault for 25 cents), ropes, nuts and bolts, jackets, overalls, peanuts (50 cents for 50 pounds), and even Copenhagen snuff (3 boxes for 25 cents). He also sold some machinery. Salesmen came to the store to take orders that would be shipped by rail to Bixby where Louis picked them up.

Louis Schisler had the first big truck in the Summit area, a chain-drive Model T, which he used to haul tin and lumber and take chickens to market in Blooming Prairie. For years the store displayed the stuffed and mounted head of a fox that Schisler had shot in Summit.[72]

Following World War II Louis's son Lawrence replaced the old wood store with a brick building. The creamery closed in 1959, although the second creamery building, built in 1918 after fire destroyed the original, was still standing in 2008. The general store eventually went out of business, but the building remained until its destruction in 2006.[73]

Anton Kubicek's blacksmith shop sat just west of the creamery on a low area of land. It remained there until Anton's marriage to Ludmilla Prokopec in 1900, when it was moved farther west.

General store, creamery, and blacksmith shop in Summit, around 1900. Courtesy of Steele County Historical Society

School District No. 51 was also located in Summit. It was in existence by 1867 and was known as the Summit School. According to Frank Kubicek's memoir, the school burned down in the winter of 1874–1875 and was replaced with a better building. The county school superintendent's report for 1879 had this summary:

> Mr. Snyder taught this school last winter after the first three weeks. Here, too, a large house has taken the place of the old log one. They have a large school and the energy of the school board in the support of a good school is commendable.

Steele Center
Steele Center is located at the north edge of the Litomysl Czech settlement and a bit east of the Moravia/Saco settlement. It started with a post office that opened in 1858 and continued operating until 1902.

A cooperative creamery organized in 1892 was located next to the post office. The following year the creamery was receiving 14,000 pounds of milk per day. The butter it produced was shipped by rail to New York. The building was replaced in 1904 with a new brick creamery.

Joseph Wolesky left the River Point creamery in 1905 to become buttermaker at Steele Center. He held the post until 1917 when he moved to Owatonna to start an automobile repair business with his brother Frank. Other Czechs associated with the creamery over the years included Wencl Kovar, L.J. Wanous, Joseph Wesely, John Simon, Lawrence Deml, Allan Kasper, and Albert Meixner.

Production at the creamery peaked around 1942 when 283,525 pounds of butter were produced. The creamery closed in 1957.[74]

A grocery store was located across the road from the creamery. Once the automobile became popular, a repair garage and gas station joined the store. Groceries were sold in the north end of the building, repairs were done at the south end, and gas was pumped out in front.[75]

A quarter mile to the north was a German Lutheran Church, which became the Somerset Town Hall in the 1930s. School District No. 40 (the Steele Center School) was nearby.

River Point

The village of River Point stood on the western edge of the Litomysl settlement. A post office was established in 1857 and operated until 1903. Frank Styndl offered blacksmith services in both River Point and Steele Center between 1886 and 1896. School district No. 37 stood at this intersection until 1921, when a bigger school was built a half mile to the south.

District 37 school, known as the River Point School, was established in 1860. It probably began as a log building, like most of the early schools. The county school superintendent's 1879 report speaks glowingly of the school:

> The citizens of this district have built a beautiful house with good blackboards and patent desks, and the house is a model. The house and furniture are in as good a condition as when new—natural wear and tear excepted. Mr. Frank Green has taught the school several terms. We are informed that Mr. O.A. Tiffany is to teach the school this winter.

In 1897 the school was a one room wooden building with a pot-bellied stove for warmth, but no electricity or running water. Students fetched water for the school's use from the kitchen of the adjacent farm owned by Joseph Kaplan Jr. (and later by his son Walter). The school had two outhouses, one for boys and one for girls. A woodshed

River Point creamery and store, 1910.
Courtesy of Steele County Historical Society

was attached to the school, and older boys brought wood from the shed to feed the stove in wintertime.[76]

In 1899 the River Point Creamery was built a half mile south of the school. The initial board of directors included local Czechs J.W. Kaplan, Wencl Jirousek, and Ferdinand Motz. The creamery was built in six weeks, an artesian well was drilled to ensure a good supply of water, and local farmers pledged milk from 400 to 500 cows for creamery use.

Buttermakers at the creamery in the early years were Joseph Wolesky from 1899 to 1905, Frank Dostal from 1905 to 1910, and Joseph Wondra from 1910 to 1917. Frank Motl took over the post from Paul Gertje in June 1918.

The creamery competed with surrounding creameries and almost closed in 1926. The directors decided to keep it going and it remained open for twelve more years, finally closing in 1938.

Soon after the creamery began, a general store opened across the street. The store had living quarters on the second story. When Joseph Wondra was the creamery's buttermaker, he also operated the store and lived above it. After he left the creamery Wondra continued to operate the store. It sold one hundred pound sacks of flour, salt, sugar, coffee, and other supplies. Farmers stopped at the store when they brought their milk to the creamery. The store was torn down in 1918 and the materials used to build a home where a younger generation (Joseph Wondra) still lives.[77]

Bixby

The village of Bixby lies about 4.5 miles east of Litomysl's Holy Trinity Church. It was created shortly after an 1890 fire destroyed the previous railroad stop in Aurora, three miles south of Pratt, and the post office in Aurora was closed. The Chicago, Milwaukee, St. Paul and Pacific Railroad decided to move the stop to a location midway between the stations in Pratt and Blooming Prairie, and settled on the farm of J.S. Bixby.

By fall 1893, the railroad had completed the station, platform, freight house, and side track. A better depot was built in 1899 and is now on view in the Village of Yesteryear in Owatonna.

J.S. Bixby rented out his farm and built a general store in the village, with an addition to serve as the family home. The Aurora post office was transferred to J.S. Bixby's house, and he was appointed postmaster.

The store was soon joined by a lumber yard, grain elevator, and feed and grain warehouse.

A creamery was opened in 1891, as John Bixby was attempting to get the village started. However, the creamery's operation was seasonal and intermittent, thus unreliable,

Frank Styndl at his anvil, 1909. Courtesy of John Styndl

Frank Styndl shoeing Mr. Malleck's horse. Courtesy of John Styndl

and the buttermaker was not popular with customers. Consequently business suffered, and eventually the creamery was destroyed by fire.

In 1894, area farmers tried again and formed the Oak Glen Creamery. A new building erected in 1895 was replaced in 1905 with a brick creamery similar in design to the one in Steele Center. The creamery operated continuously until 1978. Since then, it has changed hands and uses several times.[78]

Frank Styndl moved his family to Bixby in 1896 and opened a blacksmith shop. Frank was born in 1858 in Svinná, Bohemia, a few miles west of Česká Třebová. He was at least the fourth generation blacksmith in his family. He married Rosa Vesely from Lhotka in 1881, and they left for America in 1885. Frank operated blacksmith shops in Steele Center and River Point until 1896, when he moved to Bixby and bought a small farm. He continued as a blacksmith until about 1927, and died in 1930. Rosa died in 1933. They left three sons and five daughters.[79]

By 1897, Bixby had also acquired a wagon shop, a Presbyterian church, the Dimmick shop and home, the Zimmerman store, and the Temperance Saloon. The Bixby family lost their home and store in a January 1897 fire and left Bixby for Otter Tail County.[80]

Hope

Because the village of Hope was not founded until early in the twentieth century, beyond the primary scope of this history, I will only briefly summarize its history.

Hope developed on the western edge of the southern Czech settlement, about two miles south of Saco and ten miles south of Owatonna. The Burlington, Cedar Rapids and Northern Railroad (later the Rock Island) ran a track through the area around 1900 on the way to becoming the third railroad to service Owatonna. At the request of local farmers, a railroad stop was instituted in Hope in spring 1906 and the village grew.

The railroad initially left two boxcars on the siding as temporary stations, one for freight and one for sheltering passengers. A proper depot building soon followed.

The Speltz Company from Albert Lea built a grain elevator, coal sheds, and lumber yard on the west side of the tracks. Joseph and John Slezak built a general store on the east side across from the elevator. In 1910, the Midway Cooperative Creamery, which had begun operations in 1904 a couple of miles to the west, moved its building to Hope, locating just north of the grain elevator. Louis Schuster was appointed manager. The creamery building had an upstairs hall that for many years hosted meetings, programs and dances.

Within ten years, Anton and Louis Shuster opened another general store, a bank opened, and a new building was erected that housed a hardware store, blacksmith shop and implement dealer. The post office opened in 1916.

Lutherans in Hope met in a room above the Slezak store until the First Lutheran Church of Hope was built in 1919.

Several Czech families were closely connected with Hope, including the Srsens, Slezaks, Schusters and Hrdlichkas, Motz, Kleckers, Kubistas, Zaks and Horeckas.[81]

Blooming Prairie

The township of Blooming Prairie lay at the southeast corner of the Litomysl settlement, and at first attracted few Czech immigrants. The 1870 and 1875 censuses record only the Vincent and Anna Wencl family.

The influx of Czechs into Blooming Prairie Township occurred between 1875 and 1880. The 1880 census records 22 families with origins in Bohemia living in Blooming Prairie. Nearly all were farmers living in the township rather than the village. Their farms were located on the western edge of the township, next to Summit Township, and they were essentially the eastern fringe of the Litomysl settlement. The only non-farmer Czech resident of the township was Frank Schisler, recorded as a tailor.

The list of businesses in Blooming Prairie village in the 1879 plat book included no Czechs. However, the 1892–1893 county directory lists several Schislers living and working in the village. F.J. and John Schisler ran the Schisler and Co. livery business, and Frank Schisler was still a tailor. V. Schisler is a partner with E. Morton in a hardware and farm implement business, and F.J. Schisler apparently was a jeweler. The movement of Czechs into town continued as the twentieth century began.[82]

North Hall of Catholic Workman Lodge, Litomysl, 1935.
Courtesy of Steele County Historical Society

7

Czech Lodges and Organizations

FREETHINKERS

The period between the end of the Civil War and the beginning of the First World War was the golden age of freethinkers in America. The father of the American movement was Revolutionary War firebrand Thomas Paine, who later during the French Revolution wrote a manifesto titled *The Age of Reason*. Atheists and agnostics combined with Christians from liberal or noncomformist groups such as Unitarians, Baptists, and Methodists to fight the establishment of religion in the American Constitution, which they feared would establish Episcopalian or another denomination at the expense of smaller groups. Some smaller Christian groups had come to America to escape persecution by the established church in England, and feared a repetition of persecution in their new home.

Freethinkers and religious liberals were prominent in the abolitionist movement before the Civil War, when southern churches staunchly defended slavery as good for society, and larger northern churches avoided the issue because of its divisiveness.

After the Civil War, Unitarians, Quakers and Universalists joined freethinkers to push for women's suffrage, which was opposed or ignored by major Christian denominations. The more established churches argued, based on tradition and the writings of St. Paul, that women should be absent from the public sphere, which included voting.[1]

European freethinkers began arriving in America in considerable numbers following the failed 1848 revolutions in Europe. Many of the German refugees from a failed attempt to replace the Prussian king with a democratic government were unchurched liberals who brought their attitudes to America. As we saw in chapter 2, some of the earliest Czech immigrants were freethinkers who settled in Milwaukee, Chicago and St. Louis. They started Czech organizations and newspapers in America that later developed national followings.

The Slovanska Lipas described in chapter 2 were the earliest American organizations for Czech immigrants. They were intended for all Czechs, but since Catholics tended to center their lives around their churches, in time the Lipas became dominated by freethinkers. At conventions in 1866 and 1868 attempts were made without success to unite all the Lipas. For unchurched Czechs, 1860 to 1870 was the decade of the Lipa. In the following decade, many local organizations merged with local C.S.P.S. lodges. The Owatonna Lipa was more successful than most, and survived into the twentieth century before merging with the Owatonna C.S.P.S. lodge.[2]

For freethinking Czechs the 1870s were dominated by the Freethinker Society, an organization modeled on the German Freie Gemeinde. Several freethinker organizations formed around the country in the 1860s and, after a call in 1870 by František Zdrůbek in Chicago's Czech newspaper *Pokrok*, united to form the national Freethinker Society. From 1870 to 1872, the society published its own newspaper, the *Voice of the Freethinkers*, under the editorship of Ladimir Klácel. The paper reported the existence of a Freethinker Society in Owatonna, but apparently it was short-lived. Srsen, writing in the 1930s, said no records of it remained at that time, and that it had probably gone out of existence after the death of Klacel in 1883.[3]

C.S.P.S.

The Czech fraternal organization C.S.P.S. (Česko-Slovanska Podporující Společnost, or Bohemian Slovanic Benevolent Society) was founded in 1854 in Jakub Mottl's St. Louis tavern (named *Berlin*). The idea was to create a social group for Czechs that also offered insurance for death and disability.

At the same time in St. Louis Father Henry Lipovský was founding the first American Czech Catholic parish, and wanted the new group to be a parish organization. The membership was split between Catholics who shared Father Lipovský's idea, and others who wanted a non-sectarian Czech organization open to all. Many who opposed affiliation with the Church did so because they resented the long history of Catholic Church support of the German power structure in Czech lands. After a stalemate of a few months, the liberals prevailed, Catholics left the organization, and it was established as a secular group.

Father Lipovský, unhappy with this outcome, strongly encouraged his parishioners to resist the new organization. The Catholic former members of the C.S.P.S. founded their own organization, and agitated against the one they had left. In addition, the C.S.P.S. was modeled on secret societies such as the Odd Fellows and Masons that Catholics had been forbidden by their church to join. As a result, at first membership growth was slow.[4]

C.S.P.S. historians point out that the constitution of the original lodge required members to believe "God was the one and only ruler of the world," and new members had to swear this oath:

> I swear to God that I will love like a brother all members of our Czech society, that I will respect and obey our rules like the holiest commandments, that I will not reveal the secrets of our brotherhood, that I am taking this oath in a sound mind and not under duress, and that I call upon God to send his most dreadful curses upon me if I break this oath! Amen![5]

Many of the C.S.P.S. founders continued attending church, and had church services at their funerals. They were not atheists, but were opposed to the power of the Catholic Church in political life.[6]

The original $2 initiation fee for a new member was quickly lowered to $1.25. Monthly dues were 50 cents. The fraternal benefits were a weekly sick benefit of $2.00, soon raised to $2.50. When a member died, the society paid $20 for funeral expenses and a monthly widow's benefits of $5 until the widow died or remarried. When the widow died, the society paid a funeral benefit of $10 for her burial expenses. Only men were allowed to be members of the C.S.P.S. (see history of the J.C.D. later in this chapter.) Over time the types and amounts of the benefits and monthly fees changed due to inflation, increase in number of members, and financial solvency of the organization.

Other Czech fraternal organizations in other American cities with large numbers of Czech immigrants were content serving only individuals in their home cities. C.S.P.S. was the first such organization to expand around the country. In 1870 a second chapter was founded in the large Czech community in Cleveland. In rapid succession, new lodges were formed in Collinsville, Illinois and Pittsburgh, Pennsylvania. The Pittsburgh lodge wanted to name itself Jan Hus, after the radical church reformer of the 1400s. However, the Supreme Lodge in St. Louis feared the name would generate dissension within its membership or make Catholics feel unwelcome, and persuaded the lodge to take the name Čechie instead.

The organization had expanded to five lodges by 1874 and thirteen lodges by 1876. Most lodges were dominated by freethinkers, and some were more radical than the St. Louis Supreme Lodge. At the 1876 national convention, God was removed from the member's oath. The oath now began "I pledge this oath to my lodge" and ended with the phrase "and I guarantee this with my untainted honor."

In addition to changes in the oath, C.S.P.S. changed its official newspaper. The previous official paper (the Czech *New York News*) had gone out of business, and in 1877 C.S.P.S. chose the Cleveland weekly *Dennice Novověku (New World Journal)*. The *Journal* was edited by Vaclav Šnajdr, widely known as an excellent journalist. However, the paper's freethinker tendencies offended some conservative lodges in western states who wrote to complain.

Despite these moves, the attempt to keep C.S.P.S. inclusive for all Czechs continued at the 1883 national convention in Milwaukee. Although most members were freethinkers, and the leading rationalist publication was the lodge's official journal, religious and political discussions were strictly forbidden at meetings. The organization encouraged tolerance and understanding of all views.[7]

Another effect of the organization's tilt toward freethinkers was the call by the Czech Catholic newspaper *Hlas* for a Catholic fraternal organization to compete with C.S.P.S. This organization would offer benefits like those of C.S.P.S. to Catholics who would not have to belong to a "suspect" organization. The result was formation of the Czech Central Roman Catholic Society whose founding convention created ten lodges with 538 members. (More on this organization later)

The attitude of the Catholic Church toward the C.S.P.S. and several other Czech fraternal organizations is summed up in an article in the *Catholic Encyclopedia of 1907*, "The Bohemians of the United States":

> This organization is chiefly responsible for the loss of faith among many Bohemians of this country, having enticed thousands of well-meaning people to join its ranks under the pretext of strict neutrality in religious matters. By association with freethinkers and under other evil influences, thousands grew lukewarm in the performance of their religious duties and finally lost their faith entirely. This organization is atheistic in spirit and propagates atheism amongst its members.[8]

The *New World Journal* (in 1877) and the Slovanská Lípa society paper *Pokrok* (in 1878) issued a call for all Czech benevolent organizations around the United States to unite with C.S.P.S., and many responded. By the 1878 convention, C.S.P.S. had grown to 33 lodges with 1,446 members, and by 1880 had reached 66 lodges and 3,500 members. This explosive growth would continue through the 1880s, as well.[9]

C.S.P.S. Hall in Owatonna, today.
Michael Wolesky

C.S.P.S. COMES TO OWATONNA[10]

The spurt in new C.S.P.S. lodges around the country reached Minnesota in 1876 with the formation of the St. Paul Lodge No. 12. In 1878 it was joined by Lodge No. 30 in New Prague, and in 1880 by Lodge No. 55 in Winona.

The wave swept into Owatonna later in 1880. Eight Steele County Czechs who felt the need for a social organization with mutual protective benefits met at the farm of Anton Kovar south of Owatonna on November 14. The group, according to the 1887 Steele County history, was Anton Zajic-Donato, Joseph Srsen, Wencl Kovar, L.L. Marek, Joseph Cepelak, Frank J. Seykora, Eduard Broz and Joseph F. Racek. They decided to form a C.S.P.S. lodge in Owatonna, Lodge No. 67, named Minnesota. The inaugural meeting was held January 15, 1881, in the Odd Fellows Hall on Owatonna's Morehouse block. Members of St. Paul's Grand Lodge were present to receive the charter.

Elected as the first slate of officers were: President, Anton Zajic-Donato; Vice President, Joseph Kubat; Secretary, Joseph Srsen; Financial Secretary, John Wavrin; Treasurer, Wencl Kovar; Guide, Joseph Kaplan; Sentries, Frank Srsen and Frank Seykora.

A dance held along with the meeting to commemorate the occasion was the first of many social and cultural gatherings by the lodge over the next hundred plus years.

Grand Celebration Ball.
The Grand Celebration Ball given by the Bohemian Slavonian Benevolent Society occurred at Germania Hall last Saturday evening and nearly two hundred couples were in attendance. The gathering contained many Bohemians from the country who tripped the light fantastic as nimbly as any of their City brethren. Many of those in attendance were past middle life, whose hair had begun to silver by the severity of the winters of more than half a century; but they seemed to enjoy themselves as well as any of the young folks. Anthony Picha, of St. Paul, Grand Master of the Society for the State of Minnesota, made an able speech in the Bohemian language which was well received and enthusiastically applauded. A song was sung in that language to the great delight of all present. The music by Holden and Theimer's string band was pronounced good. A couple of couples fell down in the merry dance but got up as nimbly as they fell none the worse of the incidental slip. Prof. Donato called the meeting to order and introduced the Grand Master. The evening's pleasure was unalloyed and everything passed off pleasantly. The gallops were the most admired dances of the evening and were performed in an artistic and scientific manner.[11]

During the early years the lodge rented the Odd Fellows Hall for their monthly meetings. Attendance was encouraged by penalizing members 25 cents for every meeting missed. In 1887, annual dues were $5 per member and the charge for new members ranged from $5 to $15. Benefits were $3 per week for sick members and a payment of $1,000 upon a member's death. Membership in 1887 stood at 31. Officers that year were: Ambassador, Joseph W. Kaplan; President, Alois L. Simon; Vice President, John Dusek; Secretary, Joseph H. Soukup; Financier, Frank Horak; Treasurer, John Pichner; Guide, Joseph Kubat; Outside Guide, Joseph Svir; Inside Guide, Joseph F. Wavrin.

In 1890 the lodge acquired a library of Czech books and reading material, apparently the Slovanska Lipa collection mentioned in chapter 2. Membership had climbed to 59 by 1892, and members decided to use some of the $885 held in the treasury to buy several dozen pairs of white gloves.[12]

C.S.P.S. lodges engaged in a great deal of colorful ritual, particularly in the nineteenth century as was the norm at the time for fraternal lodges of all stripes. There were passwords, banners, signs of recognition, and several degrees of membership, each coming with a different colored sash upon its attainment. After six months of membership a new member could reach the first degree, shown by a white sash worn across the chest. After another three months the member was eligible to become a second degree member with a red sash. After three more months he was eligible to reach third degree membership with a blue sash, provided he had served as an officer for a full year or attended every meeting for a full year and owed the lodge no money. The colors were said to represent the three eras of Bohemia: white represented the coming of the Czech forefathers to Bohemia, red the history of the Hussite religious reform movement, and blue was symbolic of the Czech nationalistic awakening.[13]

Degrees of membership could only be awarded by the Supreme Lodge. Each degree was associated with certain virtues. The first, or white, degree taught members to be pure, truthful, strive for perfection, and avoid foul habits such as excessive drinking. The second, or red degree, inculcated love of the member's fellow men. The third, or blue degree, emphasized the practice of true brotherhood.[14]

As the organization grew members wanted their own lodge building. And, as Owatonna lacked a good theater, members decided the new building would also contain a theater.

In 1896 a committee was organized to find a site and money was raised from loans, contributions, fundraising dinners, dances, and donated labor. Rosalie Simek, the elderly sister of local Czech pioneer Anton Simek, donated $1,018 to the cause. The new building was opened that year with a dance that raised $254. The building, made of red sandstone and brick at a cost of $24,000, still stands along North Cedar Street in Owatonna. It became known as Auditorium Hall.

The building was finished in 1896 and stood 44 x 120 feet, with three stories. Over the street level store, in the front of the second floor, there is a meeting room 19 x 41 feet, with a hall and a room for board meetings and a library consisting of several hundred bound books. On the third floor there is a dining room. The main theater hall with balcony extends to a third floor loft and holds 700 people. The stage is spacious and outfitted for all purposes. Under the stage are two large closets. On the left arch of the stage is an oil painting of a group of pioneers in a wooded nook, and on the right side is the castle of Karluv Tyn. Both paintings were done by Frantisek Vesely to show the village green in a Czech village.[15]

The state C.S.P.S. convention was held there the next year, 1897, with 240 members participating.

Other organizations also held events in the meeting area. There was a bar in the back of the lodge hall and a projection on the top of the building accommodated the screen for the stage.

C.S.P.S lodges had meetings, dinners and dances, and dramatic and musical performances by its own members and by visiting groups of C.S.P.S. or other performers. For example, even as late as 1931, a group of Z.C.B.J. performers from St. Ansgar, Iowa presented a four-act comedy in Czech in Auditorium Hall.

Early lodge meetings usually featured singing. There were songs for opening and closing meetings and for initiation of new members. The lyrics were written by lodge members and set to the tunes of Czech folk songs familiar to everyone.[16]

The Owatonna lodge had its own musical band. An undated photo of the group shows John Pichner, John Wavrin, Joe Belina, Henry Spatenka, Louis Deml, Joe Martinek, Walter Kaplan, Ed Pichner and Victor Kaplan standing with their instruments in front of Auditorium Hall.

The Owatonna lodge followed the common C.S.P.S. practice of running a Czech language school, usually on Sundays during the summer. Earlier Czech classes at the District 23 schoolhouse were moved to Auditorium Hall after its construction.

In the early days meetings were also held on Sundays. City and county directories for 1899 and 1915–1916 list meetings of the C.S.P.S. as on the second Sunday of each month at 1 p.m.

Since many members were not affiliated with churches, weddings and funerals were performed in lodge meeting rooms. For the unchurched, a ceremony called the naming of the baby served in place of baptism. Members delivered eulogies at the cemetery for the burial of deceased members.

Nationally, the Bohemian National Cemetery Association was closely related to, but not part of, the C.S.P.S. The cemetery organization was founded by Chicago C.S.P.S. members in 1877, and many C.S.P.S. members and officers were also members and officers of the cemetery association. The same relationship existed between the Owatonna lodge and the local Bohemian National Cemetery.[17]

The feature that set the C.S.P.S. apart from earlier Czech organizations was the payment of sick and death benefits. A listing of claims for death benefits from the C.S.P.S. (later C.S.A.) in the approximately forty-nine years from September 1897 through mid-December 1946 shows 83 claims by Owatonna members.[18]

Auditorium Hall was a center of Czech culture for decades. It remained the site of the Czech language classes until they were discontinued during World War I. It hosted Czech language lectures, performances and entertainments by the C.S.P.S. or the Z.C.B.J. well into the 1930s. Frank Moravec, writing in 1932, said he and his fellow immigrants learned nothing about Czech history in Europe, but only discovered it by reading Czech books and magazines in America. He remembered some of the speakers, musicians and theater groups that performed in the Czech hall, and felt the activities at the hall kept local Czechs connected with the larger Czech community.[19]

C.S.D.P.J.

Owatonna was home to a local branch of the Czech Slovanic Workers Benevolent Society (Česka Slovanská Dělnická Podporující Jednota, or C.S.D.P.J.). This organization was founded in Minnesota in 1891, and the Owatonna Lodge 8 Ravenost was in existence by 1899 when Frank Meixner was President, and Anton Wanous was Secretary. In 1915, D. Marek was President, Anton Wanous was Secretary, and Frank Truhlar was Treasurer. Meetings were held in Auditorium Hall on the second Sunday of each month. The C.S.D.P.J. national organization was always much smaller than the C.S.P.S. (763 members in 1905 compared to 20,000 for C.S.P.S.), and the lodge was absorbed by the local Z.C.B.J. lodge around 1930 (more on that organization below).

Z.C.B.J.

The rapid growth of C.S.P.S. in the 1870s was largely in major eastern cities. Czech workers in Chicago, Cleveland, New York and other cities belonged to local lodges, many of which joined the C.S.P.S. during this decade. Many of their members were older and had begun

Blooming Prairie Z.C.B.J. members 1900: Front row from left: Frank Ruzek Sr., Alois Srsen, John Wanous Sr., Anton Wencl, John Jansa, Rudolph Motl, Frank Pechacek and Alois Renchin. Second row from left: Vincent Wencl, Joe Betlach, Frank Skalicky, Mrs. Frank Pechacek, Joe Pechacek, Mrs. Frank Ruzek, Wencl Horsky and Mrs. Agnes Moravec.
Back row from left: Joe Pirkl, Mrs. John Wanous, Frank Ruzek Jr., John Wanous Jr., Amelia Cole, Mrs. John Jansa, Mrs. Vincent Wencl, Mrs. Paukert, Rose Benes, Mrs. Frank Vavra and Mrs. Joe Betlach. Courtesy of Steve Wencl

to suffer poor health. Industrial and sanitation conditions in these large cities led to tuberculosis in particular. In the three years between the C.S.P.S. national conventions of 1883 and 1886, 150 male members died, 52 from tuberculosis; and spousal benefits were paid for 125 wives who died, 32 of them from tuberculosis.

The former Owatonna Z.C.B.J. hall, 2006. Courtesy of Don Wolesky

Beginning around 1880, younger and more rural members in recently settled western states began to push for reform. They felt that potential members should be screened for medical problems before being allowed to join, there should be an upper age limit for new members, a reserve fund should be created, and women should be allowed to join as full members.

Most of all, the western delegates wanted member dues based on age. They felt that young, healthy workers in Texas, Nebraska and other rural states were being taken advantage of if they paid the same dues as older and sicker city workers in the east. Up to the 1880s, monthly dues varied depending on how much the mortuary fund had paid out in benefits the month before; all members were charged the same amount in any given month. Western delegates felt that regular monthly dues based on age, and backed by a reserve fund to buffer against many claims in a short time, was a more financially sound and fairer system.

In addition, western delegates often were more socially conservative and did not care for the decided tilt toward rationalist or freethinker philosophy of C.S.P.S. during this period, or the number of socialists and radicals in some eastern lodges. They viewed the degrees of membership and ceremonies as pointless and elitist.[20]

While C.S.P.S. growth in the 1870s had been largely in the east, growth in the 1880s and 1890s was primarily in western states where the number of Czech immigrants kept rising. Thus, during this period the agitation for reform grew. However, apportionment of delegates to the national conventions ensured that New York, Illinois and Ohio combined had a majority of delegates and the conventions resisted any changes. A recession that started in 1894 and lasted several years worsened the crisis as members and the national lodge lost funds.

Finally, during the summer of 1897, lodges and members in western states began to break away from the C.S.P.S. to form the Západní Česko-Bratrská Jednota (Western Czech Fraternal Association), or Z.C.B.J. Core tenets of the new organization mirrored many of the membership requirements championed for years by the western C.S.P.S. lodges:

All members paid premiums based on age, along with their local lodge dues;
Women were accepted as fully insured members;
A reserve fund was created;
A medical director was employed to examine applicants.

By the end of 1897, the C.S.P.S. had lost 42 lodges with 832 members to the new organization.[21]

The Owatonna C.S.P.S. lodge did not break away from the parent organization. It continued to thrive, but it was joined by lodges of the new organization, the Z.C.B.J.

The southern Czech settlement around Litomysl had no fraternal lodges at this time, except the Catholic lodge affiliated with Holy Trinity Church. By 1880 the Czechs of Blooming Prairie had a reading society and meeting hall, but it was destroyed by wind and never replaced.[22] After that, freethinkers and the unchurched had nowhere to go for fellowship unless they traveled to Owatonna's C.S.P.S. hall. Some residents of the area decided that needed to change.

A group of men and women met with John R. Lukes on March 18, 1900, to organize Lodge number 83 of the Z.C.B.J. Charter members were: Frank Ruzek Sr., Mrs. Frank Ruzek , Frank Ruzek Jr.. Alois Srsen, John Wanous Sr., Mrs. John Wanous, John Wanous Jr., Anton Wencl, John Jansa, Mrs. John Jansa, Rudolph Motl, Frank Pechacek, Mrs.

Frank Pechacek, Alois Renchin, Vincent Wencl, Mrs. Vincent Wencl, Joe Betlach, Mrs. Joe Betlach, Frank Skalicky, Joe Pechacek, Wencl Horsky, Mrs. Agnes Moravec, Joe Pirkl, Amelia Cole, Mr. Paukert, Rose Benes, Mrs. Frank Vavra.

The first officers were President John Wanous, Vice President Joseph Subart, Recording Secretary Anton Wencl, Financial Secretary C.V. Wencl, Treasurer Jan Jansa, Guide Rudolf Motl, Inner Guard Alois Prokopec, and Outer Guard Wencl Horsky. Trustees were Joseph Subart, Frank Ruzek and Joseph Betlach.

At first they met in Blooming Prairie in a room rented from Dr. Cooly and held social events in C.V. Wencl's granary. In November 1901 members decided to build a lodge hall to be located at the northeast corner of section 30 in Blooming Prairie Township. Bids were solicited for the lumber and the winning bid was $410 from Solberg Lumber. At a special meeting on March 2, 1902, Building Committee Chairman Frank Pechacek outlined the design of the new building: it would be 30 ft. x 56 ft. and under one roof. Size and location of the bar would be decided later. Members accepted the design, as verified by Secretary Anton Wencl, and the following month members began building the new hall.

The hall held its opening ceremony on June 8, 1902, with music arranged by Anton Wencl, Alois Srsen and Frank Pechacek. In fall a new $25 stove was added and a 28 ft. x 70 ft. stable was built for members' horses. The following spring the hall was painted, and maple trees donated by Jan Jansa and willows donated by Frank Ruzek were planted by Wencl Horsky.[23]

This hall became known as South Hall and for many years was a center of social life in the southern part of Steele County. Lodge 83 of the Z.C.B.J. merged with the Owatonna Z.C.B.J. lodge in February 1967. The old lodge building was still standing as a private home in 2007.

In a 1938 letter Mrs. J.R. Popelok of the Blooming Prairie Z.C.B.J. told Milan Jerabek, a Czech American writing a doctoral thesis on Minnesota Czechs, that the Blooming Prairie lodge ran a Czech language school from 1906 to 1908. The classes were taught by Frances Vavra and the textbooks were Čítanky (reader) numbers one and two. Mrs. Popelok said the peak membership for the lodge was in 1914.[24]

Z.C.B.J. came to Owatonna two years after the Blooming Prairie lodge was founded. Owatonna lodge, no. 127, was chartered on October 5, 1902, with these twenty six charter members: Alois Horak, Katerina Horak, Wencl Krahulec, Frank Meixner, Adolf Pechacek, Joseph B. Skalicky, Joseph D. Rysavy, Edward Srsen, Joseph A. Stransky, Anezka (Agnes) Stransky, Antonia Wavrin, Frank Jasan, Otto A. Kubat, John Pavek, John Pichner, Marie Pichner, Frank Smersh, Anton W. Soukup, William Stransky, Frank

Truhlar, Wencl Shimpach, Anna B. Kubat, Frances Srsen, Alois Spinler, Rosalie Spinler and Emilie Smersh. The first officers were President Joseph A. Stransky, Vice President Rosalie Spinler, Recording Secretary Frank Smersh, Financial Secretary Joseph F. Martinek and Treasurer Frank Meixner.

By December 31, 1902, membership stood at 32 and the lodge had $27,000 worth of insurance built up. Meetings were held on the upper floors of the C.S.P.S. Auditorium Hall in downtown Owatonna until 1939, when members decided to build their own lodge hall 2½ miles south of Owatonna.

Members donated their labor to build the lodge and women of the lodge donated food for a banquet to raise funds. Janet Iverson remembers as a very young girl going to the site when the lodge was being built. Her grandparents, Joseph and Anna Wolesky, contracted terrible cases of poison ivy while clearing brush for the building. She remembers visiting her grandmother shortly after the brush clearing and finding her wrapped in gauze.

The lodge hall, a two story building at the base of a hill, was ready for use by summer 1942. An ad in the Owatonna newspaper announced the opening dance on Saturday, May 23 for the Hillside Ballroom on the Z.C.B.J. park and picnic grounds. Jerry Rypka and the Melody Kings supplied new and old time music. Admission was 25 cents until 9:30, and then was raised to 40 cents. The ad also mentions free movies every Wednesday night and another dance the following weekend, May 30, by Whoopee John and his orchestra.

A dedication ceremony seems to have been held in late July or early August 1942. A letter from the Supreme Secretary of the organization to Zdenka Rypka, dated July 22, 1942, discusses the standard way to dedicate a lodge hall. According to the letter, the president of the building committee usually dedicates the hall and then hands it over to the local lodge president. The writer says he will not be able to attend the ceremony.

The lodge hall became known locally as the Alphabet Lodge. Janet Iverson remembers many activities at the hall during her youth in the 1940s. She often accompanied her parents and grandparents who were active members. Trap shooting held on weekends on the hill behind the building attracted many Isaak Walton League members. The shooters stood on the ledge and children sat in bunkers in the ravine, coming out to reload the traps between rounds. There was a shack where shotgun shells and soft drinks were sold, and the children who set up the traps were rewarded with cold pop.

Janet recalls outdoor movies at the lodge in the days before Owatonna's drive-in theater opened. A projector was set up on the back end of a truck and a big sheet hung for a screen. These were old fashioned movies, some of them silent films. The ladies of the lodge made popcorn and ice cream cones—a nickel for a big double-dip cone. It was a family affair, parents and children sitting on blankets thrown on the ground.

*Owatonna Sokol Lodge 1912 commemorative photos.
Courtesy of Steele County Historical Society*

She also remembers daytime, weekend events called "doings" when large meals were eaten on the ground floor of the building while people danced to a polka band upstairs.[25]

The lodge building eventually became a church and later a private home.

SOKOL

The Sokol (Czech for Falcon) organization was founded in Bohemia in 1862 by Dr. Miroslav Tyrs to revive the ancient Greek ideal of combining the beauty of the body and the mind. The *American Sokol* issue for January of 2006 described the aims:

The main element of Tyr's philosophy is a free individual constantly striving to develop to the fullest all his potential strengths and abilities. This requires that the individual remain active both in a physical and mental sense throughout life and acquire a way of life in which physical and mental health, guided by high moral values, are of utmost importance. Such a life style may be best achieved within a fraternal community of like-minded individuals imbued by the same lofty ideals, enabling them to create a strong, cohesive society; its combined strength reflects the strength of its individual members and results in a continuous improvement of conditions for the development of the individual. Basic to this philosophy is the belief in man as a free individual and in the development of decent life in a free national community.

The Sokol's specialty for physical conditioning is gymnastics. Large national and international gatherings called Slets that featured gymnastic demonstrations and contests were (and are still) held every few years. The organization is humanistic and backed Czech nationalism in the 19th century. Sokol organizations formed in other Slavic nations such as Bulgaria, Poland, Russia, Serbia and Yugoslavia. The Catholic Church listed Sokol as one of the organizations that Catholics should avoid.

The organization spread to America and became popular among Czech Americans. A Sokol lodge was founded in Owatonna in 1909 (Kovar says 1904). Karel Srsen's brief history of the Steele County Czechs says that for a few years membership grew and the lodge was very active, but during World War I its purpose was forgotten, membership dwindled, and the lodge was discontinued before 1932. The 1915–1916 Owatonna and Steele County Directory lists Karel Srsen as President of the Sokol. Other officers were Secretary Walter Rypka and Treasurer A.J. Soukup. Meetings at that time were held on the second Thursday of every month at Auditorium Hall.[26]

FRATERNAL ORGANIZATIONS FOR WOMEN

Only men were allowed to join the C.S.P.S when it was founded in 1854. After the Civil War, however, the women's suffrage movement began to gain ground. Western states passed community property laws that greatly increased the property rights of married women. As traditional attitudes toward the role of women in society changed it became only a matter of time before C.S.P.S. would face the question of admitting women as members.

This question was brought up at the 1878 convention in Cleveland by the organization's

J.C.D. lodge, members 1894. Courtesy of Ann Pichner

Secretary, but was tabled without discussion by President Vaclav Rychlik. The apparent reason was that Rychlik's wife Caroline had founded a Czech women's organization in 1870 called the Unity of Czech Ladies (Jednota Ceska Dam, or J.C.D.), and did not want it absorbed by the C.S.P.S. When the question came up again at the 1880 Chicago convention, Caroline Rychlik submitted a letter on behalf of the J.C.D. asking that C.S.P.S. not admit women members because of the harm it would do to J.C.D.

The solution chosen was to continue restricting membership to men, but institute a death benefit of $250 for the death of a member's wife in addition to the $750 benefit for the death of a member. This was called the Gentlemen and Ladies Agreement and remained in force until 1904. Women finally were allowed to join the C.S.P.S. in 1909.[27]

The J.C.D. spread to other cities and became a national organization. In 1893, a lodge was established in Owatonna to "work for the progress and betterment of the whole community." Lodge 63 "Bohuslava Rajska," was founded in a schoolroom on August 27, 1893, and named after the Czech nationalist, teacher, school founder and poet Antonie Reissová, who had assumed the patriotic name Bohuslava Rajská. The nine founding members were Anna and F. Fibigar, Anna Kokaisel, Anna Soukup, Anna Dusek, Anna Kaplan, Anna Truhlar, Frances Rypka and Marie Skopp. Within two years, membership stood at twenty.[28]

In the early years it met at 1:00 p.m. on the second Saturday of each month in the C.S.P.S. Auditorium Hall. In 1899 the President was Frances Rypka, and Secretary was Anna Kokaisel. Officers in 1915 were Mrs. J.S. Stransky as President and Anna Tomsche as Vice President. In 1930 membership stood at 83. In 1977 the lodge merged with Owatonna's C.S.A. lodge (C.S.A. is the successor organization to the C.S.P.S.)

Another Czech women's lodge founded in Owatonna was the S.P.J. (Sesterská Podporující Jednota) or C.S.P.J. (Česko-Sesterská Podporující Jednota), the Czech Ladies Benevolent Society. This was also a national women's lodge founded as the women's adjunct of a men's lodge (the C.S.B.P.J.); both originated in Cleveland. The Owatonna lodge, number 27 Ratolest Svornosti, was in existence by 1899 and holding meetings on Sunday afternoons at Auditorium Hall. Its President that year was Anna Kubat and Secretary was Barbara Rypka. In 1915 the meetings were held the first Saturday of each month at the hall, and officers were Anna Tomsche as President, Anna Simon as Secretary, and Marie Motte as Treasurer. Nationally this organization was much smaller than the J.C.D. (4,000 members in 1905 compared to 13,000 for the J.C.D.) The Owatonna lodge still had 49 members in the early 1930s. The entire national organization merged with the C.S.A. in 1948 and the Owatonna lodge became part of the Owatonna C.S.A. lodge.

CATHOLIC LODGES

The success of C.S.P.S., and the allure of its insurance scheme to Catholic Czechs, led nine Catholic parish societies around the country to unite in 1877 to form the Bohemian Roman Catholic First Central Union (Česko-Rímska Katolická První Ustřední Jednota). This organization provided a Catholic alternative to nonsectarian benevolent societies. As it grew it increased its benefits, in part to compete with the benefits offered by the C.S.P.S.

Catholic First Central Union had a branch at Holy Trinity Church in Litomysl, the St. Joseph Society, formed in 1883, as well as one at Sacred Heart Church in Owatonna, St. Ivan's Lodge, founded in 1889 (for more detail, see the sections on these churches in chapter 6 and the epilogue).

Groups quickly split from the Catholic First Central Union as they had from the C.S.P.S., and for some of the same reasons—arguments over dues, age and sectionalism. One of those splits came in the 1890s when forty-eight lodges departed to form the Western Bohemian Catholic Union. Both Litomysl's St. Joseph Society and Sacred Heart's St. Ivan's Lodge left the old Catholic union and joined this new one.

Another Catholic fraternal organization, this time born in Minnesota, was the final home of the two Steele County Catholic Czech lodges. In 1890 Catholics of New Prague began organizing a St. Joseph Society to provide life insurance to members. The following year a meeting in St. Paul of the Minnesota branch of the Czech First Central Union founded a life insurance organization that settled on the name Catholic Workman (Katolický Dělnik in Czech). The St. Joseph Society of New Prague, involved in the formation of the new organization, became Lodge 1 of the Catholic Workman. The Litomysl St. Joseph's Lodge became part of the Catholic Workman in 1904. St. Ivan's Lodge at Sacred Heart finally became part of the Catholic Workman in 1930 when the entire Western Bohemian Catholic Union merged with Catholic Workman.[29]

Joe Wolesky as a child in Bohemia, with his parents, Joseph and Frantiska Wolesky, and grandmother. Photograph taken about 1884. Michael Wolesky

Epilogue

FAST FORWARD

In the period from 1881 to America's entry into the First World War in 1917, the local Czech community grew and consolidated. Immigrants continued to arrive, though at a diminishing rate, as second and third generation Czech-Americans reached adulthood and made their marks in the new land.

It is not my intention to cover the period after 1880 in great detail. This last chapter will briefly summarize the subsequent progress of the Steele County Czech settlements to the dawn of the twenty-first century.

The Stories of Selected Later Immigrants
Among the later immigrants were my forebears, the **Wolesky** (Volesky) brothers. Born in Zhoř, a small village in the hills between the cities of Česká Třebová and Litomyšl, both brothers came to the United States at the age of fourteen, Joseph in 1892 and Frank, ten years later, in 1902.

Joe was invited by his uncle, Joseph Coufal, to come to America. Joe later admitted that he was homesick when he first arrived, and would have returned to his home village if he could have paid for the return voyage. After a few months he adjusted to life in America and settled in. He first lived in Bixby and worked for area farmers, including P. Reichstetter, William Boyle and Christ Larson. In January 1894, he became an assistant butter maker at the Steele Center Creamery and decided butter-making was to be his career. He entered the butter maker course at the University of Minnesota Agricultural College in St. Anthony. After graduation he returned to Steele County and helped form the River Point Creamery in March 1899. He worked as a butter maker at the River Point, Steele Center and Cooleyville creameries until 1917, when he moved into Owatonna, apparently to run a Grant automobile dealership and repair shop with his brother Frank.

In the same year that he helped form the River Point Creamery, Joseph Wolesky married Anna Schuster (Šustr). The Schusters were from Babice, in southern Bohemia. Anna's grandparents and their younger children apparently came to America around 1877. Some of the older children followed their parents to America. One was Frank Schuster, married to Anna Yeshatek; these were Anna's parents. They came to America in 1884 with three children (and a fourth born during the voyage). Anna was three years old at the time she left Bohemia. She married Joe Wolesky at the age of 18 in the Litomysl church.

Joe and Anna Wolesky had two sons, Louis and Joseph Jr., by the time Frank Wolesky arrived from Bohemia in 1902. Joe had paid the passage for his younger brother. Frank apparently lived at first with Joe and Anna in the River Point Creamery. He attended butter maker school in St. Anthony, and worked as a butter maker at the Lemond, Oak Glen and Summit creameries.

While working at the Summit creamery, Frank met Mathilda Kubicek. Her father, Frank Kubicek, had a farm just down the road, and owned the general store next to the creamery where Mathilda and her sister Mary clerked. Frank and Mathilda married in summer 1909 in Litomysl. Frank continued as a butter maker after they were married, including a stint in Waseca County. He partnered with his brother Joe in the Grant car dealership and repair shop in 1917 and 1918, but since he remained a butter maker, he was probably only a financial partner.

In May 1918, Joe bought out Frank's share of the car business. A couple of weeks later, the Summit Creamery burned down and Frank was out of work. He moved into Owatonna to work for the post office, where he remained until retirement. Frank and Mathilda had four sons: Al, Frank, Bob and Chuck.

Joe Wolesky ran the car repair business until at least 1920, assisted by his two older sons, Louis and Joe Jr. The Joseph Wolesky family loved machines. Joe had one of the first driver's licenses in Steele County, issued in 1906 for his 1904 curved-dash Oldsmobile. Joe. Jr. and his brother Louis built and flew two kit airplanes. Federal registration records from 1930 and 1931 have entries under Wolesky for a Velie Monocoupe 113, an enclosed cabin plane similar to Charles Lindbergh's Spirit of St. Louis, and a Pietenpohl open cockpit plane. Both models debuted in 1928. Joe Jr.'s daughter Jan Iverson remembers the Pietenpohl parked in their back yard when she was a little girl.

When Joe Wolesky Sr. left the car dealership, he became an insurance salesman for the Z.C.B.J. until his retirement. His area extended to Montana. He and Anna were very active in the Z.C.B.J., and helped construct the lodge building south of Owatonna in the late 1930s.

The Wolesky brothers lived out a characteristic part of the Czech-American experience—the split between Catholics and freethinkers. Both brothers were Catholic in their younger days, but after 1920 Joe dropped out of the Catholic Church, apparently in anger over sexual misconduct by a local Catholic priest. He eventually became an atheist and lectured on the nonexistence of God. Frank and his wife remained staunch Catholics and Frank sold insurance for the Catholic Workman Czech lodge. Even though the two brothers lived within a mile of each other, they rarely socialized. However, Joe attended Frank and Mathilda's fiftieth wedding anniversary celebration in 1959, allowing some reconciliation before Joe died in 1962.[1]

Anna Kubicek married **Joseph Svercl** in Bohemia; after he died in 1881 she married Anton Mikyska. Anna and Anton came to the U.S. in 1892 with their five children plus two children from Anna's first marriage, Joseph and Frances Svercl. The family settled in the Litomysl area.

Anna's son, young Joseph Svercl was patriotic and active in his community. He had studied to be a priest while in Bohemia, and after immigrating became active in the Holy Trinity Church in Litomysl. He and his wife Christine Hruska had eight children and farmed near Bixby. He was on the Holy Trinity Church board and an officer and frequent convention delegate for the Z.C.K.J. lodge (later the Catholic Workman). He was a skilled woodworker who built his own house, which he later converted to a workshop and bathroom, and a variety of farm buildings including a barn and a silo. He hand crafted over 300 picture frames and crucifixes, and built a large Christmas scene of Dolní Dobrouč as he remembered it. Although it took up an entire side of one room, Joseph displayed the Christmas scene annually at his home. The scene featured St. Nicholas church and tiny houses, people and animals. He even devised running water to represent the Dobrouč stream that runs through the town. Joseph also carved figures, made inlaid furniture and wove rugs.[2]

Anna's daughter Frances worked in Owatonna as cook and maid for the family of Dr. Ford, the president of Pillsbury College. Her salary of $3.50 a week was very good for a maid, but her stepfather kept her earnings, giving her only enough for clothes and necessities. She learned English and became a good cook. She married John Rysavy when she was twenty-four. Frances Buryska, the author of a local memoir, was her daughter.[3]

Joseph Rysavy, a weaver from Dolní Dobrouč, with his wife Frances (Motl) and children Edward and Helen came to America in 1892. They left Bohemia to escape a hard life and diminishing livelihood in Bohemia, their trip financed by a loan from friends or family in America. They settled on a wet twenty-acre farm near Bixby in Blooming Prairie Township, and had five more children, all daughters.

Their son **Edward Rysavy** was drafted into the army near the end of the First World War. He shipped out to Europe, but the war ended before he saw action. Back in the United States, he became a carpenter, and made the acquaintance of Agnes Rajnet, a resident of Dolní Dobrouč, through Francis Paukert. Francis, a family friend, was from Dolní Dobrouč, but was in the United States studying for the priesthood. He would eventually become the pastor of Holy Trinity Church in Litomysl. Francis acted as matchmaker between Edward in America and Agnes in the new nation of Czechoslovakia.

Agnes Rajnet was the daughter of Frank Rajnet and Agnes (Rysavy) Rajnet. Before the war, she lived in a brown brick house in Dolní Dobrouč with her father and brother Rudolf and his wife Anna. The house was small and Agnes slept in the hayloft. Her bed was between the hay and the straw, and in the winter her bed was sometimes covered with snow.

As a girl Agnes worked in a textile mill and later as a hired girl for a wealthy family. When World War I broke out, Agnes' father Frank and uncle Joseph were drafted, captured by the Russians, and held prisoner for several years. During the war, part of the Rajnet house was rented to a displaced Italian family. Agnes moved in with her sister Filomena, who was married to Frank Kovar, a local baker and grocer. Frank Kovar also was drafted, and Agnes and Filomena became the village bread makers for the duration of the war. When Frank Kovar returned after the war, Agnes went back to work at the textile mill.

Edward apparently courted and proposed to Agnes by mail. In 1924 he traveled to Dolní Dobrouč to marry Agnes in the church of St. Nicholas. They considered living in Czechoslovakia, but because of a shortage of lumber there was little work for carpenters. Also, Edward felt that people stared at him because he was American. Agnes' sister Filomena tried to convince her to stay in Czechoslovakia, telling her "we have America here!" Agnes responded that the Germans may have lost, but they would rise up again in twenty years. How right she was.

Edward and Agnes sailed for America in April 1925, and upon arrival moved in with Edward's parents on the Bixby farm. Their first child, Mary, was born in October of that year, and four more children followed. Later Edward built a house for his family near that of his parents.[4]

Joseph and Agnes (Milar) Petranek were both from Dolní Dobrouč. Joseph, the only son of a silk weaver, learned the trade from his father. He was a good student, and learned to play the violin and clarinet. The local priest saw his potential and selected him for further education before he was sent to the seminary to be trained for the priesthood. When his father died, Joseph discontinued his studies and began working to support his mother.

Joseph married Agnes Miller (Milar) in 1867 and they had eight children. Joseph's work included walking to Prague (a three-day walk) to sell his rolls of fabric. Joseph and Agnes could not see a bright future for their children in Bohemia and in 1883 decided to emigrate to America. Agnes' brother Frank Miller and sister (Mrs. Frank Spinler) had already settled in Steele County and wrote that they were doing well.

In Steele County, Joseph and Agnes and their children lived and worked on other people's farms until they could pay back the money they had borrowed for their passage. Once their debts were cleared, they bought a twenty acre farm near Mineral Springs Park outside of Owatonna [5]

Doctor John Habenicht was born in Bohemia and left for America in 1867. For thirty years he lived and practiced medicine in Texas, Illinois, Michigan, Nebraska, Minnesota and Maryland. He was living in New Prague, Minnesota in 1880–1881, moved to Owatonna in 1894 where he practiced medicine for fourteen months, and then moved on again. He finally settled in Chicago in 1898.[6]

Doctor Habenicht's restless travels and literary interests served him well in the great work of his life, a large *History of the Czechs in America* published in 1910. This work covers most Czech settlements in America, many in great detail. An English language translation of the work, published by the Czechoslovak Genealogical Society International in 1996, is a wealth of information on American Czechs.[7]

Wencl Chott was born in Mytov u Novych Mitrovic in 1875. He came to America in 1904, located in Minneapolis, and worked as a tailor, hat maker and painter. He married Sylvia Edna Srsen from Steele County in 1916, and they settled in Hope where their daughter Zdenka was born.

Wencl taught violin lessons and directed the choir at the First Lutheran Church in Owatonna. In 1931, he conducted a twenty-two-voice mixed chorus that sang at the 75th anniversary celebration of the Owatonna Bohemian National Cemetery. He also taught Czech language classes.[8]

Wencl Chott's niece, Karleen Chott Sheppard of St. Paul, has spent many years gathering and translating autobiographies of Minnesota Czech immigrants from several Czech American publications. This book owes a great debt to her work.

Some Steele County Czechs came to the area when a parent died and they were sent to live with relatives or friends who had settled in the county. One such case involved the Skala family. **Frank Skala** came to America around 1908. His brother Vaclav either came with him or had come to America a few years earlier. The brothers farmed in South

Dakota for a few years, but were unsuccessful due to drought. Vaclav moved on to California, where his family prospered. Frank settled in Bagley, Minnesota west of Bemidji. He seems to have had a job hauling loads with a wagon and a team of mules.

Frank met Agnes Matejcek, who was from the Owatonna area but spent a summer in Waubun, near Bagley, helping her brother on his farm. Frank and Agnes fell in love and were married in Holy Trinity Church in Litomysl in 1912. They returned to Bagley, rented a farm, and had three children before buying their own farm in the area. Their property had no house but had plenty of stones and brush that needed to be cleared.

A fourth child, Joseph, was born in 1923. A few weeks later, Agnes died from "milk leg," a circulatory problem resulting from the pregnancy. Frank Skala tried to raise the four young children by himself. The older ones took turns staying home from school to watch over young Joseph. After two years, Frank put an ad in the paper for a bride, and a woman from Cleveland, Ohio with a three-year-old daughter came in answer to the ad. They were married in 1925 and had two more children.

A year later, Frank Skala, worn down from the work of clearing the land, died of pneumonia. His recent bride now had Frank's four children from his first marriage, her daughter from her first marriage, and their two sons from their brief marriage. She was able to find relatives to raise some of Frank's children.

Young Joseph and his sister Helen were sent to Steele County to live with their great-uncle John Kubicek and his wife Josephine (Stransky) Kubicek. The household also included Josephine's bachelor brother Joseph Stransky and her widowed mother Caroline. Although Joseph and Helen were never legally adopted, the Kubiceks raised them to adulthood. Helen became Sister Immolata in the Sisters of Notre Dame. She became the family historian for the Frank Skala family and lived until July 2009.

Joseph Skala met and wooed Mary Ann Simon, who played piano in the Staska Band with her sister Marcella who played the accordion. Their first date was at a granary dance at Klecker's farm. Joseph joined the military in 1946 and served in Korea. He and Mary Ann were married when he returned to Minnesota. They farmed a Spinler farm for a time, then rented and eventually owned both the Simon farm and the John Kubicek farm that were their childhood homes. They raised eleven children.[9]

Another instance of children sent to be raised by relatives in Steele County involved the **Kabela sisters,** Sylvia and Martha. Their parents, Christina Horcky and Immanuel James Kabela (usually called James), were married in Chicago and had a son, Immanuel James. They later moved to Limon, Colorado, where James worked for the railroad. Their twin daughters Martha and Sylvia were born December 31, 1918. Christina died when the girls were three and a half years old.

James needed someone to raise his twin daughters. Rose (Horak) Haberman from Steele County had a sister in Colorado. It was this sister who helped the twin's father arrange for them to live with Rose and her husband Jacob Haberman. The twins traveled by train from Colorado to Minnesota, accompanied by a teddy bear and the pillows their father had given them so they could nap on the train. After their parting, their father was allowed only infrequent visits to their new home in Owatonna.

Jacob and Rose Haberman lived about a block from Roosevelt School in Owatonna; the property had a big garden with apple trees behind the barn. The girls remember sleeping together in a big iron bed with a board on the side to prevent them from falling out. The house had a coal furnace, and the ceilings and walls had to be cleaned of coal dust three times a year. Rose Haberman was a nurse, and the family rented rooms to ailing boarders until Rose could nurse them back to health.

One of the recuperating boarders was Adolph Bjoraker, whom Sylvia eventually married. They had four children. Adolph Bjoraker was a truck driver for the fire department before and during World War II, and built himself a steam engine and a motorcycle. After the war, he opened a sporting goods store.

Martha was twenty-seven when she married Russell Davis. They had a daughter, Rosemary, but were divorced after two years. At age thirty-two Martha married Olaf Bjoraker, who adopted Rosemary.[10]

Broadened Career Paths

The earliest settlers in Steele County, regardless of place of origin, were nearly all farmers. Life was primitive and the goal was simply to survive. In addition, most Czechs did not have enough capital, English language skills, or higher education to earn a living any other way. However, as a result of growing up in farming villages and working on the landlord's manor, they knew how to farm. Only after about 1875, when Owatonna's economic and social life matured, did some settlers move on to other occupations.

Some early immigrants who arrived as children made several career changes. Young **Frank Kubicek**, who was born in 1865 and came to America at age seven, started by helping his father farm. At age eighteen, he decided to become a musician and took lessons from Joseph Klecker. He arranged for Joseph Petranek to buy an instrument in Bohemia and bring it to him when Petranek came to America in 1883. However, after playing for a couple years, Frank decided he was too busy with other work to be a musician.

Frank rented land from his father and farmed for a year, then decided to become a photographer. He ordered the equipment and a how-to book by mail and taught himself photography. He impressed local photographer F. Mueller who offered to let Frank live with him for six months and apprentice as a photographer. Instead Frank bought the 80 acre farm from his father.

In 1896, after several years of farming, Frank bought the general store next to the Summit creamery. He operated the store and rented out the farm, then ran both the store and farm until the store burned down in 1909. In the following years, Frank farmed in North Dakota, ran a grocery store in Blooming Prairie, farmed near Stewartville, Minnesota, and was landlord of an apartment building in Rochester. He also was handyman at the Lynard's Produce Co, and caretaker at the Sacred Heart Cemetery.[11]

Albert Kaspar was born in 1853 and came to America with his parents in 1864. He taught at the country schools of Owatonna and Somerset Townships from 1873 to 1875, farmed for a few years, then moved to Owatonna in 1880 to open a general store. He operated the store, later in partnership with Joseph Matejcek, for twenty five years. Then he briefly operated a woolen mill before returning in 1905 to the farm he owned south of Owatonna (the land later became part of the Daniel Gainey estate). After farming the land for fourteen years, Albert and his wife Rosa moved into Owatonna to retire.

Albert was on the Owatonna city council from the third ward from 1890 to 1892, and then served as city treasurer for two years. He helped create the municipal water system and the fountain in the middle of Central Park.[12]

Second generation Czech immigrants had even more options. They grew up familiar with the language and society, and with an American education. The story of one such Minnesota Czech, **Joseph Kovar**, illustrates the career option of industrial entrepreneur:

> Before my father bought the new farm, my parents arranged that the old farm would belong to me for a certain sum which I was to pay to my sisters and brothers. . . . When in my sixteenth year, I became a renter, so that I would be working for my father, I discovered that it was no longer a productive farm. I worked hard, and I knew how, but to no avail. . .
>
> At the age of seventeen I married. When I had my third harvest in stacks, there was a lot less of it than previous years. . . .
>
> When we finished the second year, I still had about 200 bushels left over. . . . So you see, dear readers, what a different method of working the soil can do. Then we got along well. In about two years, I made a planter for potatoes which I used for five years with good results. . . . A number of people looked at the potato digger I had made, but it never occurred to me to apply for a patent. . .

> When I had my 200-acre farm almost out of debt, the devil prompted me to exchange it for a mill. I did not understand milling. I had no experience in milling, and not nearly enough capital. After four years, I had a fire and inadequate insurance, and ended up $3,000 in debt. I had enough opportunities to relocate there on good farms, and in a few years I had made up for what I lost.

Later Kovar moved to Wisconsin:

> There I invented my harrow with spring teeth, which helped me a lot, and there I also spent ten years of my life. After ten years of drudgery, I had the chance to go back to a farm of 480 acres, which I bought on contract for deed, another mistake. The farm had been rented for years, and not well cared for, especially in the last two years. . . . The neighbors laughed at me because I was investing in a farm that was not even mine.

After Kovar has been on this farm for six years, the owner decides to sell it, even though Kovar still has four years on his contract. Kovar moved to a smaller farm.

> When the grain was about 18 inches tall, prominent people began coming to our place to inspect my yield, mainly the barley, which was so robust that when I was especially diligent, I cut 20 acres in 5 days and harvested 65 bushels per acre. . . . Neighbors asked me to make them a harvester like mine and I told them yes, if you underwrite me. I was seeking a patent, and when I went to order the materials, I had 39 subscribers. . . . Now I had more work making harrows, so I sold the farm and started working in town. That was six years ago and two years ago, I sold the farm for $18,000. . . .

Kovar ends his story describing his success:

> On February 14, I will be 57 years old, and we are worth half a million. I could get that much again for my patents, but I don't want to sell them.[13]

Kovar built a very successful business. A 1919 advertisement for his quack grass remover and alfalfa cultivator clamed thousands were in use throughout the United States. According to another ad from 1922, the machine was available in 24 standard sizes. By this time he was also selling a corn cultivator that carried seven patents. Another popular product was his Handy Andy 8-in-1 tool, which combined the functions of hammer and claw, vise, screw stripper and wire tenser. The company he built was still producing and exhibiting products in 1937. Kovar's tombstone in the Bohemian National Cemetery bears the inscription "invented Kovar quack grass digger."[14]

The most famous Czech industrial concern was founded by members of the pioneer **Kaplan family**. Joseph Kaplan's fourth child Bohumil (or Godfrey), born in 1861, learned the art of the blacksmith. He made his own tools, repaired items for others, and later, was a blacksmith for Owatonna Manufacturing Company. He had a shop powered by a threshing machine engine behind his house where he invented and manufactured several machines. He later bought the Washington Tool Company and renamed it North Star Iron Works.[15]

Godfrey's son Reuben Kaplan also had a mechanical bent. He worked for Zamboni's Gun and Bicycle Shop, and then ran his own bicycle repair shop. Later, he worked for Truth Tool Company in Mankato supervising the shop and designing tools. In 1925 he left after a royalty dispute and founded Owatonna Tool Company with his father Godfrey and partner Jim Peterson. The first product was a gear pulling tool that Reuben had invented, and it made his fortune. Later products were hydraulic rams and a variety of hand tools for Ford Motor Company and other clients. In 1950, Reuben and some friends purchased Truth Tool Company and moved it to Owatonna. His son Reuben W. (Buzz) Kaplan became president of Truth Tool, and later of Owatonna Tool Company.

Owatonna Tool Company was one of the largest employers in Owatonna for many years, employing nearly a thousand people. It was purchased by SPX Corporation in 1985.[16]

Cooperative creameries
Rural life in Steele County changed markedly after 1890 with the rise of cooperative creameries. Decades of growing primarily wheat in the county resulted in worn out soil and decreasing yields. In addition, great quantities of wheat were being grown in the Dakotas and other western states, resulting in oversupply and lower prices.

As described in earlier chapters, for decades farm organizations had been advocating a move away from wheat and toward dairy farming. Starting in 1869, a number of cheese factories opened in the county, and the owners encouraged farmers to increase their subsistence dairy herds to provide enough milk for the factories. Butter production also increased. By 1884 Steele County had five cheese factories and produced more than 375,000 pounds of butter annually.[17]

The cheese factories gradually converted to creameries. Although several creameries were initially started as private businesses, most began as cooperatives, and the private businesses usually converted to cooperative status after a few years. The boom years began in 1891 when eight creameries were organized. Four more followed in 1892, and seven more in 1893. Still more were created or reorganized in subsequent years.

Usually the creameries were located in a community, run by local residents, and profits shared by the members. One impetus for their formation was the feeling that some cheese factories were cheating farmers.[18] Farmers had long had the same complaint against grain elevators and railroads. Cooperative creameries allowed farmers to feel they were getting an honest payment for their production.

The county's rural creameries acted as community business centers. General stores usually sprang up near the creameries so farmers could buy supplies while dropping off their milk. Other services such as blacksmith shops might also locate near the creameries. After the rise of the automobile, gas stations and auto repair shops joined the mix.

Several of these creameries, located in the Czech areas of the county, were discussed in chapter 6. Many board members and butter makers in the Union, Steele Center, Summit, Hope, River Point and Farmers Gilt Edge Creameries were Czech-Americans.

The county creamery industry peaked during World War II, when the county had 25,200 dairy cattle. In the decades that followed, all of the creameries closed and by 1999 there were only 5,500 dairy cattle left. By then the creameries had done their work in helping develop rural parts of the county and increasing the prosperity of county agriculture.[19]

Poor Farm

Steele County followed the lead of other Minnesota counties by creating a poor farm in the fall of 1880 to provide food and shelter to the indigent who had no relatives to support them. The residents worked the farm to help pay for their keep. The farm consisted of 120 acres in Havana Township which the city purchased.

In 1883–1884, the state commissioned Hastings Hart to study the local jails, hospitals and poor farms and report back to the legislature. His report found only Hennepin County had an adequate poor farm. Most of the rest were run by farmers who got the job by being the lowest bidder, had inadequate facilities and unsanitary conditions. Presumably this included the Steele County farm at that time.

By 1910, the county history said the housing was adequate for a dozen people and the buildings were in good repair. Between 1895 and 1910 the farm received additions and remodeling and a new orchard.

Local Czech Joseph Fisher took over management of the farm in 1895 for ten years. He was succeeded by Anton Stancel for three years, and then by Samuel Pichner, who was running the farm in 1910 when it had eight residents. The history credits the good condition of the poor farm to these three Czech managers and to the head of the poor farm committee, F.G. Schuman.[20]

Sacred Heart Church in Owatonna
The eventful pastorate at Sacred Heart Catholic Church of the Czech-speaking Father Pribyl was succeeded in 1880 by a five-year stint by Father Walter Raleigh, with periodic assistance from Czech-speaking Fathers František Šulák from Chicago and Father Šimoník from Heidelberg.

Father Raleigh was transferred in 1885 and was succeeded for a few months by Father Maurice Joy, and then by Father John Solnce, a Slovenian ordained in 1884. Young Father Solnce was assigned not only Sacred Heart parish, but also the congregations in Claremont, Litomysl and Moravia. As all these parishes grew, his workload was divided with an assistant, Father Sigismund Singer, who took over stewardship of the Czech and Polish speakers in Owatonna and Litomysl while Father Solnce handled the English and German speakers.

St. Ivan's Lodge was established by members of the Sacred Heart congregation in 1889. It was a fraternal organization affiliated with the First Catholic Central Union, organized to provide insurance benefits and fellowship to Catholics. The charter members were: Rev. John Solnce, Rev. Sigismund Singer, Michael Cieszinski, Joseph Petranek, Carl Langer, Anton Kovar, Wencl Blazek, John Matejcek, John Jirele, Bernard Maixner, Charles Fisher, Frank Fisher, Frank Spinler, and Anton Pavek.

After many Midwestern lodges of the First Catholic Central Union broke away to form the Western Bohemian Catholic Union (see chapter 7), St. Ivan's Lodge switched its affiliation to the new organization in 1898. In 1929 the Western Bohemian Catholic Union merged with another Midwestern Catholic fraternal organization, the Catholic Workman. St. Ivan's Lodge continues to this day.[21]

At the end of 1889, Father Solnce was reassigned to a parish in St. Paul. Father Singer was joined at Sacred Heart in 1890 by Father Patrick Kiernan, who took over the parish as Father Singer's health began to fail. Father Singer died of tuberculosis in May 1891.

By this time, the Sacred Heart congregation had split into two ethnic and linguistic factions. The Irish and German Catholics wanted to separate from the Czech and Polish parishioners and found their own congregation. When Father Singer's replacement, Father John Pivo, arrived at Sacred Heart in June of 1891, this division was quickly arranged. Father Pivo lived with Father Kiernan in the rectory for six months while the new St. Joseph's Catholic Church and rectory were completed a few blocks from Sacred Heart. The Czechs and Poles of Sacred Heart paid $1,800 to the new congregation, which the St. Joseph parishioners claimed as their share of the funds of Sacred Heart. Father Kiernan then moved into the new rectory at St. Joseph's and became the first pastor of that parish.

Father Pivo's arrival in 1891 signaled the start of an epic pastorate. He remained at Sacred Heart for 45 years. He also sheperded the parishes in Litomysl, Moravia and Deerfield during parts of this period. His lengthy stay and forceful personality left an indelible stamp on Sacred Heart parish.

Father Pivo, Sacred Heart Church pastor, 1891 to 1936
Courtesy of Steele County Historical Society

John Nepomucene Pivo was born in 1865 in Kočin in southern Bohemia. He attended high school and college in Bohemia, and was studying at the Louvain seminary in Belgium when he met Bishop John Ireland from St. Paul, Minnesota, who was in Europe recruiting candidates for his new seminary in St. Paul. Pivo came to America in 1888, was ordained in St. Paul in 1890, and after a few months at the Catholic parish in Madison, Minnesota, he was transferred to Sacred Heart to replace Father Singer.

Father Pivo was one of those larger than life figures who frequently served as pastors during this period. If someone at the back of the church tried to leave before the Sunday service was finished, Father Pivo would call out to him by name from the pulpit and tell him to sit down until Mass was over.[22] During the time when he oversaw the Litomysl parish, his visits to the homes of parishioners could include a scolding that they were not contributing enough to the support of the parish. During one such visit, a Litomysl resident threw Father Pivo through the screen door to get him out of his house![23] The episode recounted in chapter 6 in which burial in the Holy Trinity cemetery was refused to a family behind on its pew rent was probably during Father Pivo's tenure. He assigned confirmation names and in some cases baptismal names if he did not like the names chosen by the confirmant or the parents of the baptized child.[24]

Conversant in Czech, German, Polish and English, Father Pivo said the Mass in Latin but delivered the sermon twice, once in English and once in Czech or whatever language was appropriate for the congregation that day.[25] For a time, he was not only in charge of all Catholics in Steele County, but also the flocks in Austin, Albert Lea, Waseca and New Richland. He was the living link from the frontier days of the Czech communities in Steele County, through the First World War and into the New Deal. During his tenure as pastor, the dominant language in both the Czech parishes and the fraternal lodges gradually moved from Czech to English, and new generations of increasingly Americanized parishioners grew to adulthood.

On December 17, 1901, the original Sacred Heart church building burned down. The fire apparently started from an overheated furnace. The Polish parishioners, who by this time wanted their own parish, took this opportunity to separate from Sacred Heart. They were given $4,000 as their share of the parish fund and built the Church of St. Hyacinth a block away from Sacred Heart. The remaining members of Sacred Heart, composed of 65 Czech families and 30 Bohemian German families, rebuilt Sacred Heart as a brick building. On May 21, 1903, Bishop Cotter came to Owatonna and dedicated both the new St. Hyacinth church and the rebuilt Sacred Heart.

The new Sacred Heart church building burned again on March 22, 1922, and a faulty furnace was the suspected cause. Once again the church was rebuilt as the building that still stands today.

Father Pivo, who was awarded the title of Monsignor for his long service, retired in September 1936 and moved to Jackson, Minnesota, where he remained until his death in 1960. He was briefly succeeded by Father Francis Paukert, and then the following year by Father Edward Kasal.

Father Kasal was born, educated and ordained in Bohemia, and only came to America in 1905 at the age of thirty. After fifteen months as pastor in Eastman, Wisconsin, he went to western North Dakota for three years for an eventful stay in New Hradec. His arduous work there caused the exhausted priest to be transferred to Jackson, Minnesota, where he was pastor of St. Wenceslaus parish for 22 years until being transferred to Sacred Heart in Owatonna. He served as pastor there for 28 years.

When Father Kasal died in 1965, the Catholic Church was in the middle of massive changes brought on by the Second Vatican Council. His successor pastors never again served for the lengthy terms that Father Pivo and Father Kasal had served. Most served for terms of five to ten years before transferring elsewhere. St. Hyacinth parish closed in 1952, and by 1970 the ethnic divisions between Sacred Heart and St. Joseph parishes had virtually disappeared.[26]

St. Mary's School in Owatonna

Founded in 1877 as a Catholic grade school and high school for girls (see chapter 5), St. Mary's school in Owatonna continued until decreasing enrollment and a lack of sufficient funds led to the high school's closing in 1908. The school building was heavily damaged by fire in 1913, but rebuilt with insurance money. In 1916 the high school reopened, and boys were admitted for the first time.

The boarding school was discontinued in 1925, and the school became St. Mary's Central School to serve the three Catholic parishes in Owatonna. The high school was again discontinued in 1931.

The old academy building was torn down and replaced in 1952 by the present building which housed St. Mary's Central grade school and junior high school. As the baby boom generation neared high school age, an addition was added to the building in 1958 to house the new Marian High School, which graduated its first class in 1959.

Peak enrollment for grades 1 through 12 came in 1964–1965 with a total of 1,020 students. By 1975 total enrollment had shrunk to 465 students, and the high school was again closed at the end of that school year. St. Mary's grade school continues in the 21st century.[27]

Holy Trinity Church in Litomysl

The first resident pastor of Holy Trinity Church in Litomysl was Fr. Ottmar Miller, who served there in 1898 and 1899. He was succeeded by Father Vincent Havlicek from 1900 to 1909.

The next pastor, Father Rudolf Matousek, presided at Holy Trinity from 1909 to 1932. Born in Lomnice, Moravia in 1865, he attended college and seminary in Europe. He came to America in 1888. He served in various places in Missouri until returning to Europe to recover from typhoid fever.

Once back in America, he was stationed at St. Wenceslaus Parish in Jackson, Minnesota. When Father Edward Kasal (the future pastor of Sacred Heart parish in Owatonna) was transferred from North Dakota to Jackson, Father Matousek moved on to Litomysl.

Frances Buryska remembered him fondly:

> One person who really made an impact on our growing up years was an old priest we had. He was Father Matousek, and he was in our parish for twenty years. At that time he had a small wooden church and a rectory next door, almost on the same site as our present church, but the rectory was on the north side. He was a saintly person, and all his Masses or special ceremonies were made so grand and awesome **and long**. We had Czech, Irish and German families in our parish, so he would preach a sermon in each language every Sunday, and have Benediction besides. We'd go to ten o'clock Mass and come home at one. A short way north of the church was the old North Hall, and a big horse barn nearby. In winter, when we came to church in a sleigh, the horses would be put in the barn if it was really cold.
>
> Father Matousek never learned to drive a car, and when he was called to come to visit a sick person, they would have to come and get him with a car or horses. And he would not travel in a car with a woman in it!
>
> He was a visionary. He saw in our future: a stone church built from rocks from the farmers' fields, and a school to go with it. He was laughed at for these fantasies, but the year he died [1940] saw the building of our present stone church, built from the stones from the farmers' fields, and a school was built later. Odd![28]

Father Matousek retired due to ill health in 1932 and lived in a hospital in St. James, Minnesota until his death in January of 1940. He was succeeded by Father Stephen Majerus from 1932 until February 1940.

Father Majerus was based in Geneva, Minnesota and took care of Holy Trinity and the Moravia church as mission territories. The arrangement was meant to be temporary, but he was so popular in Litomysl that he continued in this capacity for seven years. Through tireless work and fundraising he made Father Matousek's dream of a new church built of field stones a reality.

Permission to build was obtained from Bishop Kelly in October 1939. Parishioners were each to bring six loads of stones from their farms. Thorwald Thorson of Forest City, Iowa was chosen as the architect, and Anton Wacek from Holy Trinity parish was chosen as the builder.

Father Francis Tomanek was appointed pastor of Holy Trinity on February 1, 1940, as the new church was under construction right next to the old one. The cornerstone ceremony for the new church was held on June 16, 1940. The dedication was in June 1941. Upon its completion, the old church was torn down.

Another dream of Father Matousek was to build a Catholic school for the Holy Trinity parish. This also eventually came to fruition. Construction of the present day St. Isidore's School (named after the patron saint of farmers) began in fall 1957, and the school opened for its first school year in fall 1958 with 90 students. The school included grades one through eight.

St. Wenceslaus Church in Moravia (Saco)
Always a mission parish, the small St. Wenceslaus congregation was attended to by the priests of either Sacred Heart parish in Owatonna or Holy Trinity in Litomysl. The settlement never grew much due to its proximity to the services available in Owatonna, Litomysl and, later, Hope.

The picturesque building and its attendant cemetery sitting quietly in the countryside must have been a delightful place to attend Sunday services. Mary Ann Wanous recalled those times:

> I remember as a child at St. Wenceslaus Church, being dressed in white and strewing flower petals during a procession, perhaps for closing of Forty Hours. I also recall how the men sat on one side of the church and women on the other for Mass.

Once roads improved and car travel became easier, it was no problem to attend church in one of the nearby parishes. As a result, in 1952 the decision was made to close the parish. The church building was de-sanctified, and in 1962 the building and all of its vestments and furnishings were moved to the Village of Yesteryear by the Owatonna Fairgrounds.[29]

Czech lodges

The founding of the Owatonna C.S.P.S. lodge in 1881 was followed fifteen years later by the building of the impressive Auditorium Hall on north Cedar Street. (see chapter 7) The following year, Owatonna hosted the C.S.P.S. state convention in its new building.

At this time, lodges all over the western United States were breaking away to form a new organization, the Z.C.B.J. During the ensuing disruptions within the C.S.P.S., the Owatonna lodge fared well.

The national C.S.P.S. organization created ten Grand Lodges in various states during the 1870s. The idea was to create a federalist structure, akin to state governments, so there would be an intermediate level between the local lodges and the national Supreme Lodge. Grand Lodges were usually better organized and more financially solvent than other lodges in their states, and provided guidance and a good example to the other lodges. They also helped local lodges establish and maintain their lodge buildings, and often owned some of the local lodge buildings. Representatives of the Grand Lodges traveled to other lodges in their states to be present for major events such as dedications or significant anniversaries.[30]

The Minnesota Grand Lodge was created in 1878, and the position was held by the Minneapolis lodge. However, in 1897 the Minneapolis lodge broke from the C.S.P.S. and joined the new Z.C.B.J. organization. The Owatonna lodge was then designated as the new Minnesota Grand Lodge, a position it held until the Minnesota Grand Lodge was abolished in 1931.

In the early twentieth century, the Owatonna C.S.P.S. was one of the most financially sound in the country. Although other lodges had far more members (Cedar Rapids, Iowa usually topped the membership ranking), Owatonna ranked high for financial assets. In 1904, Owatonna ranked third in the nation for assets, and in 1909 it ranked second. Owatonna was still in second place as late as 1922. This was probably the reason it was chosen as a Grand Lodge.[31]

After the split between the C.S.P.S and Z.C.B.J., the national C.S.P.S. continued to thrive despite recurrent crises. The industrial depression of the 1890s caused a jump in benefit claims and a drop in the ability of members to pay their contributions; the situation was aggravated by a drop in Czech immigration.[32]

Starting in 1910, states began passing tougher insurance laws that applied to fraternal insurance organizations. These laws required financial disclosure, standardized rates and actuarial tables, and large financial reserves. Many fraternal lodges could not meet these requirements, and one proposed solution was to join many separate organizations to create one large and financially stable fraternal organization.[33]

The C.S.P.S. and the Z.C.B.J. had serious talks about reunification in 1922 at the suggestion of the C.S.P.S. Grand Lodges of Iowa and Minnesota. The major sticking point was the long standing aim of the C.S.P.S. to promote freethinking (now called rationalism). The reunification proposal stipulated that the aims of the merged organization would not be broader than the aims in the Z.C.B.J. charter, and could not be changed without approval of two-thirds of the Z.C.B.J. membership. This was to reassure the Z.C.B.J. membership that the combined organization would not promote rationalism.

Leadership of both organizations agreed to the proposed merger, although some prominent rationalists in the C.S.P.S. were upset by the elimination of rationalism as an aim. In the end, a referendum of the Z.C.B.J. members soundly defeated the merger, based largely on comments by disgruntled rationalists of the C.S.P.S.[34]

After the failure of this merger, the C.S.P.S. failed to make necessary financial changes when it had the chance in good economic times to do so. It would take the Great Depression of the 1930s to force reform.

Another recurrent issue after 1900 was the creation of English-speaking lodges. As Czech immigration to America slowed in the 1890s (and stopped during World War I), fraternal lodge members were getting older, and younger generations of Czech Americans, more comfortable with English than Czech, were not inclined to join the lodges. They gravitated instead to fraternal organizations such as the Modern Woodmen or the Foresters. The first English-speaking C.S.P.S. lodge was formed in Cleveland in 1904, but the idea did not catch on around the country until after the First World War.

The nativism and America-first attitude that arose during the world war continued after the war. Some American lodges that had recruited Czechs and encouraged them to operate locally in the Czech language now banned bilingualism and demanded the use of English. This helped break down the resistance of the C.S.P.S. and the number of C.S.P.S. English speaking lodges increased rapidly after 1920.[35]

In 1935, C.S.P.S. lodge number 418, called Minn-Tonna, was formed as an English language lodge in Owatonna. For eleven years, Owatonna had both the original, Czech-speaking, lodge and the English speaking lodge. In 1946, the original lodge converted to an English speaking lodge, and the English-speaking lodge Minn-Tonna merged with it.[36]

The financial crisis of the Great Depression finally brought about a major consolidation of Czech-American fraternal lodges. In 1932, the C.S.P.S. merged with several smaller Czech-American fraternals (but not with the Z.C.B.J.) to form the Czechoslovak Society of America (C.S.A.). The combined organization renumbered all lodges in the new organization. As a result, Owatonna's C.S.P.S. lodge 67 now became C.S.A. lodge 210.[37]

The new C.S.A.'s statutes omitted the clause in the old C.S.P.S. charter about promoting rationalism. The emphasis was now on mutual assistance and fraternity, promoting the Czech language and culture, supporting non-denominational schools and charities, and promoting "the moral, material and spiritual welfare of Czechoslovak people in the United States, and of mankind generally."[38]

At the 1934 national convention, rationalists managed to insert a clause in the organization's bylaws making it the organization's duty to support rationalism. The rationalism clause, first added to the C.S.P.S. charter in 1909, was not finally removed from the C.S.A. bylaws until the 1950 national convention.[39]

In an article from the mid-1960s about the Owatonna C.S.A. lodge, Thelma Hammel describes talking with lodge members and non-members about how the lodge was viewed in Owatonna. At that time there were 163 active members with an average age of 50 to 55, and forty inactive members with an average age of 60 to 80. Some of the officers were women, and the lodge still had a secret initiation ceremony for all members. Hammel's sources told her that many people in Owatonna still assumed the C.S.A. opposed Catholicism, and thought lodge membership was inconsistent with Catholic Church membership.[40]

The Owatonna C.S.A. lodge sold Auditorium Hall in 1978, but the lodge continues in existence in 2010 and meets at Senior Place.

There are interesting parallels between the twentieth century history of the Z.C.B.J. lodge and the C.S.P.S./C.S.A. lodge, both nationally and in Steele County. In 1932, the same year the C.S.P.S. became the C.S.A., the Z.C.B.J. decided at its national convention in Omaha to print its insurance certificates in both English and Czech, which necessitated an English translation for the name of the organization. The English name chosen was a reasonably literal translation of the Czech name—the Western Bohemian Fraternal Association.

A further modification of the name was made at the 1971 national convention. Delegates decided to change the English name to the Western Fraternal Life Association, but to keep the Czech name unchanged. These are the names of the organization at the time of this writing. A 2009 decal has the name Western Fraternal Life Association along the outer perimeter, and the initials Z.Č.B.J. in a diagonal band across the center.

The transition of the Z.C.B.J.'s meetings and publications from Czech to English was gradual. The national conventions were in both English and Czech at least as late as 1971, and the lodge journal *Fraternal Herald* had a Czech language section until the retirement of Anton Piskac in 1980.

An English speaking Z.C.B.J. lodge, Owatonna Jr. No. 338, was established in 1936. It led a parallel existence to the original Czech speaking lodge, No. 127, until long after the original lodge switched to English. The minutes for No. 127 were in Czech in May 1964, but Secretary Josephine Stransky switched to English in June 1964 without any prior announcement.

Minutes of the Bohemian National Cemetery Association west of Blooming Prairie (not as well known as the Owatonna B.N.C.) were in English in 1954, and Litomysl Z.C.B.J. Lodge 83 converted its minutes to English in 1948. However, this does not mean Czech was not spoken at meetings. Some present day lodge members remember members speaking in Czech at lodge events in the early 1960s. Even today, Czech phrases may be used by members at meetings or while socializing afterwards.[41]

The Litomysl Z.C.B.J. lodge joined the Owatonna Lodge 127 in February of 1967. The English speaking lodge No. 338 joined Lodge 127 much later. The 1997 centennial publication for the Z.C.B.J. says the two lodges stayed separate so long due to "personality conflicts," and that they finally joined in "recent times."

Czech American national publications

Czech Americans around the nation subscribed to a variety of publications in their language of origin. The larger fraternal lodges published journals for members that frequently contained member obituaries. Czechs in many large cities and some smaller towns had their own newspapers reporting on local events. Catholics and rationalists had national newspapers and journals that kept subscribers in touch with developments in public affairs and with each other. These publications informed Czech Americans of news from the old country and introduced them to life in America.

Many journals published an annual issue called the calendar that contained calendars for the upcoming year and almanac-like features, plus articles and short stories. Often they included biographical pieces written by subscribers.

The *Amerikán Národní Kalendář*, published in Chicago from 1878 to 1958, featured articles by several Steele County Czechs. An autobiographical account by Benjamin Fisher of his early years in Steele County appeared in the 1882 issue. The following year Anton Kubat submitted a brief summary of his life. Joseph Kaplan followed in 1911, and Terezie Spatenka and Frank Kovar appeared in 1925. Kovar submitted a brief history of the Steele County Czech settlements in 1933.

Another national journal read by local Czechs was *Hospodář (The Farmer)*. Begun in 1890 and published in Omaha, Nebraska, a large part of its contents were articles on farming techniques, recommendations for seeds and machinery dealers, notices of auctions and livestock sales, etc. It also contained self-help articles, cultural and social commentary, and personal memoirs. The magazine eventually moved to Texas where it is still published.

Several Steele County Czech immigrants told their stories in *Hospodář*. Karolina Broulik wrote in 1914 of her early years in Bohemia and her journey to America. She also complimented the magazine:

> Before we began subscribing to *Hospodář*, our farming amounted to nothing because we didn't understand it. In Bohemia, we both worked in a factory. The first magazine we read in America was *Hospodář*, and it provided the advice we needed.[42]

In a 1922 issue, Joseph Kovar and Frank Moravec told their life stories. Karel Srsen submitted a short history of the Steele County Czechs and a lengthy list of the local Czech settlers in 1934 to mark the 75th anniversary of the coming of the first Czechs to the area.

World War I and Aftermath
The First World War was a major divide in the evolution of Czech-American communities. It sped the process of assimilation and also began bridging the gap between Catholic and rationalist Czechs.

When the war began in August 1914, it ranged the allied powers of England, France and Russia against the Central Powers of Germany, Italy and the Austro-Hungarian Empire. The Ottoman Turkish empire allied with the Central Powers. Italy later changed sides and joined the allies. The United States attempted to stay neutral and succeeded for nearly three years.

The homelands of the Czech Americans were part of the Austro-Hungarian Empire, the nation they emigrated from. Many rationalist Czech Americans viewed the long standing alliance between the Catholic Church and the Austro-Hungarian government as oppressive and the war as a way for Bohemia to break from Austria and become a secular, independent nation. Catholic Czech Americans, of course, did not share this antipathy toward the Catholic Church, or toward the Austrian government. They had come to America for other reasons, usually economic, rather than from a sense of being oppressed in their homeland.

Rationalist Czechs rallied in New York against Austria and formed the Bohemian National Alliance in late 1914 to support the cause of the Czechs in Europe. Catholics did not immediately follow their example, and in any event, no American organization could do much to aid political causes in Europe without violating America's neutrality. However, in February 1917 the National Alliance of Czech Catholics was formed to provide aid to Bohemia and Moravia.

When America entered the war in April 1917 on the side of the Allied Powers in Europe, Czech and Slovak Americans were in an unusual position. On the one hand, they were immigrants (or descendants of immigrants) from an enemy power, and could be subject to the same suspicions that attached to German-Americans. On the other hand, they were working for the defeat of the enemy Austrian government and the breakup of the empire to create an independent Czech and Slovak nation. In this endeavor they were working with the Paris Council of exiled Czechs led by Thomas Masaryk and Edward Benes, who had organized Czech resistance, helped form a Czech army in Europe to fight with the Allies, and lobbied in America to raise funds and generate public support for an independent Czechoslovakia.

In 1918, the National Alliance of Czech Catholics, the Bohemian National Alliance and the Slovak League merged to form the Czechoslovak National Council of America. The Council aided the American war effort, gave assistance to the Paris Council of exiled Czechs, and lobbied President Woodrow Wilson on behalf of the creation of an independent Czechoslovakia.[43]

The Litomysl settlement had a unit of the National Alliance of Czech Catholics. An undated photograph of the group shows William Seykora, Joseph Svercl, Anton Wacek, Joseph Srsen, Alois Wencl, Joseph and Wencl Jirele, and Joseph Klekar.[44]

Vojta Benes, brother of future Czechoslovak President Edward Benes, was in Owatonna in 1917 and spoke at Auditorium Hall. He visited Joseph Kaplan and a photo was taken of them together. Benes was in the United States seeking help for the Czech Paris Council.[45]

In addition to some Steele County Czechs in the United States army in Europe, one local Czech traveled to Europe to join the Czech army founded by Masaryk and the Paris Council.

Bohemians for Kaiser's Defeat.
Adolph Hondl Joins Bohemian Volunteer Army to Fight in France—Alliance to Support Family.

Adolph Hondl, an alien Bohemian, left his wife and child here Monday night to join the 150,000 Bohemians of America who will form part of the Allied army in France as the result of efforts of the Bohemian Alliance of America to help defeat the Kaiser. Hondl left here for Chicago, where a large assemblage of Bohemians, many of whom are naturalized, will take special trains to New York previous to being transported to France.

Mr. Hondl is the only alien Bohemian volunteer from this city going to the front. Most of the Bohemian boys in the city are either in the service or are drafted according to Charles Srsen, one of the prominent members of the local organization of the Bohemian Alliance of America. This organization has provided for the care of Mr. Hondl's wife and boy, whom he leaves here. Mr. Srsen stated Tuesday that regardless of the payments of the Alliance, local Bohemians will provide for Mrs. Hondl and her child. Mr. Hondl came to this country just previous to the outbreak of the war. . . .

Mr. Hondl resided with his family south of town. "There are many Bohemians fighting in France" said Mr. Srsen. "There are many American Bohemians in the ranks. We who are so far away from it all and have all of our comforts do not realize what the war means. All of the members of Hondl's family are in Europe suffering as a consequence of the war. His brothers are in the ranks fighting." The Bohemian Alliance of America is doing all it possibly can do to aid in winning the war was the opinion expressed by Mr. Srsen.[46]

The Bohemian National Alliance in Owatonna met in October 1918 and immediately appropriated $200 to support the Bohemian army in Europe. It also voted to hold a fund-raising bazaar on November 2 at the C.S.P.S. hall to support the Bohemian army's fight against Germany and its allies.[47]

When the United States entered the war in 1917, Minnesota quickly created the Public Safety Commission to oversee the state's war effort. The commission mobilized materials and labor, sold war bonds, and watched for disloyalty. Each county set up a Public Safety Commission to enforce the state commission's orders and inform the state commission of local conditions. The Steele County Public Safety Commission consisted of President Thomas Cashman, Secretary W.V. Gouseff, Treasurer R.H. Back, and one representative from each township and from each ward in Owatonna. These included John Pichner from Owatonna Township and Otto Kubat from Owatonna's Third Ward.

In March 1917, former state Governor Lind resigned from the Public Safety Commission, and his place was taken by Steele County commission chair T.E. Cashman, thus giving Steele County a voice on the state commission. Cashman's replacement as head of the county commission was Owatonna businessman Fred Joesting.[48]

One of the issues considered by the state commission was regulating foreign language schools and newspapers. In a survey of 307 parochial schools in Minnesota, 94 used English exclusively and 213 were bilingual. Of the bilingual schools, German was the second language in 195, but Czech in only one.[49]

The commission debated banning foreign language newspapers and foreign language instruction in schools. However, the commission was persuaded by the argument that the foreign language press was the only way to reach some immigrants, and should be used to support the war effort.

In the end, the state commission decided against issuing an order on the subject of foreign languages. However, on May 10, 1918, it issued a rule, which was less binding than an order, specifying that English be used exclusively in public, private and parochial schools except for religious instruction or for the purpose of learning a second language.[50]

In addition to discussions of the use of German, the language of the enemy, the broader issue of Americanization picked up steam in 1918 and continued after the war's end. A study found that the U.S. contained 8 million adults who could not read or write English. In the southern part of the country, these were primarily native illiterates. In the northern United States, they were mainly aliens or immigrants who had recently become citizens. In February 1918 the Council of National Defense in Washington, D.C. issued Bulletin No. 86 on the Americanization of Aliens. The bulletin came out in favor of the national Bureau of Education's task of "welding the many races and nationalities comprising America's thirteen million foreign born and thirty-three million of foreign origin into a unified American people back of the fighting line—a task of large importance to the successful prosecution of the war."[51]

Every state was instructed to create an Americanization committee. English language classes were to be instituted in the evenings, at work over the noon hour, and in settlements. The bulletin recommended mandatory night school classes in English for aliens age 16 to 21 who were illiterate in English.[52]

The Americanization campaign came to Owatonna in October of 1918. United States Naturalization Examiner Frank Osterlind met with local officials about organizing night classes for aliens. Owatonna school superintendent W.B. Thornburgh then announced:

> Mr. Osterlind has authorized me to say: 'In the event that you are able to attend this school of citizenship, and fail to do so, the school authorities will recommend to the United States government that you be barred from becoming a United States citizen.'
>
> The organization and holding of this night school for foreigners who have not yet become American citizens, has been placed upon the public school as a duty. The school will gladly take up this work and push it successfully, hoping that we may give the men who attend, a workable basis in American citizenship.[53]

At about this time, the Czech language school in Owatonna closed forever.[54] The closing may have been ordered by the Steele County Public Safety Commission, but its records no longer survive, and the local newspapers make no mention of the issue. Alternatively, in the climate of patriotism and Americanism of the time, perhaps the local C.S.P.S. decided voluntarily to close the school.

A fitting ending to the era of Owatonna's Czech language school was the death of Joseph Kaplan in April 1918, near the time of the school's final closing. Kaplan had been the first teacher at the Czech language school when it opened in 1864.

Kaplan's funeral was conducted at his home by members of the C.S.P.S. lodge, and he was buried in the Bohemian National Cemetery, alongside many other Czech pioneers.

An obituary in the *Owatonna Journal-Chronicle* tied his life and death to the meaning of the world war then raging:

> Many of the old residents of Steele County recognize the passing of one of the county's best and oldest settlers, in the death of Joseph Kaplan, who was buried April 21, in the C.S.P.S. cemetery. The deceased represents the type of imigrant [sic] who sought a home in this country in order to improve the welfare of his own family and those of his countrymen.
>
> Joseph Kaplan came from Bohemia in 1856 and settled in this country when Owatonna was a mere settlement of a few huts. He was a college man and struggled constantly for the liberty and self development of his fellow-men, as is witnessed by his donations to endowment funds of various educational and protective institutions. He left Bohemia in order to be liberated from the oppression of the government typified by Prussia. Mr. Kaplan expressed hopes that Germany would be defeated so that the smaller countries could be free and develop into democracies. He was a staunch supporter in spirit and finance of the Bohemian National Defense League, whose object was to help the poor and war stricken people of Bohemia. Mr. Kaplan himself experienced the oppression in Bohemia when the farmers had to work with their own team for two or three days for a royal ruler. He left for America in order to escape the persecution and discriminatory laws of the Prussian ruling class. Mr. Kaplan considered the opportunity of gaining wealth in America less than the enjoyment of freedom and independence he found here.
>
> Mr. Kaplan was a member of the Minnesota Lodge, No. 67, C.S.P.S. He is survived by fifteen children, thirty grandchildren and eighteen great grandchildren.[55]

In its zeal to tie Kaplan's funeral to the war effort, the *Journal-Chronicle* styles Kaplan as a veteran of Prussian oppression when in fact Prussia never controlled Bohemia; the oppression Kaplan spoke of in his early letters to his brother in Bohemia was by the Interior Minister Bach in the government of the Austrian Emperor. The newspaper also makes the common mistake of thinking the Bohemian National Cemetery was a C.S.P.S. cemetery.

Liquor control

One of the state Public Safety Commission's major concerns was regulation of bars and saloons. Sixteen out of 48 commission orders involved regulation of alcohol. Although prohibition had not yet gone into effect, prohibition advocates believed that grain used for liquor could better be used to feed the armed forces, and time and money spent in saloons could better be used to help the war effort. They also argued that in jurisdictions where drinking was popular, the local authorities were lax in enforcing existing laws. Opponents of prohibition argued that closing saloons would be bad for morale and local economies. The commission tried to take a middle path: saloons remained open but were more closely regulated.[56]

Blooming Prairie was a regional center for alcohol sales. On December 15, 1917, after complaints by prohibition advocates, the state commission ordered Blooming Prairie saloons to close from 5 p.m. to 9 a.m., and only sell liquor for consumption on the premises. Fourteen Blooming Prairie residents traveled to St. Paul to protest the order, but were unsuccessful.

In May 1918 the commission learned that three Blooming Prairie saloons were violating the order and issued another order closing the saloons for the duration of the war. One of the saloon keepers, W.R. Carroll, got an injunction from State District Court Judge Dickson to prevent the order from going into effect. The court ordered state and local officials to appear in court on June 29 to show cause why the injunction should not issue. The commission refused to appear, and counseled local officials to do the same. Mr. Carroll, thinking he had won the day, continued to operate his saloon.

The next move was by the governor. Governor Burnquist ordered the Adjutant General to use the National Guard to close the offending Blooming Prairie saloons, which the Guard did on July 1, 1918. Judge Dickson then ordered the Governor to appear in court on July 13 to answer for disregarding the June district court order. Governor Burnquist appealed to the Supreme Court, which upheld the governor.

Still the Blooming Prairie saloons did not obey commission orders. On September 24, 1918, the commission ordered prohibition of all sales or possession of alcoholic beverages in Blooming Prairie until the end of the war and until three months after the signing of a peace treaty. All liquor licenses were revoked, and all stocks of liquor were to be confiscated. Service of the order was by state, not local, officials.[57]

Soon after the war's end, the Eighteenth Amendment to the United States Constitution was ratified prohibiting the manufacture, sale, transportation, import or export of intoxicating liquors in the United States. Its term went into effect one year later.

In 1921, 1924 and 1929, Congress passed new immigration statutes. The golden age of immigration, already interrupted by the world war, was gone forever. The 1929 law limited annual immigration to 150,000, of which only 20,000 could come from southern and eastern Europe and Asia. The days of substantial Czech immigration were over.[58]

Assimilation

With no new Czech immigrants arriving, children learning only English in school, and Czech language instruction discontinued, the attenuation of the Czech culture in Steele County was inevitable. Prohibition disrupted traditional social customs of many people, including many Czechs, and made the old life before the world war seem very distant.

However, Prohibition was often honored in the breach. Blooming Prairie, like many rural areas around the country, continued its tradition of ignoring the liquor laws, but moved from the open defiance of the war years to an assortment of illegal stills.

One huge operation in the early 1930s, located just west of the Bohemian National Cemetery off Highway 30, appears to have been operated by Chicago bootleggers in cooperation with local operators. This large alcohol factory was located in a barn and lean-to. Inside were six huge vats and a pair of two-story-tall stills, all powered by six steam engines and two boilers. The barn had a generator and electrical system. The operation was capable of making 1,800 gallons of alcohol per day. A lookout was posted atop the barn, and in case of approaching trouble, he signaled the workers below (twelve men worked during a 24-four-hour shift), who escaped through a long tunnel (actually a trench covered with boards and sod) that came out behind a haystack. An exhaust line for the used mash led to a nearby marsh.

Most locals were kept well away from the operation and treated roughly if they came too near. Local residents referred to the operators as outlaws or gangsters. When the operation was raided by federal agents, the men who ran the still left behind a sawed-off shotgun, an indication that they were professionals and meant business. Locals who did deal with the Chicago people did not go directly to the big still, but picked up their share of the alcohol production under cover of darkness at some prearranged local drop sites.[59]

Federal revenue agents finally found this still in December 1932. Their raid was detected and when they went in they found not a soul. The revenue agents destroyed equipment and poured out the alcohol; the same farm had been busted for having a big still four years before. However, treasury agents did not find most of the strictly local stills.[60]

In the decades after World War I, the paving of county roads and the proliferation of the automobile broke down time and distance barriers that had helped produce enduring and tightly knit local communities. Rural electrification made farm life much easier, and radio and movies, and later television, brought the world closer to build a national culture.

In the changed climate following the First World War, Frank Kovar looked back nostalgically at the early days. In a 1925 article in a Czech-American publication, he meditated on the changes he had seen:

> I looked around and I could see the great difference between the way the farm must have looked fifty years ago and the way it looks now. There, where once stood a log cabin of rough hewn timber and clay, where there were stables of reeds and straw, now there was a comfortable modern residence and a nice stable, silo and windmill—and around all this a little garden and small woods with green trees . . .
>
> Other farms such as Spatenka's can be seen around here, established by the first, hard-working and determined, Czech settlers. On each of the other farms there is usually a nice automobile, and most have tractors and other modern farm implements. And all this was accomplished by the diligent, skilled and thrifty hands of Czech farmers.[61]

In a later article, he speaks of visiting the grave of John Simek, the first of the Czech immigrants to Steele County to die in the new land. Srsen and several friends had visited the grave near Mineral Springs Park around 1900. Joseph Kaplan had said:

> Boys, we will take off our hats because here is buried the first Czech who died in our country. Let us give honor to his memory.

In the summer of 1931, not long before his death, Kovar again visited the grave in the company of Joseph Fisher and Frank Truhlar.[62]

A committee was created in 1930 to build a monument to the area's Czech pioneers and commemorate the seventy-fifth anniversary of their arrival. The monument was erected in the Bohemian National Cemetery south of Owatonna, and dedicated on July 14, 1931, in a public ceremony attended by Minnesota governor Floyd Olson (whose wife Ada Krejci was Czech-American). The ceremony included speeches in Czech and English, band music and singing. Following the Czech national anthem, Governor Olson spoke of how Czechs had suffered throughout history and their recent fight for freedom in the World War. He asserted that returning to the beginnings of the pioneers would answer many current questions of national economy and society. The ceremony ended with singing *America* and *The Star Spangled Banner*.[63]

As the younger generation became Americanized, old quarrels of previous generations became irrelevant. The feud between the rationalists and the Catholics slowly faded as rationalism in America ebbed and memories of the autocratic government in the old country were replaced with news of a new, democratic Czechoslovakia. Father Kasal of Sacred Heart Church attended Czech plays at Auditorium Hall, going on stage to invite audience members "including you nevěreci (non-believers)" to attend church social functions. Some did, and some even resumed attending church.[64]

An example of this coming together appeared in the October 1938 Owatonna *People's Press*, just a few weeks after the infamous Munich settlement that began the process of handing Czechoslovakia over to Nazi Germany:

Czech Program Will Be Given Here Tonight.
County Organizations to Have Joint Anniversary Program
Evening's Events to Interest only Czech-Speaking People

A completed program for the all-Czech observance planned for the Auditorium Hall tonight has been announced following a final committee meeting of representatives of the various Czechoslovak organizations in Steele County.

Worked out by the cooperative committee of the organizations, the program will be presented entirely in the Czech language, and for that reason will be of interest only to those who are capable of speaking and understanding Bohemian.

There will be no admission for the program, open to all individuals understanding the Czech language, and to be presented as follows:
Concert, Czech Concert Orchestra—George Pichner, director
Welcome—Jay Spinler
Songs—Male Quartet—Vac. Chott, director
Recitation—Jerome Rypka
Songs—Ladies Quartet
Selection—Czech Concert Orchestra
Songs—Male Quartet

Piano and Violin Solo—Effie and Alice Kovar
Recitation—Alice Jasan
Song—Ernest Rypka
Pianolog—Frank W. Dusek
Songs—Ladies Quartet
Address—Rev. Father Kasal
Living Picture—Children of St. Mary's Academy
Selection—Czech Concert Orchestra
Closing—Jay Spinler
"My County "Tis of Thee"—Audience[65]

Contact with the home country was cut off in 1939 when Hitler occupied Czechoslovakia, and then by six years of war. Following a few years of precarious freedom after the war, in 1948 Czechoslovakia fell under Communist sway and again became a place that few Americans wanted to visit. In 1953 Karel Srsen said that Czech national life in Owatonna was "completely dead."[66]

LOOKING BACK FROM THE 21ST CENTURY

Czechs have been part of European settlement in Steele County from the beginning, with Anton Simek arriving only a year after the founders of Owatonna. The local Czechs are woven into the fabric of the city and county. Marks of the Czech presence in Steele County are visible everywhere.

A 1998 list of Steele County century farms (farms owned by the same family for more than 100 years) records five farms of old Czech families in Blooming Prairie Township, eight in Owatonna Township, eighteen in Somerset Township, six in Summit Township, two in Aurora Township, and one each in Deerfield, Havana, Medford and Merton Townships. The oldest is the farm Joseph Kaplan moved onto in 1857 after his first harsh winter in Owatonna, now owned by his descendant Vernon Meixner.

Steele County businesses owned by local Czech-Americans in 2010 include Matejcek Implement, Haberman Picture Framing, Homuth Kubicek Insurance, Seykora and Born Asphalt and Paving, Skalisky Appliance, Wencl Plumbing, and Tom Wencl Accounting and Tax Service.

The biggest local Czech business, Owatonna Tool Company, is no longer owned by the Kaplan family, but is still one of the largest employers in town under the ownership of SPX.

How much Czech identity remains in the local Czech-American community? After well over a century of Americanization, and with several generations separating us from the old country, is there anything Czech remaining?

Steve Wencl points out that even in the 1950s, when Srsen said Czech national life was dead, some children still began school speaking only Czech. Many children grew up learning a fair amount of Czech from their elders who spoke it at home, church and social gatherings. Steve remembers spending whole days around the old people when hardly any English was spoken, except for a few sentences to make sure the younger generations behaved. My grandparents Frank and Mathilda (Kubicek) Wolesky spoke Czech to each other during pinochle games so that no one else could follow their moves. Czech music was very popular in Owatonna during my youth in the 1950s, and continued to be through the 1970s.

Younger generations of Steele County Czech-Americans have begun to look back to their ancestry. Alex Haley's family history *Roots* and the very popular 1970s television mini-series that grew from it started a surge of interest in genealogy and family origins. The fall of the Berlin Wall and end of the Soviet bloc in 1989 made it possible once again for Americans to visit Czechoslovakia (which after a few years split into the Czech Republic and Slovakia). The airline deregulation in the 1980s made such trips much more affordable. Finally, the rise of the internet and personal computers has greatly simplified online genealogical research. As a result, many Steele County residents of Czech descent have traveled to the Czech Republic to visit the villages and homes where their ancestors lived. They often meet with living relatives and continue correspondence with them after returning to Minnesota. The digital photos they bring back are widely shared on the internet or by email. Detailed maps and aerial photographs of small towns in the Czech Republic are easily available online. Many local families have researched and published family histories that include their Czech ancestors.

My own story is much like this. During a trip to the Czech Republic in May 2002, I visited the village of Zhoř that my grandfather Frank Wolesky left behind in 1902, as well as the town of Dolní Dobrouč from which my Kubicek ancestors had come in 1872. During that visit I had a chance meeting with the retired deputy mayor and town historian, Marie Meixner. Her stories connected me personally to that place. We corresponded until her death in 2007 and exchanged photos and family histories of people who left there to come to America.

Then, in the fall of 2002 I traveled to San Antonio, Texas, and visited the Institute of Texan Cultures where I was surprised to learn the rich history of the Texas Czechs. The Institute's bookstore carried several books on Texas Czech communities. This encounter planted the seed in my mind to search for stories of my own ancestors' journey from Bohemia to Minnesota. This book grew from that search.

While Czech lodges in many towns closed or merged with lodges in adjoining towns, Owatonna has maintained not one but two historically Czech fraternal lodges into the twenty-first century. The local C.S.A. and the W.F.L.A. have both sold their lodge buildings but remain active organizations; the C.S.A. now meets at Senior Place at the West Hills in Owatonna, and the W.F.L.A. meets at the Izaak Walton building south of Owatonna.

Every July the Holy Trinity Catholic parish in Litomysl holds its summer festival. When I attended in 2005 and 2006, the church began the event with a polka mass. A bake sale offered dozens of old fashioned buchty that tasted just like the ones my grandmother Kubicek had learned to bake in that same community one hundred years ago. These buchty were the real thing, not dinner rolls stuffed with jam that I have tasted at some Czech festivals in other towns.

The sesquicentennial celebrations for Owatonna and Steele County in 2004 and 2005 generated renewed interest in local history. Two books published for these celebrations featured photos and stories of the nineteenth century, including abundant material on the local Czechs. Events were held in Central Park with tables staffed by local lodges, and fascinating displays of old photos and lodge memorabilia in downtown store windows and the county fair. In 2005, an event at the VFW hall to commemorate the 150th anniversary of the coming of Anton Simek to Owatonna was well attended.

Blooming Prairie resident and local historian Steve Wencl has written articles about Steele County Czechs for the Czechoslovak Geneological Society International Association's journal *Naše Rodina* and for the *Owatonna People's Press*, and has assembled educational materials on the history of Czechs in Europe and Minnesota available at the Owatonna public library. He also gives talks, teaches introductory Czech language classes from time to time, collects local stories and old books, and generally is known around the county as the guy to go to for local Czech lore.

The monument at the Owatonna Bohemian National Cemetery, dedicated in 1931 to commemorate the 75th anniversary of the arrival of the first local Czechs, was badly deteriorated by the start of the new millennium. Inspired by the sesquicentennial festivities, the local lodges raised funds to rebuild it. A new granite monument, dedicated on September 13, 2009, holds the original bronze plaques from the 1931 monument, and is surrounded by paving stones etched with the names of donors or dedicatees honored by the donors.

Steele County Czechs are an important and integral part of the county, as they have been from the beginning. They are now thoroughly American, but often with a strong sense of where they came from. Many are interested in the origins and stories of their ancestors and the remnants of the Old World culture that still cling to their communities. With their roots firmly planted in a rich past, they will continue to grow and prosper in the new millennium.

APPENDIX A

A Brief History of the Czechs to 1848

The Czechs were a Slavic group who moved into central Europe from the east around 500 A.D. They moved into what is now the Czech Republic. This territory had been inhabited by the Celtic Boii in early Roman times, and later by the Germanic Marcomanni. Even today, bagpipes are played in the Czech Republic, perhaps a remnant of a distant Celtic past.[1]

Very little is known of the early centuries in the Czech lands, but around 830 an empire, which included the Czechs, started to coalesce in Moravia. The Moravian empire fell after being defeated by the Huns, but was replaced with a Czech state based in Prague under the Přemyslid princes. The Czechs were converted to Christianity around the year 900.

In the year 1002, Bohemia became part of the Holy Roman Empire. This was a loose federation of central European states with the Holy Roman Emperor as its nominal head. Usually, the emperors had little power, and the constituent states ran their own affairs without interruption. However, if the emperor was energetic, or there was a crisis in leadership in one of the member states, the emperor could step in and install new leaders.

An agreement with the Pope in 1212 raised the status of Bohemia from principality to kingdom. Later in the century, Bohemia acquired the status of elector in the Holy Roman Empire. The electors were the seven most powerful states in the empire, and had the right to choose the emperor.

Until this period, Czechs had lived primarily in the lowlands of Bohemia and Moravia. In the thirteenth century, Germans were encouraged to move in from neighboring overpopulated German states to help develop the mountainous and forested regions of the country. They brought with them more advanced agricultural methods and a highly organized feudal system in the countryside. As a result, for seven hundred years Bohemia and Moravia had Germans and Czechs living together, with the co-existence varying from smooth to rocky in different periods. However, the overall trend was that Germans gradually become more and more powerful.

During the 1200s, the culture of western Europe penetrated deeply into the Czech lands. Gothic architecture and various religious orders became widespread, and the nobles took to building castles and leading the courtly life of their European peers. In addition, the silver mines of Kutna Hora gave a major boost to the economy and to the political power of the Bohemian rulers, and enabled a currency reform which made Bohemian coinage popular all over Europe.

By mid-thirteenth century the Bohemian King Přemysl II Otakar had acquired control of Austria, Carinthia, Styria and Carniola, and was planning to become the Holy Roman Emperor. This development alarmed the other German electors, who voted in Rudolf von Habsburg as emperor instead. Bohemia was forced to give up control of Austria and the other lands it had acquired, and King Přemysl was killed in battle with the Habsburgs in 1278. His son Wenceslaus soon acquired control over Poland and Hungary, and Bohemia's power was again feared. Wenceslaus was murdered in 1308, however, and the four hundred year history of the Přemyslid dynasty was ended by lack of a male heir.

Eliška, the sister of Wenceslaus, was married to John of Luxemburg, who now became king of Bohemia. He acquired Silesia and upper Lusatia for the kingdom, and upon his death was succeeded by his son Charles, a capable and highly educated man who spoke five languages. Charles increased the power and influence of Bohemia, and eventually was crowned Holy Roman Emperor. In theory, this made him the most powerful secular ruler in Europe, with the Pope as his only peer.

Charles made Prague his capital, and began to build and beautify the city to make it worthy of being the capital of the empire. He repaired the Prague and Vyšehrad castles, built the Charles Bridge across the Vltava, and built numerous churches. He also started Charles University, which quickly became one of the great universities of Europe. During his reign, the political, cultural and economic status of Bohemia rose, and Bohemia became more closely integrated with the rest of western and central Europe.

After thirty-three years as Holy Roman Emperor, Charles died in 1378. Conditions began to deteriorate almost immediately. An outbreak of the plague in 1380 killed more than ten percent of the population of Bohemia, causing major social and economic disruptions. The new king, Charles' son Wenceslaus, was frivolous and squabbled with the church and nobles. In 1400, he was deposed from the position of Holy Roman Emperor.

These troubles gave rise to much soul-searching, and many came to believe these crises were punishment from God for the sins of the Catholic Church. The Great Schism of 1378–1417, with a Pope in Rome and a competing Pope in Avignon, scandalized Catholics all over Europe. Many felt the church had grown rich and corrupt and spent its time meddling in politics instead of saving souls and dealing with matters of the spirit.

A group of dissident intellectuals and churchmen who held these views began to coalesce around Jan Hus, a popular preacher in Prague. Hus began preaching for reform of the church in 1402.

Hus was influenced by the writings of the Englishman Wycliffe. Hus preached against indulgences, and said Christ, not the Pope, was the supreme head of the church. Popes and bishops who had committed mortal sins should not remain in their positions, and priests who committed mortal sins should be punished in lay courts. He advocated that the church be stripped of its wealth by the political powers because wealth merely corrupted the church. He favored translating the Bible into the vernacular so that everyone could read it, and giving the Eucharist to everyone (not just priests) as both bread and wine. Consequently, a chalice became the symbol of the movement. Hus is often considered to be an early Protestant, and because his backers were mainly Czechs while his strongest opponents were Bohemian Germans, there was a nationalist undertone to his preaching.

After more than ten years of preaching, and the growing fame that came with it, Hus attended a church council in 1415 to explain his views. The council found his views to be heretical, Hus refused to recant, and was burned at the stake in the same year. His friend and supporter Jerome was burned to death the following year.

Their deaths caused great tension between the many followers of Hus and the Catholic Church and its followers. This tension broke into open conflict in 1419 initiating a series of wars between Catholic rulers and the Hussites. The Pope, the Holy Roman Emperor and the King of Hungary united to try to invade Bohemia and crush the heresy. Under the leadership of the blind general Jan Žižka, the Hussites repelled attacks in 1420, 1422, 1426, and 1427. By the late 1420s the exhausted and defeated Catholic forces were looking for a way to reach an accommodation. The people of Bohemia also were worn down from the years of fighting and wanted peace.

Meanwhile, the Hussite forces had split into several factions. The Hussite nobility and intellectuals were closer to Catholicism than the general populace of Prague, and at the other end the most radical were the Taborite and East Bohemian factions. In 1434, the Bohemian Catholics and the more moderate Hussites turned on and defeated the radical Taborite and East Bohemia groups.

This defeat made peace possible, and the Compacts of 1436 were agreed to by the Hussites, the Catholic Council of Basle, and Holy Roman Emperor Sigismund (but not the Pope). The agreement made the Hussites an autonomous part of the Catholic Church, and gave Bohemians the right to practice either the regular Catholic faith or the Hussite variant of it. Emperor Sigismund became King of Bohemia.

However, in 1458, the Bohemian nobles elected George of Poděbrady, a Hussite, as king. The Pope soon declared another crusade against Bohemia. George fought the attackers until his death in 1471. He was succeeded by Vladislav of the Polish house of Jagiellon. This family ruled Bohemia until 1526, and a tense and tenuous religious toleration existed during the period, with 70% of the population estimated to have been Hussite.

Another force in Central Europe at this time was the Turks. The Ottoman Turks had begun to move from Asia to Europe in the 1300s, invading present day Greece, Bulgaria, Bosnia and Serbia. After the Turkish capture of Constantinople (Istanbul) in 1453, the process accelerated. Turkish armies continued to move north, and by 1525 had moved into present day Romania, Hungary and Austria, and were nearing Bohemia. Christian armies were defeated at the battle of Mohacs in 1526, and the Bohemian King Ludwig Jagellion was killed in the battle. He was succeeded as King of Bohemia by Austrian Archduke Ferdinand Habsburg. (The Habsburg family would remain in control of the Czech lands until 1918.)

In the early 1500s, Luther defied the Pope, and later broke with the Catholic Church, and the Protestant Reformation was underway. Luther was outlawed in 1521, and a German army sent by the Holy Roman Empire sacked Rome in 1527 and besieged the Pope in Hadrian's Tomb. Henry VIII asserted his claim to be head of the Catholic Church in England in 1534.

As Catholic and Protestant fought each other in Europe, the Turkish tide came closer to the heart of Europe. In 1529, Vienna was besieged by the Turks. When the Turks were turned back there, it proved to be the high water mark for the Turkish advance. In the centuries to come, the Austrians and Venetians slowly pushed the Turks back down the Balkan Peninsula toward present day Turkey.

Throughout the 1500s, the Protestant Reformation continued to advance. Zwingli and Calvin in Switzerland created another pole of Protestantism, the Reformed churches. They felt Lutherans were little different from Catholics and retained far too many dubious customs. Other, even more radical groups such as Anabaptists and Unitarians condemned infant baptism and even the Trinity. Some questioned the decisions of the earliest church councils, such as decisions on which books should be included in the Bible. As the century progressed, England, Scotland, Sweden and much of the German Holy Roman Empire became Lutheran or Reformed. Italy, Spain and Austria were Catholic. Central Europe, including Hungary, Transylvania, Bohemia and Moravia, were predominantly Protestant. France became largely Protestant, but after twenty years of violence and civil wars, reverted to Catholicism.

After the Council of Trent, the Catholic Church reformed many of its worst abuses, centralized discipline and priestly education, and went on the offensive against

Protestants. Jesuits founded colleges all over Europe to spread the Catholic message, and Protestants seemed on the defensive.

When the Austrian Archduke Ferdinand of the Habsburgs became King of Bohemia, he backed the Catholic side in the dispute with the Protestants. In 1547, the Habsburgs defeated a revolt by the Bohemian nobles and royal towns. In 1556, the Jesuits, vanguard of the Catholic Counter-Reformation, were brought into Prague. However, the Habsburgs agreed to the continuation of religious toleration in Bohemia in 1575 and again in 1609.

Archduke Ferdinand was systematically rolling back Protestantism in his domains from 1590 onward, gently at first and more coercively later. He was in line to replace the aging and childless Emperor Matthias, leader of the entire Austrian Empire. Events came to a head when Ferdinand began to interfere with the longstanding religious toleration in Bohemia and Moravia. Protestants all over Europe felt it was time to make a stand, and many sent expressions of support to Bohemia, the birthplace of Protestantism.[2]

In 1618, some Hussites broke into the Prague castle and threw two Catholic representatives of the Habsburg king out of the castle window. The Catholics survived unharmed, but this act ignited the Thirty Year's War, which roiled most of Europe until 1648. The old Emperor Matthias died in 1619, and was succeeded by the hard-line Catholic Archduke Ferdinand, who was determined to defeat Protestantism in Europe. In Bohemia, the Catholic Habsburgs soundly defeated the Hussites at the Battle of White Mountain near Prague in 1620. Many Czech Protestants fled to Germany, and twenty seven of the remaining leaders were executed in Prague in 1621.

After White Mountain, the Habsburgs started to systematically re-Catholicize the Czechs. Protestant lands were confiscated, and in 1627 a new constitution required all Protestants to convert to Catholicism or leave the country. Thirty-six-thousand Protestant families left the country. The long term legacy of these events was to create a strong antipathy among many Czechs toward the Catholic Church.[3]

The Thirty Years War ended in 1648 with Europe exhausted and devastated. Religious hatreds were so strong that for five years of peace talks Protestants met in one city and Catholics in another before an end was negotiated. Each part of Europe returned to the religious status it had lived under in 1624. Since in 1624 Bohemia and Moravia were legally Catholic with Protestantism outlawed, they remained so after the peace.[4]

The war affected other parts of national life besides religious affiliation. In Bohemia almost half the noble property was owned by foreign nobility. The war and the exile of nobles and Protestants had reduced the Bohemian population by a third and the economy was in bad shape.

Serf farmers were taxed at higher rates to rebuild the country, could not move without the consent of their lords, and were required to work a set number of days per year for the lord. Farmers chafed under these requirements, and rebelled several times, including in 1690. Feudalism took different forms in Europe in various times and places. The general principle was that all or much of the land in a kingdom like Bohemia was owned by the king, who granted its hereditary use and possession (but technically not ownership) to lords in exchange for payments of goods or military services. The lords then granted some of the lands to lower ranking nobility in exchange for their payments and services, and on down the line to the bottom rung of the ladder. The people who actually worked the feudal lands, the serf farmers, were also allotted particular portions to use (but not own). These farmers spent part of the year working "their" lands, and part of the year working land their noble owned directly. In essence, in a feudal system, the king was the landlord who owned the land, and everyone else leased or subleased it from him.

The Habsburg monarchy grew more powerful over time. From its base in Bohemia and Austria, it gradually moved east and south as the Turks slowly withdrew from Europe. Hungary became part of the Habsburg domain, and eventually so did all or parts of present day Poland, Slovakia, Slovenia, Croatia, Bosnia, Serbia, and Romania. This was a slow process, but as the 18th century progressed, the Habsburg territories became ever larger, more powerful, and increasingly multinational.

The Habsburg domains grew like most European nations before the modern era. From their home base in Austria, the Habsburgs acquired control over other lands by marriage or conquest. The degree and conditions of control varied from one territory to another, depending on the strength of the local nobles and towns, religious inclinations of the population, economic and social traditions, dynastic politics and other factors. Over time, the central government grew stronger and imposed more unified administration and taxation across all the territories under its control, and a modern nation slowly formed.

During the medieval era, central Europe was a collection of hundreds of kingdoms, principalities and dukedoms under no higher control except that of the very tenuous Holy Roman Empire. The growth of the Habsburg kingdom in central and southern Europe changed this by adding a strong German-led center of gravity based in Vienna.

Another German power center was developing in northern Europe. Starting from a base in Brandenburg, a strong Prussian state was emerging and growing more powerful. Between these two German kingdoms lay a patchwork of small kingdoms and principalities that were fertile ground for alliances and intrigue in the rivalry between the two big states. In the War of the Austrian Succession (1741 to 1748) with battles fought on

Bohemian soil, Austria lost part of Silesia to the Prussians. They clashed again in the Seven Years War (1756–1763), a sideshow of which was the French and Indian War in North America.

In the late 18th century, the Enlightenment mindset gave rise to a group of European monarchs known as the Enlightened Despots. These included Catherine the Great of Russia, Frederick the Great of Prussia, and Marie Theresa and her son Joseph of Austria. To keep up with modernizing currents in England and France, they undertook reforms to make their nations stronger and more competitive.

In 1774 the Habsburgs set up a national school system and decreed compulsory school attendance. Industrialization was encouraged, and was to be concentrated in Bohemia, with agriculture encouraged in Hungary. The last vestiges of Bohemia as an independent kingdom within the Hapsburg Empire were abolished by Marie Theresa, and Bohemia became just another province. Religious toleration was decreed in 1781, legalizing Lutheranism, Calvinism and the Orthodox Church.

The 1775 Bohemian peasant revolts led to the abolition of serfdom in 1781 in Bohemia and Moravia, but compulsory labor by small farmers for their lords continued. Farmers' work for their lords was not to exceed three days per week; the fact that this was considered a reform indicates the staggering burden that had led the peasants to revolt.

In 1789 Europe was electrified by the French Revolution. All the other European powers found this a dangerous contagion. The execution of the French king and his replacement by an anticlerical and rationalist regime was seen as an assault on the legal and religious foundations of Europe. France was attacked by its neighbors, but fought them off. As the revolution progressed, Napoleon Bonaparte assumed power and went on the offensive. For more than ten years, he repeatedly defeated coalitions of his rivals, the British, Russians, Austrians and Prussians, and occupied or dominated much of Europe. One of those battles, in which Napoleon defeated the Russians and Austrians, was near the Czech town of Slavkov, in Moravia (the German name of the town was Austerlitz).

After Napoleon's final defeat at Waterloo in 1815, the victorious powers attempted to put the old political system of Europe back in place, with some important differences. In 1804, Napoleon had abolished the Holy Roman Empire. Once Napoleon was defeated, nobody saw any reason to bring it back. There was no longer even a nominal head of state higher than the Prussian or Austrian kings. In addition, Napoleon had united all the many north German states except Prussia into a Confederation of the Rhine. After his defeat, this broke apart into smaller states, but the remnants were fewer and larger than what had existed in those territories before the French Revolution. This would ease the reunification of Germany later in the nineteenth century.

Britain and France continued to experiment with political and economic reforms after Waterloo, but the conservative European regimes in Prussia, Russia and Austria viewed the French Revolution and Napoleon as a close call that must never be allowed to happen again. Consequently, the appetite for reform evident during the Enlightened Despot period of the previous century was gone, and any nationalist or democratic notions were firmly quashed.

The use of the Czech language by anyone other than the poorest classes had largely disappeared between 1630 and 1800. German had become the language of government in Bohemia and Moravia, and the language of the schools, the church, the nobles and educated townspeople. That began to change around the time of the French Revolution.

The Czech National Revival was an attempt to raise consciousness and increase appreciation for Czech language and culture. It started with a society of enlightened aristocrats founded in 1769. Over the next hundred years, members of the Czech intelligentsia wrote grammars and dictionaries of the Czech language, histories and biographies of the Czech people, translated foreign literature into the Czech language, and wrote literature and poetry in Czech. Eventually, the Austrian authorities granted permission to teach the Czech language in secondary schools, although German remained the language of primary schools, which were the only schools most people attended. The National Museum was founded in Prague in 1818. Theatrical works were increasingly produced in Czech, and the composers Smetana and Dvořak composed music with Czech themes.

This nationalist revival was occurring in other European nations, which used literature, language and music to celebrate their unique cultures and contributions to history. As mid-nineteenth century neared, nationalism combined with the economic results of the Industrial Revolution and changes in agriculture to produce pressure for major political changes. This pressure came to a head in the revolutionary year of 1848 as described in the prologue.

APPENDIX B

Czech Arrivals Who Settled in Steele County

1852
Pichner, John S. and Paulina (Fibiger) and seven children, aboard *Elise*, arrived in New York December 8, 1852; lived in Freeport, Illinois until 1856.
Pichner, Joseph F. and Katerina and five children, aboard *Elise*, arrived in New York December 8, 1852; lived in Freeport, Illinois, until 1857, then in Amana Colonies, Iowa, for a year.

1854
Simek, Anton in 1854 or 1855, possibly with brother, sisters and father, aboard *Arnor*, to Boston January 5, 1854, traveling as Louis Hirscheld.
Simek, Joseph and Anna Marie (Pahl) and children Teresa and Anna, plus father John and sisters Anastasia and Rosalia, aboard *Arnor*, arrived in Boston January 5, 1854.
Kubat, Antonin and Annie (Kubista) Kubat and children Samuel and Joseph (born in Bohemia), Anton (born on the ocean), and Antonia (born in Illinois). Sailed from Hamburg to Quebec City in 1854, then probably on Great Lakes to Chicago. Lived in Freeport, Illinois, until 1856.
Renchin, Frank and Rosa and children Frank, Rosa, Joseph and Agnes. Arrived in Cedar Rapids, Iowa in 1854. Parents and some children moved to Steele County in 1862 to 1870; son Frank moved to Steele County by 1875.

1855
Fisher, Benjamin and Anna (Pichner), Antonia and Joseph, arrived in Freeport, Illinois, in 1855.
Pichner, John, son of John S. and Paulina (Fibiger) Pichner.

1856
Kaplan, Joseph and Barbora (Zednik); sailed from Hamburg aboard *Emma*, arrived at Quebec City on July 26, 1856, then on Great Lakes to Chicago.
Pichner, Vaclav; sailed from Hamburg aboard *Emma*, arrived at Quebec City on July 26, 1856, then on Great Lakes to Chicago.
Zednik, Joseph and Katerina (Kaplan) and daughter Philomena; sailed from Hamburg aboard *Emma*, arrived at Quebec City on July 26, 1856, then on Great Lakes to Chicago.

1861
Kubista, Frank and Rosalie and children Rosalie, Frank and Maria, aboard *Bavaria*, arrived in New York October 10, 1861.

Rypka, Josef, aboard *Bavaria*, arrived in New York October 10, 1861.

Slezak, Anton and Anna and children Anton and John, aboard *Bavaria*, arrived in New York October 10, 1861.

Fisher, Josef.

Horsky, Josef and Rosa and child Adelaide.

Hrdlicha, Wencl and Theresa and children Wenzel, Theresa, Frank and Joseph.

1862

Wanous, John and Anna (Jirousek) and son John, aboard *Bavaria*, arrived in New York August 13, 1862.

Belina, Wencl and Johanna and children Frank, Anton, Wencl, John and Joseph, aboard *Hansa*, arrived in New York October 15, 1862.

Kovar, Anton and Anna and children Wencl, Anton, Barbara, and Johann, aboard *Hansa*, arrived in New York October 15, 1862.

Kovar, John and Barbora and children Barbora, Anna and Marie and parents Joseph and Catherine, aboard *Hansa*, arrived in New York October 15, 1862.

Seykora, Anton and Anna and children Frank, John, Joseph and Anton, aboard *Hansa*, arrived in New York October 15, 1862.

Jirousek, Wencl and Anna and child Rosie.

1863

Belina, Frank and Paulina and children Josephine, Anna and Rosalie, aboard *New York*, arrived in New York September 2, 1863.

Fisher, Frank and Theresa (Rehak) and children Joseph and Anna, aboard *New York*, arrived in New York September 2, 1863, (by 1865, Frank was married to a Josephine).

Renchin, John and Catherine and children Frank, John S., Barbara and Franziska, aboard *New York*, arrived in New York September 2, 1863.

Wanous, Wencl and Theresa (Fisher), aboard *New York*, arrived in New York September 2, 1863.

Wavrin, Joseph A. and Paulina (Belina), aboard *New York*, arrived in New York on September 2, 1863.

Seykora, Frank and Josephine and children Frank and John, aboard *America*, arrived in New York September 28, 1863.

Seykora, John J. and Amelia and children Anna, Emilie and Rosalie, aboard *America*, arrived in New York September 28, 1863.

Seykora, Rosalie and children Frank, Franzisca, Rosalie, Anton W., John and Barbara, aboard *America*, arrived in New York September 28, 1863.

Racek, Joseph and Christina.

1864

Kaspar, Joseph and Dorthea and children Joseph, Albert, Anton, Dorthea, Mary and Jennie, aboard *Hansa*, arrived in New York June 18, 1864.

Landmichal, Anton, aboard *Hansa*, arrived in New York June 18, 1864.

Hanus, Wencl and Josefa and son Frank, aboard *Hansa*, arrived in New York June 24, 1864.

Votava, Wencl and Anna, aboard *Hansa*, arrived in New York June 24, 1864.

Motz, Ferdinand and Otillie and son Ferdinand, aboard *New York*, arrived in New York July 5, 1864.

Veith, Joseph and Rosa and children Joseph, Emilie and Frank, aboard *New York*, arrived in New York July 5, 1864.

Wondra, John and Frances (Hemerka) and children Victoria, Mary, Joseph, Frances, Clara, Anastasia and Anna, aboard *Adolphine*, arrived in New York on September 5, 1864.

Pavek, Frank and Rosa and children Wencl and Anna, aboard *Hansa*, arrived in New York October 10, 1864.

Pavek, Ignac and Rosa and children Anton, Rosa and John, aboard *Hansa*, arrived in New York October 10, 1864.

Pavek, John and Katherine and children Anna, Rosalia, Franzisca, Maria, John, Katherine, Frank and Wencl, aboard *Hansa*, arrived in New York October 10, 1864.

Simek, John and Mary, aboard *Hansa*, arrived in New York October 10, 1864.

1865

Moravec, Frank and Mary and children Frances and Frank.

Motl, Frank and Frances.

Skalicky, Frank and Matilda (Fisher) and children Frank, Matilda and Frances.

Veith, Edward.

1866

Taresh, Joseph and Catherine and children Mary and Joseph, aboard *Reinhard*, arrived in New York April 18, 1866.

Brozek, Jan, aboard *Atlantic*, arrived in New York May 28, 1866.

Blazek, Frank and Anna and children Rosalia and Mathilda, aboard *Mobile*, arrived in New York June 18, 1866.

Kaspar, Joseph and Emilia and daughter Barbara, aboard *Mobile*, arrived in New York June 18, 1866.

Kubat, Anton and Paulina, aboard *Mobile*, arrived in New York June 18, 1866.

Kubat, Frank and Thekla and children Frank, John and Anna, aboard *Mobile*, arrived in New York June 18, 1866.

Wesely, Frank and Rosalia and son John, aboard *Mobile*, arrived in New York June 18, 1866.

Simek, Frank and Anna and daughter Anna, aboard *Bremen*, arrived in New York October 9, 1866.

Brozek, Florian.

Dusek, Frank and Josepha and children Frances, Mathilda, Frank and Joseph.

Maixner, Bernard.

Pirkl, Frank and Rosalie and children Frank and John.

1867

Spatenka, Frantisek and Terezie (Jasansky) and child Anna, aboard *Hermann*, arrived in New York April 1, 1867.

Suchanek, Wencl and Anna (Srsen) and children Frank and Joseph, aboard *Kosmos*, arrived in New York May 2, 1867.

Bulver, Frank and Catherine and daughter Catherine, aboard *Northern Lights*, arrived in New York June 28, 1867; lived in Wisconsin in 1867 and came to Minnesota in 1868.

Fisher, Anton and Anna, aboard *Hermann*, arrived in New York July 13, 1867.

Moravec, Barbara and son Frank (but no sign of husband Frank), aboard *Clara*, arrived Baltimore August 3, 1867.

Maca, Anton and Marie and children Christina, Marie, Joseph and Eliza, aboard *Western Metropolis*, arrived in New York November 9, 1867.

Pribyl, Joseph and Katerina and children Mary, John, Peter, and Joseph, aboard *Western Metropolis*, arrived in New York November 9, 1867.

Smersh, Thomas and Rosa (Maca) and children Frank, Frances, Cecilia and Agnes, aboard *Western Metropolis*, arrived in New York November 9, 1867; settled in Pittsburg and Davenport until coming to Owatonna in 1878.

Habenicht, Dr. Joseph; moved to Owatonna in 1894 from elsewhere in U.S. and remained fourteen months.

Kubista, Ignac and Rosalia and three children, arrived December 1867.

Motl, Jiri (George) and Caroline and children Frank, Julia and Joseph.

Simon, Alois and Frantiska (Hanzlicek) and children Alois, Frank, Frances and Anton.

Soukop, Joseph.

1868

Matejcek, Vincent and Mary (Motl) and children Vincent, Joseph, Matilda and Frank, aboard *Quaker City*, arrived in New York July 16, 1868.

Ressler, Bernard and Josephine (Pirkl) and son Frank, aboard *Quaker City*, arrived in New York in July 1868 under assumed names (John and Maria Bendar and son Francisco); moved to Steele County in 1873 after living in Pennsylvania and Portage, Wisconsin.

Fisher, Joseph and Frances.

Maca, Joseph and Mary (Fitall), and child Theresa (at least).

Wencl, Frank J.

1869

Horsky, John, aboard *New York*, arrived in New York May 13, 1869.

Rypka, Frank, aboard *Donau*, arrived in New York July 23, 1869; lived in Cedar Rapids for three years, then moved to Steele County.

Mares, Jan, aboard *America*, arrived in New York November 1, 1869.

1870

Dostal, Frank and Mary (Watowa) and children John, Anna and Marie, aboard *Main*, arrived in New York May 23, 1870.

Pirkl, Bernard and Josephina (Matejcek) and children Joseph, Matilda, Albina, Frank, Vincent and Adolph, on a sailing ship, arrived in New York July 14, 1870.

Moravec, Frank.

Motl, Frank and Francis and children Frank and Mary.

Skalicky, Vincent and Sidonia and children Albina and Vincent.

Slavick, John and Philomena and daughter Mary.

Wavrin, John and Anna and children Anton and John.

1871

Haberman, Wencl and Rosa (Stangler) with sons Jacob, Adolf and Fred and two daughters, aboard *Rhein*, arrived in New York April 15, 1871.

Slezak, Anna (Pelinka; wife of Kaspar Slezak) and daughters Anna and Barbara, aboard *Rhein*, arrived in New York May 27, 1871.

Dusek, John, aboard *Deutschland*, arrived in New York July 24, 1871. His wife Barbara and children Peter and John came later, but before the 1875 census.

Hudrlik, Joseph and Anna (Wesely) and child Joseph.

Slezak, Kaspar (came separately from his wife and children).

1872

Kubicek, Frank and Mathilda (Kubicek) and children Frank J. and Vincent, aboard *Ohio*, arrived in Baltimore June 24, 1872; lived in Chicago until spring of 1873.

1873

Skerik, Joseph and Katherine (Janousek) and children Joseph, Anna, John and Maria, plus Joseph's sister Katherine, aboard *Leipzig*, arrived in Baltimore October 1873.

Penas, John and Josepha and child Maria, aboard *Ohio*, arrived in Baltimore November 8, 1873.

Sustacck, John and Maria and children Frank, John and Alois, aboard *Ohio*, arrived in Baltimore November 8, 1873.

Vasicek, Frank and Anna and children Wencl, Justine, Marie, Amalie, John, Frank, Alois and Franziska aboard *Ohio*, arrived in Baltimore November 8, 1873.

Blazek, Joseph and Anna and children Millie, Joseph, Josepha and Anna (arrived by 1873).

Kupka, John.

Skalicky, Josef (born about 1840) and Josephine (Seykora).

Stransky, Frank and Caroline (Svercl) and children Matilda, Agnes, Frances and Mary.

1874

Dusek, Alois aboard *Main*, arrived in New York April 20, 1874.

Dusek, Dominic and Mathilda and children Mathilda and Anna.

Benes, Anton and Anna and children Anna, Marie and Francisca, aboard *Berlin*, arrived in Baltimore May 1874.

Jansa, John, aboard *Braunschweig*, arrived in Baltimore May 23, 1874.

Jirele, John, aboard *Hohenzollern*, arrived in New York December 29, 1874.

Renchin, Anton and Frances (Seykora) and child John F.

Skalicky, Josef (born 1855).

Srsen, Frank.

Wanous, John and Katerina and children Charles, Anna, John, Frank, Henry and Mary (arrived by 1874).

1875

Herdina, Frank and Josefa and children Frank, Agnes, Frances, Matilda, Joseph, Albina and Alois, aboard *Nurnberg*, arrived in Baltimore May 17, 1875.

Dusek, Vaurin and Josephine and children Mary, Frances, Josephine and Joseph, arrived in Baltimore in late June 1875.

Klecker, Vincent and Frances (Rysavy) and children Vincent and Joseph, aboard *Nurnberg*, arrived in Baltimore March 28, 1875.

Srsen, Karel and Catherine (Mach) and children Joseph, Anton, Edward, Charles E., Anna and Frances, arrived in New York July 3, 1875.

Horak, Frank.

Klecker, Vincent and Anna.

Kubat, Josef.

Maixner, Frank.

Rybka, Josef.

Shubert, Joseph.

Skalicky, Frank and Frances (Brusenbach) and children Frank, Lenora, Mary and Joseph.

Spinler, John and Caroline and daughter Frances.

Truhlar, Anton and Anna and children Frank, Steven, Anton, Jacob, Phillip and Albert.

Vesely, Vincenc.

1876

Antel, John, aboard *Leipzig*, arrived in New York May 19, 1876.

Wanous, Anton and Frances and son Anton, aboard *Weser*, arrived in New York October 28, 1876.

Schisler, Frank and Philomena and children Frank, Joseph and Vincent.

Schuster, Matej (or Michael).

Sitz, Joseph and Agnes and children Bernard, Emma and Mary.

1877

Jerele, Wencl and Barbara (Ripka) and child Wencl.

Zdenahlik, Anton, came to Minnesota in 1885.

1878

Donato, Anton Zajic.

Fibigar, Frank.

Jirele, Anton.

Kaplan, Joseph; settled in Blooming Prairie.

Martinek, Vincent.

Matejcek, Anna (Svercl) and children John, Frank and Alois (arrived by 1878).

Miller, Frank.

Wanous, John and Barbara and son John (arrived by 1878).

1879

Moravec, Frank D, aboard *Donau*, arrived in New York March 31, 1879.

Rypka, Anton, probably aboard *Gellert*, which left Hamburg on June 4, 1879; lived for a year in Cedar Rapids, Iowa, then moved to Steele County in 1880.

Pechacek, Vincent and Frantiska with children John, Matilda and Mary.

Pic, Joseph and Anna (Matejcek) and children.

1880
Belina, Anton and Frances (Pavek) and children Josephine, Wencl and Anton (arrived by 1880).
Hondl, Jan and Anna (Groh), with son Anton J.
Maixner, Joseph and Rosa (Pavek).
Matejcek, Peregrin and Mary and daughter Mary (arrived by 1880).

1881
Kvasnicka, Joseph and Frances (Herdina) and child Joseph F.
Reichstetter, Phillip A.
Spindler, Frank and Anna (Miller) and Frank's parents.

1882
Hanzlicek, Frank and Josie (Matejcek) in late March or early April.
Slezak, Marie, Frederich and Albina, aboard *Westphalia*, arrived in New York May 11, 1882.
Slezak, Wencl and Teresa (Tomesch) and child Barbora, aboard *Westphalia*, arrived in New York May 11, 1882.
Horak, Adolf, aboard *Leipzig*, arrived in Baltimore May 1882.
Schisler, Joseph and Angelina (Brozumpavkava) and children Mary, Joseph, Anna and Frank.
Wencl, Luis.

1883
Deml, Joseph, aboard *Braunschweig*, arrived in Baltimore June 13, 1883.
Petranek, Josef and Agnes (Miller).
Ruzek, Frank and Anna (Ješatkovou) and three children.
Wencl, Frank.

1884
Ruzek, Frank and Antonia and children Cecelia, Anna and Frank, aboard *Australia*, arrived in New York September 1, 1884.
Zak, Joseph and Marie (Schuster) and children Marie, Celia, Frank, Josephine, Wencl and John, aboard *Australia*, arrived in New York September 1, 1884.
Deml, Josef and Theresa (Wesely) (Parents of Joseph Deml from 1883).
Hruska, Joseph.
Schuster, John and Mary (Adam), and children Anton, Antonia, Eliza.
Schuster, Frantisek and Anna (Yesalek).

1886
Brolek, John and Anna and child Louis.
Rysavy, Joseph and Ann (Maixner).
Styndl, Frank and Rosa (Vesely).

1887
Horak, Alois, aboard *Suevia*, arrived in New York April 11, 1887.
Matejcek, Joseph.

1888

Pivo, Reverend John.

Pechacek, Frank and Mathilda and children Frances and Frank.

Spinler, John and Frances and children Bernard and Mathilda, aboard *Bohemia*, arrived in New York June 25, 1888.

Spinler, Joseph and Rosalie and children Marie, John and Joseph, aboard *Bohemia*, arrived in New York June 25, 1888.

1890

Horak, Josef.

1891

Krahulec, Wencl.

1892

Blazek, Anton and Anezka and children Anezka, Marie and Joseph, aboard *Rhaetia*, arrived in New York April 11, 1892.

Rysavy, Frank and Marie and children Marie, Christina, Frank and Emil, aboard *Rhaetia*, arrived in New York April 11, 1892.

Wolesky, Joseph, aboard *Weimar*, arrived in Baltimore August 3, 1892.

Blazek, Adolf and Frances (Stransky) and daughter Frances.

Mikyska, Anton and Anna and children Joseph, Frances, Vincent, Louis and Anna.

Rysavy, Joseph and Frances (Motl) and children Edward and Helen.

1893

Motl, Josef and Albina and children Mary and Albina, in April 1893.

Prokopec, John and Ludmilla (Stransky).

Prokopec, Joseph.

Shimpach, Wencl and Alabeta (Zeman) and nine children.

1899

Horak, John and Anna.

1902

Wolesky, Frank, aboard *Chemnitz*, arrived in Baltimore July 20, 1902.

1904

Chott, Wencl (moved to Steele County in 1916).

1906

Broulik, Anton and Carolina and two children; Anton, aboard *Erlangen*, arrived in Baltimore April 13, 1906; Carolina and children, aboard *Neckar*, arrived in Baltimore June 26, 1906.

1908

Maixner, Frank and Matilda and children Emil, Jaroslav, Viktorie and Marie.

APPENDIX C

Origins of Local Czech Families

BABICE (near Tábor)
Schuster, John, Frank and Matej
Zdenahlik, Anton

BRANDÝS NAD ORLICÍ
Zednik, Joseph

CEREKVICE
Bulva, John
Racek, Joseph

ČESKÁ TŘEBOVÁ
Haberman, Wencl and Rose
Haberman, Wencl and Theresa
Horsky, Joseph
Jasan, Frank
Landmichl, Anton
Plotz, Joseph

DLOUHÁ TŘEBOVÁ
Belina, Frank and Wencl
Fibigar, Frank
Fisher, Anton
Fisher, Benjamin
Fisher, Joseph
Hrdlicka, Wencl
Hudrlik, John
Jansa, Anton
Jirousek, Wencl
Kaplan, Joseph and Barbora
Kovar, Anton
Kubat, Anton, Frank and Joseph
Kubista, Frank and Ignac
Marek, Anton

Mares, John
Moravec, Joseph
Motl, Jiri
Pavek, Frank
Pichner, John and Joseph
Renchin, Frank
Renchin, John
Rypka, Joseph
Seykora, Frank, Anton, John and Rosalie
Sisler, Frank
Srsen, Charles
Stransky, Anton, Frank and Joseph
Suchanek, Wencl
Wanous, John and Wencl
Wavrin, Joseph
Vesely, Vincent
Wencl, Frank J.

DOLNÍ ČERMNÁ
Betlach, Vincent

DOLNÍ DOBROUČ
Hanzlicek, Frank
Horak, Frank
Hrdina, Frank
Jansa, John
Kubicek, Frank and Vincent
Kupka, John
Matejcek, Joseph
Matejcek, Vincent, Peregryn and Anna
Meixner, Frank
Mikyska, Anna (Kubicek)
Moravec, Frank
Motl, Joseph

Pechacek, Frank
Petraneck, Joseph
Pic, Joseph and Anna
Pirkl, Bernard and Joseph
Rysavy, John
Simon, Alois
Svercl, Joseph
Skalicky, Joseph and Josephine
Skalicky, Frank and Matilda
Simon, Alois and Frances (Hanzlicek)
Spinler, John and Jaroslav
Wacek, Anton and Anna

DOLNÍ LIBCHAVY
Paukert, Wencl

HRÁDEK
Hanus, Wencl

HYLVÁTY
Simek, Anton, Joseph, John, Rosalie and Anna
Kovar, Frank

JEHNĚDÍ
Dostal, John
Skerik, John
Vasina, John

KUNČICE
Mikyska, Anton

LHOTKA
Belina
Rypka
Spatenka, Frank and Theresa
Wesely, Frank

MORAVIA
Penas, John
Sustacek, John

PARNÍK
Deml, Joseph
Hudrlik, Joseph
Rypka, Frank and Anton
Slezak, Kaspar and Wencl

PETROVICE
Dusek, John, Joseph and Alois

PRAGUE
Mikolas, Joseph

PŘÍVRAT
Stancl, Joseph and Anton
Vytlacil, Frank
Vencl, Frank
Wanous, John
Wencl, Frank
Wondra, John

ŘETOVÁ
Balcar, Frank
Rypka, Anton
Stransky, Joseph

ŘETŮVKA
Jirousek, Wencl
Pavek, John
Slezak, Anton
Wanous, John and Anton
Vasicek, Frank

SVINNÁ
Styndl, Frank

TÁBOR (in Moravia)
Maca, Joseph
Pribyl, Peter
Smrz, Thomas and Frank

ÚSTÍ NAD ORLICÍ
Brozek, John
Kaspar, Joseph
Slavik, John

ZHOŘ
Broulik, Anton and Caroline
Coufal, Joseph
Wolesky, Joseph and Frank

NOTES

PROLOGUE
1. Steve Wencl; *Bohemianism*, Wikipedia.
2. General source: *The Czechs and the Lands of the Bohemian Crown*, Hugh Agnew.
3. *Europe Since 1815*, Gordon A. Craig, p. 89.

CHAPTER 1: THE PIONEERS
1. *History of Rice and Steele Counties, Minnesota* (1910), p. 632.
2. *History of Steele and Waseca Counties, Minnesota* (1887), p. 19.
3. *Kaplan Family History*, p. 94.
4. *Kaplan Family History*, p. 87 footnote.
5. *History of Stephenson County*, Stephenson County, Illinois website; *History of Rice and Steele Counties, Minnesota* (1910), biography of John Pichner, p. 1210.
6. Kubat family tree and history by Tim Kubat; *The Czech Settlement of Steele County, Minnesota*, Karleen Chott Sheppard, p. 2; *Early Czech Settlers in Minnesota*, Karleen Chott Sheppard pp. 192–193 (life of Anton Kubat); *Family Tree of František Kubišta and Anna Šouba*, p. 5; Blooming Prairie cemetery records. Kubat family history has Anton married first to Anna Kubista until 1853, and then to Anna Renchin. However, Frank Kubista family tree says Steele County death records list the parents of Anna Kubat as Frank Kubista and Anna Šouba. Cemetery records from Blooming Prairie cemetery for Anton Kubat, born 1854 on the voyage to America, list his parents as Anton Kubat and Anna Kubista Kubat. These public records indicate that Anna Renchin was Anton's first wife, and that he came to America with his second wife, Anna Kubista.
7. *History of the Fisher Family*, 2003; Sacred Heart cemetery records. The Fisher family history lists Anna Fibiger as Benjamin Fisher's first and only wife. His second child, Joseph, born in Freeport, Illinois in 1855 is listed in Sacred Heart cemetery records as being the son of Benjamin Fisher and Anna Pichner Fisher, as are the subsequent Fisher children. Benjamin's cemetery record lists spouse number one being Anna Fibiger, and spouse number 2 as Anna Pichner. However, Anna's death record and obituaries indicate she was Anna Fibiger and that all of Benjamin's children were by her. In addition, research by Jaroslav Jansa in the Czech archives shows no indication of Benjamin having a wife die in Bohemia and his subsequently remarrying. Anna Fibiger was thus Benjamin Fisher's first and only wife and the mother of all his children.
8. *Kaplan Family History*, p. 87 footnote; Ancestry.com ship passenger lists. The Kaplan family footnote concerning Anton Simek, based in part on his police records in Bohemia, states that after his trip to America in December of 1852, he returned again to Bohemia in 1854, then left once more for America with his father, sisters, brother and brother's family. However, since his relatives all left for America in late 1853, Anton must have returned to Bohemia in 1853. The early life of Anton's brother Joseph in Bohemia and Austria is from Joseph's obituary in the May 18, 1900, issue of the *Faribault County Register* newspaper. (copy obtained from Joseph Simek descendant DD Cathcart of Sacramento, California.)
9. *Memorial Record of the Counties of Faribault, Martin, Watonwan and Jackson*, pp. 126–127, biography of Joseph Schimek.
10. *History of Steele and Waseca Counties, Minnesota* (1887), p. 339; *History of Rice and Steele Counties, Minnesota* (1910), p. 1101; obituary for May 2, 1915. Biographies of John Pichner Jr. in both county histories and in his obituary say he came to Steele County in 1855, presumably

with the Simeks. His parents and siblings came in 1856 according to pioneer accounts and the obituary of Joseph Pichner, born in 1846.

11. *Paddlewheels on the Upper Mississippi 1823–1854*, pp. 10, 11; *Acts of Congress* Ch. 113 (August 31, 1852) p. 139; Ch. 230 (August 3, 1854) pp. 535–536; Ch. 211 (March 3, 1855) p. 712. Although steamboats ran up the Mississippi well before 1854, the arrivals per year more than quadrupled between 1853 and 1857. Four railroads reached the Upper Mississippi from Milwaukee and Chicago between 1854 and 1859. In addition, the post road from St. Paul south to the Cannon River was authorized by Congress in the summer of 1852; the authorization was extended by Congress to Faribault in August of 1854, and from Faribault to Medford through the Straight River valley to Bradford, Iowa in March of 1855. It seems likely that Anton Simek went back to Bohemia in 1853, left again for America in 1853 either with his relatives or around the same time, then briefly returned to Freeport, Illinois in 1854. From there the newly opened railroads allowed him to reach the Mississippi River and catch a steamboat to St. Paul. If, as Kovar says, he took the post road south to Owatonna, he must have gone in late 1854 or in 1855. There were no European settlers in Owatonna until 1854 when Cornell and Pettit arrived. If he came in 1855 on the newly opened post road, he probably immediately filed his land claim and wrote to his relatives (who by then were in northern Iowa) and his friends in Freeport and told them to come and join him.

12. Steele County Historical Society newsletter, volume 57, issue 4, fall 2006, p. 2.

13. *Memorial Record of the Counties of Faribault, Martin, Watonwan and Jackson*, p. 127 (biography of Joseph Simek); Joseph Simek obituary in May 18, 1900 *Faribault County Register* p. 4; *History of Steele and Waseca Counties, Minnesota* (1887), p. 179; Simek family epitaphs in Bohemian National Cemetery in Owatonna. Epitaphs for Anton Simek's sisters Rosalie Simek and Anastasia Sattlau both say they arrived in Steele County in 1855. Two articles on Joseph Simek from decades later differ on the year he arrived in Steele County; he may have moved from Osage, Iowa to the Owatonna area in 1855 or 1856. His obituary says he moved to Minnesota in 1856, but his biography in the Faribault County history says he stayed in Osage, Iowa only a short time before moving to Minnesota. Steele County land records show his first land purchases at the same time as those of his brother Anton, who definitely was in Owatonna in 1855. The 1887 Steele County history lists among the new arrivals during the spring and early summer of 1855 "two Schimeks." The location of Anton Simek's initial land claim is attested to by the accounts of Frank Kovar and Joseph Kaplan, as well as by county land records.

14. The Kaplan family history states that Joseph Pichner is the father of Joseph and Jan, but cemetery records in Steele County, as well as the Pichner family genealogical research, indicate the father was Vaclav Pichner, born in 1790. He was married to Katerina Kovar who apparently died in Europe before Vaclav's departure. Vaclav is buried in the Bohemian National Cemetery in Owatonna and is the right age to be the father of Joseph and Jan. There is no burial record in Steele County of a Joseph of the right age to be their father.

15. *Kaplan Family History*, p. 91.

16. Benjamin Fisher memoir p. 1; Karleen Chott Sheppard, *The Czech Settlement of Steele County, Minnesota* p. 8; *Kaplan Family History* p. 88. Joseph Kaplan says they stayed a week in what later became Mineral Springs Park, during which time their son Joseph W. was born. His birthday was September 20. Ben Fisher says they arrived on the Feast of St. Wenceslaus (September 28), but that can't be squared with the birthday of Joseph W. Kaplan. The accounts of Anton and Anna Kubat do not mention a specific date.

17. Benjamin Fisher memoir p. 1.

18. Benjamin Fisher memoir p. 1; Karleen Chott Sheppard, *The Czech Settlement of Steele County, Minnesota* p. 8; Jensen p. 8.

19. Blegen p. 322.
20. Steele County land records; *Kaplan Family History* p. 105.
21. Benjamin Fisher memoir p. 2.
22. *Kaplan Family History* p. 88; Karleen Chott Sheppard, *Early Czech Settlers in Minnesota-Biographies* (Anton Kubat memoir) p. 4.
23. Karleen Chott Sheppard, *The Czech Settlement of Steele County, Minnesota* (Anna Kubat memoir) pp. 2, 3.
24. Wesely, pp. 13, 15; *Kaplan Family History* p. 92.
25. Karleen Chott Sheppard, *The Czech Settlement of Steele County, Minnesota* (Anna Kubat memoir) pp. 2, 3; Wesely p. 23–24; 1857 Minnesota territorial census.
26. Wesely, p. 23.
27. Benjamin Fisher memoir pp. 3, 4.
28. *Kaplan Family History*, p. 92.
29. *Kaplan Family History*, p. 93.
30. Karleen Chott Sheppard, *The Czech Settlement of Steele County, Minnesota* (Srsen memoir) p. 16–17.
31. Karleen Chott Sheppard, *The Czech Settlement of Steele County, Minnesota* (Kovar history), p. 1.
32. Naatz, Rosemary K., Joseph and Josephine Pichner family history; *History of Steele and Waseca Counties, Minnesota, An Album of History and Biography (1887)* p. 149.
33. *Kaplan Family History*, p. 93.
34. *History of Steele and Waseca Counties, Minnesota, An Album of History and Biography (1887)* pp. 113, 114.
35. Benjamin Fisher memoir, p. 6.
36. Benjamin Fisher memoir, p. 6.
37. *Kaplan Family History*, p. 95.
38. Jensen, *History of the Early Development of Owatonna 1854–1901* p. 18.
39. *Minnesota Public Statutes 1858*, Ch. 7, Sects. 95–110.
40. *Minnesota Public Statutes 1858*, Ch. 15, Sects. 1–10.
41. *Steele County Newsletter*, October 16, 1860, p. 3, second column from right.

CHAPTER 2: CIVIL WAR, COMMUNITY GROWTH, AND THE RISE OF INSTITUTIONS

1. Wesely, *Owatonna*, p. 27.
2. Folwell, *A History of Minnesota,* vol. 2, pp. 79–80.
3. Folwell, volume 2, pp. 82–84.
4. *Narrative and Roster of the First Minnesota Regiment,* pp. 8–10.
5. Steele County Probate Court records, Minnesota Historical Society microfiche, SAM 207, roll 21, frames 1632–1705; U.S. census 1850, 1860, 1870 and 1880; Minnesota Territorial Census 1857; Steele County marriage and birth records.
6. Folwell, volume 2, p. 338.
7. *Narrative and Rosters of the Minnesota Mounted Rangers and Calvary,* pp. 544–551; Folwell volume 2 pp. 295–299.
8. Second Cavalry Regiment Company C roster; Civil War Soldiers and Sailors database.
9. Souba, Gerry, unpublished Renchin family memoirs and Civil War veterans disability benefit application records.
10. April 22, 1927, obituary.
11. Chada, *The Czechs in the United States,* p. 12.

12. Chada, p. 14.
13. Folwell, *A History of Minnesota,* volume 2, p. 345.
14. Wesely, *Owatonna,* p. 26.
15. Chmelik, John, biography of Anton Slezak.
16. Chmelik, John, biography of Anton Slezak.
17. *Faribault County Register,* May 18, 1900, p. 4; emails from Delphine Cathcart (great-great granddaughter and biographer of Joseph Simek).
18. Schouweiler, *Kovar Family Story* pp. 1–5.
19. Sobotka and Sheppard, *Pioneer Stories as Related by Minnesota Czech Residents,* p. 95; 1865 census.
20. *History of Steele and Waseca Counties, Minnesota,* (1887), p. 264.
21. Souba, Renchin family history.
22. Curtiss-Wedge, *History of Rice and Steele Counties, Minnesota,* (1910), p. 1121; Wanous family tree.
23. Wesely, *Owatonna,* p. 47.
24. Holmquist, *They Chose Minnesota,* p. 340; Milan Jerabek, *Czechs in Minnesota,* p. 86; Habenicht, *History of Czechs in America* p. 288.
25. *We Remember, We Celebrate, We Believe-Church of the Sacred Heart 1866–1996* p. 16.
26. *The Story of Sacred Heart Church* (1954), p. 12; *We Remember, We Celebrate, We Believe-Church of the Sacred Heart 1866–1996,* p. 14; *History of Steele and Waseca Counties, Minnesota,* (1887) p. 238.
27. *We Remember, We Celebrate, We Believe-Church of the Sacred Heart 1866–1996* pp. 18–19.
28. Martinek, *One Hundred Years of the CSA,* p. 115.
29. Kaplan, pp. 96–97.
30. *The Story of Sacred Heart Church,* (1954) p. 24.
31. Early records and minutes of Czech-Slovanic National Cemetery, translated by Steve Wencl.
32. Chada, *The Czechs in the United States* pp. 6, 83; Capek, *The Czechs in America* pp. 83, 147, 148; Jerabek, *The Czechs in Minnesota* p. 102; Martinek, *One Hundred Years of the CSA* p. 118.
33. Sheppard, *The Czech Settlement of Steele County, Minnesota,* pp. 3, 9; Wesely, *Owatonna,* p. 41; Jerabek summary of interview with K.E. Srsen.
34. Jerabek, *The Czechs in Minnesota,* p. 103.
35. Chada, *The Czechs in the United States,* p. 83.
36. Sobotka and Sheppard, *Pioneer Stories as Related by Minnesota Czech Residents,* p. 103.
37. Sobotka and Sheppard, p. 95.
38. Sheppard, *The Czech Settlement of Steele County, Minnesota,* pp. 3, 9.
39. Dolan, *The American Catholic Experience* pp. 266–267; Folwell, *A History of Minnesota,* volume 4, p. 171.
40. Dolan p. 269.
41. Severson, *Blooming Prairie Update,* pp. 12, 13, 25.
42. Schisler, *Across the Years,* p. 13.
43. Rysavy, Paul J., *Litomysl. . . . A Dream Fulfilled,* p. 4.
44. Peller, Lorraine, *Albert Kasper: The Story of a Bohemian Immigrant,* pp. 1, 3.
45. Curtiss-Wedge, *History of Rice and Steele Counties, Minnesota* 1910, pp. 1186, 1187.
46. Fisher, Joseph, *Memories of Our Pioneers.*
47. *The Story of Sacred Heart Church, Owatonna, Minnesota,* (1954) p. 22.
48. *The Kubat Family (Frank and Thekla Belina Kubat).*
49. Steele County Historical Society newsletter, vol. 57, issue 4, Fall 2006, p. 2.
50. Karleen Chott Sheppard, *The Czech Settlement of Steele County, Minnesota* (Anna Kubat memoir) p. 2.

51. Steve Wencl, from Fisher descendant.
52. Souba, Gerry, unpublished Renchin family memoirs and Civil War veterans disability benefit application records.
53. Rysavy, Lula, *Harvest of Memories,* p. 29.
54. Fisher, Joseph, *Memories of Our Pioneers.*
55. *Kaplan Family History,* p. 92.
56. Steve Wencl, from Jerry and Vern Meixner and Dave Rysavy.
57. *Kaplan Family History,* p. 95.

CHAPTER 3: COMING TO AMERICA

1. Langer, Edward G., *Lanskroner Emigration to the American Midwest.*
2. Jansa, *Dlouhá Třebová*; Staňková, *The Region Orlicko-Trebovsko.*
3. Jansa, *Přívrat.*
4. Jansa, *Řetová* and *Řetůvka (Malá Řetová).*
5. Chaloupka, Petr, Regional Museum of Litomysl, email correspondence.
6. *Od Historie K Současnosti 1292–1992,* (Dolní Dobrouč town history) p. 37.
7. Beran and Pecháček, *Dobroučské obrázky (Dobrouč Portraits),* translated by Steve Wencl.
8. Faltýsek, Pavel, *The History of the Village of Čermná, Česke Stopy (Czech Footprints),* Vol. 4 No. 3, pp. 12–14.
9. Jerabek, *Czechs in Minnesota,* pp. 35–36.
10. Korytova-Magstadt, *To Reap a Bountiful Harvest,* pp. 3–39; Dubovický, *Ročenka* Vol. 4 2000, pp. 4–12.
11. Kaplan, p. 87 note.
12. Jerabek, pp. 49, 50.
13. Cherney, *Wisconsin's Land for the Landless,* p. 9.
14. Jerabek, pp. 48, 49.
15. *The Minnesota Guide,* pp. 64–65.
16. *Owatonna Journal,* September 3, 1868, p. 2.
17. Korytová Magstadt, pp. 23–24; Jerabek, pp. 15–16.
18. Korytová Magstadt, pp. 5–8.
19. Korytová Magstadt, pp. 17–19.
20. Sobotka and Sheppard, *Pioneer Stories,* p. 101.
21. Korytová Magstadt, pp. 22–24.
22. Jerabek, pp. 15, 21–22.
23. Jerabek, pp. 20–21.
24. Sobotka and Sheppard, *Pioneer Stories,* p. 101.
25. Sheppard, *Early Czech Settlers in Minnesota,* p. 116.
26. Korytová-Magstadt, p. 26; Jerabek, p. 16.
27. Korytová-Magstadt, p. 26; Jerabek, p. 15.
28. Korytová-Magstadt; Jerabek, p. 15—17.
29. Korytová-Magstadt, p. 25.
30. Sheppard, *Early Czech Settlers in Minnesota,* p. 116.
31. Kysilka, *The Borderland of Bohemia and Moravia,* vol. 4, p. 134.
32. Polišenský, *The Passage From Home to the Sea,* pp. 5–11; travel passes and documents of Joseph Kaplan, Joseph Kaspar, Vincenc Pechaček and Vincenz Starch; Steve Wencl.
33. Wellauer-Lenius, Maralyn A., *Bremen and Hamburg: The Ports, Shipping Companies, and Agents, Naše Rodina,* Vol. 20, No. 1, March 2008, pp. 5–8.
34. Sheppard, Karleen Chott, *A History of Czechs in Steele County, Minnesota from 1852 to 1931, The Czech Settlement of Steele County, Minnesota,* p. 2.

35. Colletta, John P., *They Came in Ships*, p. 94; Wellauer-Lenius, Maralyn A., *Bremen and Hamburg: The Ports, Shipping Companies, and Agents, Naše Rodina*, Vol. 20, No. 1, March 2008, pp. 9.

36. *Ancestry.com* internet website, Passenger Ships and Images Record.

37. From the Moravský zemský archive in Brno, furnished by Steve Wencl.

38. Kubicek, Frank Joseph, *History of the Early Days of My Life*, p. 3.

39. Horak, Tim, Petranek family memories.

40. Polišenský, J.V., *The Passage from Home to the Sea, Ročenka,* Vol. 5 (2002) pp. 5–11.

41. Aksamit, Gene, *Castle Garden-America's First Immigrant Receiving Station, Naše Rodina,* Vol. 12, No. 2, June 2000.

42. Aksamit, Gene, *Castle Garden-America's First Immigrant Receiving Station, Naše Rodina,* Vol. 12, No. 2, June 2000.

43. Vlcek, Frantisek, *Povídka Mého Života (Story of My Life), Česká Literární Společost*, St. Louis 1928 (translated by Steve Wencl, p. 96.

44. Coan, Peter Morton, *Ellis Island Interviews*, Barnes and Noble 2004, pp. 413–417.

45. Colletta, John P., *They Came in Ships*, pp. 122–126.

46. Stolarik, Mark, *Forgotten Doors*, pp. 69–71.

47. Kubicek, Frank Joseph, *History of the Early Days of My Life*, p. 3.

48. Kaplan, Joseph, *The Kaplan Family History*, p. 91.

49. Kaplan, Joseph, *The Kaplan Family History*, pp. 90–91; *Naše Rodina*, Vol. 19, No. 3, September 2007 pp. 120–121.

CHAPTER 4

1. Hobbs, Karen, *1866 War Story, Naše Rodina,* Vol. 15 No. 4, December 2003, pp. 140–148; Wikipedia.

2. Steve Wencl.

3. Craig, Gordon, *Germany 1866–1945*, pp. 2–7.

4. Pavek, Miloslav, *700 Let Obce Řetůvka*, translated by Steve Wencl.

5. Langer, Edward G., Lanskroner Emigration to the American Midwest, *Ročenka,* Volume 2, Winter 1995–1996, p. 14; Pavek, Miloslav, *700 Let Obce Řetůvka*, translated by Steve Wencl.

6. Sheppard, Karleen Chott, *Pioneer Stories as Related by Minnesota Czech Residents (1906–1930),* p. 38.

7. Sheppard, Karleen Chott, *Early Czech Settlers in Minnesota*, p. 117.

8. Justin Spinler, told to Steve Wencl.

9. Spinler, Mary Rysavy, *Life of Agnes Rajnet Rysavy* (unpublished).

10. Craig, Gordon, *Europe Since 1815*, p. 156.

11. Wesely, Edgar Bruce, *Owatonna-The Social Development of a Minnesota Community*, p. 31.

12. Folwell, William Watts, *A History of Minnesota*, Vol. 3, pp. 67–69.

13. *Owatonna People's Press*, October 4, 1878 p. 4.

14. *Owatonna People's Press*, November 15, 1878.

15. Folwell, William Watts, *A History of Minnesota*, Vol. 3, p. 33.

16. Folwell, William Watts, *A History of Minnesota*, Vol. 3, pp. 37–39.

17. Wesely, Edgar Bruce, *Owatonna-The Social Development of a Minnesota Community*, pp. 56, 58.

18. Folwell, William Watts, *A History of Minnesota*, Volume 3, pp. 47–49.

19. Folwell, William Watts, *A History of Minnesota*, Volume 3, pp. 40–56.

20. Wesely, Edgar Bruce, *Owatonna-The Social Development of a Minnesota Community*, p. 58.

21. Wesely, Edgar Bruce, *Owatonna-The Social Development of a Minnesota Community*, pp. 57, 58.
22. *Owatonna Journal*, March 20, 1873, p. 3, col. 2.
23. *Owatonna Journal*, May 1, 1873, p. 3, col. 1.
24. Wesely, Edgar Bruce, *Owatonna-The Social Development of a Minnesota Community*, p. 59.
25. Wesely, Edgar Bruce, *Owatonna-The Social Development of a Minnesota Community*, pp. 37–38.
26. Steele County school district 23 records; Hanson, Steele County country schools; *Owatonna Journal*, September 5, 1879, p. 2.
27. Steele County school district 23 records; *Owatonna Journal*, January 2, 1873, p. 3, cols. 3 and 4.
28. *Owatonna People's Press*, April 30, 1880, p. 1.
29. Sheppard and Sobotka, *Pioneer Stories as Related by Minnesota Czech Residents (1906–1930)*, p. 95.
30. *Owatonna Journal*, March 2, 1876, p. 3.
31. *Owatonna Journal*, September, 1879, p. 2.
32. Pribyl, Silvin, *My Life*, p. 1.
33. Folwell, William Watts, *A History of Minnesota*, Vol. 4, pp. 162–164.
34. Pribyl, Henry Hubert, unpublished autobiography.
35. Folwell, William Watts, *A History of Minnesota*, Vol. 4, p. 171.
36. *Owatonna Journal*, December 4, 1873, p. 2.
37. *Owatonna Journal*, February 24, 1876, p. 2, col. 3.
38. *Owatonna Journal*, March 2, 1876, p. 2.
39. Folwell, William Watts, *A History of Minnesota*, Vol. 4, p. 172.
40. Folwell, William Watts, *A History of Minnesota*, Vol. 4, p. 173.
41. Dolan, Jay P., *The American Catholic Experience*, pp. 271–272.
42. Dolan, Jay P., *The American Catholic Experience*, pp. 276–281.
43. *Owatonna Journal*, May 8, 1873, p. 3, col. 1.
44. Sheppard, Karleen Chott, *Early Czech Settlers in Minnesota*, pp. 117–119.
45. Joachim, Bonnie, Suchanek family history material.
46. Bureau, Angela Mary, *Family Tree of František Kubista I and Anna Šouba*, pp. 5–42.
47. Curtiss-Wedge, Franklin, *History of Rice and Steele Counties, Minnesota*, pp. 1101–1102, 1244; Pribyl family tree; 1870 census; Joe and Wencl Pribyl interview.
48. Kubicek, Frank Joseph, *History of the Early Days of My Life*, pp. 1–6.
49. Skalicky, Frank R., unpublished autobiography, 1932.
50. Rysavy, Lula, *Harvest of Memories*, pp. 26–32.
51. Curtiss-Wedge, Franklin, *History of Rice and Steele Counties, Minnesota*, pp. 1107–1108.
52. Reger, Theresa (Kubista), Kubista family material.
53. Falteisek, Chris, Pirkl family material.
54. Rysavy, Lula, *Harvest of Memories*, pp. 28–29; Prokopec family tree.
55. Rypka, Dorothy D., Vaclav Slezak family tree.
56. Rypka, Dorothy D., Josef Rypka family tree.
57. Curtiss-Wedge, Franklin, *History of Rice and Steele Counties, Minnesota*, pp. 1108–1109; *Krestanske Listy*, April 1920, Katerina Skerik obituary.
58. Jerabek, Milan W., *Czechs in Minnesota*, pp. 41–42.

59. Wesely, Edgar Bruce, *Owatonna-The Social Development of a Minnesota Community*, p. 52.

60. Smith, Page, *The Rise of Industrial America—A People's History of the Post-Reconstruction Era*, p. 581; Dolan, Jay P., *The American Catholic Experience*, p. 202.

61. *Owatonna Journal*, December 19, 1872, p. 2, cols. 4 and 5.

62. *Owatonna Journal*, January 2, 1873, p. 3, col. 1.

63. Folwell, William Watts, *A History of Minnesota*, Volume 3, pp. 71–72.

64. *Owatonna Journal*, January 16, 1873, p. 3, col. 1.

65. *Owatonna Journal*, January 16, 1873, p. 3, col. 1.

66. *Owatonna Journal*, January 23, 1873, p. 3, col. 1.

67. *Owatonna Journal*, March 27, 1873, p. 3, col. 1.

68. *Owatonna Journal*, April 10, 1873, p. 3, col. 2.

69. *Owatonna Journal*, July 3, 1873, p. 3, col. 2.

70. *Owatonna Journal*, November 27, 1873, p. 3, col. 3.

71. Morison, Samuel Eliot, *The Oxford History of the American People*, Vol. 3, p. 51.

72. Kann, Robert A., *A History of the Habsburg Empire 1526–1918*, p. 343.

73. *Owatonna Journal*, September 25, 1873, p. 2, col. 3.

74. Folwell, William Watts, *A History of Minnesota*, Volume 3, pp. 53, 72, 126; Josephson, Matthew, *The Robber Barons*, pp. 169–173; Gordon, John Steele, *An Empire of Wealth*, pp. 227–228.

CHAPTER 5

1. Wesely, Edgar Bruce, *Owatonna-The Social Development of a Minnesota Community*, p. 13.

2. *Owatonna People's Press*, April 16, 1880, p. 4.

3. Wesely, Edgar Bruce, *Owatonna-The Social Development of a Minnesota Community*, p. 65.

4. Wesely, pp. 53–80.

5. Wesely, p. 79.

6. Wesely, pp. 72–73.

7. *Owatonna Journal*, November 5, 1874, p. 3.

8. *People's Press*, May 4, 1878, letter on p. 1.

9. *People's Press*, January 6, 1877, p. 3.

10. *Owatonna Journal*, November 9, 1876, p. 3, col. 2.

11. *People's Press*, April 6, 1878, p. 4.

12. Wesely, Edgar Bruce, *Owatonna-The Social Development of a Minnesota Community*, p. 66; Sheppard and Sobotka, *Pioneer Stories as Related by Minnesota Czech Residents (1906–1930)*, p. 2; Holmquist, June Drenning ed., *They Chose Minnesota*, p. 349 note 31.

13. Morison, *The Oxford History of the American People*, Vol. 3, p. 81.

14. Morison, *The Oxford History of the American People*, Vol. 3, pp. 60–61; Smith, *The Rise of Industrial America*, pp. 27–33.

15. Folwell, *A History of Minnesota*, Vol. 3, pp. 113, 120, 131.

16. Folwell, *A History of Minnesota*, Vol. 3, pp. 139–140.

17. *People's Press*, April 27, 1878, p. 1.

18. Kann, *A History of the Habsburg Empire 1526–1918*, pp. 343–344, 357.

19. Sustacek, John Emil, *The Sustaceks of Minnesota*.

20. Sheppard, *The Czech Settlement of Steele County*, Minnesota, p. 6.

21. Sheppard, *The Czech Settlement of Steele County*, Minnesota, p. 7.

22. Spencer, Evelyn Dusek, *Early Life of the Dusek Family*.

23. Curtiss-Wedge, *History of Rice and Steele Counties, Minnesota*, p. 1065–1066; 1880 census; Ancestry.com ship passenger lists.

24. Sheppard and Sobotka, *Pioneer Stories as Related by Minnesota Czech Residents (1906–1930)*, p. 101.

25. Sheppard and Sobotka, *Pioneer Stories as Related by Minnesota Czech Residents (1906–1930)*, p. 101–103.

26. Sheppard and Sobotka, *Pioneer Stories as Related by Minnesota Czech Residents (1906–1930)*, p. 103.

27. Rypka, Dorothy D., Rypka family tree and history.

28. *Owatonna Journal*, November 30, 1876, p. 3, col. 1.

29. *People's Press*, June 9, 1877, p. 4, col. 2.

30. *People's Press*, June 16, 1877, p. 1, col. 1.

31. *People's Press*, October 18, 1878, p. 4.

32. *Owatonna Journal*, November 7, 1879, p. 3, col. 3; *People's Press*, November 7, 1879, p. 4.

33. *People's Press*, January 20, 1877, p. 4, col. 2.

34. *People's Press*, August 1, 1879, p. 4.

35. *People's Press*, January 2, 1880, p. 4.

36. *People's Press*, September 1, 1877, p. 1; 1880 census.

37. Peller, Loraine, *Albert Kasper: The Story of a Bohemian Immigrant 1853–1937*, p. 4 et seq.; interview with Ted Peller.

38. *People's Press*, February 10, 1877, p. 4, col. 5.

39. *People's Press*, September 8, 1877, p. 4.

40. *People's Press*, March 2, 1878, p. 1.

41. *People's Press*, May 16, 1879, p. 4.

42. *People's Press*, May 25, 1878, p. 1.

43. *People's Press*, June 15, 1878, p. 4.

44. *People's Press*, June 22, 1878, p. 1.

45. *People's Press*, September 7, 1878, p. 1 and September 21, 1878, p. 4.

46. *People's Press*, May 18, 1878, p. 1.

47. *People's Press*, July 4, 1879, p. 1.

48. *People's Press*, March 16, 1878, p. 4.

49. *Owatonna Journal*, February 21, 1879, p. 3; *People's Press*, February 21, 1879, p. 4 and February 28, 1879, p. 3.

50. *People's Press*, December 12, 1879, p. 1.

51. *Owatonna Journal*, June 4, 1874, p. 3.

52. *People's Press*, December 23, 1876, p. 4.

53. *People's Press*, August 3, 1878, p. 4.

54. *People's Press*, January 30, 1880, p. 4.

55. *People's Press*, January 30, 1880, p. 4 and February 6, 1880, p. 4.

56. *People's Press*, June 18, 1880, p. 4.

57. *People's Press*, July 2, 1880, p. 4.

58. *People's Press*, January 21, 1881, p. 4.

59. *Owatonna Journal*, December 10, 1874, p. 3.

60. *Owatonna Journal*, February 25, 1875, p. 3.

61. *People's Press*, June 4, 1880, p. 4.
62. *Owatonna Journal*, January 28, 1875, p. 3.
63. *People's Press*, December 19, 1879.
64. *People's Press*, October 1, 1880, p. 4.
65. *People's Press*, November 19, 1880, p. 4.
66. *Owatonna Journal*, July 29, 1881, p. 3; Rysavy, Lula, *Harvest of Memories*, p. 31.
67. Kubicek, *History of the Early Days of My Life*, p. 17.
68. *Owatonna Journal*, February 12, 1874, p. 3, col. 1.
69. *Owatonna Journal*, June 4, 1874, p. 3, col. 5.
70. Habenicht, *History of the Czechs in America*, p. 274.
71. *We Remember, We Celebrate, We Believe: Church of the Sacred Heart 1866–1996*, p. 15.
72. *Owatonna Journal*, February 16, 1876, p. 3, col. 1.
73. *Owatonna Journal*, February 24, 1876, p. 3, col. 2.
74. *Owatonna Journal*, March 2, 1876, p. 3, col. 1.
75. *Owatonna Journal*, August 10, 1876, p. 3, col. 1.
76. *People's Press*, December 2, 1876, p. 4, col. 2.
77. *People's Press*, February 24, 1877, p. 4, col. 4.
78. *We Remember, We Celebrate, We Believe: Church of the Sacred Heart 1866–1996*, p. 30.
79. Raiche and Biermaier, *They Came to Teach*, pp. 11, 12, 85.
80. *People's Press*, September 29, 1877, p. 4.
81. *We Remember, We Celebrate, We Believe: Church of the Sacred Heart 1866–1996*, p. 30.
82. *People's Press*, November 24, 1877, p. 4.
83. Raiche and Biermaier, *They Came to Teach*, p. 12.
84. *People's Press*, January 19, 1878, p. 4.
85. *People's Press*, January 26, 1878, p. 1.
86. *People's Press*, May 30, 1879, p. 4.
87. *People's Press*, July 11, 1879, p. 4.
88. *Owatonna Journal*, November 14, 1879, p. 3, col. 3.
89. *The Story of Sacred Heart Church*, p. 13; *We Remember, We Celebrate, We Believe: Church of the Sacred Heart 1866–1996*, p. 15; Habenicht, *History of Czechs in America*, p. 274.
90. *People's Press*, October 8, 1880, p. 4.
91. *People's Press*, November 19, 1880, p. 4.
92. *Kaplan Family History*, p. 100.
93. *People's Press*, March 28, 1879, p. 4.
94. Bichner, Ralph and Maxine, *Bichner-Pichner Family 1800–1985*, p. 2; Brewer and Wick, *History of Linn County, Iowa*, p. 851.
95. *People's Press*, October 24, 1879, p. 4.
96. Sheppard, *Early Czech Settlers in Minnesota*, pp. 4–5.
97. *Amerikán Narodní Kalendář* 1882, translated by Steve Wencl.
98. Steve Wencl.
99. *Kaplan Family History*, pp. 189–190.
100. Prague Radio, April 8, 2004; English translation of a French-language broadcast; from www.radio.cz/fr/article/52594.
101. *People's Press*, February 23, 1878, p. 4.

102. *People's Press*, March 9, 1878, p. 4.

103. Donato, A.Z., *Kolem Svéta O Jedné Noze: Cesty a Příběhy z Dráhy Umělecké*, pp. 182–183, translated by Steve Wencl.

104. Donato, A.Z., *Kolem Svéta O Jedné Noze: Cesty a Příběhy z Dráhy Umělecké*, p. 171, translated by Karleen Chott Sheppard.

105. Sheppard, *The Czech Settlement of Steele County, Minnesota*, p. 3.

106. *People's Press*, February 18, 1881, p. 4.

107. Donato, A.Z., *Kolem Svéta O Jedné Noze: Cesty a Příběhy z Dráhy Umělecké*, pp. 182–183, translated by Steve Wencl.

108. Habenicht, *History of Czechs in America*, p. 534.

109. *Owatonna Journal*, July 6, 1876, p. 3, col. 1.

110. *People's Press*, June 20, 1879, p. 4.

111. *People's Press*, July 11, 1879, p. 4.

112. Bruno, *Yield of the Years*, p. 64.

113. Holmquist, *They Chose Minnesota*, p. 338.

CHAPTER 6

1. Thiele, *Hope, Minnesota-Celebrating 100 Years 1906–2006*, p. 135.

2. Kubicek, *History of the Early Days of My Life*, pp. 10–11.

3. Miller, Frank Joseph biography.

4. Svercl, Paul, family history of Svercls and related Matejcek and Skalicky immigrants to America; 1880 and 1900 U.S. census.

5. Svercl, Paul.

6. Miller, Frank Joseph biography; *Story of Sacred Heart Church*, p. 22; *We Remember, We Celebrate, We Believe*, p. 33.

7. *Owatonna Journal*, September 5, 12, 19 and 26, 1879, p. 2.

8. Frank Kubicek, *History of the Early Days of My Life*, p. 9.

9. Buryska, Frances, interview.

10. Kubicek, Frank, *History of the Early Days of My Life*, p. 6.

11. *Owatonna Journal*, March 4, 1875, p. 3, column 1.

12. Kubicek, Frank, *History of the Early Days of My Life*, p. 7.

13. Kubicek, Frank, *History of the Early Days of My Life*, pp. 6–8.

14. *Owatonna Journal*, April 1, 1875, p. 3, col. 2.

15. *Owatonna Journal*, August 31, 1876, p. 3, col. 3.

16. Folwell, *A History of Minnesota*, Volume 3, pp. 97–103.

17. Kubicek, Frank, *History of the Early Days of My Life*, p. 8.

18. *People's Press*, April 21, 1877, p. 4, col. 2.

19. Folwell, *A History of Minnesota*, Volume 3, pp. 106–110.

20. Kubicek, Frank, *History of the Early Days of My Life*, pp. 8–9.

21. *People's Press*, February 11, 1881, p. 4.

22. Bjoraker, Martha Kabela Haberman, *Horak Family Tree*.

23. Falteisek, Jirele family tree; *History of Rice and Steele Counties, Minnesota*, p. 1090; 1880 U.S. census.

24. Falteisek, Jirele family tree; *Family Tree of Joseph and Mary Deml*; 1880 U.S. census.

25. *Amerikán* 1935, translated by Steve Wencl; *History of Rice and Steele Counties, Minnesota*, p. 1145.

26. *Owatonna Journal*, June 3, 1875, p. 3.

27. Wondra family account as told to Steve Wencl.

28. *People's Press,* March 23, 1878 p. 4 and June 8, 1878 p. 4; *Kaplan Family History,* p. 96; 1880 U.S. census.

29. *Owatonna Journal*, July 13, 1876, p. 3, col. 2.

30. Morison, *Oxford History of the American People*, Vol. 3, p. 38.

31. *People's Press*, November 11, 1876, p. 4, col. 4.

32. *History of Rice and Steele Counties, Minnesota*, p. 364.

33. *Owatonna Journal*, December 10, 1874, p. 3, col. 5.

34. *People's Press*, December 23, 1876, p. 4, col. 4.

35. *People's Press*, June 8, 1878, p. 4.

36. *People's Press*, June 8, 1878, p. 4.

37. *People's Press*, January 24, 1879, p. 1.

38. *People's Press*, January 21, 1880.

39. *People's Press*, February 13, 1880, p. 4.

40. *Owatonna Journal*, July 5, 1877, p. 3, col. 3.

41. *People's Press*, July 14, 1877, p. 1, col. 1.

42. *Owatonna Journal*, December 13, 1877, p. 3, col. 5.

43. *People's Press*, December 22, 1877.

44. *State of Minnesota v. Frank Herdina*, 25 Minn. 161, July 2, 1878.

45. *People's Press*, April 18, 1879, p. 1.

46. Kubicek, *History of the Early Days of My Life*, p. 11.

47. *People's Press*, October 27, 1877, p. 4.

48. *People's Press*, June 1, 1878, p. 1.

49. *People's Press*, October 11, 1878, p. 4.

50. *People's Press*, September 12, 1879, p. 1.

51. *People's Press*, August 13, 1880, p. 4.

52. *People's Press*, August 3, 1878, p. 4.

53. *People's Press*, December 13, 1878.

54. *People's Press*, January 24, 1879.

55. *People's Press*, March 21, 1879, p. 1.

56. *People's Press*, May 23, 1879, p. 4.

57. *People's Press*, October 17, 1879, p. 1.

58. *People's Press*, December 5, 1879, p. 1.

59. *People's Press*, February 27, 1880, p. 1.

60. *People's Press*, February 6, 1880, p. 1.

61. *People's Press*, January 21, 1881, p. 4.

62. *Owatonna Journal*, July 29, 1881, p. 3; *People's Press*, July 29, 1881, p. 4.

63. Habenicht, *History of Czechs in America*, pp. 274–276; Rysavy, *Litomysl. . . . A Dream Fulfilled*.

64. Schisler and Seykora, *Leaves of . . . Yesterday and Today: Souvenir of the Most Holy Trinity Church Cornerstone Laying Festival*.

65. *People's Press*, May 21, 1880, p. 4.

66. Buryska, Frances, unpublished memoirs

67. Rysavy, *Litomysl . . . . A Dream Fulfilled*, pp. 13–14; Rysavy, Lula, *Harvest of Memories*, pp. 31–32.

68. *Owatonna Journal*, September 5, 12, 19 and 26, 1879, county school superintendent's report.

69. Frank Ruzek, grandson of the Frank Ruzek who died in 1936, as told to Steve Wencl; obituary of Frank Ruzek in *Fraternal Herald* 1936; legal filing for cemetery association.

70. Hanson, Bernie, *History of the Creameries of Steele County*, pp. 185–186.

71. Kubicek, Frank, *History of the Early Days of My Life*; Wolesky, Donald, *Wolesky Family History*.

72. Pribyl, Joseph, telephone interview.

73. Prokopec, Carol and Bob, interview.

74. Hanson, Bernie, *History of the Creameries of Steele County*, pp. 175–179.

75. Staska, Norm, written memories of Steele Center.

76. Standke, Ione Kaplan, *Steele County: Crossroads of Southern Minnesota*, p. 126; Frances Buryska memoirs.

77. Hanson, *History of the Creameries of Steele County*, pp. 247–248; Standke, *Steele County: Crossroads of Southern Minnesota*, p. 128; Steve Wencl.

78. Hanson, *History of the Creameries of Steele County*, pp. 59–64.

79. Styndl, Frank, biography.

80. Bixby, John L., *Origin of the Village of Bixby, Steele County, Minnesota, as I Remember It After an Intermission of Seventy-Five Years*.

81. Thiele, *Hope, Minnesota-Celebrating 100 Years 1906–2006*.

82. Steele County plat book 1879; U.S. census 1880; Steele County directory 1892–1893.

CHAPTER 7

1. Jacoby, *Freethinkers*; Waldman, *Founding Faith*.

2. Martinek, *One Hundred Years of the ČSA*; Sheppard, *The Czech Settlement of Steele County, Minnesota*, p. 9.

3. Sheppard, *The Czech Settlement of Steele County, Minnesota*, p. 9.

4. Martinek, *One Hundred Years of the ČSA*, p. 33.

5. Jerabek, Milan, *Czechs in Minnesota*, pp. 109–110.

6. Martinek, *One Hundred Years of the ČSA*, p. 30.

7. Martinek, *One Hundred Years of the ČSA*, p. 135.

8. *Catholic Encyclopedia 1907*, Volume 2, internet: *The Bohemians of the United States*.

9. Martinek, *One Hundred Years of the ČSA*, pp. 35–118.

10. *Owatonna Daily People's Press*, January 22, 1931, March 19, 1931, and June 26, 2004; Fisher, Glen, 1978 speech to CSA lodge 67; *History of Steele and Waseca Counties, Minnesota*; *History of Rice and Steele Counties, Minnesota*; Hammel, Thelma, typewritten article on CSA Lodge 67.

11. *People's Press*, January 21, 1881, p. 4.

12. Fisher, Glen, speech to CSA Lodge 67.

13. Martinek, *One Hundred Years of the ČSA*, p. 85.

14. Martinek, *One Hundred Years of the ČSA*, p. 144.

15. Sheppard, *The Czech Settlement of Steele County, Minnesota*, p. 11.

16. Martinek, *One Hundred Years of the ČSA*, pp. 144–145.

17. Martinek, *One Hundred Years of the ČSA*, p. 115.
18. Sheppard, *CSPS Lodge Death Claims for the State of Minnesota September 1897 through December 15, 1946*.
19. Sheppard, *Pioneer Stories as Related by Minnesota Czech Residents*, p. 103.
20. Martinek, *One Hundred Years of the ČSA*, pp. 127–140; *Fraternal Herald* July 1972, p. 1.
21. Martinek, *One Hundred Years of the ČSA*, pp. 165–170.
22. Sheppard, *The Czech Settlement of Steele County, Minnesota*, p. 5.
23. ZCBJ Lodge 83 minutes, translated by Steve Wencl.
24. Jerabek, Milan, letters.
25. Iverson, Janet (Wolesky), interviews.
26. Sheppard, *The Czech Settlement of Steele County, Minnesota*, p. 10.
27. Martinek, *One Hundred Years of the ČSA*, pp. 109, 127.
28. *Jednota Českých Dam: ve spojených Státech Severní Americky* (Union of Czech Ladies in the United States of North America), pp. 414–415, translated by author.
29. *Catholic Workman 1891–1991*.

EPILOGUE
1. Wolesky, Donald, *Wolesky Family History*; Schouweiler, *Schuster Family Story*; interviews with Charles Wolesky and Janet Iverson.
2. Svercl, Paul, family history of Svercls and related families; Buryska, Frances, unpublished memoir.
3. Buryska, Frances, unpublished memoir.
4. Spinler, Mary Rysavy, *Reflections on My Grandfather* and *Agnes Rajnet Rysavy*; Spinler, Justin, Spinler family memories.
5. McNearney, Laurietta Miller, Petranek family memoirs.
6. Curtiss-Wedge, Franklin, *History of Rice and Steele Counties, Minnesota*, p. 1551.
7. Habenicht, Jan, *History of the Czechs in America*, p. 583.
8. Sheppard, Karleen Chott, biography of Vaclav Chott.
9. Skala, Joseph Edward, family tree and history; personal interview; 1910 U.S. census; Ancestry.com ship passenger lists.
10. Bjoraker, Sylvia Kabela Haberman, oral autobiography; Johnson, Rosemary, personal interview; 1920 U.S. census..
11. Kubicek, *History of the Early Days of My Life*; Laughlin, *Continuation of the Life of Frank Kubicek from 1909 to 1950*.
12. Peller, Lorraine, *Albert Kasper: The Story of a Bohemian Immigrant 1853–1937*.
13. Sheppard and Sobotka, *Pioneer Stories as Related by Minnesota Czech Residents 1906–1930*, pp. 26–28.
14. Sheppard and Sobotka, *Pioneer Stories as Related by Minnesota Czech Residents 1906–1930*, pp. 26–28; Wesely, *Owatonna-The Social Development of a Minnesota Community*, pp. 92, 96.
15. *Kaplan Family History*, pp. 140–142.
16. *Kaplan Family History*, pp. 151–152, 156–157; *Owatonna-Memories and Milestones*, p. 130.
17. Hanson, *History of the Creameries of Steele County*, p. 1.
18. Hanson, *History of the Creameries of Steele County*, pp. 21–23.

19. Hanson, *History of the Creameries of Steele County.*
20. Folwell, A History of Minnesota, Volume 4, pp. 410–411; Curtiss-Wedge, *History of Rice and Steele Counties, Minnesota,* pp. 850–851.
21. *Story of Sacred Heart Church, Owatonna, Minnesota,* p. 26; *We Remember, We Celebrate, We Believe: Church of the Sacred Heart 1866–1996,* p. 76.
22. Charles Wolesky interview.
23. Robert Prokopec interview.
24. Charles Wolesky interview; *We Remember, We Celebrate, We Believe: Church of the Sacred Heart 1866–1996,* p. 26.
25. Charles Wolesky interview.
26. *Story of Sacred Heart Church, Owatonna, Minnesota,* pp. 13–17; *We Remember, We Celebrate, We Believe: Church of the Sacred Heart 1866–1996,* pp. 18–29; Habenicht, *History of the Czechs in America,* pp. 274–275.
27. *We Remember, We Celebrate, We Believe: Church of the Sacred Heart 1866–1996,* p. 31.
28. Frances Buryska unpublished memoir.
29. *We Remember, We Celebrate, We Believe: Church of the Sacred Heart 1866–1996,* p. 33.
30. Martinek, *One Hundred Years of the ČSA,* pp. 117, 233, 264.
31. Martinek, *One Hundred Years of the ČSA,* pp. 198, 215, 276.
32. Martinek, *One Hundred Years of the ČSA,* p. 191.
33. Martinek, *One Hundred Years of the ČSA,* pp. 221–222.
34. Martinek, *One Hundred Years of the ČSA,* pp. 278–284.
35. Martinek, *One Hundred Years of the ČSA,* pp. 268–269.
36. Martinek, *One Hundred Years of the ČSA,* pp. 379, 449–450; *CSA Journal,* July 1976, author unknown.
37. Martinek, *One Hundred Years of the ČSA,* pp. 308–319.
38. Martinek, *One Hundred Years of the ČSA,* pp. 313–314.
39. Martinek, *One Hundred Years of the ČSA,* pp. 370, 488–489.
40. Hammel, Thelma, *Czechoslovak Society of America—Lodge 67.*
41. Steve Wencl.
42. Sheppard and Sobotka, *Pioneer Stories as Related by Minnesota Czech Residents,* p. 55.
43. Chada, *Czechs in the United States,* pp. 43–53.
44. Photo obtained from Steve Wencl.
45. *Kaplan Family History,* p. 103; *People's Press,* September 21, 1917, p. 7.
46. *Owatonna Journal-Chronicle,* March 25, 1918, p. 1, col. 3.
47. *Owatonna Journal-Chronicle,* October 11, 1918, p. 1, col. 5.
48. *Owatonna People's Press,* March 17, 1918, p. 1 col. 6 and March 19, 1918, p. 2, col. 1.
49. Chrislock, *Watchdog of Loyalty-The Minnesota Commission of Public Safety During World War I,* p. 282.
50. Chrislock, *Watchdog of Loyalty,* p. 282.
51. Council of National Defense Bulletin No. 86, February 12, 1918, p. 1.
52. Council of National Defense Bulletin No. 86, February 12, 1918, pp. 3, 4.
53. *Owatonna Journal-Chronicle,* October 4, 1918, p. 5, col. 1.
54. Sheppard, *The Czech Settlement of Steele County, Minnesota,* pp. 3, 4.
55. *Owatonna Journal-Chronicle,* May 3, 1918, p. 4, col. 3.

56. Chrislock, *Watchdog of Loyalty*, p. 109.

57. Chrislock, *Watchdog of Loyalty*, pp. 217–219; *Blooming Prairie Update*, pp. 103–107.

58. Morison, *The Oxford History of the American People*, Volume 3, pp. 234–235.

59. Steve Wencl interview.

60. *Owatonna Journal-Chronicle*, December 30, 1932.

61. Sheppard, *Early Czech Settlers in Minnesota*, pp. 119–120.

62. Sheppard, *The Czech Settlement of Steele County, Minnesota*, p. 1.

63. Sheppard, *Pioneer Stories as Related by Minnesota Czech Residents*, pp. 1–3.

64. Steve Wencl email.

65. *People's Press,* October 23, 1938, p. 8, col. 1.

66. Holmquist, *They Chose Minnesota,* p. 346.

APPENDIX A

1. General sources for appendix:

A Brief History of the Czech Lands to 2000, Petř Čornej and Jiři Pokorný; *The Czechs and the Lands of the Bohemian Crown*, Hugh Agnew.

2. *The Reformation*, Diarmaid MacCulloch, p. 485–501.

3. *The Czechs in America*, Thomas Čapek, pp. 3, 4.

4. *The Reformation*, Diarmaid MacCulloch, p. 498.

SOURCES

In addition to the individual sources listed alphabetically below, there are three broad sources I would like to acknowledge.

Steve Wencl was interested and enthusiastic about this project from the start. He has researched land and cemetery record questions in Owatonna, translated various materials from Czech to English, talked to individuals in Steele County to answer questions about their ancestors, contacted Jaroslav Jansa in the Czech Republic for family research, suggested sources, fact checked the manuscript and provided all sorts of help essential to finishing this book. He is listed below for a few specific materials he furnished, but his assistance is far broader than anything I can itemize.

Chris Falteisek of Prescott, Wisconsin, has a large collection of published and unpublished family histories of Steele County Czechs. He is building a database of the local Czechs and their relatives in other places with the hope of eventually creating an all-inclusive set of linked family trees. I furnished him typewritten information for his work, and he furnished me many, many useful family trees of the local Czechs. Although I rarely quoted from their annotations, I referred to them frequently to understand the interrelationships of the local Czechs. He also loaned me his copy of Irene Seykora's history of the John Seykora family.

Jaroslav Jansa of Dolní Dobrouč, in the Czech Republic, is a geneology researcher who trades information with Steve Wencl about the Czech families who came to Minnesota. I have gotten quite a bit of information about family origins in Bohemia from Jaroslav's work due to Steve's correspondence with him.

Adjutant General's Report, Minnesota 1866: Military Forces of the State 1861–1866, Pioneer Printing Co., St. Paul, MN 1866

Agnew, Hugh, *The Czechs and the Lands of the Bohemian Crown*, Hoover Institution Press 2004

Aksamit, Gene, *Castle Garden-America's First Immigrant Receiving Station, Naše Rodina*, Volume 12, Number 2, June 2000.

Ancestry.com, online subscription databases for geneology

Baca, Leo, *Czech Immigration Passenger Lists* (nine volumes), Minnesota Historical Society library and Czechoslovak Geneological Society International library

Beebe, Kathye and Bjoraker, Mary Jean, *Vaclav and Teresie (Fišer) Vanous, House #52, Dlouha Trebova, Bohemia to Amerika*, 2008

Beran, Miroslav et alia, *Od Historie K Současnosti 1292–1992 (700 let obce Dolní Dobrouč)*, municipal office of Dolní Dobrouč 1991.

Beran, Miroslav and Pecháček, *Dobroučské obrázky (Dobrouč Portraits)*, Vydal OFTIS s.r.o., 1996, portions translated by Jaroslav Jansa

Bichner, Ralph and Maxine, *Bichner-Pichner Family 1800–1985*

Bixby, John L., *Origin of the Village of Bixby, Steele County, Minnesota As I Remember It After an Intermission of Seventy-Five Years*, 1967

Bjoraker, Martha Kabela Haberman, *Horak Family Tree*, 1976

Bjoraker, Sylvia Kabela Haberman, oral autobiography

Blegen, Theodore C., *Minnesota-A History of the State,* University of Minnesota Press 1985

Brewer, Luther A. and Wick, Barthinius L., *History of Linn County, Iowa From Its Earliest Settlement to the Present Time* (2 volumes), Pioneer Publishing Company, Chicago, 1911

Bruno, Donald, *Yield of the Years,* Steele County Historical Society

Bureau, Angela Mary, *Family Tree of František Kubišta I and Anna Šouba,* Theos Books 2000

Buryska, Frances Buryska,

_____ Unpublished memories

_____ Personal interviews

Cathcart, Delphine, materials on life and family of Joseph Simek

Catholic Encyclopedia, Vol. 2, *The Bohemians of the United States,* 1907, from internet

Catholic Workman 1891–1991

Capek, Thomas, *The Czechs in America,* Houghton Mifflin Co. 1920

Chada, Joseph, *The Czechs in the United States,* SVU Press 1981

Chaloupka, Petr, Regional Museum of Litomysl CZ; email communications

Cherney, John J., *Wisconsin's Land for the Landless: Examining the Push and Pull Forces of Czech Immigration 1848–1870,* paper for University of Wisconsin-Madison May 1994.

Chmelik, John, biography of Anton J. Slezak, 1938, furnished by Herb Chmelik

Chrislock, Carl H., *Watchdog of Loyalty-The Minnesota Commission of Public Safety During World War I,* Minnesota Historical Society Press 1991

Coan, Peter Morton, *Ellis Island Interviews,* Barnes and Noble 2004

Colletta, John P., *They Came in Ships,* Revised 3rd Edition, Ancestry Publishing 2002

Čornej, Petr and Pokorný, Jiří A, *Brief History of the Czech Lands to 2000,* Práh 2000

Craig, Gordon A.,

_____ *The Battle of Königgrätz,* University of Pennsylvania Press 2003

_____ *Europe Since 1815* (Alternate Edition), Dryden Press 1974

_____ *Germany 1866–1945,* Oxford University Press 1978

Czechoslovak Society of America,

_____ Lodge Minnesota #210, July 1976 CSA Journal, author unknown, from Steele County Historical Society collection

_____ Brief history of the Owatonna C.S.A, 1980 speech to the lodge membership, speaker unknown, from Steele County Historical Society collection

Dalby Database, cemetery records for Steele County

De Mars, Barbara, Owatonna Bohemian National Cemetery records assistance

Deml, *Family Tree of Joseph and Mary Deml*

Dolan, Jay P., *The American Catholic Experience,* University of Notre Dame Press 1992

Donato, A.Z., *Kolem Světa O Jedné Noze: Cesty a Příběhy z Dráhy Umělecké (Around the World on One Leg: Travels and Episodes from an Artistic Career),* August Geringer (Chicago) 1895?; translations by Karleen Chott Sheppard and Steve Wencl

Dubovický, Ivan, *Czech Emigration Patterns: A European View,* Ročenka Vol. 4 2000 pp. 4–12.

Encyclopedia of Chicago, *Czechs and Bohemians,* www.encyclopedia.chicagohistory.org

Faltýsek, Pavel, *The History of the Village of Čermná, Czech Footprints* (Quarterly Publication of the Texas Czech Genealogical

Society, Vol. 4, Sept. 2004), translated by Lucy Westcott

Faribault County Register, newspaper of Faribault County, Minnesota

Fisher, Glen, speech to Owatonna CSA Lodge 67, 1978?

Fisher, Joseph, *Memories of Our Pioneers,* furnished by Rosemary K. Naatz

Folwell, William Watts, A History of Minnesota (4 volumes), Minnesota Historical Society 1956

Fraternal Herald, Official Monthly Magazine of the Western Fraternal Life Association

Gitch, Mark D., *Music in Owatonna,* Minnesota 1854–1890, 2002

Gordon, John Steele, *An Empire of Wealth,* HarperCollins 2004

Gregorova, Jaroslava, biography of Anton Zajic Donato, Radio Prague broadcast of April 8, 2004, www.radio.cz/fr/article/52594

Gross, Ganfield and Vaillancourt, *Steele County 1855–2005: Crossroads of Southern Minnesota,* Steele County Historical Society 2005 (Printed by The Donning Company, Virginia Beach, VA)

Habenicht, Jan, *History of Czechs in America,* Czechoslovak Geneological Society International 1996

Hammel, Thelma, Czechoslovak Society of America—Lodge 67, typewritten article in Steele County Historical Society collection, mid-1960s?

Hanson, Bernie,

_____ *History of the Creameries of Steele County,* Bernard D. Hanson 2001

_____ Personal interview

_____ Steele County country schools

Hanzlicek, Frantisek, memoir, *Amerikán,* 1935

History of Rice and Steele Counties, Minnesota, compiled by Franklyn Curtiss-Wedge; H.C. Cooper, Jr. and Co. Chicago 1910

History of Steele and Waseca Counties, Minnesota, An Album of History and Biography, Union Publishing Co. Chicago 1887

Holmquist, June Drenning ed., *They Chose Minnesota—A Survey of the State's Ethnic Groups,* Minnesota Historical Society Press, St. Paul 1981

Holy Trinity Church, Litomysl Minnesota: Centennial Book 1878–1978, Holy Trinity Church 1978

Horak, Tim, Petranek family memories

Houghtelin, Ronald and Robert, *Steele County Landowners of Record 1879,* Steele County Historical Society 1988

Iverson, Janet Wolesky, personal interviews

Jansa, Jaroslav,

_____ Dlouhá Třebová, brief history

_____ *History of Spinler-Horak Mill,* translated by Justin Spinler

_____ Litomyšl, brief history and origin of name

_____ Přívrat, brief history

_____ Řetová and Řetuvka (Malá Řetová), brief history

_____ Seykora (Anton) family group sheet

_____ Simek (Johann) family group sheet

_____ Spatenka (Frank) family group sheet

Jednota Českých Dam: ve spojených Státech Severní Americky (Union of Czech Ladies In the United States of North America), Jednota Českých Dam in New York, 1895

Jensen, Andrew F., *History of the Early Development of Owatonna 1854–1901;* masters thesis (copies in Owatonna Public Library) 1938

Jerabek, Milan W.,

_____ *Czechs in Minnesota,* masters thesis 1939, University of Minnesota Wilson Library

_____ Letters, Minnesota Historical Society

Joachim, Bonnie,

_____ *Czech Settlement in Steele County, Minnesota,* masters thesis Mankato State University 1979 (copy in Steele County Historical Society)

_____ Personal interview

Johnson, Rosemary, personal interview

Josephson, Matthew, *The Robber Barons,* Harcourt Brace Jovanovich 1934, Harper paperback edition 1962

Journal, Owatonna newspaper, January 1868 to March 1881, 1917–1918, Minnesota Historical Society microfiche

Kann, Robert A., *A History of the Habsburg Empire 1526–1918,* University of California Press 1980

Kaplan Family History, R. W. Kaplan 1992

Kniefel, Lorraine, Joseph and Josephine Skalicky family tree and clippings

Korytová-Magstadt, Štěpánka, *To Reap A Bountiful Harvest-Czech Immigration Beyond the Mississippi 1850–1900,* Rudi Publishing 1993

Kubat, Tim and Marcia, *Descendants of Anton Kubat,* 2003

Kubicek, Frank Joseph, *History of the Early Days of My Life,* unpublished manuscript translated from Czech by his son Frank Alois Kubicek 1969

Langer, Edward G., *Lanskroner Emigration to the American Midwest,* Ročenka Vol. 2 winter 1995-1996

Laughlin, Agnes Kubicek, *Continuation of the Life of Frank Kubicek from 1909 to 1950,* unpublished manuscript 1981

MacCulloch, Diarmaid, *The Reformation—A History,* Penguin Books 2003

Martínek, Joseph, *One Hundred Years of the ČSA-The History of the Czechoslovak Society of America* (English version by R.A. Gorman), Cicero-Berwin Press 1985

McDermott, John, pedigree charts and family tree of Wencl Jirousek family

McNearney, Laurietta Miller, Petranek family memoirs

Memorial Record of the Counties of Faribault, Martin, Watonwan and Jackson, Minnesota, Lewis Publishing Co. Chicago 1895

Meyer, Doug, *Steele County-Our Rural Heritage (Two Self-Guided Tours Through Rural Steele County's History),* 2003

Michalski, Milan, *Welcome to Česká Třebová,* Municipal Office in Česká Třebová 2001, translated into English by Ludmila Mašková

Miller, Frank Joseph, biography and family tree

Minnesota Guide, The, E.H. Burritt & Co. St. Paul 1869 (facsimile edition by Applewood Books, Bedford, MA)

Minnesota Historical Society,

_____ Bulletin 86, Americanization of Aliens, Council of National Defense, 103 L 88F Box 13

_____ Public Safety Commission of Minnesota, records, Minnesota Historical Society, 103.L.8.1.B boxes 6 through 16

_____ Steele County birth records, microfiche, SAM 207 rolls 1-6

_____ Steele County death records, microfiche, SAM 207, rolls 12-14, 145-160

_____ Steele County marriage records, microfiche, SAM 207 rolls 6-12, 127-144

_____ Steele County naturalization records, microfiche, SAM 198 rolls 1-8

_____ Steele County probate court records, microfiche, SAM 207 rolls 16-127

_____ Steele County school district No. 23 records, 1867-1961, 116.I.20.2F-116.I.20.3B

Minnesota Public Statutes, 1858

Minnesota territorial and state census records (1857, 1865, 1875, 1885, 1895, 1905), Minnesota Historical Society microfiche and Ancestry.com

Morison, Samuel Eliot, *The Oxford History of the American People* (3 volumes), New American Library (Mentor) 1972

Naatz, Rosemary K., Joseph and Josephine Pichner family history

Narrative and Rosters of the First Minnesota Regiment: A reprint from Minnesota in the Civil War and Indian War, Park Geneological Books, Roseville, MN

Narrative and Rosters of the Minnesota Mounted Rangers and Cavalry: A reprint from Minnesota in the Civil War and Indian War, Park Geneological Books, Roseville, MN

Naše Rodina (Our Family)-Quarterly of the Czechoslovak Geneological Society International

New York Times Marine Intelligencer column (from internet)

Owatonna-Memories and Milestones, Owatonna Sesquicentennial Committee 2004

Passenger lists, U.S. port arrivals and German port departures, Ancestry.com

Pavek, Miloslav, *700 Let Obce Řetůvka (700 Years of the Village of Řetůvka),* 1992, portions translated by Steve Wencl

Peller, Lorraine, *Albert Kasper: The Story of a Bohemian Immigrant 1853–1937,* written for college credit at St.Thomas University; copy furnished by author

Peller, Ted and Lorraine, personal interviews

People's Press, Owatonna newspaper, September 1876 to March 1881, 1917–1918, Minnesota Historical Society microfiche

Pichner, Anna Jasan, personal interviews

Pirkl, Paul, *Descendants of Mathes Pirkl* (family tree)

Plain Dealer, Owatonna newspaper, October 1863 to July 1866, Minnesota Historical Society microfiche

Polišenský, J.V., *The Passage from Home to the Sea,* Ročenka Volume 5 (2002) pp. 5-11.

Present Advantages and Future Prospects of the City of Freeport, Ill., Boss & Burrows 1857

Pribyl, Henry Hubert, Unpublished autobiography

Pribyl, Joseph, telephone interview

Pribyl, Silvin,

_____ *My Life,* unpublished memoir 2005

_____ Personal interviews

Primary Sources (Early accounts of life in Stephenson County, Ill.), Stephenson County Historical Society 2001

Prokopec, Carol and Bob,

_____ Personal interviews

_____ Seykora family baptisms and marriages from church records

Raiche, Annabelle C.S.J. and Biermaier, Ann Marie O.S.B., *They Came to Teach,* North Star Press, St. Cloud, MN 1994

Reger, Theresa Kubista, Kubista family tree and history

Register, Owatonna newspaper, August 1857 to February 1868, Minnesota Historical Society microfiche

Renchin, John Francis and Mary Josephine family tree 2001

Representative, Owatonna newspaper, January 1861 to March 1861, Minnesota Historical Society microfiche

Ročenka, Journal of the Czechoslovak Geneological Society International

Rypka, Dorothy D.,

_____ Descendants of Josef Rypka, family tree

_____ Descendants of Vaclav Slezak, family tree

Rysavy, Lula, *Harvest of Memories,* 1995

Rysavy, Paul J., *Litomysl . . . A Dream Fulfilled,* thesis for College of St. Thomas, St. Paul, MN 1977

Schisler, Mrs. L.B. and Irene Seykora, *Leaves of . . . Yesterday and Today: Souvenir of the Most Holy Trinity Church Cornerstone Laying Festival,* Holy Trinity Church 1940

Schisler, Marie Seykora, *Across the Years: History and Stories of the Skalicky-Seykora Family,* 1993

Schnabl, Ellen Jean, *Enduring Relevancy of Sokol Ideals,* American Sokol, Jan. 2006

Schouweiler, Carol Ann Bachman,

_____ *Kovar Family History: Bohemia to America,* 2003

_____ *Schuster Family Story: Bohemia to America* (two volumes) 2004

Severson, Harold, *Blooming Prairie Update,* First National Bank of Blooming Prairie 1980

Sheppard, Karleen Chott,

_____ *CSPS Lodge Death Claims For the State of Minnesota September 1897 through December 15, 1946,* 1994, collection of Czechoslovak Genealogical Society International

_____ *The Czech Settlement of Steele County, Minnesota-Three Accounts of the Early Czech Settlers in Steele County, Minnesota,* translated from Czech by Karleen Chott Sheppard, St. Paul, MN 2002

_____ *Early Czech Settlers in Minnesota-Biographies translated from Amerikan Narodni Kalendar* by Karleen Chott Sheppard, St. Paul, MN 2002

_____ Skerik, Katerina, obituary in *Krestanske Listy,* April 20, 1920, translated 1997

_____ Vaclav (Wencl) Chott, brief biography

Simon, Eleanor, *Wencl Family Tree* 1988

Skala, Joseph Edward, personal interview, family tree and history

Skalicky, Frank R., unpublished autobiography 1932

Slezak, Anton, memories collected by son-in-law John Chmelik, furnished by Herb Chmelik

Smith, Page,

_____ *The Nation Comes of Age—A People's History of the Ante-Bellum Years,* McGraw-Hill 1981

_____ *Trial By Fire—A People's History of the Civil War and Reconstruction,* McGraw-Hill 1982

_____ *The Rise of Industrial America—A People's History of the Post-Reconstruction Era,* McGraw-Hill 1984

Sobotka, Margie and Chott Sheppard, Karleen, *Pioneer Stories as Related by Minnesota Czech Residents-Abstracted and Translated from Hospodář (Farmer)Periodical,* Czechoslovak Genealogical Society International 2003

Souba, Gerry, materials on the life of John J. Renchin, unpublished

Spencer, Evelyn Dusek, *Early Life of the Dusek Family,* unpublished biography of Vaurin and Josephine Dusek based on 1957 interview with their eldest son Joseph W. Dusek

Spinler, Justin, Spinler family memories

Spinler, Mary Rysavy,

_____ *Reflections on My Grandfather* (Joseph Rysavy) unpublished

_____ Autobiography unpublished

_____ *Agnes Rajnet Rysavy* unpublished

Staňková, Jana, *Region Orlicko-Třebovsko at the Turn of the Millenium,* Litografie Studio KAZI and Tisk Grafické závody Hronov 2002

Staska, Norman, memories of Steele Center, 1929–1945, personal letter

Steele County directory 1892–1893

Steele County Government Center, county land and marriage records

Steele County Images: A Pictorial History of Steele County 1845–1945, Owatonna People's Press 2000

Steele County News Letter, October 16, 1860, Minnesota Historical Society microfiche

Steele County Historical Society newsletter, Volume 57 Issue 4, Fall 2006

Stolarik, M. Mark, *Forgotten Doors—The Other Ports of Entry to the United States,* Associated University Presses 1988

Story of Sacred Heart Church, Owatonna, Minnesota, The, Sacred Heart Church 1954

Sustacek, John Emil, *The Sustaceks of Minnesota,* Geneology Publishing Service 2003

Styndl, Frank, biography

Svercl, Paul, family history of Svercls and related Matejcek and Stransky immigrants to U.S.

Taylor, A.J.P., *The Habsburg Monarchy 1809–1918,* University of Chicago Press 1976

Thiele, Lori, Hope, *Minnesota—Celebrating 100 Years 1906–2006,* Lori Thiele 2006

Union Express, Owatonna newspaper, December 30, 1862, Minnesota Historical Society microfiche

United States Census records (1860, 1870, 1880, 1900), Minnesota Historical Society microfiche and Ancestry.com

Vlcek, Frantisek, *Povídka Mého Života (Story of My Life), Česká Literární Společost,* St. Louis 1928 (translated by Steve Wencl)

Wacek, Victor R., *Wacek Family Tree,* 2001

Waldman, Steve, *Founding Faith: Providence, Politics, and Birth of Religious Freedom in America,* Random House 2008

Wanous, John and Anna (Jirousek) Wanous family tree, 1994

Watchman and Register, Owatonna newspaper, July 1856 to May 1857, Minnesota Historical Society microfiche

We Remember, We Celebrate, We Believe: Church of the Sacred Heart 1866–1996, Sacred Heart Church 1996

Wellnauer-Lenius, Maralyn A., *Bremen and Hamburg: The Ports, Shipping Companies, and Agents, Naše Rodina,* Volume 20, Number 1, March 2008, pp. 1–17.

Wencl, Steve,

_____ Benjamin Fisher, autobiography in *Amerikán Národní Kalendář* 1882, translated by Steve Wencl

_____ Bohemian National Cemetery, Owatonna, Minnesota, history and translation of charter

_____ *Czech Based Fraternal Organizations to Include Halls in Steele County*

_____ *Czech Lodge Halls of Steele County,* Steele County Historical Society, Fall 2007

_____ Czech language pronunciation, regional variations, vocabulary, etc.

_____ *Early Czech Settlers in the Owatonna Area*

_____ Czech names from particular villages, with Czech spelling

_____ Frank Wencl family history material

_____ Frank Wesely family history material

_____ *History of the Fisher Family,* 2002

_____ *Immigration to the USA: The Unromantic Side of the Story*

_____ Personal interviews and emails

_____ *South Hall: Lodge Litomysl #83 ZCBJ*

_____ *Steele County Czech Settlement*

_____ *Time Line for Steele County Czech Settlement*

Wesely, Edgar Bruce, *Owatonna—The Social Development of a Minnesota Community*, University of Minnesota Press 1938

Wikipedia, http://en.wikipedia.org

Wolesky, Donald C.

_____ *Joseph F. Wolesky Family* (unpublished manuscript)

_____ *Kubicek Family* (unpublished manuscript)

_____ *Wolesky Family History* (unpublished manuscript)?

The Kubat Family (Frank and Thekla Belina Kubat)

INDEX

A
Adair, Esther
  school teacher, 100
agricultural society
  Steele County, 124
agriculture
  Bohemia, 63
  planting 1857, 16
  Steele County 1860–1870, 95
aircraft
  Wolesky brothers, home-built, 230
alcoholic beverages
  regulation, World War I and Prohibition, 255–257
Alfred, Mother M.
  Minnesota Carholic schools, establishment, 148–150
Amana Colonies
  Joseph Pichner, temporary settlement, 19
Americanization campaign
  World War I, 253–254
Amerikan Narodni Kalendar
  Czech-American publications, 249
Anti-Monopoly Party
  state convention in Owatonna, 94–95
attendance policy
  schools, 100–101
Auditorium Hall
  photograph, 213
Austrian-Prussian War 1866
  effect on Bohemia, 87–92

B
Bailey, Frank
  assault case, 185–189
Baltimore
  immigrant ports of entry, 82
Barker, William
  assault case, 185–189
Bartosch, Rosa
  marriage to Albert Kasper, 135
Belina
  Anton, 31
  Charles, 31
  school grades, 98
Frank,
  Bohemian National Cemetery, members, 38
Joseph,
  Bohemian National Cemetery, members, 38
  C.S.P.S. musical group,
Josepha,
  marriage to Frank Kovar, 131
Wencl,
  arrival, 31
  school officer, 97
Benes
  Rose, Z.C.B.J.,
    Blooming Prairie lodge, formation, 221
    photograph, 218
  Vojta,
    diplomatic visit to United States, 251
Bennett, J.K.
  buttermaker, Summit creamery, 199
Betlach
  Joseph and Mrs., Z.C.B.J.,
    Blooming Prairie lodge, formation, 221
    photograph, 218
  Joseph, Z.C.B.J.,
    Blooming Prairie lodge, officers, 221
  Vincent, town of origin, 61
Bickner, Joseph
  Civil War service, 2nd Minnesota Cavalry Regiment, 26–27
  political activities, 189–190
  political party delegate, 141
  township supervisor, 141
Bixby, 204–206
Bjoraker
  Adolph, marriage to Sylvia Kabela, 235
  Olaf, marriage to Martha Kabela, 235
Blazek
  Frank, arrival, 107
  Wencl, Saint Ivan's Lodge, 240
blizzards
  1873, 115–117
  1881, 179
Blockhus, Sam
  buttermaker, Summit creamery, 199
Blooming Prairie, 207
  alcoholic beverages,
    World War I and Prohibition, 255–257
  founding, 42
  Z.C.B.J., formation, 220–221
board of trade
  Steele County, 124
Bohemia
  Austrian-Prussian War 1866, 87–92
  brief history, 263–270
  emigration,
    process, 73–77
    reasons, 62–67
  geography, xi
  returning immigrants, 74–76, 114–115
  village life, 68–73
bohemian
  synonym for unconventional, ix
Bohemian National Alliance
  World War I, 250–252
Bohemian National Cemetery
  Blooming Prairie, 197–198
  photograph, 198
  Owatonna, 35–38
  photograph, 36
Bremen
  emigrant ports of departure from Germany, 76–77
Broulik, Karolina
  biography, Hospodar, 250
Broz, Edward
  C.S.P.S., Owatonna lodge, founding, 214
Brozek
  Florian, arrival, 105

305

John,
    arrival, 105
    residence in 1870, 45
    Joseph, Czech language, teaching, 97
Bull Run, battle
    Civil War, 24–25
Bulva, John
    residence in 1870, 45
Burlington, Cedar Rapids and Northern Railroad
    Hope, founding, 206
Buryska, Frances
    child of John and Frances Rysavy, 231
businesses
    Czech ownership, 134–139

C

C.S.A. see C.S.P.S.
C.S.D.P.J.
    Owatonna lodge, 217
C.S.P.J.
    Owatonna lodge, 226
C.S.P.S.
    breaking away of Z.C.B.J., 217–220
    early history, 210–212
    English speaking lodges, 247
    later history, 246–248
    Owatonna lodge, 214–217
        Auditorium Hall, photograph, 213
    Minnesota Grand Lodge, women, membership, 224–225
Calhoun, E.B.
    school teacher, 97
Caps, Lucinda
    school teacher, 97
Castle Garden
    immigrant station, New York City, 79–81
Catholic Church
    Czech attitudes toward, 33
Catholic First Central Union
    fraternal organizations, 226–227
Catholic Workman
    fraternal lodges, 227
    merger with Z.C.K.J., 196
Ceipult, Joseph
    assault, 140
census
    1860, 20–21
    1880, 164–166
Cepelak, Joseph
    C.S.P.S., Owatonna lodge, founding, 214
Cermna, Bohemia, 61
    cholera 1866, 90
Ceska Slovanska Delnicka Podporujici Jednota (C.S.D.P.J.)
    Owatonna lodge, 217
Ceska Trebova, Bohemia, 55
Cesko-Rimska Katolicka Prvni Ustredni Jednota
    fraternal lodges, 226–227
Cesko-Sesterska Podporujici Jednota
    Owatonna lodge, 226
Cesko-Slovanska Podporu jici Spolecnost. see C.S.P.S.
cheese factories
    Steele County, 95–96, 124
choral societies
    Owatonna, 124
Chott, Wencl
    arrival, 233
    Czech language, teaching, 39
Cieszinski, Michael
    Saint Ivan's Lodge, 240
Civil War, 23–28
Clinton Falls Township
    first European settlers, 2
Cole, Amelia, Z.C.B.J.,
    Blooming Prairie lodge, formation, 221
    photograph, 218
conscription
    Civil War, 26
Cornell, A.B.
    settlement in Owatonna, 2
Corpus Christi feast
    Holy Trinity Catholic Church, 193–196
Coufal, Joseph
    inviting Joseph Wolesky to America, 229
county coroner
    Anton Simek, election, 21

creameries, 238–239
    Midway creamery, Hope, 206
    Oak Glen, 206
    River Point, 203–204
        photograph, 203
    Steele Center, 201–202
    Summit, 199–200
crimes
    local Czechs, 139–141
Czech language, xi
    newspapers, 128
    spelling and pronunciation, xii–xiii
    teaching,
        Blooming Prairie, 221
        Bohemia, 39–40
        Steele County, 97, 162, 216–217, 254
Czech national revival, 270
Czech settlers in Owatonna Township 1858
    map, 18
Czech Slovanic Workers Benevolent Society (C.S.D.P.J.)
    Owatonna lodge, 217
Czech-American publications, 249–250
Czechoslovak National Council of America
    founding, 251
Czechoslovak Society of America. see C.S.P.S.
Czechs
    brief history, 263–270
Czeszinski, John
    horse accident, 143–144
    school report, Pavek school, 98
    school teacher, 97–99

D

Dakota Indian uprising, 25–26
Deml
    Joseph, arrival, 48
    Lawrence, Steele Center creamery, 202
    Louis, C.S.P.S. musical group, 216
diet
    Bohemia, 72

Dlouha Trebova, Bohemia, 56–57
Dolni Dobrouc, Bohemia, 58–61
   Christmas creche representing, 231
Donaldson, Ellen
   school teacher, 100
Donato, Anton Zajic, 160–163
   C.S.P.S., Owatonna lodge, founding, 214
   officer, 214
Dostal
   Anna, marriage to John Jirele, 180
   Frank,
      Bohemian National Cemetery, members, 38
      buttermaker, River Point, 203
Dusek
   Anna, J.C.D., 226
   Frank, residence in 1870, 45
   John,
      Bohemian National Cemetery, members, 38
      C.S.P.S., Owatonna lodge, officer, 215
   Vaurin,
      arrival, 131
      relocation to South Dakota, 132

E
education
   Bohemia, 71–72
Ellis Island
   immigrant station, New York City, 81–82
emigration from Bohemia, 73–77
   reasons, 62–67
English language
   teaching, World War I, 253
ethnic tensions, 125–126

F
farm laborers
   Bohemia, 69–70
feudalism, 268–269
Fibigar
   Anna,
      J.C.D., 226
      spouse of Benjamin Fisher, 4
   F., J.C.D. member, 226
Fisher
   Anna,
      death, 159
      photograph, 5
   Benjamin,
      accomodations during first winter, 10
      arrival in America, 4
      biography, Amerikan Narodni Kalendar, 249
      employment with Dr. Morehouse, 15
      journey to Steele County, 9
      later life, 159
      Minneapolis and Cedar Valley Railroad, dealings with, 19–20
      photograph, 5
      school officer, 97
      town of origin, 57
      unregistered land claim, loss, 20
   Charles,
      Saint Ivan's Lodge, 240
      scalding, 16
         Native American assistance, 52
   Frank,
      arrival, 46
      residence in 1870, 45
      Saint Ivan's Lodge, 240
   Joseph,
      description of Native Americans, 53
      management of county poor farm, 240
   Josephine, employment with John Odell, 21
   Mrs. Joseph, horse accident, 143–144
   Wencl, burial, 36
Fleckenstein, Paul
   marriage to Theresa Simek, 30
food
   Bohemia, 72
foreign language schools and newspapers
   World War I, 252–253
Fourth of July
   Czech celebrations, 164
Franciscan sisters convent, Rochester
   establishment, 150
fraternal lodges
   C.S.D.P.J., 217
   C.S.P.J., 226
   C.S.P.S. (see C.S.P.S.)
   Catholic lodges, 226–227
   J.C.D., 224–226
   Katolicky Delnik, 227
      merger with Z.C.K.J., 196
   Saint Ivan's Lodge, Sacred Heart Catholic Church, 226–227, 240
   Saint Joseph Society, Holy Trinity Catholic Church, 196, 226–227
   Sokol, 223–224
   women's lodges, 224–226
   Z.C.B.J. (see Z.C.B.J.)
Freeport, Illinois
   Czech settlers, 4–5
Freethinker Society
   Czech-American organization, 210
freethinkers, 209–210
   Czech movement, 33–34
French Revolution, 269

G
Ganser, Peter
   saloon, 136
German Bohemians
   census, 21
Germany
   unification, 118

Gertje, Paul
    buttermaker, River Point, 203
grain elevators
    discontent with, 93–95
grand riverboat excursion, 7–8
Grange, 94–95
Grisel, Joseph
    occupation in 1870, 111

H
Habenicht, Doctor John
    acquaintance with Anton Zajic Donato, 162–163
    career and residence in Steele County, 233
Haberman
    Fred, land for Bohemian National Cemetery, 197
    Jacob, raising Martha and Sylvia Kabela, 235
    Wencl, town of origin, 56
Haebell, Wencl
    saloon, 141
hail storm 1857, 16–17
Hamburg
    emigrant ports of departure from Germany, 76–77
Hanus, Wencl
    divorce, 184
    mortgage, 184
    residence in 1870, 45
Hanzlicek, Frank
    arrival, 180
Hartle, William
    living with Frank Kubicek family, 176
Havana school (District 11), 99–100
Havlicek, Father Vincent
    pastor at Holy Trinity Catholic Church, 244
Hays
    Clara, school teacher, 97
    N., school teacher, 97
health inspections
    immigrants, 80–82
Herdina
    Adolf, assault case, 185–189
    Frank, assault case, 185–189

Herman, John
    letter to Joseph Skerik, 110–111
Hickock, A.L.
    school teacher, 97
Holy Trinity Catholic Church
    establishment, 192–197
    later history, 244–245
    photographs, 194–195
    Saint Joseph Society, 226–227
Homestead Act
    effect, 67
    passage, 1862, 28
    veto 1860, 20
Hondl, Adolph
    enlistment in World War I, 251–252
Hope, 206–207
Hope school (District 12), 100
Horak
    Adolf, arrival, 179
    Alois,
        arrival, 179
        Z.C.B.J., Owatonna lodge, formation, 221
    Frank,
        arrival, 179
        C.S.P.S., Owatonna lodge, officer, 215
    Joseph, arrival, 180
    Katerina, Z.C.B.J., Owatonna lodge, formation, 221
horse accidents, 142–145
    Father Pribyl and Father Christie, 153
Horsky
    John, lawsuit, 184
    Joseph,
        residence in 1870, 45
        Somerset Township, land ownership, 44
    Wencl, Z.C.B.J., Blooming Prairie lodge, formation, 221
        officers, 221
        photograph, 218

Hospodar
    Czech-American publications, 249–250
houses
    Bohemia, 68–69
    construction, 15
Howard, L.M.
    settlement in Medford, 1
Hrdlichka
    Theresa, marriage to John Pichner, 157, 172
    Wencl,
        arrival, 171–172
        businesses, 136
        mortgage default, 113
Hruska, Christine
    marriage to Joseph Svercl, 231
Hudrlik
    Frank, photograph, facing page 55
    Joseph,
        arrival, 48
        Saint Joseph Society, charter member, 196
Hus, John
    Czech religious reformer, 265
Hylvaty, Bohemia, 57

I
Indians
    Czech encounters with, 52–54
industry
    Owatonna, 124
Ireland, Bishop John
    recruitment of Father John Pivo, 242
Italy
    unification, 118
Iverson, Janet, Z.C.B.J., Owatonna lodge, 222–223

J
J.C.D., 224–226
    Owatonna lodge members, photograph, 225
Janisch
    Frank, shoe store, 112
    John, clothing merchant, 135, 166

Jansa
- John and Mrs., Z.C.B.J.,
  - Blooming Prairie lodge, formation, 220
  - photograph, 218
- John, Z.C.B.J.,
  - Blooming Prairie lodge, officers, 221

Jasan, Frank
- Z.C.B.J., Owatonna lodge, formation, 221

Jednota Ceska Dam, 224–226

Jirele
- John,
  - arrival, 180
  - Saint Ivan's Lodge, 240
- Joseph, National Alliance of Czech Catholics, 251
- Wencl,
  - arrival, 180
  - National Alliance of Czech Catholics, 251

Jirousek
- Alois, Kubiceks staying with in Chicago, 108
- Joseph, school grades, 98
- Mary, threshing party, Owatonna, photograph, 86
- Wencl,
  - acquisition of Joseph Wondra farm, 182
  - arrival, 30
  - goose blown away in storm, 142
  - River Point creamery, officer, 203
  - school officer, 97
  - town of origin, 58

Johannsen, Peter, 17

Johnny Cake Year
- hard times 1858, 19

Joy, Father Maurice
- service at Sacred Heart Catholic Church, 240

K

Kabage, Julius
- marriage to Barbara Kovar, 184

Kabela
- Martha, life, 235
- Sylvia, life, 235

Kaplan
- Agnes, school honor roll, 114
- Anna, 17
- J.C.D., 226
- Barbora, death, 159
- Christine, marriage to Wencl Meixner, 159
- Godfrey, career, 238
- Joseph K.,
  - accomodations during first winter, 10
  - Atlantic crossing, 77
  - biography, Amerikan Narodni Kalendar, 249
  - Bohemian National Cemetery, organization, 36–38
  - Czech language, teaching, 39, 97
  - death, 254–255
  - description of Native Americans, 53–54
  - encouragement to emigrate, 4
  - journey to Steele County, 8–9
  - land claim, 11
  - later life, 159
  - marriage, 8
  - passport application, 74
  - photograph, 45
  - picnic for public, 142
  - railroad construction on property, 19
  - relocation of house, 15
  - route from port of entry, 84–85
  - Sacred Heart Church building committee, 34
  - school officer, 97
  - town of origin, 57
  - visit with Vojta Benes, 251
- Joseph W.,
  - birth in Owatonna, 9
  - C.S.P.S., Owatonna lodge, officer, 214–215
  - farm, 202
  - farm machinery dealership, 166
  - general store, fire, 137–139
  - River Point creamery, officer, 203
- Joseph, assault and disorderly conduct, 140–141
- Marie, death, 159
- Reuben W. (Buzz), career, 238
- Reuben, career, 238
- Victor, C.S.P.S. musical group, 216
- Walter, C.S.P.S. musical group, 216

Kasal, Father Edward
- pastor, Sacred Heart Catholic Church, 243

Kasper
- Albert, 44–45, 135–136
  - Czech language, teaching, 39
  - later life, 236
  - photograph, 45
  - school teacher, 97
  - Litomysl school, 197
- Allan, Steele Center creamery, 202
- Anton, 45
- Dorothy, marriage to Frank Horak, 179
- Frank, 45
- Joseph,
  - arrival, 44
  - military service, effect on emigration from Bohemia, 63
  - occupation in 1870, 111
  - town of origin, 57
- Mary, marriage to Frank Moravec, 133

Kasper and Matejcek general store, 136

Katolicky Delnik
- fraternal lodges, 227
- merger with Z.C.K.J., 196

Keller, Father George
- Sacred Heart Church pastor, 34–35

Kiernan, Father Patrick
- pastor, Saint Joseph Catholic Church, 240–241

Klekar, Joseph
    National Alliance of Czech Catholics, 251
Knickerbocker, W.R.
    assault case, 185–189
Kokaisel, Anna, J.C.D., 226
Koniggratz, battle of, 89–90
Kovar
    Anna, threshing party, Owatonna, photograph, 86
    Anton,
        arrival, 30–31
        Bohemian National Cemetery, directors, 37
        C.S.P.S.. Owatonna lodge, founding, 214
        Saint Ivan's Lodge, 240
        school officer, 97
        threshing party, Owatonna, photograph, 86
        town of origin, 57
    Barbara, marriage to Julius Kabage, 184
    Francis, school grades, 98
    Frank,
        arrival, 131
        biography, Amerikan Narodni Kalendar, 249
        threshing party, Owatonna, photograph, 86
        town of origin, 57
    John,
        arrival, 31
        lawsuit, 184
    Joseph,
        careers, 236–238
        school experiences, 99
        Mrs., robbery and assault, 139
    Wencl,
        C.S.P.S. Owatonna lodge, founding, 214
        officer, 214
        Steele Center creamery, 202
Kovar farm machinery company, 237–238
Krahulec, Wencl
    Z.C.B.J., Owatonna lodge, formation, 221

Kroulik, John
    assault case, 185–189
Kubat
    Anna,
        Atlantic crossing, 77
        C.S.P.J., 226
        death, 158
        employment at Sanford House, 13–14
        employment at Winship House, 21
        marriage to Frank Miller, 171
        memories of Native Americans, 52
        photograph, 7
    Anna B., Z.C.B.J., Owatonna lodge, formation, 222
    Anton,
        arrival, 4, 107
        biography, Amerikan Narodni Kalendar, 249
        birth, Atlantic crossing, 77
        Bohemian National Cemetery, members, 38
        entry into United States, 85
        grand jury service, 113–114, 141
        horse theft, 139
        journey to Steele County, 9
        later life, 158
        photograph, 7
        political party delegate, 141
        residence in 1870, 45
        school officer, 97
        town of origin, 57
        township treasurer, 141
    Antonia, birth, 4
    Catherine, spouse of Joseph Pichner, 4
    Frances, marriage to Anton Rypka, 133
    Frank,
        arrival, 47–48, 107
        residence in 1870, 45
    Joseph,
        C.S.P.S., Owatonna lodge, officer, 214, 215

        coping with blizzard of 1881, 179
        horse accident, 182–183
        partner in meat market, 134
        saloon, 136, 166
        school officer, 97
        theft of coat, 139
        township treasurer, 114
    Josephine, employment with David Potwin, 21
    Otto A., Z.C.B.J., Owatonna lodge, formation, 221
    Otto, Public Safety Commission of Minnesota, World War 1, 252
    Rosa, marriage to Frank Miller, 171
Kubicek
    Anna, marriage to Anton Mikyska, 231
    Anton, blacksmith shop, 200
    Frank,
        ancestral home, Dolni Dobrouc, Bohemia, photographs, 59
        arrival, 107–108
        Atlantic crossing, 78
        careers, 235–236
        entry into United States, 82
        first years in America, 175–176
        horse accidents, 144–145
        marriage to Caroline Stransky, 173
        Summit creamery, officer, 199
        Summit store, 200
    John, raising Joseph and Helen Skala, 234
    Joseph, death in battle of Koniggratz, 90
    Mary, marriage to Adolf Ressler, 200
    Mathilda,
        arrangements for voyage to America, 170
        marriage to Frank Wolesky, 230

Vincent,
    arrival, 108
    hosting brother Frank
        Kubicek, 175
Kubista
    Anna,
        marriage to Anton Kubat,
          30
        spouse of Anton Kubat, 4
    Catherine, marriage to John
        Renchin, 30
    Frank,
        arrival, 29–30
        newspaper ad for stray
          horse, 118
        Sacred Heart Church
          site, 34
    Ignac,
        arrival, 30, 106–107
        contribution, Dlouha
          Trebova church, 57
        residence in 1870, 45
    Sarah, marriage to Frank
        Wencl, 118
Kumpost, John
    letter to Joseph Skerik, 111

L

land claims
    Homestead Act, 28
    process, 11
land ownership
    Czech settlers, Steele
        County, map, 168
Langer, Carl
    Saint Ivan's Lodge, 240
Langmichel, Michael
    death in wagon accident,
        117–118
Lanskroun district,
    Bohemia, 55
    map, 60
Leary, William
    Sacred Heart Church
        building committee, 34
Lhotka, Bohemia, 56
libraries
    Slovanská Lípa organization,
        39
Litomysl school (District 57),
    100, 197

Litomysl settlement
    growth,
        1870 to 1875, 123
        1875 to 1880, 165–166,
          174–179
    new arrivals,
        1875–1881, 179–180
    origins, 43–47
Litomysl, Bohemia, 58
local government
    Bohemia, 69–71
locust invastion 1873-1877,
    177–178
Locust Point
    immigrant station,
        Baltimore, 82
Lonergan, James
    Sacred Heart Church
        building committee, 34
Lull, Chauncey
    settlement in Medford, 1

M

Maca, Anton
    arrival, 107
    living with Frank Kubicek
        family, 175–176
Majerus, Father Stephen
    pastor at Holy Trinity Catholic
        Church, 244–245
Mala Retova, Bohemia, 58
Marek
    D., C.S.D.P.J. lodge,
        officer, 217
    L.L., C.S.P.S.,
        Owatonna lodge,
        founding, 214
Martinek
    Emil, partner in saloon
        with Adolf Horak, 179
    Joseph F., Z.C.B.J.,
        Owatonna lodge, officers,
        222
    Joseph, C.S.P.S. musical
        group, 216
Masser, Anton
    residence in 1870, 45
Matejcek
    Alois, relocation to North
        Dakota, 172

Anna,
    arrival, 172
    marriage to Joseph Pic, 172
Frank, marriage and relocation
    to North Dakota, 172
John,
    marriage to Mary Vasicek,
        172
    Saint Ivan's Lodge, 240
    Saint Joseph Society,
        charter member, 196
Joseph,
    general store, 136
    partnership with Albert
        Kasper, 236
    photograph, facing page
        55
Josepha, marriage to Bernard
    Pirkl, 172
Josephine, marriage to Frank
    Hanzlicek, 180
Peregrin, arrival, 172
Vincent, arrival, 172
Matejcek school (District 69), 100
    superintendent's report, 173
Matejcek-Ressler store
    photograph, facing page 55
Matousek, Father Rudolph
    pastor at Holy Trinity
        Catholic Church, 244
McAlona, Frances
    school teacher, 97
Medford Township
    first European settlers, 1
Meixner
    Albert, Steele Center
        creamery, 202
    Benjamin, wagon business,
        135, 166
    Bernard, Saint Ivan's Lodge,
        240
    Frank,
        C.S.D.P.J. lodge,
          officer, 217
        Z.C.B.J., Owatonna lodge,
          formation, 221
          officers, 222
    Joseph, marriage and
        relocation, 172
Midway creamery
    Hope, 206

Mikyska, Anton
    arrival, 231
    military land warrants
        land claims, 11
    military service
        effect on emigration from Bohemia, 63, 92
Miller
    Agnes, marriage to Joseph Petranek, 233
    Father Ottmar, pastor at Holy Trinity Catholic Church, 196, 244
    Frances, arrival, 171
    Frank,
        arrival, 170–171
        role in Catholic worship in Saco, 173
Mineral Springs Park
    photograph, 10
Minneapolis and Cedar Valley Railroad, 19–20
Minnesota
    growth 1880, 128–129
    recruitment of immigrants, 65–66
    routes from ports of entry, 84–85
    map, 83
    statehood, 19
Minnesota Central Railroad
    arrival in Owatonna, 32
    construction, Blooming Prairie, 42
monument to Czech pioneers
    dedication, 258
    rededication, 261
Moravec
    Agnes, Z.C.B.J.,
        Blooming Prairie lodge, formation, 221
        photograph, 218
    Frank,
        arrival, 47, 132–133
        Austrian-Prussian War 1866, memories, 91
        biography, Hospodar, 250
        education in Bohemia, 71–72
        marriage to Mary Kasper, 133

    reasons for emigration, 70
    remarriage and relocation to North Dakota, 172
    residence in 1870, 45
    Marie, Czech language, teaching, 39
    Otilie, Czech language, teaching, 39
Moravia settlement. see Saco
Morehouse, Doctor
    employment of Benjamin Fisher, 15
Motl
    Frank,
        buttermaker, River Point, 203
        residence in 1870, 45
        residence in Saco, 173
        Saint Joseph Society, charter member, 196
    George,
        death, 192
        residence in 1870, 45
    Rudolph, Z.C.B.J.,
        Blooming Prairie lodge, formation, 220
        officers, 221
        photograph, 218
Motte, Marie, C.S.P.J., 226
Motz, Ferdinand
    River Point creamery, officer, 203
music
    Belina family, 31
    Owatonna, 124

N
names
    spelling and pronunciation, xii–xiii
National Alliance of Czech Catholics, 250–251
National Grange of the Patrons of Husbandry, 94–95
Native Americans
    Czech encounters with, 52–54
naturalization
    1876, 127
New York City
    ports of entry, 79–82

newspapers
    Czech and German languages, 128
North Dakota
    Matejcek relocation, 172
North Hall, Litomysl, 196–197
    photograph, 208
Novotny, Vincent
    assault, 134

O
Oak Glen creamery
    Bixby, 206
occupations
    Czechs in 1880, 165–166
Our Lady of Lourdes Catholic School
    Rochester, establishment, 149–150
overseer of the poor
    Anton Simek, election, 21
Owatonna City
    first European settlers, 2
    growth,
        1855, 16
        1856–1857, 17
        1860, 20
        1880, 124–125
    incorporation, 19
Owatonna Tool Company, 238
Owatonna Township
    Czech settlers,
        1858, map, 18
        growth 1870 to 1875, 123
        growth 1880, 164–166
    first European settlers, 2

P
Pachl, Agnes
    marriage to Joseph Horak, 180
Panic of 1857, 17
    Minneapolis and Cedar Valley Railroad, 19
Panic of 1873, 119–120
Paris Commune, 119
parish fair
    Sacred Heart Catholic Church, 145–147, 150
Parker, C.M.
    school teacher, 97

passports
    Bohemia, emigration, 73–74
Paukert
    Father Francis,
        introduction of Edward Rysavy to Agnes Rajnet, 232
        service at Sacred Heart Catholic Church, 243
    Mr., Z.C.B.J.,
        Blooming Prairie lodge, formation, 221
    Mrs., Z.C.B.J.,
        Blooming Prairie lodge, photograph, 218
    Wencl, farm fire, 191
Pavek
    Anton, Saint Ivan's Lodge, 240
    Catherine, burial, 36
    Frank,
        Bohemian National Cemetery, members, 38
        residence in 1870, 45
    Ignac, residence in 1870, 45
    John,
        Bohemian National Cemetery,
            members, 38
            site, 37
        school officer, 97
        Z.C.B.J., Owatonna lodge, formation, 221
    Wencl, donation of land for church, 173
Pavek school (District 23), 97–99
    photograph, 98
Pechacek
    Adolf, Z.C.B.J., Owatonna lodge, formation, 221
    Frank and Mrs., Z.C.B.J.,
        Blooming Prairie lodge, formation, 220–221
        photograph, 218
    Frank, Z.C.B.J.,
        Blooming Prairie lodge, building committee, 221

Joseph, Z.C.B.J.,
    Blooming Prairie lodge, formation, 221
    photograph, 218
Vincent, passport application, 74
Pehler, Anton
    saloon, 136
Petranek, Joseph
    arrival, 232–233
    Atlantic crossing, 78
    furnishing musical instrument to Frank Kubicek, 235
    Saint Ivan's Lodge, 240
Pettit, W.F.
    settlement in Owatonna, 2
Pic, Joseph
    arrival, 172
Pichner
    Catherine,
        death, 157
        employment at Winship House, 14
        employment with A.B. Cornell, 21
        sister of Anton Kubat, 4
    Edward, C.S.P.S. musical group, 216
    John,
        arrival in America, 4
        Bohemian National Cemetery,
            members, 38
            officers, 37
        C.S.P.S., Owatonna lodge,
            musical group, 216
            officer, 215
        Czech language, teaching, 97
        journey to Steele County, 9
        later life, 157–158
        marriage to Theresa Hrdlichka, 172
        Public Safety Commission of Minnesota, World War 1, 252
        route from port of entry, 84
        school grades, 98
        school officer, 97
        town of origin, 57

        township supervisor, 114
        Z.C.B.J., Owatonna lodge, formation, 221
    Joseph,
        arrival in America, 4
        arrival in Steele County, 19
        lawsuits, 141–142
        route from port of entry, 84
        Somerset Township, land ownership, 44
        tombstone, photograph, 3
        town of origin, 57
    Marie, Z.C.B.J., Owatonna lodge, formation, 221
    Pauline,
        death, 158
        school teacher, 97
    Rosalie, mother of Anton Simek, 2
    Samuel, management of county poor farm, 240
    Wencl,
        burial, 36
        death, 154
        election as township supervisor, 190
    William, death, 154
Pirkl
    Bernard, arrival, 109, 172
    Joseph,
        marriage to Josephine Skalicky, 193
        Saint Joseph Society, charter member, 196
        Z.C.B.J.,
            Blooming Prairie lodge, formation, 221
            photograph, 218
Pisorna, Rosa
    marriage to Ignac Kubista, 106
Pivo, Father John
    photograph, 241
    Sacred Heart Catholic Church, 240–243
poor farm, 239–240
Popelok, Mrs. J.R., Z.C.B.J., Blooming Prairie lodge, member, 221
ports of departure from Germany, 76–77

ports of entry
  immigrants to United States, 79–82
prairie fire
  autumn 1856, 12
preemption
  land claims, 1, 11
presidential election
  1860, 21
  1876, 183–184
Pribyl
  Father Francis,
    Corpus Christi feast in Litomysl, 194
    ministering to Litomysl Catholics, 193
    Sacred Heart Catholic Church,
      departure from Owatonna, 154–156
    first resident pastor, 35
    horse accident, 153
    literary talent, 154
    pastor, 146–156
    public speaking, 151–153
  J.B., Summit creamery, officer, 199
  John, burial, 36
  Joseph, arrival, 107
  Silvin, school experiences, 100
Privrat, Bohemia, 57
Prokopec
  Alois, Z.C.B.J.,
    Blooming Prairie lodge, officers, 221
  Ludmilla, marriage to Anton Kubicek, 200
  Public Safety Commission of Minnesota
  World War 1, 252–255
public schools
  Catholic attitude toward, 40–41, 101–104
  secularization, 103–104

R
Racek
  Joseph, C.S.P.S.,
    Owatonna lodge, founding, 214
    school officer, 97
  Mary, school honor roll, 114
railroads
  arrival in Owatonna, 32
  discontent with, 92–95
  Minneapolis and Cedar Valley, 19–20
  recruitment of immigrants, 65
Rajnet, Agnes
  early life and marriage to Edward Rysavy, 232
Raleigh, Father Walter
  pastor, Sacred Heart Catholic Church, 154, 240
recreation
  Owatonna, 125
recruiting agents
  emigration from Bohemia, 64–66
religion
  Bohemia, 71
religious affiliation
  Czech immigrants, 33–34
Renchin
  Alois, Z.C.B.J.,
    Blooming Prairie lodge, formation, 221
    photograph, 218
  Anna, spouse of Anton Kubat, 4
  Anton, contribution, Dlouha Trebova church, 57
  Catherine, memories of Native Americans, 52
  Frank, 50–51
    residence in 1870, 45
  John,
    arrival, 31
    Atlantic crossing, 77
    Civil War Service, 1st Minnesota Infantry Regiment, 27
    lawsuit, 184
    residence in 1870, 45
    route from port of entry, 85
Ressler
  Adolf, marriage to Mary Kubicek, 200
  Bernard,
    arrival, 109–110
    photograph, facing page 55
  Josephine, memories of Native Americans, 52
Retova, Bohemia, 58
returning to Bohemia
  immigrants, 74–76, 114–115
Retuvka, Bohemia, 58
Revolution of 1848, xiv–xv
  effect on emigration from Bohemia, 62, 64
River Point, 202–204
River Point school (District 37), 100, 202–203
Rock Island Railroad
  Hope, founding, 206
Ruzek
  Frank,
    funeral, 198
    Z.C.B.J.,
      Blooming Prairie lodge, officers, 221
  Frank and Mrs., Z.C.B.J.,
    Blooming Prairie lodge, formation, 220
    photograph, 218
  William, burial, 197
Rypka
  Anna, marriage to Joseph K. Kaplan, 159
  Anton,
    arrival, 110, 133
    marriage to Frantiska Kubat, 133
  Barbara, C.S.P.J., 226
    marriage to Wencl Jirele, 180
  Frances, J.C.D., 226
  Frank,
    arrival, 110
    books, donation, Slovanská Lípa organization, 39
  Joseph,
    horse accident, 143
    Somerset Township, land ownership, 44
  Walter, Sokol,
    Owatonna lodge, 224
  Zdenka, Z.C.B.J., 222
Ryshavy
  Agnes Rajnet, hiding food in wartime, 91
  Alois, fatal accident, 190

Edward, early life and
marriage to Agnes Rajnet,
232
Frank, marriage to Mary
Wondra, 182
Joseph D., Z.C.B.J.,
Owatonna lodge,
formation, 221
Joseph, arrival, 231

S
Saco
growth 1866-1880, 169–174
origins, 47–48
Saco school (District 69), 100
superintendent's report, 173
Sacred Heart Catholic Church,
240–243
dedication, 147
destruction by fire, 242
founding, 34–35
growth, 145–150
photograph, 148
Saint Ivan's Lodge, 226–227, 240
Saint Columbanus Catholic
Church
Blooming Prairie,
founding, 42
Saint Hyacinth Catholic
Church
closing, 243
founding, 242
Saint Isidore's Catholic
School
founding, 245
Saint Ivan's Lodge
Sacred Heart Catholic
Church, 226–227, 240
Saint Joseph Catholic Church
founding, 240–241
Saint Joseph Society
Holy Trinity Catholic Church,
196, 226–227
Saint Mary's Catholic School
establishment, 148–150
later history, 243
photograph, 148
Saint Wenceslaus Catholic
Church of Saco, 245
establishment, 173
photograph, 174

saloons
Anton Zajic Donato, 162
Czech ownership, 136
Sanford House
Anna Kubat employment,
13–14
Sattlau, Anton
death, 117
marriage, 18
Somerset Township, land
ownership, 44
Scheve, Father Clement
Sacred Heart Church pastor,
35
Schimek. see Simek
Schisler
family, Blooming Prairie
businesses, 207
Frank, Summit store, 200
Lawrence, Summit store, 200
Louis, Summit store, 200
Schoen, Charles
Sacred Heart Church
building committee, 34
schools
Owatonna Czech settlement,
97–100
Schuster
Anna, marriage to Joseph
Wolesky, 230
Anton, Hope general store,
206
Frank, arrival, 230
Louis, Hope general store, 206
Seykora
Anton,
arrival, settlement in
Somerset Township,
43–44
land donation for Holy
Trinity Catholic
Church, 193
Saint Joseph Society,
charter member, 196
town of origin, 57
Frank,
arrival, settlement in
Somerset Township,
43–44
blacksmith shop, 136–137,
166

Bohemian National Cemetery,
directors, 37
Civil War service, 2nd
Minnesota Cavalry
Regiment, 26–27
death, 192
farm machinery dealership,
166
general store, fire, 137–139
lawsuit, 184
Saint Joseph Society,
charter member, 196
town of origin, 57
township treasurer, 141
Frank J., C.S.P.S.,
Owatonna lodge,
founding, 214
officer, 214
John,
arrival, settlement in
Summit Township, 43
Bohemian National
Cemetery, officers, 37
residence in 1870, 45
Saint Joseph Society,
charter member, 196
town of origin, 57
Joseph,
connection with Srsens,
169–170
Saint Joseph Society,
charter member, 196
school grades, 98
Josepha, burial, 36
Rosa,
arrival, 43
marriage to Wencl
Hrdlichka, 171
William, National Alliance of
Czech Catholics, 251
Sheppard, Karleen Chott
Czech immigrant autobio-
raphies, editing and
translation, 233
Shimeck. see Simek
Shimpach, Wencl
Z.C.B.J., Owatonna lodge,
formation, 222
Shubart, Joseph
Z.C.B.J.,
Blooming Prairie lodge,
officers, 221

Index • 315

Simek
- Anastasia,
  - arrival in America, 5
  - inheritance, 25
  - later life, 157
  - marriage to Anton Sattlau, 18
  - marriage to Peter Johannsen, 17
- Anna,
  - inheritance, 25
  - marriage to Wencl Jirele, 180
- Anton,
  - arrival in America, 4
  - assistance to Benjamin Fisher, 15
  - bringing family to America, 4–5
  - character, 16
  - county coroner, election, 21
  - death, 25
  - early life, 2
  - enlistment, 1st Minnesota Regiment, 23
  - land claim, 11
  - last will and testament, 25
  - overseer of the poor, election, 21
  - police surveillance of, 3, 65
  - property sale, 22
  - relocation, 17
  - restless nature, 64
  - route from port of entry, 84
  - scouting place to settle, 7
  - settlement in Steele County, 8
  - town of origin, 57
- Frank,
  - arrival, 105
  - Bohemian National Cemetery, members, 38
  - experiences in Austrian-Prussian War 1866, 91
- John,
  - arrival, 5, 46
  - blizzard of 1873, temporary shelter for Edward Veith, 116
  - death, 17
  - father of Anton, 2
  - residence in 1870, 45
  - visits to grave of, 257
- Joseph,
  - arrival in America, 4
  - departure from Steele County, 30
  - home in Cedarville, Illinois, 5
  - later life, 157
  - photograph, 6
  - settlement in Steele County, 8
  - Somerset Township, land ownership, 43
- Rosa,
  - arrival in America, 5
  - Auditorium Hall, contribution, 215
  - inheritance, 25
  - later life, 157

Simon
- Alois,
  - arrival, 107
  - C.S.P.S., Owatonna lodge, officer, 215
  - making firebreak for Frank Kubicek, 176
- Anna, C.S.P.J., 226
- John, Steele Center creamery, 202
- Mary Ann, marriage to Joseph Skala, 234

Simonik, Father
- ministry to Owatonna Catholics, 154, 240

Singer, Father Sigismund
- ministry to Owatonna Catholics, 240

Skala
- Frank, arrival, 233–234
- Helen, life, 234
- Joseph, life, 234
- Wencl, arrival, 233–234

Skalicky
- Frank,
  - Saint Joseph Society, charter member, 196
  - Z.C.B.J.,
    - Blooming Prairie lodge, formation, 221
  - photograph, 218
- Frank and Frances, arrival, 109
- Frank and Matilda, arrival, 108
- Joseph,
  - arrival, 109
  - boarding visiting priests, 196
  - land donation for Holy Trinity Catholic cemetery, 193
  - Saint Joseph Society, charter member, 196
- Joseph B., Z.C.B.J., Owatonna lodge, formation, 221
- Josephine, marriage to Joseph Pirkl, 193
- Mary, marriage to Frank Matejcek, 172
- Mathilda, marriage to Anton Zajic Donato, 161–163
- Vincent, residence in 1870, 45
- Wencl, arrival, 109

Skerik, Joseph
- arrival, 110
- Bohemian National Cemetery, members, 38

Skopp, Marie, J.C.D., 226

Slavick, John
- residence in 1870, 45

Slezak
- Amelia, marriage to Francis Smersh, 132
- Anton,
  - arrival, 29
  - involvement in Joseph Wondra shooting, 181–182
  - route from port of entry, 85
- John, Hope general store, 206
- Joseph, Hope general store, 206
- Kasper,
  - arrival, 110
  - saloon, 166

Slovanska Lipa organization, 38–39, 210

Smersh
- Emilie, Z.C.B.J., Owatonna lodge, formation, 222

Francis,
    marriage to Amelia Slezak, 132
    practice of medicine, 132
Frank,
    blacksmith, 166
    Z.C.B.J., Owatonna lodge,
        formation, 221
        officers, 222
Jerome, practice of medicine, 132
Thomas, arrival, 132
Smith, Amanda
    school teacher, 97
social conditions
    Bohemia, 69
    Owatonna, 125–128
social life
    Bohemia, 72–73
Sokol
    Owatonna lodge, 223–224
Solnce, Father John
    service at Sacred Heart Catholic Church, 240
Somerset Township
    European settlement, 43
Soukup
    A.J., Sokol, Owatonna lodge, 224
    Anna, J.C.D., 226
    Anton W., Z.C.B.J.,
        Owatonna lodge,
        formation, 221
    Joseph H., C.S.P.S.,
        Owatonna lodge,
        officer, 215
    Joseph, Czech language, teaching, 39
Spatenka
    Frank,
        arrival, 105–106
        Bohemian National Cemetery, members, 38
        town of origin, 56
    Henry, C.S.P.S.
        musical group, 216
    Leopold, employment in flour mill, 166
    Terezie,
        biography, Amerikan

Narodni Kalendar, 249
    dancing in Bohemia, 73
    education in Bohemia, 72
Spinler
    Alois, Z.C.B.J.,
        Owatonna lodge, formation, 222
    Frank,
        arrival, 131–132
        Saint Ivan's Lodge, 240
    Rose, Z.C.B.J.,
        Owatonna lodge, formation, 222
        officers, 222
    Rudolf, hiding food in wartime, 91
Srsen
    Alois, Z.C.B.J.,
        Blooming Prairie lodge, formation, 220
        photograph, 218
    Edward, Z.C.B.J.,
        Owatonna lodge, formation, 221
    Frances, Z.C.B.J.,
        Owatonna lodge, formation, 222
    Frank, C.S.P.S.,
        Owatonna lodge, officer, 214
        employment as laborer, 170
    Joseph,
        agent for Hamburg America Line, 170
        C.S.P.S., Owatonna lodge, founding, 214
        officer, 214
        employment as store clerk, 166
        National Alliance of Czech Catholics, 251
        raised by Suchaneks, 106
    Karel,
        arrival, 169–170
        biography, Hospodar, 250
        Czech language, teaching, 39
        Sokol, Owatonna lodge, 224
    Sylvia, marriage to Wencl Chott, 233

Stancl, Anton
    management of county poor farm, 240
    threshing party, Owatonna, photograph, 86
steamships
    Atlantic crossing, 77–78
Steele Center, 201–202
Steele Center school (District 40)
    location, 202
Steele County
    European settlement pattern, 41
    first European settlers, 1
    formation, 16
    geography, 1, 2
    growth,
        1860, 20
        1870, 111
        1880, 164–166
    presettlement vegetation, map, xvi
Steinbauer, Joseph
    Saint Joseph Society, charter member, 196
Stransky
    Agnes, Z.C.B.J., Owatonna lodge, formation, 221
    Caroline, remarriage to Frank Kubicek, 173
    Frank, Saco resident, 172–173
    John,
        assault, 134
        butcher, 166
        partner in meat market, 134
    Joseph A., Z.C.B.J.,
        Owatonna lodge, formation, 221
        officers, 222
    Mathilda, marriage to Joseph Meixner, 172
    Mrs. J.S., J.C.D., 226
    William, Z.C.B.J.,
        Owatonna lodge, formation, 221
Strong, Emily
    inheritance, 25
Styndl, Frank
    arrival, 48, 206
    blacksmith, 202

photographs, 204–205
town of origin, 56
Suchanek
    John, injury in threshing accident, 106
    Wencl, arrival, 106
Sulak, Father Frank
    ministry to Litomysl Catholics, 193
    ministry to Owatonna Catholics, 154, 240
Summit, 199–201
    photograph, 201
Summit school (District 51), 100, 201
destruction by arson, 176
Summit Township
    Czech settlement 1870, 45
Sumtrey, Reverend Felix
    Catholic priest, death, 154
Svercl
    Frances, marriage to John Rysavy, 231
    Frank, arrival, 172
    Joseph,
        arrival, 231
        National Alliance of Czech Catholics, 251
Svir, Joseph
    C.S.P.S., Owatonna lodge, officer, 215
Swissholm, Jane Grey
    Owatonna, description, 20

T
temperance movement, 125
textile industry
    Bohemia, 64
Thirty Years War, 267
threshing party, Owatonna
    photograph, 86
Tichy, Father Frank
    ministering to Litomysl Catholics, 192–193
Titus, Mary
    school teacher, 97
Toher, Michael
    Sacred Heart Church building committee, 34
Tomanek, Father Francis
    pastor at Holy Trinity Catholic Church, 245

Tomsche, Anna
    C.S.P.J., 226
    J.C.D., 226
trade board
    Owatonna, 94
transcontinental railroads, 119
Traverse de Sioux treaty, 1
Truhlar
    Anna, J.C.D., 226
    Barbara, threshing party, Owatonna, photograph, 86
    Frank,
        C.S.D.P.J. lodge, officer, 217
        Z.C.B.J., Owatonna lodge, formation, 222
    Mary, threshing party, Owatonna, photograph, 86

U
Umlauf, John
    altar paintings donated for Holy Trinity Church, 193
Usti nad Orlice, Bohemia, 57

V
Vasicek, Mary
    marriage to John Matejcek, 172
Vavra
    Frances, Czech language, teachers, 221
    Mrs. Frank, Z.C.B.J., Blooming Prairie lodge, formation, 221
        photograph, 218
Veith
    Edward,
        death in blizzard, 116–117
        residence in 1870, 175
    Joseph,
        assault, 140
        residence in 1870, 45, 175
Velebny, Joseph
    Czech language, teaching, 39
Velka Retova, Bohemia, 58
Vesely
    Frank,
        Auditorium Hall, paintings, 216
        town of origin, 56

    Rosa, marriage to Frank Styndl, 206
Veverka, Frank
    Czech language, teaching, 39
village life
    Bohemia, 68–73

W
W.F.L.A. see Z.C.B.J.
Wacek
    Anton,
        builder of Holy Trinity Catholic Church, 245
        National Alliance of Czech Catholics, 251
    Dominic,
        mortgage, 184
        residence in Saco, 173
wagon train
    photograph, Owatonna 1864, 48
Wanous
    Anton, C.S.D.P.J. lodge, officer, 217
    John,
        arrival, 32
        fatal accident, 191
        military service, effect on emigration from Bohemia, 63
        Z.C.B.J., Blooming Prairie lodge, officers, 221
    John and Mrs., Z.C.B.J., Blooming Prairie lodge, formation, 220
        photograph, 218
    L.J., Steele Center creamery, 202
    Thomas, employment in shoe store, 165–166
    Wencl,
        Saint Joseph Society, charter member, 196
        Somerset Township, land ownership, 44
Watowa, Wencl
    Civil War Service, 1st Minnesota Infantry Regiment, 27
    saloon, 134, 136, 166
Wavrin
    Anton, marriage to Frances Wondra, 114

Antonia, Z.C.B.J.,
    Owatonna lodge,
        formation, 221
John, C.S.P.S.,
    Owatonna lodge,
        musical group, 216
        officer, 214
Joseph,
    Bohemian National
        Cemetery, officers, 37
    C.S.P.S.,
        Owatonna lodge,
            officer, 215
    school officer, 97
Weiseler, Father Laurence
    Sacred Heart Church pastor, 35
Wencl
    Alois, National Alliance of
        Czech Catholics, 251
    Anna, contribution,
        Privrat church, 58
    Anton, Z.C.B.J.,
        Blooming Prairie lodge,
            formation, 220
        officers, 221
        photograph, 218
    C.V., Z.C.B.J.,
        Blooming Prairie lodge,
            officers, 221
    Frank,
        court cases, 191
        marriage to Sarah Kubista, 118
    Vincent,
        residence, 207
        1870, 42
    Vincent and Mrs., Z.C.B.J.,
        Blooming Prairie lodge,
            formation, 221
        photograph, 218
Wencl, election as township supervisor, 190
Wesely
    Anna, marriage to Joseph Hudrlik, 48
    Frank,
        arrival, 48, 107
        Bohemian National
            Cemetery, directors, 37
        residence in 1870, 45

Joseph, Steele Center
    creamery, 202
Paulina, marriage and arrival, 48
Rosalie, marriage to Frank Styndl, 48
Theresa, marriage to Joseph Deml, 48
Western Bohemian Catholic Union
    fraternal lodges, 227
Western Czech Catholic Union
    formation, 196
Winona and St. Peter Railroad
    arrival in Owatonna, 32
Winship House
    Catherine Pichner
        employment, 14
winter 1856-1857, 12–15
Wolesky
    Anna, Z.C.B.J.,
        Owatonna lodge, 222
    Frank,
        arrival, 229–231
        buttermaker, Summit creamery, 199
        military service, effect on emigration from Bohemia, 63
    Joseph,
        arrival, 229–231
        building aircraft, 230
        buttermaker,
            River Point, 203
        Steele Center creamery, 202
        photograph, 228
        Z.C.B.J., Owatonna lodge, 222
    Louis, building aircraft, 230
Wondra
    Anna, marriage to Anton Slezak, 182
    Frances,
        later life, 182
        marriage to Anton Wavrin, 114
    John,
        arrival, 31–32
        divorce action, 184
        later life, 182
        residence in 1870, 45
        town of origin, 58

Joseph,
    buttermaker,
        River Point creamery, 203
        Summit creamery, 199
    injury in wagon
        accident, 117–118
    shooting death, 181–182
Mary (Pribyl), marriage to
    Frank Rysavy, 182
Wood, W.
    school teacher, 97
World War I
    effect on Czech-Americans, 250–255

Z
Z.C.B.J.
    Blooming Prairie,
        formation, 220–221
        photograph, members in 1900, 218
    formation, 217–220
    later history, 248–249
    Owatonna,
        formation, 221–223
        photograph, building, 219
Z.C.K.J.
    formation, 196
Zajic-Donato, Anton, 160–163
    Czech language, teaching, 39
Zapadni Cesko Katolicka Jenota
    formation, 196
Zednick
    Anna,
        marriage and arrival, 30–31
    Catherine, later life, 160
    Joseph,
        accomodations during first winter, 10
        burial, 36
        later life, 160
    Philomena, later life, 160
Zhor, Bohemia, 57